# Reading Instruction and the Beginning Teacher

## A Practical Guide

Edited by

### James F. Baumann

Purdue University
West Lafayette, Indiana

### Dale D. Johnson

University of Wisconsin–Madison

 **Burgess Publishing Company**
Minneapolis, Minnesota

Consulting editor: Alden J. Moe
Acquisitions editor: Wayne E. Schotanus
Assistant editor: Sharon B. Harrington
Production editor: Anne E. Heller
Copy editor: Marcia Bottoms
Art coordinator: Priscilla Heimann
Production: Morris Lundin, Pat Barnes
Composition: Cold Type Setters Inc.
Cover concept: James F. Baumann
Cover illustration: Catherine Cleary
Cover design: Priscilla Heimann

Library of Congress Cataloging in Publication Data

Reading instruction and the beginning teacher.

    Includes bibliographies and index.
    1. Reading (Primary)      2. First year teachers.
I. Baumann, James F.      II. Johnson, Dale D.
LB1525.R36  1984      372.4'1      83-15213
ISBN 0-8087-4092-X

Burgess Publishing Company
7108 Ohms Lane
Minneapolis, Minnesota 55435

JIHGFED

# Contents

# Preface

Our purpose in developing this volume is to fill a void in materials for college-level reading instruction. Many fine reading methods textbooks are on the market, all of which contain the basic information needed for training teachers in reading instruction. For example, the texts already available contain strategies for teaching word identification, vocabulary, and comprehension skills; procedures for assessing and diagnosing reading ability; and information about the various methods and materials used in reading instruction and about management and organizational options available to teachers.

In working with preservice teachers in reading methods courses, however, we have found that our students are frequently overwhelmed with the great volume of information contained in general methods texts and frustrated when authors present an extensive array of methods and materials for teaching reading but fail to recommend what is sensible and practical for a beginning teacher to use. In other words, beginning teachers want to know which *specific* procedures and techniques will be effective for them, given their limited experience.

*Reading Instruction and the Beginning Teacher: A Practical Guide* is a unique reading textbook and one that we believe fills this void. Rather than presenting teachers a potpourri of methodological materials and options, this guide includes only tried and tested procedures known to be effective and appropriate for teachers with limited experience. All of the contributing authors are professional reading educators who have had many years' experience as classroom reading teachers. Each chapter is written in a nontechnical, readable style and presents a specific set of teaching strategies or organizational guidelines that is not only based on current research and theory but also, and more important, is educationally sound, easily managed, and realistic for a novice teacher to implement.

Do not be misled; this text is not simply an "idea" book or a reading "cookbook." Although this book presents many concrete teaching strategies, it offers a *select set* of instructional procedures—those known to be appropriate and feasible for a teacher of limited experience, a beginning teacher.

The text is organized into four parts. Part I presents teaching strategies for the development of basic reading skills: word identification, vocabulary, and comprehension skills. Part II contains information and procedures whereby beginning teachers can assess and diagnose their students' reading strengths and weaknesses and then use this information to make sensible instructional decisions. Part III presents organizational and management plans that are known to be effective but are also feasible for a beginning teacher to implement. Part IV describes numerous strategies for motivating children to read both in school and at home. We refer the reader to the introductions that precede each of the sections for additional preview information.

In addition to the content of our text, we believe several other features distinguish this book from others. As previously mentioned, there are introductions for each of the four parts of the text. Chapter introductions also provide the reader an abstract of each chapter and relate and link one chapter to the next. We are perhaps most proud of the many activities, exercises, and case studies contained in this book. Our authors have made a conscious effort to *involve* readers with the chapters by requiring them to *do* while they *read*. These activities enable readers to apply information as they are learning it. Each chapter concludes with a recommended readings section, a brief annotated bibliography of additional related readings.

As its title indicates, this book is aimed toward the needs of beginning teachers—undergraduate (or graduate) preservice teachers in teacher-training programs. Recent graduates of education programs—those with five or fewer years of teaching experience—may also find this text useful and informative. Experienced teachers wanting to update their knowledge of reading instruction, especially practical teaching strategies, also may be interested in this text.

Given such an audience, this text is appropriate for undergraduate reading methods courses as well as for beginning graduate-level developmental reading courses that bring teachers back to university classrooms after they have acquired some teaching experience. As a final note on the use of this text, we envision a university instructor using this book either in conjunction with a basic developmental reading methods text or even in lieu of such a text when classroom lectures, activities, and demonstrations address topics not covered by this book.

We wish to thank all the contributors to this guide for their efforts in translating their knowledge of reading instruction into practical instructional techniques, for the ultimate goal of true educators is to bring theory and knowledge to practitioners. We also sincerely thank Wayne Schotanus, our editor, for his encouragement and guidance, and Sharon Harrington, Anne Heller, Marcia Bottoms, and other members of the Burgess staff for their competence and cooperation in the production of this text.

James F. Baumann
Dale D. Johnson

# PART I

# Teaching Basic Reading Skills: Word Identification, Vocabulary, and Comprehension Strategies

*Part I deals with the development of basic reading skills in the areas of word identification, vocabulary, and comprehension. Chapters 1 and 2 present strategies that beginning teachers can use in teaching children basic skills in word identification. Chapter 3 and part of Chapter 4 provide suggestions for expanding children's meaning vocabulary. Chapters 4, 5, and 6 address the complex task of teaching children to comprehend what they read. Chapter 4 provides suggestions for teaching comprehension at the word, sentence, and passage levels; Chapter 5 presents strategies teachers can use to engage children actively in comprehension instruction; and Chapter 6 describes activities appropriate for the development of critical reading skills. Chapter 7 explains the use of poetry as a medium for teaching a wide range of reading skills, and Chapter 8 provides beginning kindergarten and first-grade teachers numerous suggestions for the development of literacy skills in young children.*

CHAPTER 1

# Helping Children to Identify Words by Using All Three Cue Systems of the Language

Dixie Lee Spiegel
University of North Carolina at Chapel Hill

*The ultimate goal of reading instruction is to develop readers who can skillfully comprehend what they read. In order to achieve a high level of competence in reading comprehension, however, readers need to be able to read individual words. In other words, the ability to identify words is a necessary (but, to be sure, not sufficient) condition for reading comprehension. In this chapter, Dixie Lee Spiegel discusses three cue systems that readers can use to help them identify words: the semantic system (what "makes sense"), the syntactic system (what fits grammatically), and the graphophonic system (how letters are translated into sounds). Spiegel presents not only a clear discussion of what each cue system involves but also provides many concrete ideas for teaching children to apply each cue system. In addition, the reader will find exercises that help children to monitor their word identification skill, to integrate two or three cue systems when appropriate, and to be flexible in switching from one cue system to another according to the particular unknown word.*

This chapter introduces the three cue systems of the English language and describes practical activities that will help children to develop the ability to use all of these cue systems effectively when reading. Teaching word identification in the elementary grades is too often perceived as a matter of teaching only phonics, and children learn primarily to huff and puff at isolated words in the name of reading. Unfortunately, such children are trained in using only one cue system of the language: the graphophonic cue system. A good reader is able to use all three cue systems of the language: the semantic (meaning), the syntactic (word order or grammatical), and the graphophonic (letter/sound) systems. A good teacher gives children the tools to use these cue systems and provides them ample opportunity to practice using the tools.

2

# THE SEMANTIC SYSTEM

The semantic system is the meaning system of language. It is the semantic system that allows us to decide that the missing word in "I was cold, so I put on my _____" could be *sweater, scarf,* or *gloves* but not *shovel, glasses,* or *earrings.* A child's ability to use the semantic system to identify an unknown word in a sentence depends a great deal on the child's concept of what reading is all about. If a child does not think of reading as a process of finding meaning, she[1] might make a miscue (a deviation from the expected response [Goodman and Burke, 1972]), for example, inserting *glasses* in place of *gloves* in the example above. If the child views reading only as making noises based on the letters on the page, the child is likely to abandon the semantic system in favor of the graphophonic system (the letter-sound patterns of the language). The child is apt to provide nonsense words that have the *sounds* of the printed letters but that do not mean anything. For example, if the word *gloves* were part of the sample sentence above, a child who relies only on the graphophonic system might pronounce this word *glōves* (rhyming with *coves*).

The child who perceives reading as a process of finding meaning, however, uses the semantic system as an aid to word identification (in conjunction with the other cue systems, as we will see). That child might miss the exact word, substituting perhaps *sweater* for *scarf,* but the miscue would still make sense. The miscue might not represent the precise meaning that the writer intended, but the basic meaning-getting nature of reading would not be violated.

A child's ability to use semantic cues also depends on the child's experiential background. A child who has lived in Florida since birth would be less likely to be able to identify *stiff* in "The cold wind made our faces feel *stiff*" than would a native Minnesotan. Unless one has experienced minus 30 °F on a windy day, the word *stiff* does not spring to mind.

The great advantage of a broad experiential background is that the reader is better able to *predict* which word would make sense in a given slot than a reader who knows nothing about the topic. Readers who are able to use the semantic system effectively often can predict the next word before they see it.

Try this example to see how your own experiential background helps or hinders you.

The whiffling marfweezel has four legs, striped fur, and p_____ eyes.

Naturally, you supplied the right word, *plaid.* What? You did not? You put in *purple?* One would think you had never even heard of a whiffling marfweezel.

Try again.

The body of the bald eagle is covered with black or dark brown feathers, while its head is all wh_____.

How did you do this time? Did you put in *white?* Of course, you did.

A child who has no experience with the concepts presented in a story is at the same disadvantage as you were in reading about the mythical whiffling marfweezel. To be able to use the semantic system to identify unknown words, the reader must have a meaningful store of relevant experience from which to make predictions.

---

[1]To avoid the use of sexist language or intrusive substitutes in this textbook, the feminine pronoun has been used alternately with the masculine pronoun throughout.

## THE SYNTACTIC SYSTEM

The syntactic system is related to the grammar of the English language. Word order is an important aspect of the syntactic system. Because English is a highly positional language, only certain word classes (parts of speech) can fill certain spots in a sentence. In "I was cold, so I put on my _____," only a noun makes sense in the slot. A guess of *hers, into,* or *mumbles* would violate the syntactic system, since none of these words is a noun, and the resulting sentence would not "sound right." That is, it would not sound like the English language. *Red,* an adjective, would be acceptable syntactically only if the slot were followed by a noun.

If a child put a verb into a slot that could only be filled by a noun, you would immediately wonder what that child thinks reading is all about. A good reader knows that the end result has to sound like real language, even if he is not sure of all of the words.

In addition to the child's understanding of the relationship of language to reading, the child's familiarity with the syntactic patterns of printed material can be an important factor. For example, "Betty Sue, who was the oldest girl in the third grade, was the smallest child in the class, despite her age" is so complex and convoluted that even you may have had trouble reading the sentence and understanding it. If the syntactic patterns are not familiar to the child, then the child may have trouble using the syntactic system to help identify unknown words.

## THE GRAPHOPHONIC SYSTEM

In English, the letters used to spell a word often give some indication of the way that word is pronounced. Unfortunately, the graphophonic system does not always work. The common words *some, said,* and *do,* for example, should be pronounced *sōmĕ, sāĭd,* and *dŏ,* according to phonic "rules." Therefore, unlike some languages (e.g., Spanish), English does not have a reliable one-to-one correspondence between sounds and symbols or, conversely, between symbol and sound. The "long *e*" sound can be written as *e* (*be*), *ee* (*see*), *y* (*city*), *i* (*ski*), *ie* (*piece*), and *ea* (*bead*). The letter *a* can represent an equally bewildering array of sounds, as in *star, walk, father, assess, game,* and *bead,* to name a few examples.

On the other hand, the letters in a word often can give enough clues for identification of the word, especially when the word occurs in a meaningful context and the word is part of the child's speaking or listening vocabulary. For example, although *put* does not follow the common consonant-short vowel-consonant rule (CV̆C), most children would be able to identify that word in "Put that book over there" simply by using the consonant cues (*p* and *t*) and the context. Using the graphophonic cues (especially consonants) frequently helps readers get close enough to the target word to identify it when the word is used in context and is familiar.

Some children pay little attention to the graphophonic system when attempting to identify unknown words. These children might substitute *coat* for *sweater* in "I was cold, so I put on my coat" if they were attending only to the semantic and syntactic cues. Such children could use practice in integrating the use of graphophonic cues with the use of the other two systems. A few children disregard all three systems, with disastrous results, such as "I was cold, so I put on my *special.*"

Other children pay too much attention to the graphophonic system. These children are not concerned about whether their reading makes sense or whether it sounds like language; they just want to "sound out" those words. As a result, they might say, "I was cold, so I *putt* on my gloves." These children need work with materials that deny them graphophonic cues and so force them to rely on context.

## THE USE OF ALL THREE CUE SYSTEMS TOGETHER

Reading is not just "barking at print" (i.e., pronouncing words by using only the graphophonic system). Reading involves receiving the writer's message; therefore, it must use the semantic system of the English language. Reading also involves understanding that what one is reading is language; therefore, the use of the syntactic system is important. Reading also involves being able to select the writer's precise meaning from all possible choices; therefore, the graphophonic system often comes into play. Overreliance on any one of the cue systems can cause problems in reading.

Children need to be *taught* to use the cue systems interactively. They need to be shown how these systems are interwoven, and then they need to be given a great deal of practice in anticipating words through using the semantic and syntactic systems and in confirming these anticipations through using the graphophonic system. They need to be *taught* strategies for changing their decisions when subsequent information proves them wrong.

### A Practice Exercise

Teachers should be able to recognize opportunities to help children practice the use of the three cue systems. Teachers should also recognize when one cue system offers more efficient clues than another, and they should be able to guide children toward using the most appropriate cue system. To help judge your own expertise in selecting the appropriate cue system, complete the exercise that follows. (The answers can be found after the exercise.) When completing this exercise, assume the following: (1) The child can read every word in the sentence except the one set in italics. (2) The child has read as far as the italic word and stopped, looking to you for help. (3) The child has had phonics training in consonant sounds and major vowel patterns. For each sentence, indicate what you think would be the *one* best way to help the child to identify the italic word. Mark *S*, *T*, or *C* in the blank for each example according to this system:

Put *S* on the line preceding the sentence if you would tell the child to *"sound the word out" by using BOTH consonant and vowel cues.*

Put *T* on the line if you would simply *tell the child the unknown word.*

Put *C* on the line if you would have the child use *context* (i.e., *tell the child to finish the sentence and see what makes sense*).

_____1.   I like *suede*.

_____2.   That is *enough* cake for me, thank you.

_____3.   The *hat* is very tall.

_____4.   I *have* to go now.

_____5.   Did you *praise* him?

_____6.   We went to the *ballet*.

_____7.   Because Mother asked me, I used the *broom*.

_____8.  *Give* it to me.

_____9.  Sam will *come* to my party.

_____10.  Billy has a new *one*.

*Answers*

| | | | |
|---|---|---|---|
| 1. | Tell | 6. | Tell |
| 2. | Context | 7. | Sound |
| 3. | Sound | 8. | Context |
| 4. | Context | 9. | Context |
| 5. | Sound | 10. | Tell |

To understand why certain answers are more appropriate than others, look at items 1, 2, and 3. In item 1, "I like *suede*," *suede* is a phonically irregular word in which the *u* does not "say its name" but makes an entirely unpredictable sound. Neither can the child use the "when two vowels go walking, the first one does the talking" rule for *ue*. Therefore telling her to sound the word out is inappropriate. In item 1, the context is also useless for identifying *suede*. If *suede* were followed by *shoes*, the context would offer some clue. Such a minimal context as this is, however, of no help. The child must be told the word, since none of the cue systems offers an adequate clue.

In item 2, "That is *enough* cake for me, thank you," *enough* is also phonically irregular. (Does it rhyme with *cough, through, bough,* or *rough*?) Sounding the word out, therefore, would not work. In item 2, however, context is helpful. Because of the placement of the word before "cake for me," only one word really fits. If two word slots were available, *too much* would also fit, but only one slot needs to be filled. Telling the child to finish the sentence and see what makes sense (from context) would almost guarantee the correct identification of the word.

*Hat*, in item 3, "The *hat* is very tall," follows the consonant-short vowel-consonant generalization, and, therefore, the child can use phonic cues successfully to identify the word. Context cues are not very helpful. Any noun denoting something capable of being tall would fit.

As you work with children, be sure that you think about the kinds of cues you suggest. Following an ineffective cue in one instance discourages them from using that kind of cue when it is appropriate.

## GUIDELINES FOR HELPING
## CHILDREN TO USE ALL THREE CUE SYSTEMS

The three guidelines that follow should help you to prepare yourself for working with children in developing their use of the three cue systems. The guidelines should be used both when planning formal instruction and when interacting with children in reading groups or in those spontaneous "teachable moments" (e.g., when a child seeks help in identifying a word).

1.  *Avoid using words in isolation.* A reader cannot use the semantic and syntactic systems to identify a word when the word is not in a natural language context. Lack of context forces the reader to rely on only one cue system, the graphophonic. You should always put words in phrases, at least, and preferably in sentences or paragraphs, so that the child can make use of all three cue systems.

2. *Think before you offer a child help with a word.* You should think first about whether you should even be offering help. Rowe's (1969) classic study on teachers' wait time showed that teachers frequently do not give children enough time even to think about an answer before they provide the word (that is, before they become a "helpful Harriet or Harold" and come to the rescue). To put it emphatically: Be quiet until the child has had at least five to ten seconds to work on the word without help. (This means that you also should control Sally Sunshine and Helpful Harry, who always want to enhance their own self-esteem by blurting out the correct word.) After five to ten seconds, you may ask the child whether he is ready for help. If the child wants more time, provide it. Either go on to a different task with another child or just sit patiently for a little while longer. Some children work things out more slowly than others. Give them *time*.

The second thing you should think about is the *kind* of help you offer. Earlier in the chapter, several examples were discussed in which some kinds of assistance were more appropriate than others. Be sure that you can recognize when one cue system is more applicable than another, and then *use* this knowledge. Do not fall into the trap of simply telling the child the word in order to get on with the lesson (Spiegel and Rogers, 1980).

3. *Give children instruction and practice in using all three cue systems together.* Many children need to be "walked through" the use of various cue systems, since they may not have developed the all-important ability to monitor their own responses to see how these responses fit in with the available semantic, syntactic, and graphophonic cues. You may need to do a lot of oral work playing "how can you tell" games, such as "How can you tell this word isn't *sunglasses?* in 'I was cold, so I put on my s_____'" or "How can you tell this word isn't *gloves?*" Guided oral work on using all three cue systems interactively can help children to develop independence in word identification.

Another reason for helping children to practice with all three cue systems at once is that certain cues in a particular context help some individuals but not others. Over-emphasis in a lesson on using one cue system presumes that the teacher is infallible in identifying the one most effective cue for all readers. Presenting all three sets of cues and helping the children to select the combination of cues that works for them is more effective in the long run than insisting that there is one right way to identify the target word. (If a child is unwise in choosing appropriate cues, however, the teacher needs to impose her judgment to show the child more effective techniques.)

## ACTIVITIES FOR IMPROVING WORD IDENTIFICATION ABILITIES

Several kinds of inappropriate word identification strategies in which readers either ignore one or more cue systems or rely too heavily on one cue system have already been discussed in this chapter. For each of these ineffective strategies, several activities designed to help readers develop more appropriate strategies will be described.

### Excessive Reliance on the Graphophonic System

Readers who rely too heavily on the graphophonic system need to attend to meaning as well as to letter/sound relationships. One way to keep the reader from overrelying on the letters is simply to remove the letters. Cloze exercises, in which the word of interest has been replaced by a blank, effectively force the reader to attend to the other two cue systems, the semantic and the syntactic.

### Activity 1

Present a sentence with a blank that could be filled with just one word and no other.

Everyone has two ears and _____ nose.

A little dog is called a puppy and a little cat is called a _____.

Ask the reader to identify the missing word. When the reader has done this successfully, ask how he was able to tell which word belonged there when all the letters were missing. If necessary, lead the reader toward the conclusion that often one can figure out what a word is just by thinking about what makes sense.

### Activity 2

Give the reader a booklet made of three three-by-five-inch pieces of construction paper stapled together. (See Figure 1.1.) On the first page, write an open-ended sentence and leave several spaces to be filled in by the child according to whatever makes sense to her. For example, *skate, read, cook, eat,* and *swing* would logically complete "I like to . . . ."

On the second page, add words that make the context more specific, such as "At school I like to . . . ," thus narrowing the range of possible answers. The child is to copy only the answers from the first page that still make sense (e.g., *read, swing,* and *eat*).

On the third page, the context should be even more limiting ("During recess at school I like to . . ."), so that the child can use only the words from the second page (if any) that are still meaningful within the new context (e.g., *swing*). Children can then compare and defend their answers.

### Activity 3

Since many children mispronounce the vowels in words, these children should be taught to forget the vowels and rely primarily on meaning and language cues plus consonant cues. Let the child discover that he can identify the partial words below simply by attending to the cues that *are* there.

For Chr-stm-s I got a new doll.  ·

My dog rolled on the gr--nd.

I read my b--k.

### Activity 4

When a child asks for help when reading or when you are listening to oral reading, tell the child to skip the unknown word, finish the sentence, and *then* go back and try to figure out the word. If the reader still cannot figure out a word that conforms to the grapho-phonic, semantic, and syntactic cues, tell the child to put in a word that makes sense, even if it does not follow the letter cues, and keep reading.

Some children may find it helpful to say something in place of the word, such as "Oh, nuts!" instead of just skipping the word. Many children (and some adults!) think that it is inappropriate to skip an unknown word and to use only the context to identify it. These readers need to realize that this is not only acceptable but also that it is the way "good readers" read.

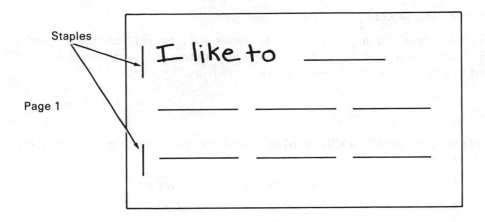

Staples

Page 1

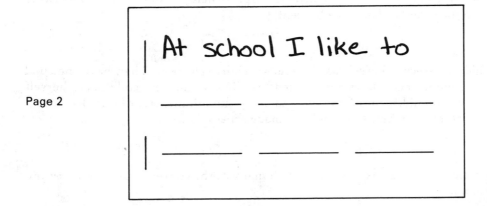

Page 2

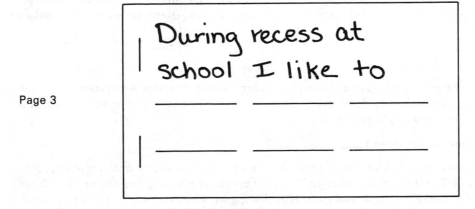

Page 3

Figure 1.1. An exercise for readers who rely too heavily on graphophonic information.

### Failure to Monitor What Is Read

The reader who does not monitor what she reads lives by the "anything goes" philosophy. Such readers are perfectly happy with providing a nonsense word for an unknown word or a real word that does not make sense (e.g., "I was so cold I put on my *shovel*").

#### Activity 1

Have the reader first identify a silly word in a sentence and then suggest a sensible substitute for that word.

> I opened the stove to let in more air (substituting *window* for *stove*).
>
> The man gargled at the joke (substituting *laughed* for *gargled*).
>
> Ted drives a big tent (substituting *truck* for *tent* or *has* for *drives*).

Always explore apparently wrong answers. The child's reasoning may be just as good as yours; he simply may have focused on a different aspect than you did (which could easily occur with a sentence like "Ted drives a big tent").

#### Activity 2

Let the child tape-record herself as she reads a short selection. Then have the child listen to the tape while she follows the printed text. Every time the child hears herself make a miscue, she should turn off the tape, identify the miscue, figure out the correct word, and then determine whether the miscue made sense.

#### Activity 3

Provide practice with cloze exercises in which many of the context clues come *after* the blanks. For example:

> When I fell, I broke my _____ and then I couldn't write.
>
> The little _____ went "quack, quack."

A variation of this activity is to cover up the context after the blank (with a tagboard strip), have the child guess a word, and then ask the child to see whether that guess still makes sense with the rest of the sentence.

#### Activity 4

Play the "how can you tell" game. Give the reader a sentence from which one word has been omitted and in which only the initial consonant or consonant cluster is presented, and then have the reader try to guess the word.

> For dinner we ate roast t_____.

After the child has correctly identified the missing word, ask questions of these two types: "How can you tell that it is not *take* or *target*?" (with the aim of eliciting the response "Those words don't make sense" or "It doesn't sound right"), and "How can you tell it's not *beef* or *pork?"* (with the hope of eliciting the response that these choices "don't start with the right letter").

### Failure to Perceive the Relationship Between Language and Reading

When a child substitutes a part of speech into a slot in which that part of speech can not "fit," the child does not understand that what he reads must sound like real language. Such children need a lot of practice judging whether a sentence "sounds right." However, children should not be asked to get any more technical than "That doesn't sound right" or "People don't talk like that." A child who could respond with "That's incorrect because I have placed a noun where only a verb can go" probably does not need these exercises anyway!

### *Activity 1*

Guthrie, Siefert, Burnham, and Caplan (1974) suggest using a modified cloze technique called maze to help students attend to syntactic cues. In a maze sentence, the reader is not confronted by a blank but by three choices, each a different part of speech. For example:

> The (is, into, ice) is cold.
>
> I have a (new, running, hat) red coat.

### *Activity 2*

Language experience stories, in which the child dictates a story and the teacher records *exactly* what the child says, can be useful in emphasizing the relationship between language and reading (i.e., that what is read involves *language,* just as speaking and listening do). When a child sees her own oral language being transformed into print, she realizes that print can also be changed back into oral language. You should recognize how important it is to use the child's own, unedited language to cement this relationship. If you are trying to help the child understand that reading must "sound right," you cannot change his language to something that sounds right to *you* but not to the child. "I don't have any" may sound lovely to you, but "I ain't go no" may be what sounds right to the child. So grit your teeth and write it down just as the child says it!

### *Activity 3*

Allow the child to manipulate word or phrase cards to make sentences. Give the child enough cards so that more than one sentence is possible, but give few enough cards so that the child does not become overwhelmed.

### *Activity 4*

Take plain wooden blocks and put a peel-off label on each face of each block. For any given block, each face should have a word with the same part of speech on it. For example, block A might have all nouns (*dog, house, mother, elephant, car, cake*), block B might have all verbs, and so on. Be sure to have one or two noun-determiner blocks (*the, my, their, this, our, her*) and some adjective blocks. The child rolls all the blocks at once and then arranges the words that fall faceup to make a sentence. The child gets one point for every block used. Then, the child judges whether the sentence is "silly" (i.e., sounds like language but does not make sense) or "makes sense." Blocks with the words *yellow, our, eats, mother, cat, the, jumps,* and *in* could become: "Our mother eats the cat" (which is a silly sentence), "The yellow cat jumps our mother" (which might be a meaningful sentence if the child could explain it), or "The yellow mother cat eats" (a sentence that truly does make sense).

The peel-off labels should be changed periodically to incorporate new sight words that the children are practicing.

### Failure to Use Graphophonic Cues

Some readers are perfectly content to use only semantic and syntactic cues to acquire the general meaning of a sentence or a word. Such readers do not concern themselves with accuracy and tend to ignore the graphophonic cues that would enable them to pronounce words and to determine the writer's exact meaning. They need to work with materials in which minor changes in word identification can have major consequences. For example, substituting *Greenville* for *Greenland* in a study of other lands or *sixty* for *six* when reading about insect legs would result in significant changes in meaning. Content area materials (social studies and science books) are particularly useful in this regard. Note that these exercises are appropriate *only* for students who *have* the ability to use graphophonic cues but *do not*. These activities would be entirely inappropriate for students with undeveloped phonic skills or for students not yet secure in their use of semantic and syntactic cues.

### *Activity 1*

Develop an activity that forces students to use graphophonic cues to identify words in context. On a two-by-four-inch piece of construction paper, write an open-ended sentence, such as "We opened the _____" or "The big _____ swayed across the clearing." Instead of leaving a blank, however, provide a specific word, such as *package* or *giraffe*. Make a sliding cover out of construction paper that fits snugly around the paper with the sentence and is just wide enough to cover the word of interest (in this case, *package* or *giraffe*) (Figure 1.2).

Ask the child to read the entire exposed portion of the sentence and to make a guess at the covered word. Then, expose the initial letter of the word, and ask the student to judge whether her guess was right or wrong. Then, without telling the student whether she was right, uncover the entire first syllable, and have the student judge again. If at any time the student decides that the guess was wrong, she should make a new guess based on the available graphophonic cues. When the student's guess has been correct for two successive exposures of word parts, expose the whole word for a final check.

Be sure to use sentences in which several words would make sense. If at all possible, select target words that have beginning letters that are the same as those of other reasonable guesses. For example, for "We opened the _____," the student might guess *door*, but when the initial letter *p* is exposed, he might change the guess to *presents*. However, the next exposure would reveal *pack-*, thus narrowing the choice to one specific word (*package*).

Double piece of paper taped at ends

Figure 1.2. An exercise for inaccurate readers who ignore graphophonic cues.

### Activity 2

Many students who ignore all graphophonic cues in favor of relying exclusively on context are capable of decoding the exact words, but they cannot be bothered to be that careful. (This assumes that the student has the ability to use graphophonic cues.) For such readers, games in which the first spoken guess counts can be useful. The reader gets only one chance to name a word in context.

One such game uses an all-purpose game board like the one in Figure 1.3. Tagboard cards (two by three inches) should be prepared with sentences containing underlined words. To play, a child rolls a die, draws the top card from the deck, and moves the number of spaces indicated on the die after identifying the underlined word.

The sentences should be like the ones described in the previous exercise. In addition, the underlined word should be one of the less predictable words for that context. For example, for "My favorite dessert is chocolate _____" choose *pie* instead of *cake* or *ice cream.* Similarly, for "My mother was very _____ when I dropped the book" supply *amused* instead of *angry.* In this way, you are forcing the reader away from making reasonable but inaccurate predictions based solely on context.

### Activity 3

Play a version of Password in which each player writes a word of her choice on a separate one-inch-square piece of construction paper for each letter. The squares are placed in front of the player in order, facedown, and the children alternate, making guesses about each other's words. To begin, player A gives a general clue about his hidden word, such as "It's something to eat." (The children may need practice in giving general rather than specific clues.) Player B then makes a guess at the word (*food*). If the guess is incorrect, player A exposes the first letter of the word (*b*). Then, player B makes another guess. If player B is still wrong, player A gives another general clue ("It's yellow") and exposes the last letter of the word (*r*). Thereafter, a player exposes the other consonant letters in any order, saving the vowels until last.

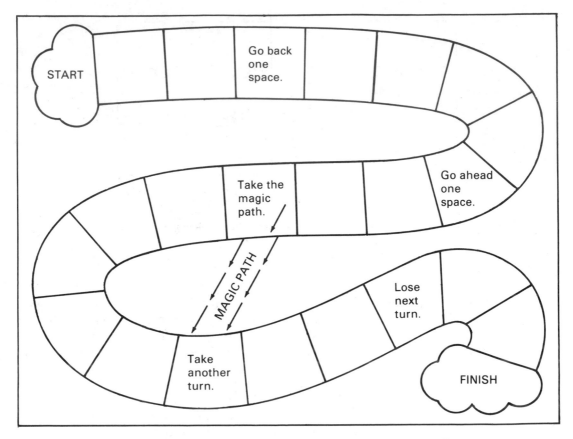

Figure 1.3. A sample game board for an activity to help readers who rely too heavily on context cues.

The object of the game is to identify the word exactly with as few cues as possible, thereby receiving a *low* score. A player receives one point for each letter that is exposed for her, and she also receives five points for every guess after the first guess that does *not* correspond to the beginning and ending (when available) letters. (Penalizing students for mistakes with internal letters is too demanding. The game then becomes simply a spelling contest.) The player with the lowest score wins the round. Note that a player may not be the first to identify his word but still may have the lowest score since no wild guesses were made. A player may decline to make a guess on any turn rather than make a guess inconsistent with the exposed letters.

### Activity 4

To encourage children to use the graphophonic system to obtain accuracy, write a description of a mythical creature or an imaginary object, using as many unpredictable descriptive words as possible. For example:

The snuffling wileywoss has five long legs. One leg has three toes. One leg has seven toes. The other legs all have four teeth. The snuffling wileywoss has two large striped eyes. Its three small ears are placed on one side of its head. The nose looks like a fried tomato.

Have the children first read the description silently and then draw a picture that includes all of the details provided in the description. Children who fail to use the graphophonic system and rely only on context may draw five-toed wileywosses or noses like french fries.

## SUMMARY

Good readers possess a flexible repertoire of word identification strategies based on the three cue systems of the English language. Reading teachers must make sure that the students are able to use each of these cue systems and that they are able to switch strategies according to the particular unknown word and the specific context in which the word appears. The guidelines and activities described in this chapter should help teachers to develop confident, flexible readers.

## REFERENCES

Goodman, Y., and Burke, C. *Reading miscue inventory manual: Procedure for diagnosis and evaluation.* New York: Macmillan, 1972.

Guthrie, J. T., Siefert, M., Burnham, N. R., and Caplan, R. I. The maze technique to assess, monitor reading comprehension. *The Reading Teacher,* 1974, **28,** 161-168.

Rowe, M. B. Science, silence, and sanctions. *Science and Children,* 1969, **6,** 3-8.

Spiegel, D. L., and Rogers, C. Teachers' responses to miscues during oral reading by second-grade students. *Journal of Educational Research,* 1980, **74,** 8-12.

## RECOMMENDED READINGS

Durkin, D. *Teaching young children to read.* (3rd ed.)
   Boston: Allyn and Bacon, 1980.
   Chapter 10, "Using Contexts," provides an excellent overview of the use of integrated cue systems for word identification. Durkin supplies several examples of lessons designed to help children use both written and spoken contexts.

Goodman, Y. M., and Burke, C. *Reading strategies: Focus on comprehension.* New York: Holt, Rinehart and Winston, 1980.
   This well-organized book combines theory and practice in a down-to-earth manner that will enable even beginning teachers to implement their ideas and to understand *why* these ideas are important. The major portion of the book is made up of specific reading-strategy lessons focusing on the development of the ability to use the three cue systems to predict and to confirm meaning.

Spache, E. B. *Reading activities for child involvement.* (3rd ed.)
   Boston: Allyn and Bacon, 1982.
   This book has over 200 pages of activities for developing and reinforcing reading skills. The sections entitled "Composing Stories and Experience Charts" and "Contextual Analysis" are particularly relevant for developing the use of all three cue systems to identify words.

Spiegel, D. L. Meaning-seeking strategies for the beginning reader. *The Reading Teacher,* 1978, **31,** 772-776.
   In this article, the importance of risk taking, self-monitoring, and self-correction in reading is described. Activities are outlined for developing each of these strategies to help children use information from all three cue systems.

# CHAPTER 2

# Developing Intensive Word Practice Exercises

Alden J. Moe
Louisiana State University
Baton Rouge

John C. Manning
University of Minnesota
Minneapolis

*The strategies for identifying words presented in Chapter 1 were generalizable and transferable; that is, they were not tied to any particular word but rather enabled a reader to identify many new words. In Chapter 2, Alden Moe and John Manning also deal with word identification but present strategies for teaching children to identify and learn the meaning of* specific *words. Their intensive word practice exercises are designed to teach children to recognize words prior to their exposure to the words in instructional materials such as basal readers. In contrast to traditional preteaching of vocabulary, which typically involves only an oral presentation of the words, the intensive word practice exercises are designed to maximize students' attention and to require them to attend to words in a trimodal fashion—through visual, auditory, and tactile or kinesthetic senses. By requiring students to attend to new words through several modes, the likelihood is greater that such words subsequently will be recognized, pronounced, and understood.*

The purpose of this chapter is to describe the development and use of intensive word practice exercises that help students recognize and learn the meaning of new words. The exercises and the procedures for using them are "intensive" in that the students practice using new words in several contexts and through two or three sensory modes *before* they are encountered in a story or a reading selection.

The techniques presented in this chapter may be used at most grade levels and in most content areas where new words must be learned before the text can be understood. For some students, the techniques may be more intensive than necessary; in these instances, modifications or shortcuts to the procedures are recommended.

## OBTAINING AND MAINTAINING THE LEARNER'S ATTENTION

Consider one of the most common methods the teacher uses to introduce the new vocabulary either in a basal reader or a content area lesson. The teacher writes the new words on the chalkboard. For our purposes, let us next consider how the teacher teaches just one new word. The teacher pronounces the word and asks the students to do likewise. If he is concerned about the meaning of the word, the teacher clarifies the meaning and leads students in a discussion. Often, students are asked to use the new word in a sentence orally, and in some instances, the students are also directed to the page and the sentence in the text where the new word is used. The teacher proceeds to the next word, then the next, and so on.

The problem with this method is that some students will attend, using their ears to listen to the teacher's directions and their eyes to focus attention on the word, but many will not attend. *Such inattentive behavior, however, may not be apparent to the teacher.*

Because it is possible to repeat a new word spoken by the teacher without looking at the word, many children simply use their short-term, auditory memory and only *appear* to be following the teacher's direction to "look at the word." It is necessary, therefore, to use techniques that ensure that students attend *visually* to the task of learning the new words.

An essential factor in the use of intensive word practice activities is the maximization of the students' attention. When appropriately used, these activities employ what Manning (1980) calls the trimodal reading method, which enlists the students' tactile or kinesthetic (i.e., touching or moving) sense to ensure the visual and auditory attention of the learner. The major focus in developing such activities is to determine what overt responses (such as underlining a word) the student should make during the period when the teacher directs the instruction.

## PREPARING AND USING THE EXERCISES

The student exercises can take many forms. It is essential, however, to use procedures —those that are suggested or similar procedures—that require students to pay visual attention to the new words.

The exercises may be wholly teacher made, or they may be adapted from exercises available in student workbooks. The development and use of two teacher-made exercises and one adapted exercise are described here.

### Example 1 (Lesson Made Up by Teacher)

Consider a situation in which the teacher must prepare second-grade students for a short selection entitled "The Octopus and the Ax" (Stone and Burton, 1960). The teacher has read the selection and identified six words, *ax, bottom, honesty, octopus, silver,* and *thanks,* that she considers new and difficult words. Individual flash cards for these words, large enough to be seen by the group or class, should be prepared. These six words are then discussed so that the students develop some understanding of the meanings of the words before they are encountered in the exercise. She may wish to hold up a card, say the name of the word on the card, and discuss its meaning.

These six words, together with three words the students definitely know as sight words (in this case, *he, cat,* and *one),* are then incorporated into an exercise sheet like the one presented in Figure 2.1. The section with the four sentences at the bottom of the exercise sheet should be folded on the dotted line so that it is hidden behind the rest of the exercise.

For this particular exercise, three lines of three words each are used. However, more lines and more words could be included in the exercise, depending on the number of new words to be taught and on the skill and independence of the learners.

The numerals next to each box serve to guide the students from one box to the next. Students are directed to the group of words in box 1 and instructed as follows while the teacher *shows* the word on a flash card as she *says* the word aloud.

"In the first line, circle the word *ax.*"

"In the second line, circle the word *thanks.*"

"In the last line, circle the word *honesty.*"

"Now back to the first line. Draw a line under *silver.*"

"In the second line, draw a line under *octopus.*"

"In the last line, draw a line under *bottom.*"

Students are then directed to the second group of words in box 2, for which the teacher only *shows* the word on a flash card and gives the following instructions.

"In the first line, circle this word" *(silver).*

"In the second line, circle this word" *(octopus).*

"In the last line, circle this word" *(bottom).*

"Back to the first line. Draw a line under this word" *(ax).*

"In the second line, draw a line under this word" *(thanks).*

"In the last line, draw a line under this word" *(honesty).*

Students are then directed to the next group of words in box 3, for which the teacher only *says* the word.

"In the first line, circle *silver.*"

"In the second line, circle *thanks.*"

"In the last line, circle *bottom.*"

"Back to the first line. Draw a line under *ax.*"

"In the second line, draw a line under *octopus.*"

"In the last line, draw a line under *honesty.*"

Next, students are directed to the last group of words in box 4, for which, depending on the students' need, the teacher either defines each word and directs the students to circle or underline the defined word or, if additional practice on word meanings is unnecessary, simply says, "Circle all the words we have been working on today."

If the teacher chooses to do so, he may collect all the completed exercises and examine them. The completed exercises should look like the example shown in Figure 2.2.

The next step in this intensive word practice activity is to use the four sentences that have been folded behind the exercise page. These sentences have been taken directly from the selection "The Octopus and the Ax."

Students are directed to sentence 1 and told to follow along as the teacher reads it; some will follow along and some will not, but the students' short-term auditory memories can be put to good use since their attention is immediately focused on the sentence. After reading the sentence, the teacher says: "Draw a line under *octopus.*" "Draw two lines under *silver.*" "Draw a circle around *ax.*" Similar directions are then given for sentences 2, 3, and 4. Refer to the bottom portion of Figure 2.2 to see what this part of the completed exercise should look like.

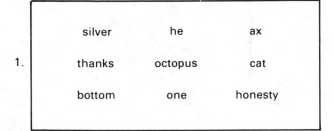

1.

| silver | he | ax |
| thanks | octopus | cat |
| bottom | one | honesty |

2.

| he | ax | silver |
| octopus | cat | thanks |
| honesty | bottom | one |

3.

| ax | silver | he |
| octopus | thanks | cat |
| one | honesty | bottom |

4.

| silver | he | ax |
| thanks | octopus | cat |
| honesty | one | bottom |

· · · · · · · · · · · · · · · · · · · · · · · · · · · · · · · · · · · · · · · · · · · · · · · · · · · ·

1.  The octopus had a silver ax.
2.  The octopus went down to the bottom.
3.  "Your honesty is all the thanks I need," said the octopus.
4.  The octopus went back to the bottom of the sea.

Figure 2.1. A response sheet for a teacher-made lesson, example 1.

1.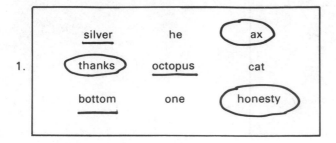

2.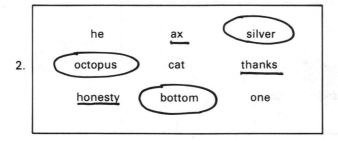

3.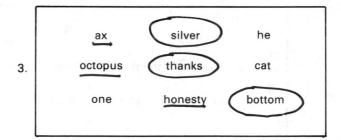

4.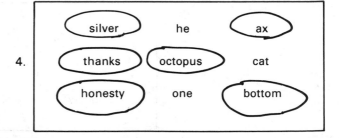

1.  The <u>octopus</u> had a <u>silver</u> (ax.)
2.  The <u>octopus</u> went down to the (bottom.)
3.  "Your <u>honesty</u> is all the (thanks) I need," said the <u>octopus</u>.
4.  The (octopus) went back to the <u>bottom</u> of the sea.

Figure 2.2. A completed response sheet for a teacher-made lesson, example 1.

## Example 2 (Lesson Made Up by Teacher)

Another word practice activity, less intensive than the one just described, presents the words to the students in a different format. Assume that there are ten new words to be introduced to the students before they read the selection. These ten words are listed on a response sheet like the one presented in Figure 2.3.

Every student is provided a copy of the response sheet, and the teacher may pronounce each word in order. Then, the teacher begins by saying, "Find the word *election* in the first group of words. Can anyone tell us the meaning of *election?*" If it is apparent that the students understand the meaning of the word *election,* then the teacher should have them write a number one in the space before the word. The teacher proceeds in a similar manner with all the words in each group.

After all the words have been introduced, the teacher might wish to provide additional practice by defining the words and directing the students as follows.

"In the first group of words, underline the word that names things you can drink" *(beverages).*

"Circle the word that names someone who works for a newspaper or a book publisher" *(editor).*

Appropriate definitions are then given for the remaining words on the list.

If additional practice is still needed, the teacher could define a word, ask the students to find the word in the list, and then require that the word be written in the blank to the right of the word. After one word has been defined, the students and teacher proceed to the next. This practice method holds the students' attention as they spell out the words correctly and thereby gain additional practice with the words.

## Example 3 (Lesson Adapted From Workbook)

The use of workbooks, study books, practice books, duplicating masters, and the like has been of some major concern to classroom teachers and administrators for a considerable time. In most instances, these materials are a single-page reading skill reinforcement activity. The procedures for using these materials are commonly understood. Usually, the teacher provides some initial direction or instruction using one or two of the skill items as examples, and the pupils then complete the rest of the exercise independently "at their seats."

Such skill-type materials are found in most classrooms, most commonly at the primary-grade levels. Some dissatisfaction with the use of such materials, however, exists, and often their effectiveness is dismissed by labeling such activities as "seatwork" or "busy work."

In some schools, administrators or curriculum specialists prohibit the use of such reading skill materials. In some schools, the materials are tolerated although not endorsed. In other schools, these reading skill materials are intelligently, sensitively, and creatively used. In still other schools, the use of such materials is excessive, ill-advised, and abused. This section attempts to cast some light on appropriate uses for such reading skill materials so that classroom practitioners may use their talents to extend these sample procedures into more meaningful word practice and reinforcement activities.

_____ editor          _____

_____ cartoon        _____

_____ election        _____

_____ beverages     _____

_____ signatures     _____

_____ strategy        _____

_____ hesitate        _____

_____ baggage        _____

_____ excess          _____

_____ celebrate     _____

Figure 2.3. A response sheet for a teacher-made lesson, example 2.

Workbook, study-book, skillbook, and practice-book pages can be used with several significant objectives: (1) to improve listening ability and ability to follow directions, (2) to improve word recognition abilities, (3) to improve spelling and related handwriting skills, and (4) to increase attention to and understanding of written directions.

The following practice-book page (Figure 2.4), intended for use with second-graders, demonstrates some model instructional procedures. The procedures for using the page, as described in the teacher's manual, are fairly simple. The pupils are to fill in the open circle before the word that makes sense in the sentence. The teacher's manual refers to this exercise as a context, consonants exercise.

To obtain maximum pupil participation and response to this exercise, however, "teacher-directed" methods must be employed. The teacher leads the students through the exercise to ensure their attention and participation. To begin, teachers can give directions using the exact exercise page so that the teacher can be confident that the directions are being followed properly. For example, pupils could be directed to circle the numbers in

Daisy Days
Use after page 95

NAME _____

Mark the word that makes sense in the sentence.

1. The g_____ is eating grass.
   (a) game        (b) goat        (c) sheep

2. Our school is in the c_____.
   (a) cent        (b) town        (c) city

3. The bird sat on its n_____.
   (a) nest        (b) note        (c) branch

4. The girl put on her sh_____.
   (a) sandal      (b) shed        (c) shoe

5. We saw a z_____ at the zoo.
   (a) seal        (b) zebra       (c) zigzag

6. The v_____ grew on the wall.
   (a) van         (b) bush        (c) vine

7. Dad gave me milk in a th_____.
   (a) thermos     (b) cup         (c) thread

8. Our baseball team w_____ the game.
   (a) wave        (b) played      (c) won

9. A k_____ can jump very high.
   (a) kite        (b) mouse       (c) kangaroo

Figure 2.4. An original workbook page. (From *Scott, Foresman Basics in Reading,* "Daisy Days" Workbook by Ira E. Aaron et al. Copyright ©1978, Scott, Foresman and Company. Reprinted by permission.)

front of each sentence in random order: "Circle the number six," "Circle the number eight," and so on. The purpose of this initial activity is to gain the pupils' attention before the actual directions involving reading skill development are given.

The pupils are then directed to draw a long line after the period in each sentence as the teacher reads the sentence. The purpose of this activity is to provide a model of fluent reading and allow enough space to print or write the correct word response. For example, some pupils might not be able to print the correct answers to items 5, 7, and 9 in the spaces provided on the exercise page.

Next, the teacher reads two or three times each of the three answer choices below the first sentence. Then, the teacher gives these instructions.

"Print a number two in front of the word *goat.*"

"Print a number one before the word *game.*"

"Print three before *sheep.*"

"Underline the word *sheep.*"

"Underline *game.*"

"Underline *goat.*"

"Circle *game.*"

"Circle *sheep.*"

"Circle *goat.*"

The teacher then reads the sentence, deleting the word choice, and she asks pupils for the correct response. The students print or write the word on the line drawn after the sentence.

The remaining eight sentences would be completed in a similar manner. When all the sentences have been completed, the teacher could further direct attention to any particular sentence. For example: "Look at sentence number two." The teacher reads the sentence and then directs the students to draw a line below and between the words *cent* and *town* and a line below and between the words *town* and *city.* By having the students indicate each word, additional recognition practice is achieved, and the teacher's reading of the sentences provides another fluent model. It should be evident, even at this point, that the amount of pupil practice in word recognition tasks has been increased dramatically.

After all the lines have been draw below and between all the word choices for each sentence, the teacher would say: "I'm going to give you a sentence number and one of the words below that sentence. You are to print [write] that word on one of the lines you have drawn." The teacher would then *by random sentence number* indicate one of the other two nonchoice words from that sentence.

"Sentence 2, print *cent.*"

"Sentence 5, print *seal.*"

"Sentence 7, *cup.*"

"Sentence 3, *note,*" and so on.

The teacher would continue in this manner until all 18 of the nonchoice words had been printed or written. When completed, the exercise page would look like the exercise reproduced in Figure 2.5.

Daisy Days
Use after page 95

NAME _____

Mark the word that makes sense in the sentence.

1. The g——— is eating grass. *goat*
   1 ⓐ (game)   2 ⓑ (goat)   3 ⓒ (sheep)
   *game*      *sheep*

2. Our school is in the c———. *city*
   1 ⓐ (cent)   2 ⓑ (town)   3 ⓒ (city)
   *cent*      *town*

3. The bird sat on its n———. *nest*
   1 ⓐ (nest)   2 ⓑ (note)   3 ⓒ (branch)
   *note*      *branch*

4. The girl put on her sh———. *shoe*
   1 ⓐ (sandal)   2 ⓑ (shed)   3 ⓒ (shoe)
   *sandal*      *shed*

5. We saw a z——— at the zoo. *zebra*
   1 ⓐ (seal)   2 ⓑ (zebra)   3 ⓒ (zigzag)
   *seal*      *zigzag*

6. The v——— grew on the wall. *vine*
   1 ⓐ (van)   2 ⓑ (bush)   3 ⓒ (vine)
   *van*      *bush*

7. Dad gave me milk in a th———. *thermos*
   1 ⓐ (thermos)   2 ⓑ (cup)   3 ⓒ (thread)
   *cup*      *thread*

8. Our baseball team w——— the game. *won*
   1 ⓐ (wave)   2 ⓑ (played)   3 ⓒ (won)
   *wave*      *played*

9. A k——— can jump very high. *kangaroo*
   1 ⓐ (kite)   2 ⓑ (mouse)   3 ⓒ (kangaroo)
   *kite*      *mouse*

Figure 2.5. A completed workbook page. (From *Scott, Foresman Basics in Reading,* "Daisy Days" Workbook by Ira E. Aaron et al. Copyright ©1978, Scott, Foresman and Company. Reprinted by permission.)

# SUMMARY

Other examples of intensive word practice activities are provided in publications listed in the Recommended Readings for this chapter. The development and use of such activities, however, is limited only by the creativity and resourcefulness of the individual teacher. Through direct instruction, during which attention to the learning task is ensured, these exercises facilitate the students' learning of the new words and the subsequent acquisition of the new words.

# REFERENCES

Manning, J. C. *Reading: Learning and instructional processes.* Geneva, Ill.: Paladin House, 1980.

Stone, C. R., and Burton, A. E. *New practice readers: Book A.* St. Louis: Webster, 1960.

# RECOMMENDED READINGS

Dale, E., O'Rourke, J., and Bamman, H. A. *Techniques of teaching vocabulary.* Addison, Ill.: Field Educational Publications, 1971.
A work providing a wealth of excellent activities, sample lessons, and word games for vocabulary instruction, this comprehensive volume also includes separate chapters on testing, figures of speech, and dictionary use. Lists of common prefixes, suffixes, and common root and derived words are also provided.

Deighton, L. C. *Vocabulary development in the classroom.* New York: Teachers College Press, Columbia University, 1959.
This 65-page paperback provides suggestions of value to intermediate grade and junior high school teachers.

Heilman, A. W., and Holmes, E. A. *Smuggling language into the teaching of reading.* Columbus, Ohio: Charles E. Merrill, 1972.
Many sample lessons that may be used or adapted for reading vocabulary development are included in this brief paperback.

Henderson, E. H. *Learning to read and spell: The child's knowledge of words.* DeKalb, Ill.: Northern Illinois University Press, 1981.
Henderson's book reviews the theoretical background and research behind our current knowledge of child development in the areas of reading and spelling. The author also provides a critique of current methods of instruction.

Hopkins, C. J., and Moe, A. J. Game books for reading instruction. *Reading Horizons,* 1977, **18**, 75–77.
This article provides a list of excellent sources for teachers who are interested in developing a variety of motivating instructional activities for reading.

Ives, J. P., Bursuk, L. A., and Ives, S. A. *Word identification techniques.* Chicago: Rand McNally, 1979.
Both background information on word identification techniques and examples of sample lessons are included in this publication. A glossary of commonly used terms in reading vocabulary is also provided.

Johnson, D. D., and Pearson, P. D. *Teaching reading vocabulary.* (2nd Ed.) New York: Holt, Rinehart and Winston, in press.
Many sample lessons and suggested activities in most areas of reading vocabulary instruction are included in this paperback, which also contains separate chapters on phonics and structural analysis.

Manning, J. C. *Reading: Learning and instructional processes.* Geneva, Ill.: Paladin House, 1980.
This comprehensive book on instructional methods provides excellent sample lessons for reading vocabulary instruction. Also included are many suggested activities for helping students attend to the desired learning tasks.

McCormick, S., and Moe, A. J. The language of instructional materials: A source of reading problems. *Exceptional Children*, 1982, **49**, 48–53.
   Particularly helpful to teachers who work with learning disabled students, this article discusses differences between oral language and written language.
O'Rourke, J. P. *Toward a science of vocabulary development.* The Hague, The Netherlands: Mouton, 1974.
   O'Rourke's book is particularly appropriate for those who seek a theoretical background for vocabulary instruction at the advanced levels, especially the high school levels.

# CHAPTER 3

# Expanding Vocabulary Through Classification

Dale D. Johnson
University of Wisconsin–Madison

*Chapter 1 presented strategies for teaching children to develop generalizable and transferable word identification skills, and Chapter 2 described techniques for directly teaching children to identify specific words. Chapter 3 also deals with instruction in specific words, but it focuses on* meaning vocabulary, *that is, on directly teaching children the meanings of specific words. Research has demonstrated that the best predictor of a reader's ability to comprehend is word knowledge. Meaning vocabulary links the skills of word identification and comprehension, for it is essential that readers understand the meanings of individual words before they can grasp the meanings of larger units of text. In this chapter, Dale Johnson discusses several prior knowledge strategies for developing a reader's meaning vocabulary in which readers are taught new concepts (words) by relating them to those they already know. Specifically, he recommends classification exercises (semantic mapping, semantic feature analysis, and analogies) as sensible and efficient ways to help children learn entirely new words and add meanings to words known only in a limited context by requiring them to relate new words and meanings to known words and meanings.*

The purpose of this chapter[1] is to describe three types of instruction that have repeatedly proved effective in building students' vocabularies. You are invited to begin this chapter by participating in a demonstration of a fact about the way humans learn. Please read the following passage and answer the question "What is this passage about?"

---

[1]Concepts in this chapter have appeared previously in *Teaching Reading Vocabulary* (Dale D. Johnson and P. David Pearson, Holt, Rinehart and Winston, 1978) and *Three Sound Strategies for Vocabulary Development* (Dale D. Johnson, Ginn Occasional Paper number 3, Ginn and Company).

The procedure is actually quite simple. First you arrange things into different groups. Of course, one pile may be sufficient depending on how much there is to do. If you have to go somewhere else due to lack of facilities that is the next step, otherwise you are pretty well set. It is important not to overdo things. That is, it is better to do too few things at once than too many. In the short run this may not seem important but complications can easily arise. A mistake can be expensive as well. At first the whole procedure will seem complicated. Soon, however, it will become just another facet of life. It is difficult to forsee any end to the necessity for this task in the immediate future, but then one can never tell. After the procedure is completed one arranges the materials into different groups again. Then they can be put into their appropriate places. Eventually they will be used once more and the whole cycle will then have to be repeated. However, that is part of life (Bransford and Johnson, 1972, p. 719).

The passage, intentionally ambiguous, has been used in research studies designed to demonstrate the importance of relating new knowledge to prior knowledge and experience in the comprehension of printed text. Bransford and Johnson (1972) asked adult readers to read the passage in the same way you were asked to do so. Other adults received help—they were given a title for the passage. Readers who were first shown the title read the passage with much greater comprehension than those who were not shown the title. The title for the passage could be "Washing Clothes" or "Doing the Laundry."

Now that you have been given a title, try reading the passage a second time. Chances are on the second reading you found the passage much more understandable and much less ambiguous. Why? Because the title enabled you to relate unfamiliar printed text to a familiar experience—to prior knowledge. (This conclusion assumes that you are familiar with the tasks involved in doing the laundry.)

## VOCABULARY DEVELOPMENT: RELATING THE NEW TO THE KNOWN

What this simple demonstration shows is that we cannot learn much of anything unless we can relate something new to something we already know. This fact of human learning begins when we are in the cradle. And how do we relate new knowledge to prior knowledge? We depend on classification. We classify concepts by comparing them to one another on the basis of our prior knowledge and by discerning how they are alike and how they are different.

Classification activities lie at the heart of vocabulary development. Classification is absolutely essential for dealing with our world. If each new stimulus in life, each concept, each experience had to be treated as unique, learning would be incredibly inefficient, sluggish, and uninsightful. Consider these two statements:

1. An albassa is a plant of the lily family that has an edible bulb with a strong, sharp smell and taste.
2. An albassa is a large onion, grown in Africa, which, when sliced, is great on a hamburger.

The first statement, though containing some classification (lily family, edible bulb), is essentially a unique description. The second statement places an albassa directly in a class (onion family), enabling you to draw on prior knowledge and assign all kinds of already-known attributes to the new concept (e.g., thin, brown skin; makes me cry). Learning accomplished through classification is much more complete, personal, and generalizable.

## THE RELATIONSHIP BETWEEN VOCABULARY AND COMPREHENSION

Classification activities are among the most vital and important that a teacher can use to help children expand their meaning vocabularies, that is, the words for which students have some semantic association (to be discriminated from their only being able to decode, or pronounce, a word). Before specific classification activities are described, however, the importance of vocabulary to comprehension should be emphasized. Numerous studies carried out during recent decades have supported the finding of a landmark study done by Davis in 1944. Davis found that the most critical skill related to reading comprehension was a reader's vocabulary. That is, word knowledge—meaning vocabulary—is the *key* to comprehension. Common sense tells us the same thing: if you do not know the words, you are not going to understand the passage.

Vocabulary instruction is an essential component of any reading program. Teachers and researchers agree that students with limited vocabularies do not read well. During their early years in school, students learn words that they sense are necessary since they are used in everyday situations. Because of their frequent use in a variety of ways, these words are often easily learned. A systematic program of vocabulary development, in which students are exposed to new words and are taught techniques for independent vocabulary acquisition, usually improves reading comprehension and other language abilities. Vocabulary development can lead children to broader experiences that generate new experiences. Learning new words and using them in a variety of ways is a *dynamic* process, for when our vocabularies change, we change!

What students have read, what experiences they have had, and how their minds function are reflected in their vocabularies. Therefore, teachers must devote instructional time to helping students add more words to their vocabularies.

## CLASSIFICATION ACTIVITIES FOR VOCABULARY DEVELOPMENT

Classification involves the systematic arrangement of words, objects, and experiences in groups (categories) according to some established criterion. When humans are introduced to a new stimulus, they usually identify it by relating it to the class to which it belongs and by assigning to it the attributes of that class. We assimilate new information by relating it to past experiences and prior knowledge when such are available. Classification activities are among the most helpful that teachers can plan and implement in any developmental vocabulary program. In this chapter, three types of classification activities for vocabulary development are described: semantic mapping, semantic feature analysis, and analogies.

### Semantic Mapping

Semantic mapping as a successful method for vocabulary expansion extends knowledge by displaying, in categories, words related to other words (i.e., how words "go together"). Learning new words, seeing "old" words in new lights, and seeing the relationships among words are the desirable and inevitable outcomes of semantic mapping.

The following steps constitute the procedure, but the teacher should keep in mind that the procedure can be varied to suit different purposes.

1.  First, select a word central to the story to be read or from any other source of classroom interest or need (e.g., a science, social studies, or health textbook chapter).
2.  Then, write the word on the chalkboard.
3.  Next, ask the students in the class, working as individuals, to think of as many words as they can that in some way are related to the word you have written. Have them write the words, arranged in categories, on paper.
4.  Then, ask individuals to share the words they have written, and as they do, you should write the words on the board in categories. In addition to eliciting words and subcategories from the students, you should feel free to add additional words, especially those considered critical to later reading (i.e., important words from the basal story or content textbook chapter). For example, if the category word you wrote on the board were *school,* the resultant class semantic map might look like Figure 3.1.

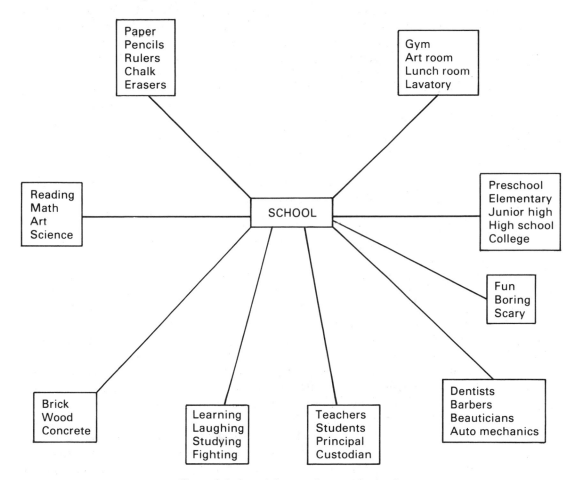

Figure 3.1. A partial semantic map of *school.*

5. Next, you might want to number the categories and have the students name them. For example: (1) school subjects, (2) things we use in school, (3) places in school, (4) kinds of schools, (5) things school can be, and so on.

6. Discussion, you should remember, is *crucial* to the effectiveness of semantic mapping. You might ask, for example, "What does *studying* (or *custodian* or *concrete*, etc.) mean? When do we study? Why? What is an antonym of studying?" You should be ready for some disagreement; you may have put a word in one category when it could just as logically have been placed in a different category. Some words will end up in several categories, and new words will be added as the discussion ensues.

7. As the discussion concludes, it often becomes necessary to focus attention on one or two subcategories mapped from the central concept. For example, for the semantic map exemplified in Figure 3.1, you might need to say something like this: "We've prepared quite a map about *school,* and have listed words in nine categories! That's great! The selection we're going to read, though, is about the different kinds of schools to be found in our society. It describes public, private, and parochial schools as well as trade schools and specialty schools. Which two lists on our semantic map contain words descriptive of different kinds of schools? Let's talk about these words." This type of "focusing" discussion, which directs students' attention to particular words on the map, is appropriate when you are using semantic mapping as an activity to develop vocabulary before reading a story or chapter. In addition, semantic mapping is often done for general vocabulary development (e.g., when a current event, holiday, or film is used as the central concept). At such times, focusing is not a necessary part of the discussion.

8. You might also find semantic mapping a good "postreading" activity. After fifth-graders had read a social studies chapter on the Civil War, for example, a map with *Civil War* as the central concept would help students organize concepts and vocabulary about the Civil War. Categories students might develop could include battles, dates, generals, armaments, and the like.

### Semantic Feature Analysis

Semantic feature analysis, like semantic mapping, capitalizes on the reader's prior knowledge and the ways it is organized and stresses the relationship among concepts within categories. Unlike semantic mapping, which explores how words are *alike,* semantic feature analysis requires the reader to explore how related words *differ* from one another. Like semantic mapping, semantic feature analysis can be helpful to students of any age. This instructional practice, which capitalizes on the reader's prior knowledge (and the ways it is organized), has been shown to have considerable potential for greatly expanding vocabulary in a logical and sensible way.

The procedure is simple. The teacher begins with a list of known words (within a category) that share some features or attributes. For example, he might begin with kinds of tools when the words *hammer, saw, scissors, hoe,* and *pliers* are known to the children. These words are listed in a column on the chalkboard or on paper. Next, he has the children suggest features that at least one of the words usually possesses. These features are listed in a row across the top of the board or paper. Then, the children fill in the matrix by putting a plus or a minus for each word under each feature, as is shown in Figure 3.2. When a word *usually* has a particular semantic feature, it is given a plus; when it usually does not have that feature, it is given a minus.

What this semantic feature grid shows is that a hammer is usually used to pound, is used with wood, and has a handle. It is usually not used to cut or grip or with dirt. A hoe, on the other hand, is a tool with a handle and is usually used to cut in dirt.

We favor the use of plus and minus to indicate whether a word *usually* has a given feature even though we realize that many features of words are not truly dichotomous but rather exist in varying degrees. As children learn to read better and become more skilled with feature analysis, a scale of numbers can be appropriately substituted for pluses and minuses. (For example, 0 = none or never, 1 = few or some, 2 = many or most, 3 = all or every.) This system allows for even greater precision. Teachers of young children may wish to use smiling faces in place of pluses and either sad faces or blank spaces in place of minuses.

After the grid has been completed, several activities could be added. The children could be asked to suggest other words that share some of the same features (*screwdriver, rake, beater, thimble, file, blade*) and then to suggest additional features shared by some of these words (*metal, kitchen, garden, two hands*). The students usually run out of space or time before they run out of features or words.

Next, the children complete the remainder of the grid by adding pluses and minuses. Finally, the teacher helps them to discover that no two words have identical patterns of pluses and minuses and thus that no two words are identical in meaning. With even the most synonymous pairs or clusters of words, the pattern eventually becomes different once enough semantic features have been listed. In addition to discovering the uniqueness of words, children learn new words within a category and new semantic features that they had not considered before. Group discussion of the words and their features is *essential*. For example, asking questions such as "Which two words are the most alike?" or "Which two words are the most unalike?" stimulates discussion. Even putting down an arbitrary row of pluses and minuses and then trying to figure out whether a word "fits" that description (although there will not always be such a word) makes the class's discussion interesting.

Topic: Tools

Features

| Words | Pounds | Cuts | Grips | Wood | Cloth | Dirt | Handle |
|-------|--------|------|-------|------|-------|------|--------|
| Hammer | + | – | – | + | – | – | + |
| Saw | – | + | – | + | – | – | + |
| Scissors | – | + | – | – | + | – | + |
| Pliers | – | – | + | + | – | – | + |
| Hoe | – | + | – | – | – | + | + |

Figure 3.2. A partial semantic feature analysis grid for *tools*.

Children asked to list the semantic features of the word *carrot* might quickly mention "something to eat," "something to cook," "something to chew," but eventually they might add "something to plant," "something to sell," "something to cut," "something to buy," and so on. In other words, they begin to discover what they already knew but had not immediately thought about, and they begin to view words in more complex and precise ways.

Semantic feature charts can be constructed for any category of words. Categories that are concrete and within the experiences of the students are a good place to start. Later, students can progress to more abstract or less familiar categories. Beginning categories could include:

| | | |
|---|---|---|
| Games | Vegetables | Pets |
| Jobs | Food | Clothing |
| Tools | Buildings | Animals |
| Plants | Vehicles | Furniture |
| Fruits | | |

Subsequently used categories could include:

| | | |
|---|---|---|
| Moods | Sizes | Entertainment |
| Feelings | Shapes | Musical Instruments |
| Commands | Modes of communication | Machines |

In summary, semantic feature analysis involves the following steps.

1.  Select a category (*tools*).
2.  List, in a column, some words within the category (*hammer, saw*).
3.  List, in a row, some features shared by some of the words (*pounds, cuts*).
4.  Mark a plus or a minus for each word beneath each feature.
5.  Supply additional words.
6.  Think of additional features.
7.  Complete the expanded grid with pluses and minuses.
8.  Remember that discussion is *crucial* to semantic feature analysis. Through discussion children learn the meanings of words by seeing how they are alike and how they are different from other words within the same category and by relating these new words to prior knowledge.

It is also recommended that the teacher provide an adequate supply of single-page grid sheets so that they are available for individual or small-group use (Figure 3.3).

Semantic feature analysis works with learners of all ages, preschool (as an oral activity) through college. It is a powerful procedure for use with content-area materials as well as with intensive vocabulary instruction. For example, in conjunction with a chapter on rocks and minerals in a science textbook, semantic feature analysis could be used to classify various rocks and minerals (e.g., granite, limestone, gold, coal, pumice) according to a number of relevant features (e.g., igneous, sedimentary, valuable, hard).

Reading comprehension involves processing textual material and integrating it with the experiences, prior knowledge, and attitudes already in one's mind. Comprehending is, metaphorically, "building bridges from the new to the known." Semantic feature analysis as a process for vocabulary development is based on this metaphor.

Topic: _____

**Features**

| Words | | | | | | | |
|---|---|---|---|---|---|---|---|
| | | | | | | | |
| | | | | | | | |
| | | | | | | | |
| | | | | | | | |
| | | | | | | | |

Figure 3.3. A sample grid for use in semantic feature analysis.

### Analogical Reasoning

Analogies portray the meaning of a word through comparisons that show its relationship to other words. For example, *"coop* is to *chicken* as *hutch* is to *rabbit,"* that is, *home* to *animal.*

There are several categories of analogies. Among the most common are the following: (1) characteristics (e.g., *"rain* is to *wet* as *sun* is to *dry"),* (2) part/whole (e.g., *"leaf* is to *tree* as *feather* is to *bird"),* (3) whole/part (e.g., *"cup* is to *handle* as *clock* is to *hands"),* (4) location (e.g, *"teacher* is to *classroom* as *sailor* is to *ship"),* (5) action/object (e.g., *"run* is to *track* as *swim* is to *pool"),* (6) agent-action or object (e.g., *"teacher* is to *student* as *doctor* is to *patient"),* (7) class or synonym (e.g., *"smell* is to *sniff* as *see* is to *look"),* (8) familial (e.g., *"uncle* is to *nephew* as *aunt* is to *niece"),* (9) grammatical (e.g., *"hear* is to *heard* as *see* is to *seen"),* (10) temporal or sequential (e.g., *"fifth* is to *first* as *twenty-fifth* is to *fifth"),* and (11) antonyms (e.g., *"smile* is to *happy* as *frown* is to *sad").*

Analogies provide a means of joining new knowledge to what is already known. They are powerful organizers and should be taught as early as possible. Five-year-olds are capable of completing an analogy such as *"rabbit* is to *bunny* as *cat* is to _____."* Generally, activities in analogies can be used as soon as students know that a baby cries and an older child talks. They are then ready to learn that crying serves the same function for a baby that talking does for an older child.

When the teacher is introducing new concepts to students, analogies can be extremely helpful. For example, suppose a group of students knows that a microscope is looked through to discover information. The comparable discovery method for a stethoscope is to listen. Thus, the analogy—*look/microscope, listen/stethoscope*—summarizes an important comparison between these two instruments.

Practice sheets for analogies can be planned in various ways. One method is for each item to consist of three parts of the analogy for which students choose or create a fourth (e.g., *automobile/road—train/*_____). Alternatively, students can match one half of an analogy with the other half (e.g., *astronomy/universe—*_____/_____). The activities outlined below are intended to encourage the general expansion of meaning vocabulary, but the teacher may also find them appropriate for teaching specialized content vocabularies.

### Activity 1: Sentence Comprehension

1. _____ is to female as buck is to doe.
2. _____ is to fishes as air is to humans.
3. One is to _____ as solo is to duet.

### Activity 2: Related Word Lists

Either have the children match the two lists or give them a few examples and have them add additional words to each list.

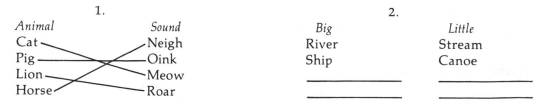

1.

| Animal | Sound |
|--------|-------|
| Cat | Neigh |
| Pig | Oink |
| Lion | Meow |
| Horse | Roar |

2.

| Big | Little |
|-----|--------|
| River | Stream |
| Ship | Canoe |
| _____ | _____ |
| _____ | _____ |

### Activity 3: Supply the Titles

This activity is similar to the preceding one, only this time the matched lists are provided and the children supply the appropriate titles for the lists (animal/home, clothing/body part).

| _____ | _____ |
|-----------|-----------|
| Bear | Cave |
| Human | House |
| Deer | Forest |
| Lion | Den |

| _____ | _____ |
|-----------|-----------|
| Hat | Head |
| Shoes | Feet |
| Pants | Legs |
| Dress | Body |

### Activity 4: Traditional Analogies

Probably the most versatile format is the traditional analogy format. The blank can go in any of the four slots, although varying the position may be confusing for young children. Students either can select a response from a list of choices that is provided ("easier") or can be asked to supply their own answers ("harder").

1. duck/quack—bird/_____
   (peep, neigh, meow, road)
2. cabbage/vegetable—_____/fruit
   (lettuce, apple, beet, tree)
3. month/year—hour/_____
4. _____/feet—fishes/fins

*Activity 5: Fill in the Blanks*

There are numerous variations on the theme that involve analogies.

A _____ is like a _____, only bigger.

    (hotel)           (house)

    (sheep)          (lamb)

   (mountain)       (hill)

A _____ is like a _____, only longer.

   (kilometer)       (centimeter)

Red is to pink as brown is to _____.

Tallahassee is to Florida as _____ is to Arizona.

Mouse is to _____ as cricket is to insect.

A teacher works in a _____. A nurse works in a _____.

A _____ works in an office. A _____ works underground.

An engineer drives a _____. A chauffeur drives a _____.

## SUMMARY

The use of the three instructional strategies discussed in this chapter—semantic mapping, semantic feature analysis, and analogical reasoning—is increasing in elementary classrooms. Evidence from empirical research (Johnson, Toms-Bronowski, and Pittelman, 1982), teachers' testimonials, and common sense tell us that classification is critical to concept learning, and these strategies help students learn new words through classification. Many other classification activities work but have not been described here, just as many other procedures can be used in vocabulary development (e.g., synonym-antonym relations, denotation-connotation, context, compounds, homophones).

## REFERENCES

Bransford, J. D., and Johnson, M. K. Contextual prerequisites for understanding: Some investigations of comprehension and recall. *Journal of Verbal Learning and Verbal Behavior,* 1972, **11,** 717–726.

Davis, F. B. Fundamental factors of comprehension in reading. *Psychometrika,* 1944, **9,** 185–197.

Johnson, D. D., Toms-Bronowski, S., and Pittelman, S. D. *An investigation of the effectiveness of semantic mapping and semantic feature analysis with intermediate grade level children* (Program Report 83-3). Madison, Wis.: Wisconsin Center for Education Research, 1982.

## RECOMMENDED READINGS

Bush, C. *Language remediation and expansion.* Tucson, Ariz.: Communication Skill Building, 1978. This practical resource for teachers is filled with lists of words and activities in such vocabulary categories as compounds, homophones, homographs, synonyms, antonyms, analogies, and classification.

Durkin, D. *Teaching word identification.* Boston: Allyn and Bacon, 1976.
Durkin's book contains especially helpful chapters on structural analysis and contextual analysis in vocabulary development.

Johnson, D. D., and Pearson, P. D. *Teaching reading vocabulary.* (2nd ed.) New York: Holt, Rinehart and Winston, 1984 (in press).
Johnson and Pearson's paperback book for teachers contains separate chapters covering sight vocabulary, meaning vocabulary, phonic analysis, structural analysis, contextual analysis, and the use of the dictionary and thesaurus. Each chapter describes a variety of instructional strategies.

# CHAPTER 4

# Teaching Comprehension Skills in the Reading Program

Marvin Klein
Western Washington University
Bellingham

*The chapters in Part I of this book, which deal with basic reading skills, progress from an emphasis on decoding to an emphasis on meaning, that is, from word identification skills to meaning vocabulary development to comprehension. In this chapter, Marvin Klein completes the transition to comprehension by presenting strategies for teaching children to comprehend at three linguistic levels: the word, sentence, and passage levels. Klein's strategies for word-level comprehension extend Johnson's discussion in Chapter 3 of meaning vocabulary by requiring readers to attach new information to already-existing concepts. The sentence comprehension section includes strategies that help children understand how simple and more complex sentence patterns are related and how the different functions sentences play can affect meaning. The final section on text or passage comprehension presents exercises that help children to learn how sentences themselves are related to one another, how stories are constructed, and how cohesive elements tie sentences and paragraphs together.*

The purpose of this chapter is to provide a range of activities and techniques for teaching reading comprehension skills at three levels: word comprehension, sentence comprehension, and text (passage) comprehension. These skill development activities and techniques are all based on certain fundamental assumptions about how reading comprehension functions and how it develops. Three of these fundamental assumptions are the following.

First, reading comprehension is a language-based operation. The reader brings to the reading important oral language skills, a range of experiences, and a variety of past contacts with written language. Many human experiences, in fact, have come through language rather than through direct contact with events, places, and so on. Therefore, our comprehension of new information and ideas in reading forces us to call up past events experienced primarily through language.

Second, the various language-producing (speaking and writing) and language-comprehending (reading and listening) skills are interrelated, and reading comprehension skill development should capitalize, to whatever extent possible, on these interrelationships. Reading skill development does not take place in a vacuum, and the human brain does not operate in a linguistically piecemeal fashion. Therefore, reading, writing, speaking, and listening exercises mutually reinforce one another and ought to be part of an integrated reading and language arts program.

Finally, reading comprehension skills are most effectively developed when there is a conscious effort on the part of the teacher to provide a stimulating learning environment, to utilize the experiential background of the learner, and to ensure a close examination of the text. This process requires sensitivity, directness, and good materials and activities planned by the teacher.

## WORD COMPREHENSION

To some extent, the term "word comprehension" is a misnomer. Words are seldom—some people would contend *never*—used in isolation. Either a sentence context is provided by the writer, or one is intended, and thus imposed, by the reader. It is reasonable to consider, however, that the heart of meaning, in at least one sense, is in the individual word. Although a knowledge of the meanings of individual words does not *guarantee* that comprehension occurs, it is safe to say that word knowledge is *necessary* for the comprehension of sentences, paragraphs, and stories. In addition, the teacher can help the learner develop word comprehension skills in a number of ways.

### Classification Activities

As discussed in Chapter 3, classification activities are critical to both cognitive development and reading comprehension skills development. Therefore, they can be incorporated into all subject matter areas, not just that subject typically designated as reading instruction. The following activities are intended to help students develop word comprehension skill by requiring them to classify words.

### *Branching Trees*

Branching trees require students to associate words with one another according to some word relationship. One such relationship is the class-example relationship represented by the following word tree.

Cow
Holstein    Jersey

Either an overhead projector or activity sheets can be used to provide students with an array of branching trees to complete. For example:

Automobile
?                ?

Or:

$$\overset{\displaystyle ?}{\diagup\ \diagdown}$$
Kawasaki     Harley-Davidson

Discussions of responses allow students to share words with one another (e.g., *motorcycle, bike, chopper*) and, hence, to expand their vocabularies. Variations of branching trees can be introduced. One variation would require that words at the nodes (ends of the branches) be semantic contrasts. For example:

Human
Man     Woman

Feelings
Love     Hate

Run
?     ?

Texture
Rough     ?

?
Hot     Cold

?
Sweet     Sour

Branching trees can also go beyond two levels. Consider, for example, how the following might be completed.

Animal
?       ?
?   ?   ?   ?

### Abstraction Ladder

Another interesting version of the branching tree is the abstraction ladder, in which a general category—for example, *transportation*—is gradually transformed to more specific examples; that is, it moves from the general to the specific.

| |
|---|
| Transportation |
| Vehicle |
| Car |
| Ford |
| Two-door sedan |
| Escort |

The teacher can prepare activity sheets and control their complexity by increasing or decreasing the number of rungs on the ladders. Try completing the following ladders.

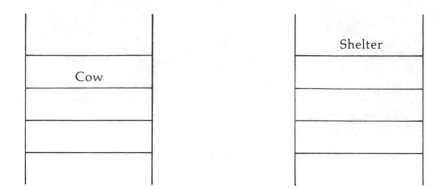

### Category Fixing

"Category-fixing" activities are designed to help the reader develop a number of skills critical to reading comprehension. Searching for set membership features and attributes in one group as opposed to another assists the learner in associating and contrasting important ideas and concepts in the text. Categorizing activities also helps the learner to develop skills in projecting ahead and in examining possible larger frameworks or idea groups into which less abstract ones can be placed.

Both inductive and deductive reasoning processes are recognized as important to analytical reading. The ability to categorize in a variety of ways is also basic to the development of these more-advanced reasoning skills.

Category fixing involves using the branching tree model and asking students to answer questions such as those that follow this "branched tree." (All of the activities in the classification section can be altered to increase or decrease their complexity, depending on the developmental level of the learners and the purpose of the particular instructional effort.)

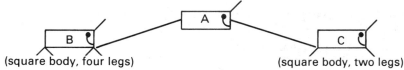

1. Is the relationship depicted general to specific or whole to parts? (general to specific)

2. What features or attributes do A, B, and C all have? (square bodies, eyes, antennae)

3. What kinds of "animals" could not belong to your "family"? (round bodies, triangular bodies, etc.)

If △, ☐, ☐, and ☐ are in one group and ◯, ✐, and ◯ are in another, what is the requirement for membership in each? (Answer: straight lines and angles in one; curves and circles in the other.)

Or: If *nice, pretty, gentle,* and *happy* are in one group and *mean, ugly, sad,* and *violent* in another, what is the requirement for membership in each?

Look at the parade of words:

Rocks   Sand   Stones   Fishes   Trees   John   Chevy   Clouds
(1)      (2)      (3)        (4)        (5)       (6)      (7)        (8)
Sun   President   Bike
(9)      (10)         (11)

1. How many categories can you create?
2. What are the requirements for membership in each?
3. Can some members belong in more than one category at the same time?

## Word Building

Knowledge of vocabulary remains one of the most critical basics for reading comprehension skill development. Therefore, the reading teacher needs to provide a wide variety of word-building activities for students. The activities should include attention to spelling, to word parts, such as prefixes and suffixes, and to treatment of word connotations and denotations (implied meanings and literal meanings). Several sample activities that focus on different aspects of word building follow.

### Word Squares

The teacher provides the class with word squares of various types. A number of cards of varying complexity (e.g., 9 square, 12 square) are distributed to the students, who are asked to create as many words as they can (the same letter can be used more than once if desired). Word squares can be made on duplicating masters or on transparencies for group activities (Figure 4.1). One interesting possibility using this idea is to build word squares, or word searches, around a key social studies concept, such as *occupations*. Hidden words could include *teacher, mechanic, doctor, grocer,* and so on. Themes are also interesting. For young students holidays are popular. Halloween and Christmas provide excellent word-square options, for example, *pumpkin, mask, ghost, goblin,* and *spook.*

### Hink Pinks and Hinky Pinkies

Hink pinks consist of two single-syllable words that rhyme and redefine a common word at the same time. For example, an *obese feline* is a *fat cat.* Hinky pinkies follow the same format but consist of two-syllable words. A hinky pinky for a *fish doctor* is a *sturgeon surgeon,* a *tired flower* is a *lazy daisy* or a *dozey posey,* and so forth. Proficient hinky pinkiers can produce some rinky-dinky-hinky-pinkies (e.g., a *bigger-than-normal, black-marking, name-brand writing instrument* for a *larger darker Parker marker*).

### Jonathan Swifties

Jonathan Swifties are sentences in which the structure or meaning of a specific word gives a distinct clue to other referents in the sentence. For example: "'He sure is smart,' said Lincoln *ably,*" or "'We have a flat,' he said *tiredly.*" Students can create their own Swifties in a variety of different contexts.

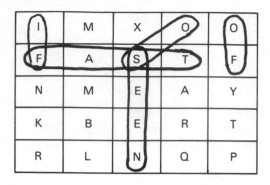

Figure 4.1. An example of completed word square.

### Irregular Conjugations

Irregular conjugations are activities in which the learner restates the same idea in three different versions, with each version being less positive than the previous. In this way, learners practice abstracting skills and develop word connotation.

This activity is also self-motivating and helpful for developing synonym relationships. Consider the following examples: "I am regular in physical features. You are rather plain. He's been whipped with an ugly stick!" and "I am pleasantly plump. You are obese. He is a blimp!"

It is important to note that word play is an inherent part of most of the word-building activities described in this section. Their role, however, involves more than simple entertainment. The activities promote the development of vocabulary and word comprehension skill. Just as important, all these activities possess excellent motivational power.

## Context Generating

Context provides readers powerful clues to the meanings of words. The following activities help readers develop their ability to use context clues to determine the denotative and connotative meanings of words.

### Slotting and Embedding

Activity sheets for students reproduce a paragraph such as the following.

The _____ girl found a _____ in the street. She
   (tiny, huge, mean, little)       (dog, puppy, animal)
_____ away from it at first. Then, she went back to _____
(ran, walked, skipped)               (look, stare, see)
again, because she was _____ .
      (sorry, sad, happy)

Students fill in the slots with words from the options given. The students then read their papers aloud and compare how the meaning of the paragraph changes when different words are inserted. The students should consider how both the denotative and connotative meanings change with the different words.

### Word Meaning Inference

The word meaning inference activity, which uses a nonsense word in a meaningful context, helps students to learn the importance of utilizing the surrounding linguistic environment to infer a logical meaning for a word. For example, a transparency or handout with short paragraphs like the following includes nonsense words.

> Mary got out of bed one morning and decided to wear her <u>zimps</u> to school. After her bath, she put the pair of <u>zimps</u> on—first, her left leg in, then her right. The <u>zimps</u> felt good on her legs. It was a cold morning, and wearing them was a better idea than wearing a dress.

Students "guess" what *zimps* are after reading the paragraph. Are they slacks? How do you know? Could they be tights? Why or why not? What were some clues that helped you?

Students can also be asked to write their own paragraphs with nonsense words embedded in them. These can then be duplicated and shared with others.

### Word Charting

Word charting helps learners to comprehend and use metaphors and analogies accurately. Students can file such charts (for example, Figure 4.2) for later reference.

In the example in Figure 4.2, students fill in appropriate human attributes that parallel those of the sun. The students' word charts can serve as idea generators for writing activities. Also, word charts can focus on different semantic roles. The sample chart deals with subjects and verbs. Similar charts can address modification or other grammatical constructs. For example, adjectives appropriate to both sailboats and humans include *trim, sleek,* and *smooth;* for cars and humans, *noisy, banged up,* and *clean.*

## SENTENCE COMPREHENSION

The effective and efficient reader knows how to look beyond the word for meaning in print; that is, skilled readers are able to grasp language in chunks (syntactic and semantic units, such as clauses, phrases, and sentences). Quality reading programs should include activities and techniques that help students to develop comprehension of these linguistic units. The following examples should prove helpful in developing this skill.

### Sentence Combining

Sentence combining is the practice of taking a series of short, choppy sentences and combining them into more complex sentences by deleting some words and changing others or by doing both. Although sentence-combining activities are most commonly used to teach composition (writing) skills, they are also useful in helping readers to understand how writers combine and integrate a series of thoughts into a clause or sentence.

| Actions of the Sun and Humans | |
| --- | --- |
| Sun | Humans |
| rises | wake up |
| sets | go to bed |
| is overcast | ? |
| shines | ? |

Figure 4.2. An example of a word chart.

The simplest variety of sentence combining is the open-ended type, in which students must take all the information in a series of sentences and combine it into one sentence. For example, sentences 1, 2, 3, and 4 could be combined into sentence 5.

1. The puppy was cute.
2. The puppy was mean.
3. The puppy ate the food.
4. The food was soggy.
5. The cute mean puppy ate the soggy food.

Or the combination of sentences 6, 7, 8, 9, and 10 could result in sentence 11.

6. The rain fell on the street.
7. The rain was slow.
8. The rain was chilly.
9. The street was narrow.
10. The street was old.
11. The slow, chilly rain fell on the old, narrow street.

A more structured version of sentence combining is the cued variety, in which a cue word is placed in parentheses after the sentences that are to be combined. The cue word must be used when the sentences are combined. For example, the relative pronoun *who* is used to combine sentences 12 and 13 into sentence 14.

12. The children were tired.
13. The children were hungry. (who)
14. The children who were hungry were tired.

The cue word can also be a verb with an inflectional change that produces a participial modifier. For example, sentences 15 and 16 could be combined into sentence 17.

15. The woman was happy.
16. The woman sips a soda. (sipping)

17.   The woman sipping a soda was happy.

Sentence-combining clusters can be designed in simple or complex sets. They can be made more challenging by increasing the number of sentences to be combined, by scrambling the order of those to be combined, or by varying the difficulty or complexity of the cue words provided.

In addition, sentence-combining activities can be used to teach comprehension of specific semantic or grammatical constructs. For example, students would need to discover an implicit cause-and-effect relationship when combining sentences 18 and 19.

18.   The team lost the game.

19.   Their pitcher was ill.

A likely result of combining these sentences would be sentence 20.

20.   The team lost the game, because their pitcher was ill.

Another sentence-combining activity presents readers with a mixed array of sentences. Then, three tasks must be completed. First, the sentences must be reordered. Second, the sentences must be clustered into related groups. Third, the related sentences must then be combined. For example, sentences 21 through 29 could be clustered into three related groups: groups A, B, and C.

21.   He raced along the road.

22.   The road was narrow.

23.   The boy jumped on the motorcycle.

24.   The boy was big.

25.   The garage was old.

26.   The road was curvy.

27.   The motorcycle was red.

28.   He stopped by the garage.

29.   The garage was near his home.

Reordered and clustered, the array would appear in the following order.

23.   The boy jumped on the motorcycle. ⎫
24.   The boy was big.                    ⎬  Group A
27.   The motorcycle was red.            ⎭

21.   He raced along the road.           ⎫
26.   The road was curvy.                 ⎬  Group B
22.   The road was narrow.               ⎭

28.   He stopped by the garage.          ⎫
25.   The garage was old.                 ⎬  Group C
29.   The garage was near his home.      ⎭

A likely three-sentence paragraph resulting from these clusters would be the following.

> The big boy jumped on his red motorcycle [group A]. He raced along the narrow, curvy road [group B]. He stopped by the old garage near his home [group C].

Another variation of sentence combining requires the teacher to choose a sentence from a basal reader, short story, or novel. This sentence is then reduced to a series of short sentences. For example, the following is the opening sentence from "Hands" in Sherwood Anderson's *Winesburg, Ohio:* "Upon the half decayed veranda of a small frame house that stood near the edge of a ravine near the town of Winesburg, Ohio, a fat little old man walked nervously up and down." We can reduce this sentence to the following sentences, which incorporate its basic meaning and structure.

30.  A man walked up and down.
   31.  The man was little.
   32.  The man was fat.
   33.  The man was old.
   34.  The man walked nervously.
35.  The man was on the veranda of a house.
   36.  The veranda was half decayed.
   37.  The house was small.
   38.  The house was frame.
39.  The house stood near the edge of a ravine.
   40.  The ravine was near the town of Winesburg, Ohio.

Students can then be asked to combine these short sentences into one sentence designed to evoke a sad or tragic tone to a story. After they have shared their results, the teacher can point out that the original sentence opened the story of "Hands," from Sherwood Anderson's *Winesburg, Ohio.* This technique is an excellent one for teaching the relationship of sentence structure and meaning to the tone or mood of a story.

## Uses of Sentences

Students need to look at sentences from the perspective of a reader concerned with acquiring the overall meaning and purpose of the sentence. For example, does the sentence assert something (describe, explain, propose), or does it make an inquiry? These uses should not be confused with the relatively simple differences between statements and questions, for all assertions are statements and yet their semantic roles are different. For example, sentence 41 is a descriptive assertion, sentence 42 is an explanatory assertion, and sentence 43 is a propositional assertion (i.e., it proposes something).

41.  The ball is red.
42.  The ball is red, because it was painted with that color.
43.  The ball should be red, because it can then be used in this new game I've invented.

Readers must note the role of critical cue words used in sentences. Words such as *feel, think, believe,* and *want* denote propositional use; *because* and *if* and *then* denote explanatory use; and *to be* verbs denote descriptive roles.

The following activities are helpful for the development of sentence comprehension skill.

### Activity 1

Ask students to identify sentences according to semantic function: D = describe, E = explain, P = propose. Then, have students underline key words and be prepared to explain why the words are important. For example, sentences 44, 45, and 46 demonstrate the three semantic functions.

44.   The girl <u>ate</u> the apples.

45.   I didn't go to town, <u>because</u> I was ill.

46.   I <u>think</u> we should have a new mascot for our team.

### Activity 2

Have students complete assertions, such as the following, and tell what type they are.

47.   I saw _____. (describe)

48.   I think that _____. (explain)

49.   The dog looks like _____. (describe)

50.   We should save our money, because _____. (propose)

Remember that skill in perceiving such assertion functions helps the reader to comprehend main ideas in the text and to detect the writer's purpose.

## Turning Inward on Sentences

Metalinguistic awareness and sensitivity are generally conceded to be important characteristics of the efficient reader. The reader needs to recognize that the language is a construct in itself as well as a conveyor of information about ideas and events in the physical world. Students should be engaged in a variety of activities and exercises designed to enhance and develop this metalinguistic awareness.

Activities in language play, such as puns and riddles, in which a turn of meaning evokes humor, help students to develop this awareness and knowledge. Throughout the grades, metalinguistic activities need to be built in to the reading program for another reason. That reason is that activities requiring the reader to attend to the structure, form, and/or semantic character of words or sentences help to develop facility in close, precise reading—attention to critical detail or to important cue words or phrases. The good reader, like the good writer, knows how to manipulate and exploit the potential of language. Activities such as the following are appropriate for developing this skill.

### Self-Referencing Sentences

A self-referencing sentence is one that refers to itself rather than to something in the object world. For example, sentences 51, 52, and 53 refer to themselves or to content within themselves.

51.  I once spent three months in Spanish before being translated back into English.

52.  If I were six words shorter, I would be six words long.

53.  "Snow is white" is true if and only if snow is white.

Notice that reference in these sentences is always inward—focused on themselves and not on something outside the sentences. Students should try to produce some sentences of their own.

### Self-Contradictory Sentences

Students can be asked to think of self-contradictory bumper stickers, such as the following.

1.  Make Haste Slowly.

2.  Eschew Obfuscation.

3.  Illiterate? Write for Help.

4.  He Who Hesitates Is . . . Uh . . . Er . . . Hu . . . Lost!

Students can work in pairs or groups, each reading samples produced by others and interpreting the meaning for the others.

## TEXT COMPREHENSION

The most demanding, and the most important, of the various reading comprehension skills are those required to understand passages of discourse, commonly referred to as texts. Technically, many reading educators use the term "text" to refer to any unit of discourse. Thus, a single sentence could be a text. For our purposes, however, "text" refers only to units of discourse or writing of paragraph length and longer.

Texts occur in one of three major modes of discourse: expository, narrative, or creative. Essays, reports, and persuasive or argumentative writing make up exposition. Narration is the extended subjective description that can be found in both fictional and nonfictional writing. The creative mode includes prose, poetry, and drama.

### Text Development

Well-written text reflects a logical development in which ideas are presented in a sequential fashion. It is important for developing readers to practice perceiving logical relationships within texts.

The following structural model includes a *what* (claim) sentence, several *why* (support) sentences, and a *so* (conclusion) sentence.

I.  What (Claim) Sentence
    We should buy a gerbil for our classroom.

II.  Why (Support) Sentences
    1.  Our class had a cookie sale, and we made $50.
    2.  All the children agreed to take turns feeding and caring for a new pet.
    3.  We couldn't agree on where to go for a trip with the money, so we decided not to do that.
III.  So (Conclusion) Sentence
    So, we'll get our gerbil next week.

Initially, the teacher might compose a paragraph on the board by brainstorming with the students. Next, the students could consider the order of the *why* sentences and how some may not support the claim sentence. Then, using handouts, students could progress through the following two exercises.

### Exercise 1

What is the best conclusion sentence for the following? Choose one and tell why it is best.

#### Claim Sentence

We should be allowed to have a gerbil for our room.

#### Support Sentences

We had a cookie sale and made $50. Our parents donated the cookies, and we worked at the school fair to sell them.

#### Conclusion Sentences

1.  So, we should go to the pet shop and buy a gerbil.
2.  So, our room really needs a pet.
3.  So, gerbils are easy to care for.
4.  So, we all like gerbils.

### Exercise 2

Below are a number of sentences that include a *what* (claim) sentence, *why* (support) sentences, and a *so* (conclusion) sentence. They are mixed up. Reorder the sentences so that the *what* sentence is first, the *why* sentences follow, and the *so* sentence comes at the end. Then, label each sentence *what, why,* or *so.*

1.  There has been a lot of rain. _____
2.  The spring came earlier. _____
3.  We did not have any late frost. _____
4.  Our corn crop will be a good one this year. _____
5.  It looks like we will do well. _____
6.  The corn weevil has not been a problem this summer. _____

### Additional Activities

Additional follow-up activities can include exercises in which the teacher provides *what* and *why* sentences and students infer a reasonable conclusion sentence or exercises in which the teacher provides *what* and *so* (conclusion) sentences and has the students fill in with appropriate *why* (support) sentences.

Using the claim-support-conclusion model is an excellent technique for teaching critical logic and inference skills for comprehending a wide range of texts in both expository and narrative modes and throughout grades 1 through 12. Its simple and straightforward nature make it a versatile teaching tool.

### Text Comprehension of Stories

Stories have a structure or grammar. Comprehension of stories is facilitated when readers are aware of the structure of stories and use this structure when reading. Story structure (or grammar) has been described in many different ways, but most story grammars include the following elements: setting, protagonist and antagonist development, plot development, conflict development, climax, and denouement.

Readers need experience in examining, exploring, and probing stories to be good comprehenders of fiction. The following activities are designed to help students acquire this experience.

#### Activity 1

A tape recorder is a useful tool for teaching story grammar. Several activities are possible. For example, have students compose stories orally by using the tape recorder. Older children could be asked to transcribe the stories from the recordings. The transcribed stories, typewritten and duplicated, could then be used as language experience readers with the original young authors.

#### Activity 2

Provide picture sequences (e.g., comic-strip-type drawings without the dialogue balloons) for the students to complete. The children write appropriate dialogue to develop a story that matches the pictures. The stories could be exchanged and critiqued, with the students' critiques answering the following questions.

1. Where and when is the story taking place?
2. Who are the main characters in the story?
3. What is the main idea of the story?
4. Is the ending a good one?

#### Activity 3

Have students make up a character who might appear in a story or play. Ask them to write descriptions of their character so that readers not only know what the character looks like but also what kind of person he or she is (e.g., mean, kind, cowardly, brave, etc.). Students then exchange these character descriptions. They outline a story with the character from the description they received playing a central role. The outline should be organized by using the following questions.

1.   Where and when will the story take place?
2.   Who will be the important characters?
3.   What will the story be about?
4.   Will there be a conflict in the story? If so, what kind (e.g., personality, physical)?
5.   How will the story end?

The character descriptions and proposed story outlines are then returned to the original authors. The students discuss whether the story outlines agree with those conceived by the originators of the characters.

### Activity 4

Have students read a story (or read a story to them), and then ask them to make up and discuss an additional character who might fit in the story.

## Text Cohesion

Sentences that make up a text should cohere, or be tied together, in a number of ways. Backward and forward referencing is one form of cohesion that is accomplished through the use of particular transitional words, which the developing reader must learn to detect. Commonly used transitional words include *so, after, before, and, but,* and *since.*

One of the most common and important cohesion devices, however, is the pronoun. Notice their extensive use in the following story, in which arrows depict reference ties.

The lion jumped out of its cage. It then ran across the street, where several people were standing. They quickly ran away, because they feared him.

Pronouns help reduce redundancy in text by providing alternate ways of referring to the same thing or topic. If students have difficulty associating referents to pronouns, however, comprehension can be seriously impaired.

The following activities help students to comprehend cohesive devices in text better.

### Back-Referencing Sentences

Students circle the appropriate word and connect it to its referent by an arrow.

1.   The <u>kitten</u> chased the yarn. It was cute.
2.   The kitten chased the <u>yarn</u>. It was on the floor.

These examples can be made more complex by leaving out the underlining, by increasing the exercises to paragraph length and beyond, and by embedding increasingly complex referential ties through going beyond simple pronominal ties. For example, *the water, the lake, the shore,* and *the waves* could all be cohesive ties for the same concept.

### Cloze Paragraphs

Students complete cloze passages in which the pronouns have been deleted. For example:

> Once upon a time a little old lady lived alone in the forest. _____ was kind and gentle, and the animals all loved _____. _____ would often come to visit at _____ cottage. _____ would feed _____ nuts and fruit.

Students insert the correct pronouns and read their completed paragraphs aloud. They should discuss any differences in pronoun use that surface.

### Linking Sentences

Students are challenged with passages from which important transitional sentences have been deleted. They are asked to compose a sentence that is suitable for the slot provided. For example:

> (1) The girl slid down the hill on her sled. (2) She was having fun in the snow. (3) All of a sudden, a big tree was in front of her. (4) _____ _____. (5) She laughed as the sled stopped.

Notice that the transitional sentence needed in this example must help the reader make an unexpected shift from an anticipated conclusion to one that is surprising.

### Linking Paragraphs

Students study a series of paragraphs that need intervening paragraphs to help them cohere into one complete text. For example:

P. 1 { The children enjoyed the trip to the zoo. They got to see many unusual animals they had never seen before.

P. 2 {

P. 3 { They decided that the anteater was the strangest even though they all liked the giraffe, too.

Students provide a transitional paragraph. They can do this individually, in pairs, or in small groups. Then, they exchange their papers and discuss in pairs the appropriateness of the paragraphs they wrote.

Additional activities linking paragraphs (and sentences) can be designed, reproduced on ditto masters, and filed for use in appropriate contexts. The teacher should keep in mind the advantages of including texts from different subject matter areas (e.g., science, social studies, health) and in the different discourse modes (e.g., expository, narrative, and creative).

## SUMMARY

The reading teacher should follow these guidelines for an effective program in comprehension skills.

First, remember that the activities and techniques in this chapter are not intended to constitute an entire or total reading program. Instead, they are intended to serve as *models* for the development of a range of lessons that can enrich and enliven an ongoing program in reading comprehension.

Second, observe that all of these activities have a considerable range in difficulty and complexity. They can be used throughout most grades by adjusting vocabulary, content, and grammatical complexity.

Third, consider the possibility of incorporating oral discussion, writing, and small-group and large-group formats when using these reading comprehension development activities. They make the linguistic environment richer and more productive.

Finally, remember to extend, create, and add to these activities. Over the years, you will discover that your reading program becomes livelier, reflects greater variety, and is generally more fun as well.

## RECOMMENDED READINGS

Pearson, P. D., and Johnson, D. D. *Teaching reading comprehension.* New York: Holt, Rinehart and Winston, 1978.
The teacher gains from this book a solid rationale for teaching comprehension, along with useful ideas for implementing the rationale.

McCracken, M., and McCracken, R. *Reading, writing and language: A practical guide for primary teachers.* Winnipeg, Man.: Peguis Publishers Limited, 1979.
This is an excellent resource for designing language-based activities for the reading program in the primary grades.

Moffett, J., and Wagner, B. *Student-centered language arts and reading, K–13.* Boston: Houghton Mifflin, 1976.
Interesting for its theoretical and conceptual base, this book contains a wide range of useful ideas for teaching reading comprehension skills within a comprehensive language arts and reading program.

Smith, F. *Reading without nonsense.* New York: Teachers College, Columbia University, 1978.
A theory of how the reading process takes place is described in Smith's book.

Strong, W. *Sentence-combining and paragraph-building.* New York: Random House, 1981.
Strong's helpful book provides sentence-combining activities for students from the middle grades on up.

# CHAPTER 5

# Engaging Students in Reading Comprehension Instruction

William E. Blanton
Appalachian State University
Boone, North Carolina

Karen D. Wood
University of North Carolina at Charlotte

*Chapter 4 presented strategies for teaching children to comprehend at the word, sentence, and passage levels. In Chapter 5, William Blanton and Karen Wood also deal with comprehension, but they assume a slightly different perspective. They begin by discussing current practices in reading comprehension; then they present a definition of comprehension that takes into account several factors that influence comprehension, such as the reader's prior knowledge, interest, and ability to anticipate and make inferences. In the heart of the chapter, Blanton and Wood discuss the traditional "directed reading" strategy for teaching comprehension, and then they present an alternate comprehension instructional strategy. Their strategy consists of three stages: prereading, reading, and postreading. For each of these instructional stages, several procedures and activities are described that not only help children to comprehend before, during, and after reading but also to engage them in comprehension instruction, that is, activities teachers can employ to force students to become actively involved in making sense out of connected text.*

Before reading this chapter,[1] react to the following statements by marking each with a plus if you agree with a statement or a minus if you disagree with a statement. After you have read the chapter, again indicate your agreement or disagreement with each statement.

[1]Some of the materials in this chapter are based on an article by Karen D. Wood and J. A. Mateja, "Adapting secondary level strategies for use in elementary classrooms," *The Reading Teacher*, 1983, **36**, 492–496.

*Before*　　*After*

————　　————　　1.　Reading comprehension involves simply reading a selection and
————　　————　　　giving correct answers to questions.

————　　————　　2.　Comprehension develops through instruction in a sequence of
　　　　————　　　specific skills.

————　　————　　3.　A best answer to all comprehension questions always exists.

————　　————　　4.　The best way to teach reading is to rely as much as possible on
　　　　　　　　　the basal reader manual and the directed reading lesson format
　　　　　　　　　within the manual.

————　　————　　5.　One can answer comprehension questions without understand-
　　　　　　　　　ing the material that was read.

Beginning teachers often feel overwhelmed by the challenge of providing students with instruction on how to comprehend written material. Similarly, many veteran teachers remain puzzled about answers to questions related to reading comprehension instruction. For example, many novice and experienced teachers are uncertain about answers to questions such as the following.

1.　If reading comprehension is not answering questions asked about material read, what is it? Do not most teachers ask students questions?
2.　Will asking students questions after reading improve their comprehension?
3.　What are the important phases of a reading comprehension lesson?
4.　What are some reasonable alternatives to workbook assignments and other activities suggested in the teacher's manuals for basal reader programs?

The purpose of this chapter is (1) to provide a practical discussion of what reading comprehension is, (2) to review some current practices in comprehension instruction, (3) to discuss three steps in comprehension instruction, and (4) to describe alternative strategies for engaging students in reading comprehension instruction.

## WHAT IS READING COMPREHENSION?

Reading comprehension is not simply answering questions about material one has read. It seems to be a fact, however, that most teachers believe that asking questions is one of the better strategies for *teaching* reading comprehension.

In a recent study, Durkin (1978–1979) observed 17,977 minutes of reading instruction in elementary classrooms. Her findings revealed the degree to which teachers use questions. She found that, while teachers spent less then 1 percent of their time on comprehension instruction, they devoted 17 percent to asking students "low-level" questions (i.e., factual, literal, detail questions) about what they had read and having them complete worksheet activities. In particular, Durkin noted that very little time was devoted to direct instruction in *how* to comprehend written material.

In an effort to understand why teachers were devoting so much time to asking questions, Durkin (1981) followed her classroom observational study with an intensive analysis of the teacher's manuals for five leading basal reading series. Her findings indicated that the manuals devoted a major portion of their instructional suggestions to directing teachers to ask low-level questions, to make reading assignments, and to give out worksheets. More important, Durkin noted that the manuals contained few suggestions on how to *teach* reading comprehension.

### Is Reading Comprehension Asking Questions?

During the early part of this century, reading instruction focused on teaching students word-attack skills. The goal of reading instruction was simply to provide students with the skills necessary to pronounce words. As early as 1913, educators began to develop and administer tests that were to become the building blocks for standardized reading tests. As might be guessed, early reading tests used the technique of asking students questions about what they had read. Understandably, many students performed poorly, and educators became concerned. More emphasis was placed on comprehension as an instructional goal after 1920.

From its early introduction until the present day, the idea of reading comprehension has undergone many changes. For example, the initial view of reading comprehension was that it was simply the ability to answer factual questions about material read. This view was later expanded to the more global goal of understanding what was read, or to getting the intended meaning of the writer. Concepts such as inferential comprehension, critical reading, interpretive reading, evaluation of material read, reorganization of material read, and response to literature followed later.

As noted previously, the early concern over reading comprehension was prompted by the poor performance of students on tests that consisted solely of comprehension questions. It seemed reasonable, therefore, to conclude that reading comprehension instruction should center around having students answer questions after reading. In addition, concluding that the questions asked should be based on recalling, inferring, interpreting, evaluating, and reorganizing material read—broad categories of reading comprehension—seemed logical. In other words, practice in answering different kinds of questions, it was believed, should develop reading comprehension.

Thus, using questions as a major part of reading comprehension instruction became important for a number of reasons. First, the intention of educators was to provide students with practice on difficult comprehension tasks. Second, publishers of basal reading programs suggested that the use of questions was very important in comprehension instruction.

Clearly, the use of questions represents an excellent instructional strategy for developing purposes for reading, stimulating discussion about material read, and determining whether the reader is understanding written material (Pearson 1981). On the other hand, the overuse of questions suggests a misunderstanding of the comprehension process.

1. Reading comprehension involves more than answering questions.
2. Questions do not automatically "teach" students to comprehend.
3. Good comprehension questions do not have right and wrong answers.
4. Answering questions does not mean that written material has been understood.

5. To many students, comprehension questions "all look alike."
6. A good comprehension lesson is centered around many activities, only one of which is asking questions.

## If Reading Comprehension Is Not Answering Questions About Material Read, What Is It?

From our perspective, *reading comprehension is intentional thinking stimulated by written material.* The first intention of the reader is to bridge the gap between what she knows *before* reading and the new information presented in written material. In other words, the goal of the reader is to make sense out of written material by relating new information to that which is already known.

The second intention of the reader is to think *with* the information obtained by reading. The kinds of thinking abilities used by the reader depend on the purposes the reader generates for reading or the purposes given to the reader for reading. The thinking skills a reader might use include the following:

1. Recalling and recognizing information read, such as details, sequence of events, and other facts.
2. Reorganizing information obtained through reading by classifying, outlining, summarizing, synthesizing, paraphrasing, and associating.
3. Making inferences by using information known before reading and information gained through reading to make predictions.
4. Evaluating information gained through reading by using background experiences, prior knowledge, and values to make judgments about its worth, validity, and usability.
5. Interpreting and applying information gained through reading to solve personal problems and problems confronting society.
6. Creating with information gained through reading by integrating it with already-known information to develop new expressions and forms.

The degree to which the reader can bridge the gap between what he already knows and new information and think with information obtained through reading is influenced by a number of factors. Among these are the reader's use of prior knowledge, level of interest in the material to be read, ability to make predictions about the material, capacity for making inferences, and understanding of reading comprehension.

### Using Prior Knowledge

Current research (Rumelhart and Ortony, 1977; Rumelhart, 1980; Spiro, 1977, 1980) clearly points out that the more a reader knows about what is to be read, the more sense the reader will make out of what is read. For example, a person who has served in the army's field artillery understands exactly what is meant by the following paragraph.

> Fire mission! Deflection two, niner, zero. Shell H.E. Charge seven. Lot number two, zero, zero. At my command, elevation four, zero, niner. Fire! Repeat elevation!

In the preceding example, comprehension questions about this paragraph could be answered even if the reader lacked a complete understanding of the material. For example, consider the following questions.

1.   What is happening? Answer: A fire mission.
2.   What is H.E.? Answer: A shell.

The following questions, however, are more difficult to answer.

1.   Who is saying, "Fire mission?"
2.   What is shell H.E.?
3.   What does "Repeat elevation!" mean?
4.   What is a niner?
5.   How many times are the guns fired?

Answers to these questions and, more important, an understanding of what is happening require prior knowledge on the part of the reader.

In this example, a field artillery fire direction officer is sending a fire command to a gun battery. Commands such as "elevation" and "deflection" tell each gun crew the direction in which to aim their guns, along with the kind of shell to load and fire.

Most readers would probably understand that the guns were fired. Not so easily understood, however, are "At my command," and "Repeat elevation!"

The most important command to a gun crew is the elevation command. Unless the elevation given to a crew is preceded by the phrase "at my command," the crew automatically fires the gun when it is loaded. In this example, the crew waits for the fire direction officer to give the command "Fire!"

What happens after the command to fire? Note that the command, "Repeat elevation!" is given. This command tells each crew to reload its gun exactly as before. Each crew will fire its gun as soon as it is loaded, however, and continue to reload and fire until given the command, "Cease Fire!"

### Having Interest in Material

An interest in the material to be read is not necessary for reading comprehension. If the reader is interested in the material to be read, however, one can predict that she will probably spend more time on the comprehension task and that she will probably be willing to expend more energy on the comprehension task (Asher, 1980). Hence, interest can indeed enhance reading comprehension.

### Making Predictions About Material

An essential ingredient for reading comprehension is the ability to make predictions about material being read (Smith, 1975). This then provides the reader a purpose for reading. The extent to which the reader makes meaningful confirmations of predictions tells him that the material is being understood. Realizing that the material is or is not understood causes the reader to make different predictions, to look for additional information, to go back and read again, to read slower, to read faster, or to use other strategies.

*Making Inferences*

Skilled readers virtually cannot read without making inferences. In making inferences, the reader combines information she already knows with information gained through reading to make probable or plausible statements about what was known before reading (Trabasso, 1981).

For example, consider the following sentence: "Tom was a good old fellow who rarely created a problem with his playmates around the neighborhood." At first reading, one might infer that Tom is a boy or a man. This inference could be correct. Certainly, it is logical. Tom is a name usually given to males, and we usually infer gender from names. What about the reader who infers that Tom is a cat? This is also a logical inference. People often name their male cats Tom. To make the correct inference the reader must obtain additional information. The point we want to stress, however, is that inferential thinking is already occurring.

*Understanding Reading Comprehension*

Current research (Brown, 1982) indicates that one of the differences between good and poor comprehenders is that good comprehenders appear to have a notion of what reading comprehension is: a process of getting meaning from material relevant to the reader's purpose and the author's purpose. Instructional strategies, therefore, should lead students to perceive reading comprehension in this manner. Students must realize that there are no best interpretations of a passage. Rather, what is important is the line of reasoning and the thinking processes used to reach an answer or interpretation. Opportunities to discuss reading material and to talk about how an answer or interpretation was reached help develop this understanding. In addition, thinking and discussing enable the reader to evaluate what and how he is comprehending in relation to what other students are comprehending.

## ENGAGING STUDENTS IN READING COMPREHENSION

For many years, the most widely used approach to teaching reading comprehension has been a generalized procedure commonly called the directed reading lesson. All basal readers have incorporated a variation of the directed reading lesson into their teaching strategy. In general, this lesson plan has the following parts:

1. Relating the reader's background of experiences to the reading selection.
2. Introducing new vocabulary.
3. Setting purposes and questions for reading.
4. Reading the selection as a whole or in parts.
5. Discussing the selection in relation to purposes and questions for reading.
6. Guided rereading for new purposes and additional understanding.
7. Skill instruction followed by practice exercises or other activities or both to develop comprehension skills.

Although this instructional strategy can be effective, it has some weaknesses. First, the notion that students may already know a great deal about what they are going to read is not emphasized. Instead of helping readers *bring* what they know to reading, we typically spend a great deal of time *telling* them what we think they should know before they read.

Second, as we discussed earlier, we devote a great deal of time to asking questions. As a result, students spend a great deal of their time answering questions. We suggest to students that reading comprehension is nothing more than a passive process to be completed in order to answer questions. Consequently, students fail to grasp the idea that reading is an active, constructive process to which they bring a great deal of significant information. Last, but not least, reading comprehension instruction that follows the same lesson plan day after day becomes very boring. Students, then, may not approach reading with excitement and anticipation.

## Reading Comprehension Instruction

Reading comprehension is more than a series of ordered skills that result in proficient reading. An analogy to the teaching of swimming may prove to be helpful in explaining this point. Merely demonstrating, first, the arm movements, second, the kicking movements, and, third, the breathing components of the swimming act does not ensure that the learner, when placed in the water, will be able to swim. Likewise, students who are assigned workbook exercises or ditto sheets covering a series of skills (e.g., main idea, drawing conclusions), purported to be component skills of reading comprehension, will not necessarily be able to apply these skills when faced with actual reading material.

As mentioned earlier, reading comprehension is intentional thinking stimulated by written material. The goals of reading comprehension are to bridge the gap between what the reader already knows and new information and to think with information obtained through reading. The role of the teacher is to serve as a mediator who bridges the gap between the reader's background knowledge and the new information presented by the author and who provides instructional strategies that emphasize the thinking abilities the reader must use. In short, the teacher must provide instructional strategies that enable the reader (1) to activate prior knowledge and associate it with the material to be read, (2) to anticipate that the material to be read will be meaningful, (3) to make predictions about the material to be read, (4) to make logical inferences about the material to be read, and (5) to develop an interest in the material to be read.

This approach suggests that reading comprehension instruction is much more than merely asking questions at the end of a reading selection. Instead, reading comprehension instruction is an activity that consists of three stages: (1) the prereading stage, (2) the reading stage, and (3) the postreading stage. The final sections of this chapter present a number of instructional strategies that can be used to teach the three stages of reading comprehension.

## Prereading Stage

The prereading stage of a comprehension lesson may be the most important stage. Here, the framework for new knowledge is provided. The teacher must bridge the gap between new information presented in the text and information already possessed by the student. Also, during this stage, the purposes for reading are determined, and students are introduced to new vocabulary. Two instructional strategies that can be used to accomplish these purposes are the anticipation guide (Bean and Peterson, 1980; Herber, 1970) and possible sentences (Moore and Arthur, 1981). These strategies, which are described below, can be used as adjunct aids to basal reader instruction.

### Anticipation Guide

The anticipation guide is a study guide designed to familiarize students with the major concepts and ideas in a reading selection *before* they begin reading. It requires that students state their opinions about a series of statements. Used during the prereading stage, the anticipation guide can serve as a method for activating students' prior thinking on a given topic and stimulating group discussion. Used again after reading, the guide can help clarify misconceptions about a given topic as well as help students to recognize changes in their opinions resulting from new information gained by reading.

The development of an anticipation guide involves five steps (Wood and Mateja, 1983). The guide illustrated in Figure 5.1 was developed for a second-grade selection entitled "Girls Can Be Anything" (Klein, 1979). This basal reader story is about a young girl who is deciding what she wants to be when she grows up. She chooses from professions typically thought of as male dominated. The teacher has the option of allowing students to read the selection when they are capable of doing so or of reading the selection to them, thereby concentrating on their listening skills.

The procedures for developing an anticipation guide are the following.

1. Determine the major concepts and significant details in the story, expository selection, poem, or other material selected for reading.
2. Develop approximately five to eight general statements that are somewhat ambiguous in nature or that reflect a common misconception about the topic of

---

*Directions:* Look at the sentences on this page. The sentences have numbers from 1 to 6. Read each sentence. If you think what each says is right, print YES on the line under the word BEFORE. If you think the sentence is wrong, print NO on the line under the word BEFORE. Do the same thing for each sentence. Remember how to do this, because you will do it again after reading.

| Before Reading | After Reading | |
|---|---|---|
| _____ | _____ | 1. Nurses are always women. |
| _____ | _____ | 2. Most fathers think their daughters should not work. |
| _____ | _____ | 3. It would be great to be a king or a queen, since they have a lot of power. |
| _____ | _____ | 4. Only men can become presidents. |
| _____ | _____ | 5. Many women have become airline pilots. |
| _____ | _____ | 6. When you are flying in an airplane, a stewardess always serves your meals. |

---

Figure 5.1. An anticipation guide for "Girls Can Be Anything."

the reading. These statements may be either correct or incorrect but should be designed in a way that stimulates thought and discussion.

3. Before the students read the story, present the guide on paper, chalkboard, or overhead projector and allow students to agree or disagree with the statements. Initially, permitting students to work in small groups often facilitates discussion and fosters a tolerance and understanding for the opinions of others.

4. Encourage students to discuss their responses and to provide a justification for their individual opinions. Imagine the responses of second-grade students to the statements "Nurses are always women" and "Only men can become presidents."

5. Return to the anticipation guide after students have read the selection to determine whether they have changed their minds. Encourage them to discuss the reasons why they changed or did not change their responses.

### Possible Sentences

The possible sentences technique is a strategy teachers can use to provide direct instruction on the unfamiliar vocabulary of a reading selection by drawing on students' existing knowledge of the new vocabulary. The main purpose of this strategy is to assist students to determine independently the meanings and relationships of new words by using the context of the reading selection. Since students are to use their prior knowledge to predict relationships among new vocabulary items, their motivation to read the assignment is increased, and a mental set is developed for reading the new material.

Possible sentences exercises are comprised of four steps. These steps are presented below, along with a sample lesson applying the strategy to a basal reader selection.

1. Visually display the key vocabulary of the selection on the chalkboard, poster paper, or the overhead projector. Vocabulary words are often underlined or listed in the teacher's guide of a basal reader. In addition, teachers may want to focus on additional vocabulary words not highlighted by the authors.

2. Ask the students to compose a sentence that uses two or more of the vocabulary words in a sentence that they think may *possibly* appear in the selection to be read. In other words, based on their prior knowledge of the topic and the vocabulary presented, they are to predict some *possible sentences*. Write each sentence on the board exactly as dictated by the students, even though the information may be inaccurate. Continue this procedure until the students are unable to produce any more sentences.

3. Have the students write the number of each sentence on their paper. Then, have them read the selection and determine whether the possible sentences are true or false. Next to each number, have the students write *T* if they believe the sentence is true, *F* if they believe it is false, and *DK* if they do not know whether a sentence is true or false.

4. As an oral activity for the whole class or for groups, ask students to make the necessary revisions in the existing sentences to comply with the selection they read, that is, to rewrite the sentences to make them true. Should disagreements emerge, have the students check the text. After the final modifications have been made complete, students may want to record the sentences in their notebooks or folders.

The following sample lesson uses the possible sentences strategy. It is based on the first part of a third-grade basal story entitled "Ma Lien and the Magic Brush" (Kimishima, 1979). The target vocabulary was derived from that listed by the basal authors in addition to vocabulary a teacher might choose to emphasize.

### Target Basal Vocabulary

| | | |
|---|---|---|
| peasant | portrait | frightened |
| artist | mandarin | famous |
| coin | brush | wolves |

Using the words presented above, students might generate the following possible sentences in the prereading stage. After reading the selection, they should have labeled the sentences with a *T, F,* or *DK* as shown in the examples below.

**F** 1. Ma Lien was a *famous artist.*

**T** 2. The *peasant* did not have a single *coin.*

**DK** 3. The *famous artist* used a magic *brush* for painting.

**F** 4. The *wolves frightened* Ma Lien.

**F** 5. A *mandarin* was in the *portrait* he painted.

After modifying and revising the sentences to make them true according to the selection read, the sentences might resemble these.

1. Ma Lien dreamed of being a famous artist.
2. The peasant boy, Ma Lien, did not have a single coin.
3. The famous artist used a magic brush for painting. (We do not know at this point whether it is a magic brush.)
4. The famous artist frightened Ma Lien away when he asked for a brush. So Ma Lien used a stone to draw pictures of wolves, cows, chickens, and sheep.
5. A mandarin, or a powerful official in China, was in the portrait the famous artist painted. (The teacher will want to fill in with further definitions not clearly determined from the context of the story.)

## Reading Stage

For many students, the reading stage of a comprehension lesson is a difficult task. The amount of printed information contained in a typical passage, unit, or chapter is often overwhelming, especially for those students reading below grade level. One possible remedy for this problem is to reduce the amount of print a student must deal with at a given time by interspersing questions throughout the text. The Guide-o-rama (Cunningham and Shablak, 1975) is an easily constructed device that is used for this purpose. A second procedure, the guided reading procedure (Manzo, 1975), also helps students in the reading stage.

### Guide-o-rama

The Guide-o-rama is a study guide developed to help students process the major points and concepts of a selection *while they are reading.* Since it is impossible to provide one-on-one assistance to an entire class, the Guide-o-rama serves as a "tutor in print" that helps students to identify significant ideas, to ask questions, and to guide their thinking and responding. By adhering to a six-step procedure (Wood and Mateja, 1983), teachers can provide students with a reading road map that emphasizes both comprehension and reading rate.

A sample Guide-o-rama for reading a chapter about the War for Independence, taken from a fifth-grade social studies textbook (King et al., 1978), is reproduced in Figure 5.2.

The six steps for developing a Guide-o-rama follow.

1.  Determine the overall purpose for reading a particular assignment. In our illustration, the teacher's purpose was to help students understand the events leading up to the War for Independence.
2.  Select those sections that are necessary to the purpose for reading and that may prove to be confusing to the students.
3.  Develop questions or informative statements that may help students to understand the selection. Teachers of older elementary students may want to suggest the speed at which they should read (for example, "skim," "slow down," "think") to develop the idea that one reads at different speeds for different purposes.
4.  Design a guide format that is novel enough to stimulate the interest of students. For example, a Guide-o-rama for a selection on automobiles might be in the shape of a speedway.
5.  Present the guide to students, usually in the form of a dittoed sheet, and explain its purpose as an adjunct guide to their textbooks. It is recommended that teachers "walk" students through the guide at first to familiarize them with the procedures. Allowing students to work in pairs or small groups may also help them develop skill in using a Guide-o-rama.
6.  After the students have completed the Guide-o-rama, call on them to discuss and explain their answers. This step provides additional reinforcement and allows students to make oral and written contributions to the assignment.

### Guided Reading Procedure

The guided reading procedure is used to help students to recall information read and to improve students' abilities to organize information. The guided reading procedure should be used after the prereading stage has been completed. When the teacher is sure that the students have a background sufficient for processing new knowledge and that they understand their purpose for reading an assignment, the following five-step procedure can be implemented.

1.  Tell the students that they are to read and remember all they can about the selection. (Basal stories or content area passages can be used for this purpose. It may be necessary, however, to divide the passage into short sections.) After the students have read one section, have them turn the material facedown on their desks.
2.  Ask the class to recall whatever comes to their minds about the selection they read. This recalled information is recorded on the board in the order given, usually in an abbreviated form to save time.

3.   When the students are unable to recall any more information, allow them to skim over the selection for the purpose of expanding and amending the information already listed. Throughout this step as well as the remaining steps, continue to ask the students for more information that may or may not be explicitly stated in the selection. This forces students to make inferences and helps them to understand the material beyond the literal level.

(Interview with a colonist) Purpose: Imagine that you were a colonist when Great Britain controlled America. Describe how you felt during each of the events you read about on pages 159-164.

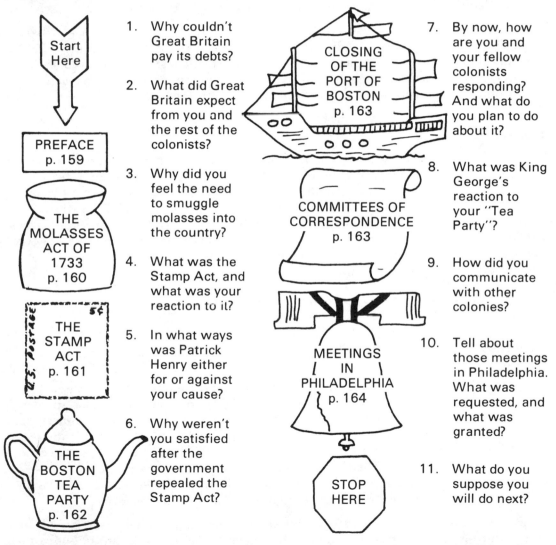

1.   Why couldn't Great Britain pay its debts?

2.   What did Great Britain expect from you and the rest of the colonists?

3.   Why did you feel the need to smuggle molasses into the country?

4.   What was the Stamp Act, and what was your reaction to it?

5.   In what ways was Patrick Henry either for or against your cause?

6.   Why weren't you satisfied after the government repealed the Stamp Act?

7.   By now, how are you and your fellow colonists responding? And what do you plan to do about it?

8.   What was King George's reaction to your "Tea Party"?

9.   How did you communicate with other colonies?

10.   Tell about those meetings in Philadelphia. What was requested, and what was granted?

11.   What do you suppose you will do next?

Figure 5.2. A Guide-o-rama for a fifth-grade chapter in American history, "The English Colonies." (From Karen D. Wood and J. A. Mateja, "Adapting secondary level learning strategies for use in elementary classrooms," *The Reading Teacher*, 1983, **36**, 492-496.

4.  Instruct students to reorganize and modify the material they recalled. This modification may involve having them reorganize the information in the sequence originally presented by asking questions such as "What happened first?" or "When did this occur?" How the information is reorganized depends on the kind of selection read and the comprehension task to be stressed. For example, when the material is largely factual, it may be more appropriate to reorganize it around main ideas and supporting details. Similarly, when the material describes characters, the reorganization process may emphasize specific character traits.
5.  As an optional, follow-up activity, a short quiz can be given to check the short-term memory for the major concepts introduced in the selection.

The guided reading procedure, when used selectively (no more than once or twice a week), is an excellent way to engage the entire class in the learning process. Since all students are not expected to remember the same information, students of all ability levels can participate in the activity. Each bit of recalled information sets off a chain reaction that causes other students to associate and recall other significant events.

## Postreading Stage

The postreading stage of a reading comprehension lesson must not be neglected. During this stage, the important vocabulary of the lesson is reviewed and reinforced, and major concepts are synthesized. The teacher can further extend the lesson by engaging students in activities that accomplish more than one instructional goal. Such strategies as list-group-label (Taba, 1967) and capsule vocabulary (Crist, 1975) are multipurpose activities that reinforce vocabulary, comprehension, and writing simultaneously. They are versatile and practical, because they take little advance preparation and can be used to supplement any reading material.

### List-Group-Label

List-group-label is a technique that uses association and categorization as a means of organizing the significant concepts of a lesson. The steps for list-group-label are described below.

1.  Ask students to think of all the words they can remember from a story they have read, and then record the responses on the board. The initial associations will promote additional responses by other students. Depending on the concept load of the material used, students may produce as many as 25 to 30 associations.
2.  Next, ask students to organize the words into groups of words based on a common element. Then, ask them to provide a label for each group.
3.  To extend the lesson further, allow the students to choose a label and to write a paragraph or short paper using the words from a single group.

Below is a list of the initial associations students might give after reading a selection from a third-grade basal reader. "Child of the Navajos" (Reit and Conklin, 1979) is a story about modern life on an Indian reservation in Arizona.

| | | |
|---|---|---|
| Navajo | Arizona reservation | School Father |
| Modern | American Indian | School Mother |
| Mesa | School | Wool |
| Grazing | Spinning | Meals |
| Cattle | Weaving | Fried bread |
| Sheep | Legends | Language |
| Pupils | Goats | Jerry |
| Miss Dodge | Charlene | Typical |

Using these associations, students might group and label words in the following manner:

1. *Sheep, goats, cattle:* animals that graze.
2. *Spinning, weaving, wool:* making rugs.
3. *Pupils, Jerry, School Mother, School Father:* Navajo Indians.
4. *Language, Arizona, school, modern, pupils, typical, Miss Dodge:* Rough Rock School.

The ability to generate terms, concepts, and details and to categorize them on the basis of some common element is a high-order thinking skill. The use of list-group-label with a reading comprehension lesson, therefore, enhances and expands the students' understanding of material read by eliciting the collective, yet individual, responses of the class. In addition, this strategy engages students in a meaningful review of the material read.

## Capsule Vocabulary

Another strategy—which is built around the use of associations and involves the communication processes of reading, writing, listening, and speaking—is capsule vocabulary. This strategy can be used during the prereading stage of an instructional lesson to stimulate the students' thinking about a selection, or it can be used during the postreading stage as a culminating activity to allow the students additional practice with significant vocabulary words.

The steps for using capsule vocabulary are presented below. These steps are explained in conjunction with a basal reader selection entitled "The King of the Frogs" (Harman, 1979). This story is about the change that occurs when a disorderly colony of frogs takes on a crocodile as their king.

1. After the class has read a selection (from a basal or a content area textbook such as social studies or science), ask the students to free-associate, that is, to think of all the important words they can remember from the story they just read. Write these words on the chalkboard, adding any terms of conceptual significance not mentioned by the class (15 words maximum).
2. Focus the attention of students on each word by using it in a sentence in an informal conversational manner and discussing definitions. Enlist the aid of the students in this activity whenever possible. Some representative sentences based on the sample passage include: "My grandfather is my *elder*, since he is much older than I," "We are supposed to *respect* our *elders*," and "*Africa* is another *continent* thousands of miles away."

3. Have the students copy the list of words off the board and inform them that they will use this list to "talk" to the person sitting next to them. Give them five minutes in which to use as many words from the list as possible. Have them check off the words as they are used by their partner (they should switch roles back and forth throughout the conversation).

4. A natural follow-up to this oral language activity is transferring the "conversation" into a coherent composition. Using a time limit as an incentive, give the students ten minutes to write a paragraph using as many of the words as possible.

5. Organize the students in small groups and have them read their papers aloud. In some instances, the compositions may resemble events in the selection that has been read, but in other cases, students may choose to deviate from the topic and create an original story.

Below is a sample list of words students might produce during a free association based on "The King of the Frogs."

| Wise | Crocodile | Respect | Frog | King |
|------|-----------|---------|------|------|
| Elders | Commission | Croak | Africa | Drowsily |
| Jaws | Gaped | Boulder | Creature | Splash |
| Scandalous | | Waterweeds | Mossy | Gigantic |

The following sample paragraph could have been written by students who had completed step four of the capsule vocabulary activity.

> Africa was the home of the wise, old creature. He was one of the elders now, so everyone showed him respect. Crocodiles splashed their tails for him, and frogs croaked in his honor. He lived amidst the mossy waterweeds and only came out if something scandalous was going on. Even then he just drowsily peeked out from behind the gigantic boulder to see what was the matter. But it was his gaping jaws that caused law and order in the city and made everyone call him "King."

## SUMMARY

We have underscored a number of points about reading comprehension and comprehension instruction. First, we stressed the point that reading comprehension is not simply answering questions about material one has read. Rather, we suggested that reading comprehension is intentional thinking stimulated by written material. The goal of the reader's intentional thinking is to bridge the gap between known and unknown information and to think with information obtained by reading. Next, we pointed out that the teacher is a mediator between the student and the written material. In this mediation role, the teacher must provide instructional strategies designed to activate the student's prior knowledge, to help the student relate her prior knowledge to new information, and to engage the student in thinking with information obtained by reading. Finally, we presented examples of instructional strategies designed to engage students in reading comprehension before reading, during reading, and after reading.

# REFERENCES

Asher, S. R. Topic interest and children's reading comprehension. In R. Spiro, B. Bruce, and W. Brewer (Eds.), *Theoretical issues in reading comprehension.* Hillsdale, N.J.: Lawrence Erlbaum Associates, 1980.

Bean, T. W., and Peterson, J. Reading guides: Fostering reading in content areas. *Reading Horizons,* 1980, **21,** 196–199.

Brown, A. L. Learning how to learn from reading. In J. Langer and M. Smith-Burke (Eds.), *Reader meets author: Bridging the gap.* Newark, Del.: International Reading Association, 1982.

Crist, B. I. One capsule a week: A painless remedy for vocabulary ills. *Journal of Reading,* 1975, **19,** 147–149.

Cunningham, D., and Shablak, S. L. Selective reading Guide-o-rama. *Journal of Reading,* 1975, **18,** 380–382.

Durkin, D. What classroom observations reveal about reading comprehension instruction. *Reading Research Quarterly,* 1978–1979, **14,** 481–533.

Durkin, D. Reading comprehension instruction in five basal reading series. *Reading Research Quarterly,* 1981, **16,** 515–544.

Harman, H. The king of the frogs. In W. K. Durr, J. M. Lepere, B. Niehaus, and B. York, *Keystone.* Boston: Houghton Mifflin, 1979.

Herber, H. *Teaching reading in content areas.* Englewood Cliffs, N.J.: Prentice-Hall, 1970.

Kimishima, H. Ma Lien and the magic brush. In W. K. Durr, J. M. Lepere, B. Neihaus, and B. York, *Tapestry.* Boston: Houghton Mifflin, 1979.

King, A. Y., Dennis, H., and Potter, F. *The United States and other Americas.* New York: Macmillan, 1978.

Klein, N. Girls can be anything. In W. K. Durr, J. M. Lepere, B. Niehaus, and B. York, *Sunburst.* Boston: Houghton Mifflin, 1979.

Manzo, A. V. Guided reading procedure. *Journal of Reading,* 1975, **19,** 287–291.

Moore, D. W., and Arthur, S. Possible sentences. In E. Dishner, T. Bean, and J. Readence (Eds.), *Reading in the content areas: Improving classroom instruction.* Dubuque, Iowa: Kendall/Hunt, 1981.

Pearson, P. D. *Asking questions about stories.* Ginn Occasional Paper Number 15. Lexington, Mass.: Ginn and Company, 1981.

Reit, S., and Conklin, P. Child of the Navajos. In W. K. Durr, J. M. Lepere, B. Niehaus, and B. York, *Tapestry.* Boston: Houghton Mifflin, 1979.

Rumelhart, D. Schemata: The building blocks of cognition. In R. Spiro, B. Bruce, and W. Brewer (Eds.), *Theoretical issues in reading comprehension.* Hillsdale, N.J.: Lawrence Erlbaum Associates, 1980.

Rumelhart, D., and Ortony, A. The representation of knowledge in memory. In R. Anderson, R. Spiro, and W. Montague (Eds.), *Schooling and the acquisition of knowledge.* Hillsdale, N.J.: Lawrence Erlbaum Associates, 1977.

Smith, F. The role of prediction in reading. *Elementary English,* 1975, **52,** 305–311.

Spiro, R. J. Remembering information from text: Theoretical and empirical issues concerning the "state of schema" reconstruction hypothesis. In R. Anderson, R. Spiro, and W. Montague (Eds.), *Schooling and the acquisition of knowledge.* Hillsdale, N.J.: Lawrence Erlbaum Associates, 1977.

Spiro, R. J. Constructive processes in prose comprehension. In R. Spiro, B. Bruce, and W. Brewer (Eds.), *Theoretical issues in reading comprehension.* Hillsdale, N.J.: Lawrence Erlbaum Associates, 1980.

Taba, H. *Teacher's handbook for elementary social studies.* Reading, Mass.: Addison-Wesley, 1967.

Trabasso, T. On making inferences during reading and their assessment. In J. Guthrie (Ed.), *Comprehension and teaching: Research reviews.* Newark, Del.: International Reading Associaton, 1981.

Wood, K. D., and Mateja, J. A. Adapting secondary level learning strategies for use in elementary classrooms. *The Reading Teacher,* 1983, **36,** 492–496.

# RECOMMENDED READINGS

Clymer, T. What is reading?: Some current concepts. In H. M. Robinson (Ed.), *Innovation and change in reading instruction, 67th Yearbook of the National Society for the Study of Education.* Chicago: University of Chicago Press, 1968. Clymer presents a readable discussion of the theories behind reading comprehension and a description of reading comprehension skills.

Durkin, D. What classroom observations reveal about reading comprehension instruction. *Reading Research Quarterly,* 1978-1979, **14,** 481-533. Durkin's article is a controversial report on reading comprehension instruction and how it is being provided in the classroom.

Durkin, D. Reading comprehension instruction in five basal reading series. *Reading Research Quarterly,* 1981, **16,** 515-544. This article analyzes reading comprehension instruction as treated in leading basal reading series.

Durkin, D. What is the value of the new interest in reading comprehension? *Language Arts,* 1981, **58,** 23-43. This article constitutes a practical review of the new emphasis on reading comprehension.

Guthrie, J. T. (Ed.). *Comprehension and teaching: Research reviews.* Newark, Del.: International Reading Association, 1981. Frontier knowledge on reading comprehension processes, skills, instructional practices, and programs is discussed cogently in this book.

Jones, L. L. An interactive view of reading: Implications for the classroom. *The Reading Teacher,* 1982, **35,** 772-777. Jone's article discusses one approach to reading comprehension instruction.

Langer, J. A. From theory to practice: A prereading plan. *Journal of Reading,* 1981, **25,** 152-156. Strategies for activating and evaluating the prior knowledge of students before they read are explored in Langer's article.

Langer, J. A., and Smith-Burke, M. T. (Eds.). *Reader meets author: Bridging the gap.* Newark, Del.: International Reading Association, 1982. Langer and Smith-Burke's book discusses ideas that should influence reading comprehension instruction.

Lapp, D., Flood, J., and Gleckman, G. Classroom practices can make use of what researchers learn. *The Reading Teacher,* 1982, **35,** 578-585. This article emphasizes the use of new findings on reading comprehension in the classroom.

Pearson, P. D. *Asking questions about stories.* Ginn Occasional Papers number 15. Lexington, Mass.: Ginn and Company, 1981. This publication discusses the purposes of questions in reading comprehension instruction and provides clear examples of how they can be developed and used in the classroom.

Pearson, P. D., and Johnson, D. D. *Teaching reading comprehension.* New York: Holt, Rinehart and Winston, 1978. Reading comprehension instruction is the topic of this volume.

Russell, D. H. *The dynamics of reading.* Waltham, Mass.: Ginn-Blaisdell, 1970. Russell provides a rare and meaningful analysis of reading comprehension in this book.

Sadow, M. W. The use of story grammar in the design of questions. *The Reading Teacher,* 1982, **35,** 518-522. Examples of questions used in reading comprehension instruction are provided in this article.

Santa, C. M., and Hayes, B. L. (Eds.). *Children's prose comprehension: Research and practice.* Newark, Del.: International Reading Association, 1981. This is a recent book on children's reading comprehension.

Schwartz, E., and Sheff, A. Student involvement in questioning for comprehension. *The Reading Teacher,* 1975, **29,** 150-154. How students can be involved in asking their own questions before reading is discussed in this article.

Singer, H. Active comprehension: From answering questions to asking questions. *The Reading Teacher,* 1978, **31,** 901-908. The role of readers in developing their own questions for reading comprehension is explored.

Smith, F. The role of prediction in reading. *Elementary English,* 1975, **52,** 305-311. The role of prediction in reading is discussed in this article.

Spiegel, D. L. Six alternatives to the directed reading activity. *The Reading Teacher,* 1981, **34,** 914-920. The strengths and weaknesses of the directed reading lesson are reviewed and descriptions of useful alternatives are provided in this article.

Stauffer, R. S. *Teaching reading as a thinking process.* New York: Harper and Row, 1969. Reading comprehension instruction is one of many topics in this book.

Strange, M. Instructional implications of a conceptual theory of reading comprehension. *The Reading Teacher,* 1980, **33,** 391-397. One theory of reading comprehension and its implications are discussed in this article.

# CHAPTER 6

# Teaching Critical Reading Skills

Bernard L. Hayes
Utah State University
Logan

*In Chapter 4, the comprehension of words, sentences, and passages was discussed, and Chapter 5 presented an alternative to the directed reading strategy that provides teachers a structure for actively engaging students in comprehension instruction. Chapter 6 also deals with reading comprehension, but this chapter emphasizes critical reading skills—the "higher-level" comprehension skills that distinguish a mature, fluent reader who not only is capable of comprehending on the literal and inferential level but is also able to evaluate and interact with print. In this chapter, Bernard Hayes presents five different facets of critical reading skill that involve a reader's sensitivity to the source of the material, ability to discriminate between fact and opinion, understanding of an author's purpose, awareness of an author's use of language, and ability to detect propaganda techniques. In each of these areas, Hayes presents concrete, practical teaching activities that teachers can use to develop students' critical reading ability.*

The ultimate goal of reading instruction is to produce mature, fluent readers who not only are skilled at word identification and basic comprehension skills but also are capable of evaluating what they read, that is, readers who interact with, or critically read, the print they encounter. Teaching students to read critically, however, is perhaps the most difficult task a teacher faces in reading instruction, for critical reading depends on, but goes beyond, literal comprehension and interpretive comprehension.

What does a critical reader do? A critical reader is one who can separate fact from opinion, one who can detect an author's purpose, bias, and intent in writing a passage even when it is not clearly stated. A critical reader is one who understands the meaning of words used and the fine shades of meaning words may have in different contexts. Critical reading, therefore, involves many different reading skills and demands that the reader evaluate and make a personal judgment on the quality, value, accuracy, and truthfulness of what is read. The purpose of this chapter is to assist the teacher in helping students make more and better critical judgments about what they read.

Critical reading is the evaluation of written material. It involves comparing the ideas discovered in written passages with established criteria (i.e., the reader's attitudes and values) and arriving at conclusions regarding the accuracy, appropriateness, and timeliness of the selection. The critical reader must be an *active* reader who uses the skill of questioning as a way to understand a writer, to determine a writer's purpose, and to evaluate a writer's ideas. Critical readers actively read between the lines of written material. They search with certain questions in mind. To help guide students in critical reading, this chapter provides key questions that critical readers might ask themselves and some instructional procedures for teaching children to use these questions effectively. The questions that follow require that readers (1) examine the source of the materials they read, (2) be sensitive to statements of fact and opinion, (3) consider an author's purpose in writing, (4) critically examine the language an author uses, and (5) be aware of propaganda techniques.

## THE SOURCE

Readers should keep three questions in mind as they read written material: What is the source of the material? Is the material reliable? And is the material up-to-date? The first task of critical reading is to examine the source of the material being read. Most readers expect printed material to be written by knowledgeable individuals. A critical reader, however, must evaluate the source of the material and attempt to appraise the qualifications of authors whenever possible. Students should be aware that some authors express strong opinions that might differ from their own. Critical readers must also examine the material itself. Is it published by a reputable source, or is it material sponsored by a special interest group? Is the material current or timely, or is it out-of-date?

### The Author

Perhaps the most important concern facing a critical reader is analyzing the writer of the material. If information about the author is given or available, it should be carefully studied.

#### Author's Qualifications

The credibility of written material is affected by the expertise of the author. In questioning the qualifications of an author, students should be instructed to ask about her background, experience, and education. Do other persons who write on this topic respect her? For example, a recognized physician writing about an area of medicine that he has studied could be considered a qualified source.

#### Author's Bias

The critical reader will want to determine whether an author has been an active member of organizations related to the topic about which she is writing. The reader will want to know also whether the author holds strong or controversial views that would prejudice any opinions about a topic in one way or another. For example, a professional hunter writing an article against gun control in a hunting magazine would be considered a biased source.

### The Publisher

Many times, no information about the author is given in material we read. Sometimes, even the name of the author is not provided, as is frequently the case in newspapers and magazines. When no information about the author of the article is given and the reader has no prior knowledge of the author, the reader must seek other sources of information to judge the reliability of the material. Students should consider examining information about the publisher of the material. Does the publication represent the views of a specific organization? Does the publisher have a reputation for printing certain types of articles? Is the publisher known for printing reliable or unreliable information? The reader's own experiences with specific publications will be his best guide in judging the value of the information they contain.

### Timeliness of the Material

Finally, in examining the source, the critical reader must determine *when* the material was published. Is it current or out-of-date? Because of the rapid changes taking place in the world today, knowing when the material was published is often important. For example, an outdated article from a medical journal may refer to a disease as incurable when, in fact, a cure has recently been found. Sometimes, however, the fact that an article is recent does not indicate that its information is more reliable than older material. A contemporary account of the construction of the Panama Canal, for instance, might be more reliable than one written in 1983.

## FACT, OPINION, AND INFERENCE

The ability to identify fact, inference, and opinion is a skill vital for critical reading. Uncritical readers may unquestioningly accept as fact anything they read in print and accept as fact statements or positions with which they strongly agree. Good readers, however, determine whether an author uses statements that are primarily facts, opinions, or inferences. Students must be helped to develop a clear and concise idea of what constitutes fact, inference, and opinion.

### Fact

A fact is a statement that can be verified. If a statement cannot be proven by observation, official records, or scientific experimentation, it is not a fact.

Remember, also, that although a statement may be presented as a fact, it may not be true. Incorrect statements of fact (i.e., false facts) appear when the writer is uninformed or when she simply wants to deceive the reader. The reader must learn to rely on external sources for verification of facts when he suspects that the reading material contains false facts or misinformation. In such cases, checking one or two of the facts through a source the reader believes to be reliable is prudent.

## Opinion

Students need to recognize that an opinion is a statement of belief that may or may not have support. For a variety of reasons, opinions cannot be verified. Take, for example, the statement "Our dog is the smartest dog in town." This statement cannot be verified and is, therefore, an opinion. It would be impossible for all dog owners in a town to agree on what the standards for a smart dog might be and to judge each dog on that scale of smartness.

The teacher should also help students become aware of specific key words that alert them to statements indicating opinions. Qualifiers such as *I think, I feel, in my opinion, I believe,* as well as words such as *should, ought,* and *must* signal opinions. For example, two such clues denote opinions in the following sentences: "*I think* the Badgers were the best team in 1981," and "You *should* buy this bike."

It may be helpful to students if the teacher points out such cues and gives the students opportunities to practice locating them in written material. Students must also learn that not all opinions are of equal value. Opinions based on fact and careful thinking are much more valid than those that are unsupported or based on biases.

## Inference

When introducing students to inference, teachers must communicate that an inference is a judgment based on careful thinking about what is known to be fact. Students should understand that the more support, or facts, that an author presents for an inference, the more likely it is to be valid. For example, when a politician attempts to persuade people to vote for her by telling them facts about her background, she is using inference. She provides support (facts about her background) to give people confidence in the inference that she is the candidate best qualified for the office.

In discussions of the critical reading of inferences, it should be emphasized that opinions and inferences are many times as valuable as facts. They allow the author to present ideas that encourage thinking and interaction between the writer and the reader.

# THE PURPOSE

## To Inform

One reason an author has for writing is to inform. Students should learn that, when providing information is an author's primary purpose, the written statements are mainly factual and the style and tone, objective. For example, an author writing to inform usually presents information in an organized manner, as in *The Book of Lists,* airline schedules, telephone directories, and *The Guiness World Book of Records.*

## To Instruct

A good deal of what students read is meant to instruct them. The teacher should help students determine whether an author's writing is instructional. If material is intended to instruct, it should be accurate, unbiased, to the point, and up-to-date.

## To Persuade

Students come in contact with a good deal of material that is written to persuade them that what the author (or interest group) believes to be true is true. The teacher can help students to identify persuasive writing by indicating that such writing usually contains a good deal of factual information. Persuasive writing, however, contains more inferences and opinions than material written to inform or to instruct. Persuasive writing may also include more connotative language. Students should be taught to understand that an author may write to persuade the reader for two different reasons. One is for humanitarian purposes, and the other is for self-interest. For example, an author may write about the dangers of smoking and (for humanitarian purposes) suggest that the reader should not smoke. On the other hand, an author may write about the dangers of smoking and suggest (for purposes of self-interest) that the reader should use a certain cigarette filter.

## THE LANGUAGE USED

The style and tone of the material should match the purpose of the selection. Students need the teacher's help to become sensitive to the author's style or the literary devices used, such as figurative language, symbolism, repetition, understatement, exaggeration (hyperbole), personification, irony, and pun. Students also should become aware of the use of connotative language—the emotional overtones of words—and they should learn to evaluate the validity of such statements. For example, the words *prance, strut, saunter,* and *shuffle* all denote walking, but each has a unique connotation. Students should understand that the critical reader is one who *suspects* a possible bias on the part of the author who relies heavily on the use of connotative language. For example, compare "Redskins steal the game from Cowboys" to "Redskins defeat Cowboys."

The writer's tone and use of emotional words do much to move a reader toward or away from a point of view or attitude. For example, note the effect of these two sentences.

*Writer 1:* The wolflike beast growled viciously as we walked by its cage.

*Writer 2:* The large dog barked loudly as we walked by its kennel.

## RECOGNITION OF PROPAGANDA TECHNIQUES

Readers are constantly asked to respond to printed material that attempts to influence their thoughts and actions. Much of this material may serve a good purpose, although some may serve a bad one. Instruction and activities should be planned with the goal of helping students look for propaganda techniques that writers use to sway readers' opinions about a cause or point of view.

Students should learn that the use of propaganda means that the author has *deliberately* attempted to persuade a reader to accept a point of view or to take a particular action. The use of propaganda itself, however, is not inherently bad. The critical reader must decide whether the action or the point of view that is being expressed is consistent with the readers' beliefs. Propaganda is used in all types of reading material—newspapers, magazines, books, billboards, and ads—and on television.

Listed below are some undesirable devices authors sometimes use to persuade or to influence the reader. Good critical readers should be acquainted with each.

1. Appealing to emotion over reason (name calling, appealing to sympathy). Example: "It is appallingly clear that America the beautiful has fallen into the hands of political madmen."

2. Inferring a relationship between persons, objects, or events that does not exist (associating a well-known and respected person or organization with a project, product, or idea in an effort to transfer that fame or respect). Example: "Arnold Palmer plays golf and owns property just two miles from our new Hidden Fairway Estates subdivision."

3. Using glittering generalities (using vague phrases to sway a point of view without discussing specific detail). Example: "Shooting Star cleanser has style on the outside and power on the inside."

4. Emphasizing the plain folks approach (relating a person or product to the common people in an effort to gain their support). Example: "Finally, a car that is built for you and me, a car that meets the basic transportation needs of the average, everyday driver."

5. Offering endorsements (using a prominent person to endorse a product or project). Example: "Mark Damp, Olympic swimmer, brushes with new, improved 'Tastie Teeth' toothpaste."

6. Using the bandwagon approach (encouraging one to do what others are doing). Example: "Hurry while the offer lasts. Don't miss out on this chance to be one of the growing number of people to own land at Wagon Creek Ranch."

7. Omitting facts (card stacking by telling only one side of a position while ignoring positive facts related to the opposing point of view). Example: "Unlike most other models of home computers, our 101 model can be purchased for under fifty dollars."

8. Avoiding the source of information (providing facts to support a position or product while not discussing the origin of the information). Example: "According to the latest poll, most people support the President's new program."

## CRITICAL READING ACTIVITIES

Critical reading skills are essential if we are to function in a society that increasingly demands that we make well-informed and intelligent decisions about what we read. Students need to learn to read critically so that they acquire the necessary skills to make the many decisions society will soon expect of them as adults.

To develop critical reading skills in the classroom, the teacher should encourage students to read with these questions in mind:

1. What is the source? What do we know about the author's qualifications, the reputation of the publisher, and the date of publication?
2. Is the author's primary purpose to inform, instruct, or persuade?
3. Are the statements in the material primarily facts, inferences, or opinions?
4. Does the author rely on a heavy use of connotative words that may indicate a bias?
5. Is the author using any negative propaganda techniques?

The following five activities correspond to these questions. Although specific materials are used to describe the activities, alternate reading materials appropriate for the reading ability and interests of the students could be substituted.

## Activities for Examining the Source

### Activity 1

Have students identify authors who are writing about specific topics and discuss whether or not their writing should be accepted. Make sure students determine why an author may be reliable or unreliable. For example, consider an article discussing a popular new diet plan. Would the well-known Hollywood star who has used the plan or the nutrition expert who has studied the diet be considered the more reliable source? In this example, the star might be able to discuss the diet plan's success in helping one to lose weight but would likely be much less well informed than the nutrition expert about other positive or negative effects the diet might have on the health of an individual.

### Activity 2

Ask the class or a group of students to review selected written material and develop criteria (such as author's background, experience with the topic, and date of publication) for determining the competence of the author. For example, have students determine how much attention should be given to the views or statements of the following writers on the stated subjects.

1. A sports expert writing in the summer issue of a sports magazine, on what might be "the nation's top ten teams" in the upcoming football season.
2. The English physician, John British (1578–1648), on the causes of lung disease.
3. A young, attractive television star, on the face cream that is best for your complexion.
4. A society page columnist, on the merits of a presidential candidate.
5. A police officer with 20 years of experience, on the trends in law enforcement.
6. The president of a large labor union, on a proposed law to limit collective bargaining.
7. The chairperson of the National Association of Manufacturers, on a proposed law to limit collective bargaining.
8. A Nobel Prize–winning economist, on the long-range effects of a new tax program.

### Activity 3

Provide students with several different publications, such as the *Washington Post*, the *Midnight Globe*, and a local newspaper. Lead students in evaluating each newspaper's reputation for containing "uncolored reports" and on the paper's reputation for presenting facts accurately. Have students "research" two different publications, such as the *New York Times* and the *National Enquirer*, in an effort to determine what awards or recognition each has received for their reporting. They should try to determine whether the publication appears to report predominantly public issues or to focus on sensational events or topics and famous personalities' private lives.

*Activity 4*

Find reports in newspapers or magazines with views on a subject and discuss why an author's view may be reliable or unreliable. For example, have students read the following two letters written to the editor of a large newspaper regarding a change in child labor laws.

## Letter 1

A proposal to increase by one-third the hours that 14- and 15-year-olds may work during a school week could significantly damage the youngster's family life, school performance, and health. The social and psychological costs of working are directly related to the amount of time the youngster spends in the work place.

Based on our 3-year study of 539 high school students in Orange County, we found that the negative effects of working increase sharply, on the average, after 15 hours a week for 15-year-olds.

I. M. Bright, Ph.D.
O. K. Wythme, Ph.D.
Department of Child Psychology
Bakersfield State University

## Letter 2

Can the labor department really be serious when it proposes easing work rules for children? Of course, it can. Why shouldn't an administration that believes we no longer need to watchdog nursing homes or guard against high lead levels in gasoline decide whether it's all right for 14- and 15-year-olds to work longer hours for substandard pay.

Since the early part of this century, the U.S. of A. has moved to limit the workday for children and to protect them from hazardous and inappropriate work. There is no justification for removing any of these protections from a group so ill equipped to protect itself.

The Committee to Protect Our Youth
Joe Goodworthy, Chairman

Students should note that, even though the writers' views may be similar, as in the above example, the reliability of the authors may vary a great deal.

## Activity for Determining the Purpose

Provide students with a list of reading selections and have them indicate whether each was intended to be primarily instructional, informative, or persuasive. An example follows.

| *Informative* | *Persuasive* | *Instructional* |
| --- | --- | --- |
| An article in a newspaper about child being bitten by large dog. | An editorial in a newspaper about large dogs running loose on the streets. | A book about dogs that describes the personality and pedigree of various breeds of large dogs. |

| *Informative* | *Persuasive* | *Instructional* |
|---|---|---|
| A magazine article describing the need for new energy sources and nuclear energy as one of many possible sources. | A document on atomic energy distributed by Citizens for a Safe Environment. | An encyclopedia entry on nuclear energy. |

## Activities for Identifying Fact or Opinion

### Activity 1

*Directions:* Read each sentence carefully. Decide whether the statement is a fact or opinion. If the sentence states a fact, write *F* on the line in front of the sentence. If the sentence is an opinion, write *O*.

_____ 1. Pete Rose is the best baseball player.

_____ 2. There are 30 days in September.

_____ 3. I think we should have better shows on television.

_____ 4. Jill is a secretary.

_____ 5. Jill is a great secretary.

_____ 6. The money spent on space exploration has been a wise investment.

_____ 7. If the plane is on time, it will arrive at 7:15 A.M.

_____ 8. State will have a basketball team this year.

### Activity 2

Magazine or newspaper editorials are good materials for students to use in identifying statements of fact and opinion. Statements in editorials can be underlined and marked with an *F* for a fact and an *O* for an opinion. Groups or individuals can discuss their determinations and decide which opinions seem to be most valid.

### Activity 3

Students should also be alert to statements offered as facts but that are not facts. In the following example, students are to identify the "true facts" and the "false facts" by writing a *T* or an *F* on the line in front of the sentence. (This type of activity will probably require that students *verify* the facts they are asked to believe.)

_____ 1. The 1960 Olympic games were held in Rome, Italy.

_____ 2. One out of every two cars sold in the United States during 1982 was an import.

_____ 3. Chicago has the world's two tallest buildings.

_____ 4. Utah is the largest copper-producing state in the United States.

_____  5.  The United States has had a Republican-controlled House of Representatives for the last ten years.

_____  6.  Indiana won the 1981 NCAA basketball tournament.

## Activities for Language Used

### Activity 1

Have students compare and contrast certain groups of words to see how words lend themselves to generating biased attitudes or feelings. Have students examine the following pairs of words for their connotative meanings and discuss how the meanings of sentences in which they might appear would differ. The following is an example.

> The man *preyed* upon the deer.
>
> The man *hunted* the deer.
>
> policeman—cop
>
> politician—public servant
>
> burly—large
>
> chef—cook
>
> preyed upon—hunted
>
> disgust—upset
>
> stubborn—cautious
>
> clutch—hold
>
> demagogue—leader

### Activity 2

As a follow-up activity, have students write pairs of sentences that would indicate the connotations of these words. An example follows.

> The *large policeman* was a *cautious public servant* when it came to law enforcement.
>
> The *burly cop* was a *stubborn politician* when it came to law enforcement.

## Activities for Propaganda Techniques

### Activity 1

List on a worksheet a number of widely used propaganda techniques. Compile a list of statements that illustrate the techniques. Have the students match the techniques to the statements.

1.  Emotional appeal (name calling, etc.)
2.  Implied relationship
3.  Glittering generalities

4. Plain folks approach
5. Endorsements
6. Bandwagon approach
7. Omitting facts
8. Avoiding the source of information

_____ Mary Cliner, world champion tennis player, says, "The Zippo sportswear has been my first choice for years."

_____ The present administration is dangerous and misinformed.

_____ The results of independent tests indicate that this car is your best buy.

_____ Two out of ten dentists think that our toothpaste will help prevent tooth decay.

_____ Don't be the last person on your block to install our Sunny Solar System.

_____ Vote for Sam Price—a man who, like you, knows what it is like to work for his money and send children to school.

_____ Enjoy the world, travel, experience life, join the U.S. Army.

_____ We brought you the best-selling cereal on the market, and now we offer you the best-tasting toothpaste.

*Activity 2*

After students have become familiar with propaganda techniques, they can be given the opportunity to analyze magazine, newspaper, and television advertisements. It is recommended that this activity be introduced in the following sequence.

1. Select several advertisements that utilize a specific propaganda technique. Ask students to identify the propaganda technique used in the advertisements.
2. Have students, working in teams, select a certain propaganda technique. Then, have the groups find examples of the techniques in newspapers and magazine advertisements. Have groups evaluate each others' advertisements to determine whether they agree that the ads are examples of the specified propaganda techniques.
3. Have students find examples of propaganda techniques in material other than advertisements. Newspaper editorials, printed political campaign material, and various organizations' printed material all may employ propaganda techniques students can recognize.
4. Have students write their own advertisements, editorials, campaign speeches, or other materials to illustrate one or more propaganda techniques.

## SUMMARY

This chapter has introduced skills and strategies required for efficient and effective critical reading. A series of questions that students should be taught to ask themselves as they read critically to judge the soundness of written material was offered. The teacher, however, must be the one who carefully guides the students in the use of these questions as they critically read new material. Much thoughtful modeling and discussion using a wide range of materials is needed to introduce the skills of critical reading to students.

## RECOMMENDED READINGS

Altick, R. D. *Preface to critical reading.* (5th Ed.) New York: Holt, Rinehart and Winston, 1969. Although a useful text on critical reading intended for college students, Altick's book includes an excellent discussion of critical reading and many fine examples of exercises in critical reading that upper-grade elementary teachers could adapt to their students' abilities.

Eller, W., and Wolf, J. G. *Critical reading: A broader view.* Newark, Del.: International Reading Association, 1972. This annotated bibliography contains references to many useful texts and materials related to critical reading.

Pearson, P. D., and Johnson, D. D. *Teaching reading comprehension.* New York: Holt, Rinehart and Winston, 1978. Pearson and Johnson's paperback book for teachers includes an excellent chapter on critical reading factors, as well as very useful activities for involving students.

Rosenbaum, J. *Spotlight on reading: Critical reading.* New York: Random House, 1978. This series of materials for students' use contains many interesting activities for developing critical reading skill.

Stauffer, R. G., and Cramer, R. *Teaching critical reading at the primary level.* Newark, Del.: International Reading Association, 1968. Practical suggestions for developing habitually critical readers are provided in this publication.

Walling, E. *Reading comprehension: Critical reading (levels A–D).* New York: Scholastic Book Services, 1979. This series of skill books provides students with practice in and application of several critical reading skills discussed in this chapter.

# CHAPTER 7

# Using Poetry to Improve Reading Ability

Richard J. Smith
University of Wisconsin-Madison

*Chapters 1 through 6 presented teaching strategies that beginning teachers can use to teach basic word identification, vocabulary, and comprehension skills. Chapter 7 continues this same theme, but here Richard Smith suggests how teachers can use the medium of poetry to teach reading skills. Smith argues that some reading skills may be more effectively taught with poetry than with prose. Using his own poetry as examples, the author offers teaching suggestions for instruction in nine different reading skills: performing expressive oral readings, using context clues, finding main ideas, using mental imagery, recalling sequence, taking part in thoughtful discussions, becoming aware of the poet as a person, anticipating outcomes, and thinking creatively. In addition, Smith discusses how other sources of published poetry and original poems by teachers and students can be used for reading skill instruction.*

The value of poetry in the reading curriculum can lie in more than the aesthetic experience that comes from reading it. Poems can be used successfully to improve reading ability. Indeed, certain reading skills (e.g., sequencing information, finding main ideas, making predictions) can often be taught more effectively with poetry than with prose. The purpose of this chapter is to encourage teachers to find and use poetry for improving their students' reading skills as well as for providing them enjoyment.[1]

---

[1]The poetry used, with permission, in this chapter was written by the author and originally published in *Instructor* magazine.

## WHY POETRY FOR READING INSTRUCTION?

Perhaps teachers overlook poems as vehicles for reading skills development because they have stereotyped poems as fragile creations. Poems are often presented to children as though they had to be mouthed gently and touched only by questions of appreciation: "Did you like this poem?" "Tell me why you liked it." Often, the artwork that accompanies poems in instructional materials furthers the stereotype by dressing them in gossamer and lace. Who would dare to pull apart or dig into such a lovely thing? Material used to *teach* reading skills, however, must be pulled apart and dug into, at least a little.

The stereotype and what it implies for reading instruction are misguided. Most poems can be grasped, squeezed, and thrown about without breaking them. They can be given to children for the purpose of skills development as well as for appreciation. The fact is, however, that they rarely are. Terry (1974), after a study of fourth-, fifth-, and sixth-graders' reading preferences, concluded, among other things, that "teachers rarely read poetry to their students and seldom provide opportunities for them to write their own poems" (p. 56). Apparently, many teachers have not yet discovered the full value of poetry.

## USING POETRY TO DEVELOP EXPRESSIVE ORAL READING

One valuable characteristic of poems for purposes of reading development is their rhythm. Beginning readers and students with reading problems often have difficulty learning to read orally with good expression. Teachers are all too familiar with the monotonous, word-by-word reading that provides the reader with neither joy in reading nor good comprehension. Poems can be used to help students to use the intonation system of the English language as it works to convey meaning. The "feel" of reimplanting the melodies of the language the poet had in mind when he wrote is an important discovery for all students. Beginning readers or students who experience difficulty reading prose orally with good expression may be able to perform better with poems that have a definite rhythm than with prose. With a little encouragement and practice, students can learn to let their voices ride along on the rhythm in poems. For example:

### Don't Catch the Flu

*Shivering is what you'll do*
*If you should go and catch the flu.*
*And you'll be hot and thirsty too*
*If you should go and catch the flu.*

*Throwing up is what you'll do*
*If you should go and catch the flu.*
*And you'll be dizzy, shaky too*
*If you should go and catch the flu.*

*It's terrible the things you'll do*
*If you should go and catch the flu.*
*And what I say I know is true*
*'Cause I just went and caught the flu.*

## USING POETRY TO DEVELOP CONTEXT CLUE SKILLS

Rhyme is another characteristic of some poems that makes them good for reading development. Poems that rhyme can be used to help students learn to use context clues and to anticipate information as they read. Such poems are excellent material for the construction of cloze exercises. There can be little doubt about the deleted words in the stanzas below.

### Geraldine Jackson

*For a kid who loves to eat*
*Geraldine Jackson can't be beat.*
*All considered, bite for bite,*
*She has a monstrous _____.*
*Smack!*

*Geraldine always cleans her plate.*
*For dinner time she's never late.*
*Neither her mother nor her pop*
*Ever tells her, "Time to _____ "*
*Burp!*

*Once she ate three lemon pies.*
*I don't know how she closed her eyes.*
*Drank a milk shake so darn thick*
*Even Geraldine got _____.*
*Ugh!*

*I saw her eat a whole fried chicken,*
*And then she even got to lickin'*
*Off the bones 'till they were bare.*
*Wouldn't you think her clothes would _____?*
*Rip!*

*Geraldine just makes me cry.*
*Yes, I cry. Do you know why?*
*Geraldine can eat like that*
*And never gain an ounce of _____.*
*Sob!*

## USING POETRY TO TEACH FINDING MAIN IDEAS

The content of most poems is rich with emotional tone. The interplay between thoughts and emotions heightens both. Consider the following stanzas.

*If you think I'm never sad*
*I'll tell you what let's do.*
*You be me for just one day,*
*And I'll in turn be you.*

*You just hop inside of me,*
*And be me for a while.*
*Think my thoughts and do my jobs,*
*Find out what makes me smile.*

*By the way, while you are me*
*As one day passes by,*
*You'll also learn behind that smile*
*I sometimes want to cry.*

Asking students to state the message in this poem in their own words or to supply a title for it provides them excellent practice in finding main ideas.

## DEVELOPING MENTAL IMAGERY THROUGH POETRY

Much enjoyment and comprehension of printed material are the result of mental imagery, which is a behavior students can learn. The language of poetry stimulates mental imagery when students are asked to read for that purpose. Students could be asked to pause and form mental pictures after each stanza in the following poem.

### What Happened?

*What happened to our yard last night?*
*Come here and look around.*
*Why, you can see all kinds of things*
*Lying on the ground.*

*Sidewalk full of half-drowned worms,*
*Street all muddy-wet,*
*Grass all strewn with parts of trees,*
*Garbage cans upset.*

*Water's dripping everywhere—*
*Sliding from green leaves,*
*Gliding down slick window panes,*
*Slipping off the eaves.*

*Trickling down the driveway,*
*Two streams of water meet,*
*And search beneath some leaves and twigs*
*Before they find the street.*

*I know what's happened to our yard.*
*It's had a bath I'll bet.*
*All the dirt's still in the tub,*
*And the water's not out yet.*

At the conclusion of their reading, students could be asked to tell which stanza or words gave them the clearest or prettiest mental pictures. They could be asked what different colors they "saw" or what sounds they "heard." They could describe the pictures they formed and compare their perceptions with the perceptions of other students. They could even be asked to draw the picture they most enjoyed.

## TEACHING SEQUENCE SKILLS THROUGH POETRY

Learning to recall the sequence in which ideas are presented by an author is an important objective in the reading curriculum. Many poems contain sequenced ideas that students can be asked to recall in the order in which they were presented. The following is a good example of such a poem.

### Once I Did

*Once I drove a racing car*
*Three hundred miles an hour.*
*Once I jumped right to the top*
*Of New York's highest tower.*

*Once I threw a ball so far*
*It landed on the moon.*
*And once I ran to India,*
*And got back home by noon.*

*Once I fought a grizzly bear*
*And sailed through seven gales.*
*I'll bet by now you must have guessed*
*I also tell tall tales.*

## USING POETRY TO DEVELOP THOUGHTFUL READING

Many instructional reading materials do little to foster thoughtful reading. That is, students are more impressed by the packaging, multiple-choice questions, and self-answer keys in some workbooks and kits than they are by the ideational and emotional content of the reading selections themselves. In some cases, this is not difficult to understand, because the content of the selections is not thought provoking. A characteristic of most poems is that they contain ideas that foster thoughtfulness and warrant thinking about. The following poem could be used to promote a discussion about students' dreams and how dreams affect their lives.

### My Dreams

*Sometimes my dreams are very merry.*
*Other times they're very scary.*
*I've danced at balls with queens and kings,*
*Been chased and caught by monstrous things.*

*Where am I when I'm asleep?*
*I know my body's snuggled deep*
*Beneath the covers on my bed.*
*But where's the inside of my head?*

*Do my thoughts go out walking*
*When I stop my daytime talking?*
*Do they visit strange new places?*
*See different lands and different faces?*

*I think that they don't stay at home,*
*For in my dreams I often roam*
*Through areas unknown to me—*
*I've climbed a mountain, sailed a sea.*

*I never dream that I'm asleep,*
*Under covers snuggled deep.*
*I know my dreams are in my head,*
*But does my head stay in my bed?*

The following questions could be used as discussion starters: (1) What question does the poet ask? (2) What causes dreams? (3) Would people be better or worse off without dreams? (4) Do you have a recurring dream? (5) What is the best dream you ever had? (6) The worst?

## USING POEMS TO INFER CHARACTERISTICS OF THE POET

Poets are often more visible in their poems than are writers of prose in their writing. Speculations about the age, dress, occupation, hobbies, and other personal characteristics of the writer of the following poem could lead students to a discovery of the personal element in reading material. What can be imagined about the author of the following poem?

### Imagining

*Imagining is what I do*
*When walking by the sea,*
*Imagining I'm lots of things*
*That I can never be.*

*Imagining that I'm a wave*
*Washing this white beach,*
*Stretching water fingers out*
*As far as they will reach.*

*Imagining that I'm a shark,*
*The biggest ever seen;*
*Scaring fishes left and right,*
*'Cause I'm so hungry-mean.*

*Imagining that I'm a gull*
*Resting on a piling, then*
*Flapping up above the waves,*
*Fishing while I'm flying.*

*Imagining that I'm a fish,*
*A dolphin with a snout;*
*Sewing up an ocean path*
*By dipping in and out.*

*Imagining I'm anything*
*That's part of this old sea,*
*Until a sand burr bites my toe*
*And then I know I'm me.*

# USING POETRY TO TEACH OUTCOME PREDICTION

Good readers anticipate or speculate as they read. Thinking ahead keeps their minds from wandering and promotes careful reading. Poems in which the subject is undisclosed until the final stanza, riddle poems, and poems that unfold information or a story a stanza at a time are good vehicles for teaching students to make predictions as they read. Students could read the following poem a stanza at a time, pausing between stanzas to speculate about what is outside the tent.

## Outside My Tent

*Outside my tent I hear something pawing,*
*Clawing and gnawing, hungrily mawing.*
*Maybe it's friendly, a friendly old deer,*
*Hungry or curious. I've nothing to fear*
*From a deer in search of a midnight snack*
*Who found the cookies left in my pack.*

*Outside my tent I still hear it pawing,*
*Clawing and gnawing, stealthily mawing.*
*But now it sounds smaller. A hungry raccoon*
*Searching for food by the light of the moon?*
*Raccoons don't hurt people. No need now to fear.*
*I'm sure it's a raccoon—or maybe that deer.*

*Outside my tent that creature's still pawing,*
*Clawing and gnawing, greedily mawing.*
*What's that I can smell? A skunk on the loose?*
*Oh how could I ever have been such a goose*
*As to trade my bed for this tent under trees,*
*To lie here all worried, sniffing the breeze.*

*Outside my tent the thing won't stop pawing,*
*Clawing, gnawing, ferociously mawing.*
*Now it sounds huge. It must be a bear,*
*Hungry and mean and ready to tear*
*Me to pieces before I can flee.*
*Oh, please! Someone, anyone, come rescue me.*

*Outside my tent no end to the pawing,*
*Clawing and gnawing, persistent mawing.*
*I cannot stay here. I must look and see*
*The creature that may make a supper of me.*
*Bear or deer, raccoon or skunk—*
*I see it! Good grief—it's a tiny chipmunk.*

The riddle poem that follows is also good for making the reader think ahead.

## The Bravest Thing I Know

*It has a long, long way to go,*
*And it must travel very slow.*

*Danger lies on every side,*
*There's no way it can catch a ride.*

*High above, a hungry hawk!*
*It cannot run. It still must walk.*

*On the left, a speeding car!*
*It can't turn back. It's gone too far.*

*It has no fear of getting lost,*
*Inch by inch the road is crossed.*

*What's the bravest thing I know?*
*A caterpillar on the go!*

## FOSTERING CREATIVE THINKING THROUGH POETRY

Another major objective of reading programs is fostering creative thinking about reading material. What better way than to use a poem and questions that ask for divergent thinking.

### A Scary Book

*Take a look inside this book*
*If you think you dare.*
*For in this book, this very book*
*Scary things are there.*

*You'll meet a beast that's running loose.*
*It broke out of its cage.*
*And there's a monster in this book*
*On almost every page.*

*My poem about a wicked witch*
*Will surely make you shiver.*
*She catches little girls and boys*
*And makes them eat raw liver.*

*How about a creature who*
*Comes to your house one night,*
*And crawls right into bed with you*
*When you turn out the light.*

*I really cannot tell you more.*
*Please put this on a shelf.*
*I've written down such terrible stuff*
*I've even scared myself.*

What other terrible stuff might be in a scary book? What might be the title of this scary book? What might the book jacket on this scary book look like? The children could draw a picture of the creature "who comes to your house one night."

## SUMMARY

In the preceding discussion, a single skill or behavior was identified for each poem. However, each poem has the potential for being used to teach at least several of the skills or behaviors that were specified. Teachers who want to use poems to improve reading ability have no difficulty determining the potential of any poem for attaining one or several reading program objectives.

Through informal studies done with elementary teachers in several schools, I have found the skills and behaviors illustrated in this chapter to be those for which it is easiest to find suitable poetry: doing expressive oral reading, using context clues, finding main ideas, developing mental imagery, recalling sequence, having thoughtful discussions, becoming aware of the author as a person, anticipating outcomes, and thinking creatively. These are also the skills and behaviors for which questions and activities can be constructed with relative ease. Therefore, teachers are advised to start their reading development work using poetry with these nine skills or behaviors as primary objectives.

The poems used as examples in this chapter were all written by the author. Basal series collections of children's poetry and children's magazines, however, are excellent sources of poetry for improving reading ability. In fact, it is a rare poem that cannot be used for reading development as well as for enjoyment and literary appreciation. A list of collections of children's poems teachers have found to be valuable in reading improvement is provided in the Recommended Readings at the end of this chapter.

The learning of cognitive reading behaviors (e.g., finding main ideas, sequencing, using context clues) is enhanced with material that is enjoyed by the learners. The study referred to earlier in this chapter (Terry, 1974) identified students' preferences for poetry. Teachers who are selecting poems for their students can be guided by the findings of that study. Children in grades four through six respond more favorably to contemporary poems than to traditional ones, to poems dealing with enjoyable experiences familiar to them, to poems that tell stories or have a strong element of humor or both, to poems with rhythm and rhyme, and to poems that do not rely too heavily on complex imagery or subtly implied emotion.

Another source for poems is the teacher herself. Children love to read and to learn to read with poetry written by someone familiar. Reading and studying poetry written by their teachers is a learning treat. Most teachers can write poems (which need not rhyme or have a definite rhythm) for their students, and many can write poems their students like better than those that come from commercial sources.

Thus far nothing has been said about the reading of poetry leading to the writing of poetry. The experience of teachers who have made special efforts to improve students' reading ability with poetry has been that reading poetry can be the beginning of writing poetry. Teachers have found that most students change their roles as readers to writers more readily with poetry than with prose. They write their own poems, read them to their classmates, listen carefully to their classmates' poems, and offer criticisms gently. Their writing and listening experiences also have a positive effect on their reading development.

Poems are marvelous creations for touching the feelings of readers. They can also be marvelous creations for helping readers improve their reading ability. Armed with a collection of poems and a repertoire of instructional activities to use with them, teachers can teach their students how to be better readers as well as how to enjoy poetry.

## REFERENCE

Terry, A. *Children's poetry preferences.* Urbana, Ill.: National Council of Teachers of English, 1974.

## RECOMMENDED READINGS

Fowke, E. *Riddles in rhyme: Ring around the moon.* Englewood Cliffs, N.J.: Prentice-Hall, 1977, pp. 21–32.

Hoberman, M. A. *Bugs.* New York: Viking Press, 1976.

Kuskin, K. *Any me I want to be.* New York: Harper and Row, 1972.

Morrison, L. *Black within and red without.* New York: Thomas Y. Crowell, 1953.

Rees, E. *Riddles, riddles everywhere.* New York: Abelard-Schuman, 1964.

Schenk de Regniners, B. *It does not say meow and other animal riddle rhymes.* New York: Seabury, 1972.

Silverstein, S. *Where the sidewalk ends.* New York: Harper and Row, 1974.

Smith, W. J. Seal. In *Laughing time.* New York: Delacorte, 1980, p. 73.

Wilner, I. Money. In *The poetry troupe: An anthology of poems to read aloud.* New York: Scribner's, 1977, p. 115.

Worth, V. *More small poems.* New York: Farrar, Straus and Giroux, 1976.

Worth, V. *Still more small poems.* New York: Farrar, Straus and Giroux, 1978.

# CHAPTER 8

# Beginning Teachers and Beginning Readers

Janet K. Black
North Texas State University
Denton

*The last chapter in Part I addresses a special aspect of basic reading skill instruction: reading instruction for beginning readers. Many of the instructional procedures discussed in Chapters 1 through 7 are appropriate for young children, but Janet Black, a specialist in early childhood education, in this chapter addresses the unique needs of beginning readers and appropriate teaching strategies for meeting those needs. Although beginning kindergarten teachers are Black's primary audiences, many of her suggestions are appropriate for first-grade reading instructors as well. After a discussion of the knowledge, skills, and abilities beginning readers already possess, numerous specific strategies and activities are presented for the development of a classroom environment conducive to the development of literacy in young children. Detailed descriptions of the infusion of literacy skills into classroom learning centers are included, in addition to ideas for the direct instruction of reading and writing skills. Suggestions for modeling reading and writing behaviors, evaluating the acquisition of literacy skills, and reporting to parents are also offered in this chapter.*

Respond to the following questions as honestly as possible.

1. As a new teacher, how do you feel about teaching beginning readers?
2. What do you know about beginning readers?
3. What will you do to help beginning readers?

After thinking about these questions, you may be asking, "Why did I ever decide to teach beginning readers?" You may feel somewhat frightened about your responsibilities and unsure about how to help your students become readers. The purpose of this chapter

95

is to offer some possible answers to the above questions by (1) reassuring you that your anxious feelings are normal (and even helpful), (2) providing you with information about beginning readers, and (3) giving you specific ideas and strategies you can use to teach beginning readers. This chapter is aimed toward kindergarten teachers, but many of the ideas may also be useful to those who teach preschool or first grade.

## WHAT ARE BEGINNING TEACHERS OF BEGINNING READERS LIKE?

Beginning teachers have had different backgrounds and experiences, they have practice taught in different situations, and they have taken different college courses preparing them to teach reading. Yet, in some ways they are alike. They are probably excited about being teachers, and they probably had similar reactions to the first question asked at the beginning of this chapter, "How do you feel about teaching beginning readers?"

I imagine that most beginning teachers, if they responded honestly, admitted that they felt frightened about teaching beginning readers. I know I felt that way. Teaching a group of young children to read is a big responsibility. Our society places a great deal of emphasis on the importance of learning to read. Newspapers frequently carry stories about declining literacy in America, often using test scores to substantiate their claims. The desire of parents and administrators to see *every* child reading "on grade level" also causes stress for teachers. (See Chapter 10.) It is no wonder you feel somewhat anxious. Real pressures have been placed on you by society as well as by your community and school.

Although this discussion so far may seem negative, realizing that this feeling of apprehension can be positive is important. After I had been teaching young children for eight years, the principal of my school sent a memo to all the teachers on the first day of the school year. In this memo he asked, "On this first day of school, I wonder how many of you have butterflies in your stomach?" He went on to say that he, as a principal, still had butterflies in his stomach. Furthermore, he said, "This feeling is a good sign. It is a sign that you care, that you are concerned, that you want things to go well for the children and you." He concluded by saying that he hoped that those butterflies never completely flew away.

A little anxiety can be a positive motivating factor in working with children. No one would want to be anxious to the extent that he could not carry out his teaching responsibilities. The purpose of this chapter is to provide information and ideas so that you have a small but healthy amount of anxiety left in you.

## WHAT ARE BEGINNING READERS LIKE?

### Their Feelings

Beginning readers are in many ways like beginning teachers. They have different backgrounds and experiences (more about this later). They are excited about going to school. Yet, like the beginning teacher, they are frightened. They ask themselves, "Will my teacher like me?" "What will the school and my classroom be like?" "Will the other kids like me?" "Will school be fun?" "Will I do well in school?"

Realizing that young children who are coming to school for the first time feel this way suggests the importance of (1) creating a positive relationship with children, (2) making them feel at home in the classroom and school environment, (3) helping children feel that they are an important part of the group, (4) providing interesting experiences for learning, and (5) emphasizing what children can do, not what they cannot do.

These suggestions can go far to relieve young children's initial feelings of anxiety about coming to school. When you help children feel comfortable within the classroom, you feel comfortable, and learning can begin.

## Their Backgrounds

Learning to read does not begin at school but at home. Many teachers as well as parents do not realize this fact. Yetta Goodman (1980) commented about this early reading behavior:

> I believe that the beginnings of reading development often go unnoticed in the young child. Neither children nor their parents are aware that reading has begun. This lack of sensitivity occurs because the reading process is misunderstood; because learning to read print and being taught to read it have been conceived as a one to one correspondence; and because we have been led to believe that the most common sense notion about learning to read suggests that it begins in a formalized school environment (p. 9).

Apparently, then, most children come to school with some print awareness. That is, they demonstrate through their behavior that they are aware of print in books and their environment. Although the degree of print awareness varies from child to child, most children realize that print conveys meaning. Many indicate other kinds of knowledge about print: that it goes from left to right and from top to bottom, that type style varies, and that groups of letters can be words.

### Awareness of Environmental Print

From birth, children live in situations in which they see persons around them responding to print. They see adults and older children reading signs and maps or looking for specific products and services. Children observe others looking and talking about signs that advertise products, tell people what to do, or designate the names of places and objects. By the age of two years, many children recognize meaningful and commonly occurring words such as *Coke, McDonald's,* and *Lucky Charms.* Children at ages three and four may want to write words that are important to them. As Goodman (1980) noted,

> Preschoolers are not passive bystanders. They are fitting all these experiences into what they are learning about the world. They ask themselves questions about the world of print in which they live. "What does it do? How can I use it? What does it say? Can I use print to tell others?" (p. 6).

### Awareness of Book Print

While children are developing awareness of print in the environment, they usually are also developing print awareness in response to books, newspapers, magazines, mail, and so forth. Generally, these print experiences are somewhat different from the ones just discussed. The print in a story is different from the print on a McDonald's sign or a stop sign. Print in a book goes on and on. It is connected. Children become aware that handling print in this context is somewhat different from handling environmental print. Generally speaking, when children have been read to from an early age and see adults reading, they begin to pick up certain notions about the nature of reading. They learn that books, magazines, newspapers, television logs, and mail have meaning. They develop book-handling knowledge. They recognize the front of the book, they know how to open it, they learn to skip the copyright and title pages, and they understand where the story begins. They probably have read along with adults and older siblings. Many children "play at reading," and can predict words or phrases in stories. Some children even know how to read when they come to school.

### Awareness of Writing

Studies suggest that many early natural readers are also early writers (Durkin, 1966; Clay, 1972; Clark, 1976; Price, 1976). The early reader's interest in writing appears before or during the time she learns to read. Recent child development research seems to support the notion that young children develop an interest in writing around the age of three or four years (Temple, Nathan, and Burris, 1982). When this interest is encouraged naturally in meaningful contexts, the writing seems to *help* children with their reading. In other words, children read what they write when they are allowed to write what is meaningful to them.

### Awareness of Vocabulary About Reading and Writing

By interacting with print in the environment, by having books read to them, and by experimenting with writing, children begin to use and understand such words as *read, write, name,* and *book.* Some children come to school understanding these terms, which are important in learning to read and write.

The point of the preceding discussion is that many children come to school with some knowledge about print. These children are not necessarily high-socioeconomic-status children. Harste, Burke, and Woodward (1981), for example, found that many children from lower socioeconomic groups have access to print in home environments. In fact, early readers come from a variety of socioeconomic groups and are not always children with high IQs.

Beginning teachers need not feel that they are starting from the beginning. Many children have been working on reading for several years before they come to school. Remembering this can be helpful to the beginning teacher of beginning readers. It can help in (1) planning appropriate learning experiences, and (2) relieving the overwhelming feeling of having to start at the beginning.

Although children often know more about print than teachers assume, a word of caution is appropriate. Just as there are wide variations in children's physical, socio-emotional, and cognitive development, there is a broad range in their print awareness. Some children may not know the front of a book from the back. Others may be able to read it from beginning to end. Beginning teachers should not expect *all* children to have a high print awareness.

## WHAT BEGINNING TEACHERS CAN DO TO HELP BEGINNING READERS

The following section provides ideas that kindergarten and early childhood teachers can use in providing appropriate learning experiences for beginning readers. Strategies for meeting children's varying stages of development are also presented.

## Know and Apply Child Development Information

Contemporary knowledge of child development suggests the importance of play and children's interests and experiences in the learning process. Integrating reading and writing along with children's play, interests, and experiences seems to provide the basis for the development of literacy.

### Play Is Basic to the Development of Literacy

If beginning teachers are to help beginning readers, they must know what young children are like and then provide appropriate experiences. The young child does not think like an adult (Elkind, 1978). Although adults often learn in quiet ways (reading or listening), young children need real and concrete experiences. Piaget and Inhelder (1969) said that active physical involvement (play) with real objects promotes thinking, or mental activity, in the young child. Through repeating these experiences, the child's behavior is internalized; that is, the child can do mentally what he could previously do only through physical movement.

Thus, it is through play that children learn to think, which then facilitates language development (Piaget and Inhelder, 1969). Language is the primary vehicle through which children communicate their thoughts to others. If children have the opportunity to become competent in their oral language, reading can emerge naturally (Bettelheim, 1978). Vygotsky (1978) sees play as important in the development of written language. He wrote that through the child's use of gesture in play, then through drawing, the representation of speech in written form emerges. In summary, play is necessary for the development of thought and language. Thought and language are prerequisites for reading and writing. In short, play is basic to the development of literacy. The relationships between play, thought, and language are depicted in Figure 8.1.

### Reading and Writing Should Be Taught Together

Writing and reading are complementary; therefore, they should be taught together (Chomsky, 1971). Writers think and then write for themselves or other readers. Writers read and reread what they have written. Readers read and think about what writers thought and wrote. Thus, it would seem that writing facilitates reading in young children, and vice versa.

### Children's Interests and Experiences Provide the Motivation to Read and Write

Often, good reading is perceived by young children as something that is done fast and without mistakes. The goal of reading, however, should be to gain information, pleasure, and comfort. For this to occur, children must bring understanding *to* the written word. Such understanding is developed in the young child through play and active involvement in the home, school, and community. If children are encouraged to talk about their ideas and if these thoughts are written down, they will (1) learn that print conveys meaning, (2) become aware of letter-sound relationships as well as other conventions of writing, and (3) begin to read what was recorded. Children can begin to write about their own experiences, thoughts, and feelings. The confidence children gain in using their own words and thoughts provides the motivation for them to learn to read and write. Contrived experiences are not necessary.

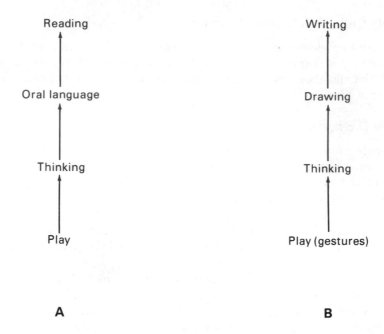

Figure 8.1. The development of literacy: (A) according to Piaget and Inhelder (1969) and Bettelheim (1978) and (B) according to Vygotsky (1978).

### *Children Have Unique Rates and Patterns of Development*

Finally, it is important to note that there seem to be many ways in which children learn to read and write. Each child is unique and comes to school with her individual learning style and background experiences. Thus, the manner or sequence in which one child learns to read and write may not be best for other children. Likewise, the rates of development vary from child to child. Some children develop in spurts, while others seem to mature in an even manner. Consequently, it is not appropriate for a teacher to impose a single set of expectations on all children at the same time.

### Think Carefully About Using Structured Reading or Prereading Programs

From the preceding discussion, it should be obvious that highly structured reading and prereading programs may not be appropriate for all young children. Often, such programs intensively teach phonics: letter-sound correspondences and rules for word pronunciation. Thus, phonics programs involve seeing words in a part-to-whole relationship. Many young children, however, have not developed the cognitive structures required to deal with the various parts of a word (Wolfgang and Freeman, 1977). Also, many such programs involve the learning and application of rules. Although according to child development research (Hersh, Paolitto, and Reimer, 1979) many kindergartners and first-graders are in a rule-oriented stage of development, they have difficulty comprehending exceptions to rules. Thus, young children may find it difficult to conceptualize that one letter (or spelling pattern) may have two or more pronunciations, or that some phonic "rules" have exceptions to them. For example, if a teacher taught a child that the letter *e* corresponds to the short *e* sound as in *hen*, the child might become very confused when he encountered the long *e* sound in words such as *he* and *me* (Donaldson, 1979, p. 108). Or, if the child internalized the *cv̄ce* "rule" as in *bike*, *take*, and *cube*, exceptions to the rule (e.g., *love*, *some*, *have*) might seem very confusing. Donaldson (1979) has suggested that children need to understand that the English language system contains *options* rather than hard-and-fast *rules*. For example, children can be helped to become aware that the hard *k* sound can be spelled in several different ways (e.g., *keep*, *cat*, *back*, *character*).

The emphasis on obtaining high scores on achievement tests also encourages some kindergarten teachers to use materials, teaching strategies, and learning experiences that are more appropriate for older children. Young children need not consciously understand the form or structure of language. They need to become *literate*, not *linguists*. Most children enter school competent in their oral language without having learned about nouns, verbs, and adjectives. Likewise, children can be taught to read without acquiring a formal knowledge of the vocabulary of reading (e.g., grapheme, phoneme, digraph, diphthong, schwa). Although a certain amount of vocabulary is required for reading and language instruction (e.g., letter, word, sentence, story), teachers should attempt to keep the vocabulary to a minimum and to state directly what these terms mean when they are used.

In conclusion, many prepackaged reading programs may not be suited for young children. The programs, therefore, should be examined closely and used judiciously. Young children need to be actively involved in concrete experiences (play) that are of meaning and interest to them. These experiences should be used to help children with language, reading, and writing. Instruction should develop *naturally* from the young child's interest and curiosity. In fact, representatives of many of the leading professional organizations interested in the development of language and literacy skills in young children have expressed concern over the current trend toward using highly structured prereading and reading programs. These organizations have prepared a joint statement that articulates their concerns. This joint statement, which includes both the concerns and recommendations is reproduced here.

### Create Meaningful Classroom Environments

The kindergarten classroom needs to be organized in such a way that children are involved in concrete active experiences that facilitate thinking, oral language, reading, and written language. This whole-language approach involves the integration of concrete oral and written language activities designed to help the children to understand that print conveys a message and that writing is used for communication.

### *Learning Centers*

One way to organize the environment for the young child is to create learning centers that encourage print awareness and use. In setting up these centers, the teacher needs to provide materials that encourage thinking, using language, reading, and writing. Then, after the centers have been arranged, the teacher needs to listen and observe children so that she knows when to intervene (e.g., ask a question or make a suggestion) and when to

## Reading and Pre-First Grade

A Joint Statement of Concerns and Present Practices in Pre-First Grade Reading Instruction and Recommendations for Improvement

- American Association of Elementary/Kindergarten/Nursery Educators
- Association for Childhood Education International
- Association for Supervision and Curriculum Development
- International Reading Association
- National Association for the Education of Young Children
- National Association of Elementary School Principals
- National Council of Teachers of English

### A Perspective on Pre-First Graders and the Teaching of Reading

Pre-first graders need...

opportunities to express orally, graphically, and dramatically their feelings and responses to experiences.

opportunities to interpret the language of others whether it is written, spoken, or nonverbal.

Teachers of pre-first graders need...

preparation which emphasizes developmentally appropriate language experiences for all pre-first graders, including those ready to read or already reading.

the combined efforts of professional organizations, colleges, and universities to help them successfully meet the concerns outlined in this document.

### Concerns:

1. A growing number of children are enrolled in pre-kindergarten and kindergarten classes in which highly structured pre-reading and reading programs are being used.

2. Decisions related to schooling, including the teaching of reading, are increasingly being made on economic and political bases instead of on our knowledge of young children and of how they best learn.

3. In a time of diminishing financial resources, schools often try to make "a good showing" on measures of achievement that may or may not be appropriate for the children involved. Such measures all too often dictate the content and goals of the programs.

4. In attempting to respond to pressures for high scores on widely-used measures of achievement, teachers of young children sometimes feel compelled to use materials, methods, and activities designed for older children. In so doing, they may impede the development of intellectual functions such as curiosity, critical thinking, and creative expression, and, at the same time, promote negative attitudes toward reading.

5. A need exists to provide alternative ways to teach and evaluate progress in pre-reading and reading skills.

6. Teachers of pre-first graders who are carrying out highly individualized programs without depending upon commercial readers and workbooks need help in articulating for themselves and the public *what* they are doing and *why*.

### Recommendations:

1. Provide reading experiences as an integrated part of the broader communication process that includes listening, speaking, and writing. A language experience approach is an example of such integration.

2. Provide for a broad range of activities both in scope and in content. Include direct experiences that offer opportunities to communicate in different settings with different persons.

3. Foster children's affective and cognitive development by providing materials, experiences, and opportunities to communicate what they know and how they feel.

4. Continually appraise how various aspects of each child's total development affect his/her reading development.

5. Use evaluative procedures that are developmentally appropriate for the children being assessed and that reflect the goals and objectives of the instructional program.

6. Insure feelings of success for all children in order to help them see themselves as persons who can enjoy exploring language and learning to read.

7. Plan flexibly in order to accommodate a variety of learning styles and ways of thinking.

8. Respect the language the child brings to school, and use it as a base for language activities.

9. Plan activities that will cause children to become active participants in the learning process rather than passive recipients of knowledge.

10. Provide opportunities for children to experiment with language and simply to have fun with it.

11. Require that pre-service and in-service teachers of young children be prepared in the teaching of reading in a way that emphasizes reading as an integral part of the language arts as well as the total curriculum.

12. Encourage developmentally appropriate language learning opportunities in the home.

change materials or provide new materials. Suggestions about how to incorporate writing and reading into the usual kindergarten learning centers follow.

### Sociodramatic Center

The sociodramatic area provides the opportunity for children to assume various roles and use oral language in a variety of ways. Props usually include dress-up clothes, furniture, dishes, dolls, tools, and cleaning equipment. Additional props that encourage reading and writing behavior can also be provided in the sociodramatic center. Such materials could include the following:

1.  Note paper for messages (telephone number, grocery lists, etc.)
2.  Paper and envelopes for writing letters
3.  A pencil holder with a variety of pens and pencils
4.  Newspapers, television logs, magazines, books, cookbooks
5.  A mailbox with junk mail
6.  Checkbooks (some banks will provide these)
7.  Attaché cases with legal pads and pencils
8.  Recipe cards
9.  A noteboard or chalkboard or both

The kindergarten teacher initially could establish the environment by encouraging the children to explore some of these materials, for example, by having mail in the mailbox, a note on the chalkboard, a grocery list on the refrigerator, and a recipe card laid out with cooking utensils.

Props can be added or changed throughout the school year. For example, at Christmas and Hannukah time, I put a tree, ornaments, stuffed animals, and other objects for presents along with boxes, wrapping paper, ribbons, and materials for making cards in the sociodramatic area. Much decorating, list making, present wrapping, and card making resulted.

Adjacent sociodramatic centers such as a bank, restaurant, various kinds of offices, stores, and a post office can provide extended opportunities for children to speak, read, and write. Signs and props can be used in these areas.

### Block Center

The block area usually contains large and small blocks for constructing. In addition, various vehicles, boats, planes, miniature animals, and human figures are included to enrich the themes of block play. Opportunities to write, however, often emerge from the theme of block play. Block players, therefore, need to know where they can find writing materials, or the teacher needs to provide them at the block center. I once had a group of kindergarten children who decided to construct a doughnut shop. It soon became apparent that they needed a sign for the outside, price signs on the inside, and money as well as doughnuts. Much writing and drawing then took place in the process of constructing the appropriate signs.

Another idea is to have a notebook available so that sketches and descriptions of constructions (with the names of the architects and builders) can be recorded for other children to see and perhaps duplicate. Children at one school that had split-day kindergarten classes enjoyed leaving drawings and instructions of their constructions for children in the other session.

### Art Center

The art center usually has a wide variety of materials that commonly includes scissors, crayons, felt pens, pencils, chalk, paints (tempera, water, and finger), various kinds of paper (construction, manila, newsprint, tissue, crepe), as well as a variety of fabric scraps and junk for constructions and collages. The following activities encourage reading and writing behavior in this area and with these materials.

1.  After children have drawn or painted a picture, they may wish to write a story about it. This may be accomplished by (a) having the children dictate the story to the teacher, an older child, or an adult volunteer who writes down the child's story as the child watches or (b) having the children write their own stories.
2.  Children can make cards (birthday, holiday, get well) for school friends and write notes in the cards.
3.  A display area can be set up where various creations can be exhibited, and the title and the name of the artist can be displayed on a card. At times, a description of the process the artist used may also be appropriate.

### Science Center

The science center usually provides some items that are permanently available for children to observe, such as fishes, gerbils, guinea pigs, hamsters, and various plants. Children can be encouraged to draw and write about the habits, behavior, and appearance of these living things. One kindergarten class had fun weighing and then charting the weight gain of a baby guinea pig. Another group measured and recorded the growth of different kinds of plants. Various scientific experiments or demonstrations can be assembled in empty ice cream containers and appropriately labeled: for example, magnets, sea shells, nuts and seeds, and so forth. Books and pictures with captions can also provide children with science information, as well as print awareness.

### Math Center

The math center contains a variety of materials for counting, sorting, classifying, weighing, and measuring. Various numerals (made out of felt or sandpaper) as well as math games and counting books can be a part of this learning area. Large plastic tubs filled with wet sand, dry sand, and water, along with miniature toys and containers for measuring and filling, can encourage lively discussions. Paper and pencils should be provided for children who wish to write numerals and record their experiences with various math materials. Some children may wish to dictate their experiences to the teacher. For example, children could group red, blue, and white plastic disks into sets and count them. The resulting information could be dictated to the teacher, who could record the data in a math center notebook.

Another activity that children love, and that helps with math concepts as well as oral and written language, is the survey. A child or teacher writes a survey question at the top of a large sheet of paper and then lists alternative answers under the question. For example, "What is your favorite color?" (See Figure 8.2.) The child then goes around the classroom and asks his classmates the survey question. He then enters a tally by the response. Other possible survey questions include:

1.  What is your favorite pet?
2.  What is your favorite dessert?
3.  What is your favorite flavor of ice cream?

# What is your favorite color?

| | | |
|---|---|---|
| blue | ⫴⫴ | 5 |
| red | ⫴⫴ ‖ | 7 |
| green | ‖ | 2 |
| yellow | ‖ | 1 |
| purple | ‖‖ | 4 |
| brown | ‖ | 1 |
| black | | 0 |
| orange | ‖‖ | 4 |
| other | ‖ | 2 |

Figure 8.2. A math survey.

4.  What is your favorite soft drink?
5.  What is your favorite fast-food restaurant?
6.  What is your favorite sport?

Children can also create their own survey questions. After the survey is completed, children (with adult help if needed) can transfer the information into a report or a bar graph as represented in Figures 8.3 and 8.4, respectively.

# Our Favorite Colors

5 children liked blue.

7 children liked red.

2 children liked green.

1 child liked yellow.

4 children liked purple.

1 child liked brown.

0 children liked black.

4 children liked orange.

Figure 8.3. A report based on the math survey in Figure 8.2.

## Writing Center

The writing center should be located in a place in the classroom where children almost run into it. Research suggests that writing centers that are out of the way are not used as much as those that are located near main traffic areas (Harste, Burke, and Woodward, 1981). A variety of writing materials should be made available in this center to encourage various types of writing. Suggestions include these materials:

1. Paper and envelopes for letters
2. Paper for writing stories (used computer printouts work well)

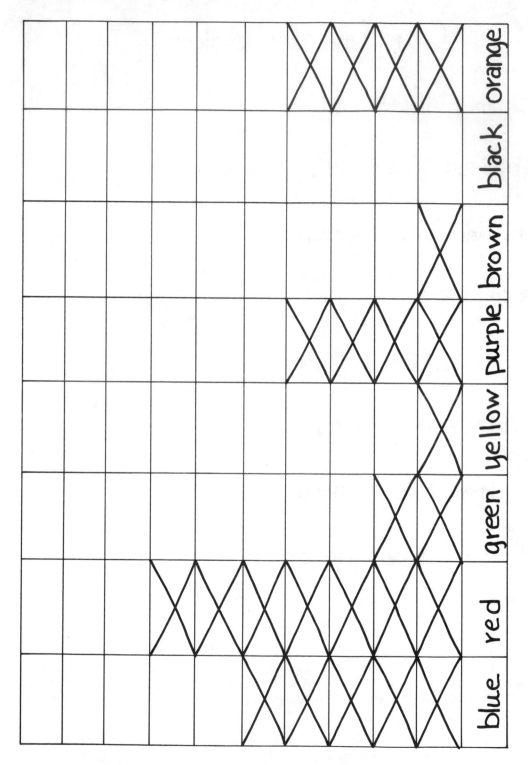

Figure 8.4. A bar graph based on the math survey in Figure 8.2.

3. Note pads
4. Memo paper (this can be dittoed, see Figure 8.5)
5. Various blank books
   a. One kind can be made up of several pages of typing paper folded together and stapled
   b. Bound books made by adult volunteers or with the help of older children (see Figure 8.6 for instructions)
6. Various pencils, crayons, pens, and felt pens
7. Chalkboards and chalk
8. Printing stamps and ink pads
9. Typewriter
10. Magnetic letters

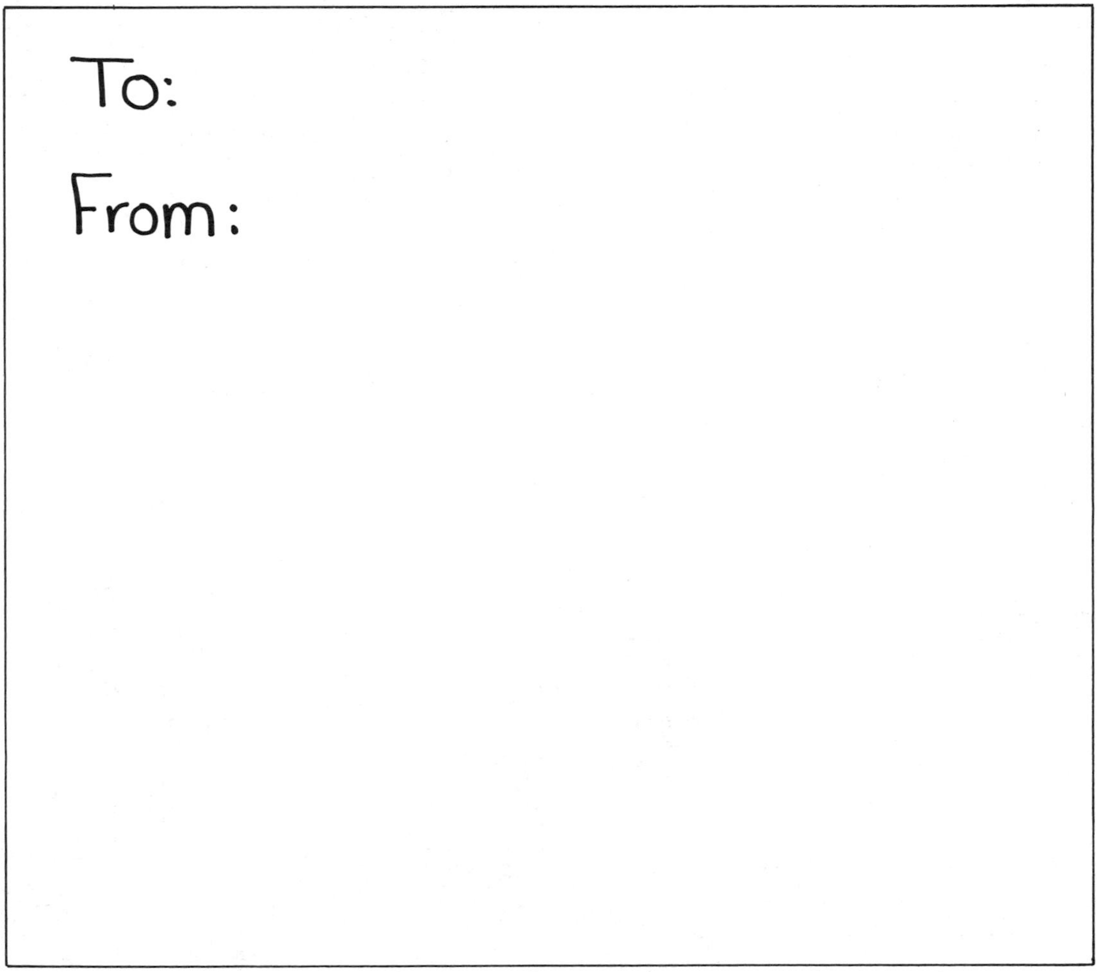

To:

From:

Figure 8.5. A blank memo form.

**Materials:** Paper, stiff cardboard, white glue or contact cement, stapler or needle and thread, fabric (twice the size of book) or contact paper, ruler

**Procedure:** (1) After you have finished writing and illustrating your book, add one blank page at the front and back of the book. Then, staple or sew the pages together about a quarter of an inch in from the left side. (2) Cut two pieces of cardboard for covers. Cut the covers so they extend a quarter of an inch beyond the edges of the book pages. (3) Cut two pieces of cloth (or contact paper) three quarters of an inch larger than the cardboards placed side by side. (4) Now, fold over the edges and glue the cover material to the cardboard. Start by turning down the "ears" (or corners). Then, fold over the rest of the edge. (5) Center the book pages over the cardboard or cloth covers. Glue the blank page at the front of your book to the cardboard on the left side and glue the blank page at the back to the right side. Place the book under a stack of heavy textbooks for several hours to press it flat.

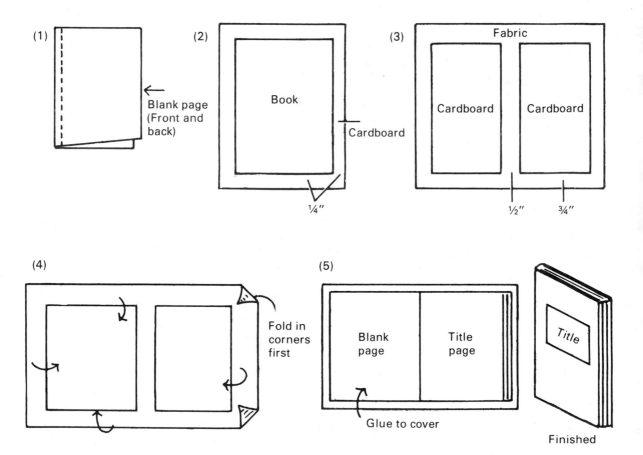

Figure 8.6. Instructions for constructing hard-bound books.

Children can be encouraged to use this center to write notes or letters to family members (to be taken home) or school friends (to be put in individual mailboxes). Classroom experiences (e.g., taking a trip to the farm, watching the birth of gerbils, or copying a recipe from the cooking center to take home) can also provide opportunities for children to come to the writing center. The blank books can be used for writing similar stories read at story time (e.g., a group a kindergarten children did a take-off on Bill Martin's *Brown Bear, Brown Bear* involving jungle animals and the sounds they heard). Chalkboards serve as an easy place for children to write, correct, or revise. Chalkboards also give the children a place to write important messages for the whole class (e.g., "Toda is mi brfda" [Today is my birthday] or "I haf a nu babe bruthr" [I have a new baby brother]).

### Reading Center

A variety of good children's books (picture books, wordless picture books, and informational books) and children's magazines (e.g., *Kids Magazine, Highlights* and *Ranger Rick*) should be made available at all times. In addition, books that the children have constructed themselves should be a part of the classroom library collection. Children enjoy reading to themselves and to their friends books they have written and illustrated. Books that contain drawings and writing about the class's experiences (e.g., *We Made Butter* or *Our Trip to the Planetarium*) can also be displayed in the reading center. Covers for such books can be made out of heavy cardboard and laminated. Photographs of various classroom activities with captions can be put into picture albums for children to look at and read.

Another part of a good reading center is a listening table. Listening posts, at which children can hear records or tapes of favorite stories taken from shared book experiences or predictable books (more about these later), are good sources that help children to understand the repetitive nature of stories. Next to books, the tape recorder is probably the most important tool in promoting literacy (Chomsky, 1976). Martin and Brogan (1972) have suggested that beginning readers need a number of familiar books that they can easily and quickly read. The tape recorder can help children to become familiar with many of these predictable books.

Children also enjoy checking out books and taking them home to read. In addition to regular trips to the school library (yes, even for kindergartners), a sign-out system can be set up so that the children take responsibility for checking out books from the classroom reading center.

## Meaningful Literature Experiences

Kindergarten children should be read to at least once a day and preferably more often. Books to be read aloud should be previewed and should be appropriate for young children. A large-group story time provides a sense of community and helps children become aware of various story structures and types of literature. In large and small groups as well as in individual story times, however, the teacher needs to make sure that children become familiar with print. This can be accomplished in several ways.

### Large-Group, Small-Group, and Individual Story Times

In any of these group contexts, the teacher needs to follow these steps.

1. Talk about the author—this person had an idea for a story and then wrote it down.

2. Talk about the illustrator.
3. Point out the title.
4. Point out the print that tells the story.
5. Point to the page that is being read.
6. Sweep your hand in the direction of the print.

Suggestions 4, 5, and 6 should be handled in a casual, nonritualistic fashion.

All children need to be read to in an intimate way. This experience provides many children with an awareness of print as well as a love of reading. Those children who have not been read to at home especially need these kinds of experiences. Older children, parent volunteers, or senior citizens can help by providing one-to-one story times, that is, one person reading to only one child at a time.

Follow-up questions are an important part of the literature experience. While the teacher flips back through the book, she may ask several children some of these kinds of questions.

1. What happened on this page?
2. What happened first?
3. What happened next?
4. What happened at the end of the story?
5. What did you like about this book?
6. What didn't you like about this book?
7. What was your favorite part?
8. Has anything like this ever happened to you?
9. How did this story make you feel?
10. Does this story remind you of another story we have read (similar plot, characters, illustrations, etc.)?

These ten questions are important for several reasons. First, they help young children to recall the events in the story. Recall serves as a basis for later (in the primary and intermediate school years) comprehension of higher-level questions regarding content material. Questions also help children to become aware of story structures (e.g., setting, plot, and resolution). Meaningful ties between the child's background and the literature experience can also be accomplished through asking questions. Finally, questions help children to realize that literature can provide informaton, comfort, and pleasure—an important concept in developing a love of reading.

### Shared Book Experience

The shared book experience is an attempt to improve upon the usual large-group story time. This approach can be particularly helpful during the first half of the kindergarten year. Drawing on the idea of the oral tradition, Holdaway (1979) has suggested using the shared book experience with the entire class. He claimed that "reading to a group of children in school has little instructional value simply because print cannot be seen, shared, and discussed" (p. 63). In the shared book approach, large books (including illustrations) are constructed by the teacher and are based on such stories as *The Three Billy Goats Gruff, The Gingerbread Man, Over in the Meadow,* or Bill Martin's *Brown Bear, Brown Bear.* The print is made large enough for all children in the group to see. The teacher initially reads the story, pointing to the words as he reads. Then, the children are encouraged to read the story aloud along with the teacher. Because the children are reading in a group, they have no fear of making mistakes. This is different from traditional "round-robin" reading in the reading circle (see Chapter 23) in which each child takes a turn reading aloud. Later, the children, working individually or in small groups, read the large books. Eventually, they read regular-sized books. These stories can also be recorded and the books used at the listening table. Refer to the Holdaway reference in the Recommended Readings at the end of this chapter for more information about the shared book experience.

### Predictable Books

Predictable books are books that help children to learn that authors frequently establish writing patterns. Using these books helps children to learn to predict what the author is going to say next. Generally, after a few pages have been read, children cannot resist the urge to join in with the reader. Characteristics of predictable books include repetitive or cumulative patterns as well as familiarity of story, story line, or story sequence. In predictable books, "The language flows naturally and the vocabulary and content reflect what children know about their world and language" (Rhodes, 1981, p. 513). Repeated readings, with the teacher pointing to the sentences in the book, help children to realize the importance of print. Children, working in small groups or individually, can then read these books themselves or listen to them at the listening table. Gradually, children learn to locate various words, phrases, and sentences (that is, learn some words by sight) after reading predictable books. Some examples of predictable books include Pam Adams's *This Old Man,* Marcia Brown's *The Three Billy Goats Gruff,* Eric Carle's *The Grouchy Ladybug* and *The Very Hungry Caterpillar,* Remy Charlip's *Fortunately,* and Mercer Mayer's *If I Had . . . .* For a more extensive list of predictable books and a description of how they can be used to stimulate children's writing, refer to the article by Rhodes (1981) listed in the Recommended Readings.

### Language Experiences

A teacher's recording of a child's own language describing an experience can help the beginning reader to realize that oral language can be written down. Language experience stories (and drawings) can be displayed around the room or on bulletin boards for children to read to their friends. If the class has shared a field trip or group experience, the children's illustrations and recorded oral descriptions can be compiled in a book that can be enjoyed in the reading center (e.g., *Our Trip to the Zoo*).

An extension of the language experience idea is the key vocabulary approach (Ashton-Warner, 1963). The teacher elicits key or important words from the child. These are then written on cards and placed alphabetically in a file box. The child can use the words in making sentences to read or copy.

### Story Dictation

Although language experience can be a powerful tool in helping the child to realize that oral language can be recorded, it is important to note that written language is not merely talk written down. Spoken language is usually supported by the physical and social situation in which it occurs as well as by the nonverbal behaviors of the speakers. Such situational support is usually lacking in written language (Holdaway, 1979). Children need to learn to incorporate those elements that make a story stand on its own. Encouraging children to engage in extended monologues can be facilitated through the use of story dictation. Writing down the children's stories can tell the teacher whether the children are aware that written language is different from oral language. Because many kindergarten children are still somewhat egocentric, they do not always attend to the necessary elements of a story. As they become more social, however, their stories become more complete. Collecting dictation at periodic intervals helps the teacher to become aware of the children's development of story structure and of their understanding of written language.

## Model Reading and Writing Behaviors

Current research seems to suggest that young children who *see* parents or teachers reading and writing are aided in developing reading and writing behaviors (Bissex, 1980; Clark, 1976; Clay, 1972; Graves, 1982). The teacher should read for her own enjoyment in the presence of children. Some schools and classes reserve times during the day for all children and teachers to read books of their own choice. Similarly, teachers who write about their own experiences help children to understand the uses of writing.

When a teacher values children's reading and writing, he takes care to see that his appreciation is communicated directly and indirectly to the children. Some additional activities that create an atmosphere encouraging reading and writing in the kindergarten classroom include these:

1. Writing letters to the children at their homes before school starts
2. Having the children sign in for attendance
3. Having the children sign up for milk
4. Having individual mailboxes so teacher and children can send letters, notes, messages, and cards or return and turn in papers
5. Having a message board (a chalkboard will do) on which children can write messages or share important events with each other
6. Writing plans for trips, projects, centers, cooking, and so on
7. Attractively displaying children's stories and art in the classroom

## Plan for Appropriate Evaluation

Evaluating young children's reading and writing is a necessity. Assessment helps the teacher to plan appropriate experiences and provides documentation of the child's progress. Formal as well as informal methods can be used to provide the teacher with information about the child. An assessment measure, however, should be administered only when the results are to be used to make an instructional decision. (Implicit here is the requirement that the instrument being used is valid, i.e., accurate.) Also, all children in the classroom need not be given all forms of evaluation.

### Formal Evaluation

Many schools use reading readiness tests to determine which children are "ready to read" and which children need to participate in a readiness program. Although this form of assessment may be of some value, several precautions are worth noting.

Goodman (1980) described three first-graders who were beyond the beginning reading stage and yet who, according to the readiness test, needed more readiness experience. Durkin (1982) reported that, at times, nonreaders perform *better* than readers on readiness tests, particularly when the nonreaders are used to completing workbook pages. Durkin (1982) specified several specific problems with readiness tests: (1) the lack of agreement among authors of readiness tests concerning what the basic subskills for beginning reading are, (2) the lack of reliability resulting from the small number of items on a subtest, (3) the lack of relevance of some subtests for the reading task, and (4) the lack of diagnostic information one obtains from tests that are primarily predictive instruments. Durkin's findings certainly suggest that instructional decisions should *not* be made *solely* on the basis of reading readiness test scores. Other data must also be considered.

Children who are diagnosed as "not ready" do not need more typical readiness activities (e.g., finding likenesses or differences on a worksheet or completing a geometric shape); they need to be exposed to *real print in meaningful contexts.* According to Clay (1972), "The transformation at the early reading stage takes place only in the presence of print when the child actively seeks to discover how oral and written language are related" (p. 5). In other words, even if some of the students are not "ready" to read, as determined by a readiness test, they should not be denied the opportunity to have experiences with print. If anything, they should be given *more* opportunities to learn what written language is about.

## Informal Evaluation

The following are some questions that can serve to guide the teacher in the informal evaluation of young children's language, responses to books, and writing behavior.

### Observing Children's Oral Language

1. How does the child use language in various school settings: the playground, the lunchroom, as well as within various classroom situations?
2. Can the child talk easily about a variety of topics?
3. Does the child use language for a variety of purposes: to express need, to give information, to question, to interact, to be creative?
4. Can the child talk with a variety of people: various children and adults?
5. Does the child's nonverbal behaviors, actions, gestures, facial expressions, and body movements support and enhance her oral language?

When the teacher determines that a child needs help in the area of oral language, the following suggestions may be of some help.

1. The child must have the opportunity to talk in a variety of settings, for example, the various centers in the classroom or the playground at snack time or lunch time. Children learn to use language by using oral language, that is, by talking. Quiet classrooms do not facilitate language development.
2. Creating interesting centers within the classroom should provide children with the motivation to talk about a variety of topics as well as learning to use language for a variety of purposes (e.g., "I need a pair of scissors," "Today is my birthday," "Why are the gerbil's cheeks so fat?" "Let's sing 'Hickory Dickory Dock'").
3. Talking with a variety of people, classmates as well as children from other classrooms and adults, encourages children to learn to control conversation about

a variety of topics with a variety of people (e.g., the principal, school nurse, secretary, cooks, and custodians or sixth-grade buddies, parent volunteers, and senior citizen aides who come to read or help with a special project).

4. Activities such as pantomime, creative dramatics, and movement, as well as sociodramatic play, can facilitate the child's use of appropriate nonverbal behaviors, actions, and gestures.

5. If the teacher thinks that the child may have a severe oral language problem, he may wish to talk with the school's speech pathologist or other resource personnel.

### Observing Children's Responses to Literature

Children's responses to books can provide information about their attitudes toward books. Other kinds of information include the children's comprehension and awareness of book print. The following questions can be of help.

1. Does the child seem to enjoy books in group as well as individual situations?
2. Does she use the classroom library?
3. Does he talk about books read at home?
4. Does the child remember and listen to stories?
5. What are the child's responses to stories?
6. Can the child retell a story?
7. Does the child repeat appealing phrases or words from stories?
8. Does the child understand what the author and illustrator of a book do?
9. Does the child know where to begin reading a book?
10. Does the child understand the directionality of print (left to right, top to bottom)?

Oral language use helps the child to learn about the structure of language. Exposure to literature also facilitates the child's learning about language and the types of literature as well as the mechanics of handling books. Children learn subconsciously. Nevertheless, their tacit knowledge of the structure of language, of what books can be about, and of how to go about using a book is crucial for success in beginning reading. When a child's response to books and literature lacks enthusiasm, one of the teacher's best approaches is the lap method. The lap method involves reading to the child while she sits on a lap (the teacher's, an older child's, or a volunteer's). This approach needs to be used daily. For more specific suggestions, refer back to the section on meaningful literature experiences.

### Observing Children's Writing

Children read what they write if they are encouraged to write about what is of interest to them. The best way to find out about children's writing is to observe them writing. The following questions can guide the teacher making observations.

1. Does the child read his writing or scribbling (understand that writing is a form of communication)?
2. Does the child demonstrate a knowledge of the uses of writing (e.g., notes, labels, letters, stories, etc.)?
3. Does the child demonstrate directionality (e.g., make her writing go from left to right and from top to bottom on the page)?
4. Does the child write letters, words, and sentences?

5. Does the child point to each word as he reads his writing?
6. Does the child differentiate print from drawings?
7. Does the child use the terms "letter" and "word"?
8. Does the child rehearse (talk or draw) before she writes?
9. Does the child feel comfortable asking the teacher or other children for assistance when writing?
10. Does the child give evidence of the development of spelling?
    a. Spelling inventions—"mi" for *my*, "fit" for *fight*, "snac" for *snake*.
    b. Transitions—"si" for *is*, "houes" for *house*.
    c. Conventions—words spelled conventionally.

If after observing the child in the writing situation, the teacher thinks that the child needs additional help or if he notices that the child is not participating in writing experiences, he may want to try some of the following techniques.

1. Make a written record of the child's oral language in as many contexts as possible (e.g., write down what the child tells you about a picture she has drawn, write down her description of what she built with blocks, write down the child's favorite foods, television programs, names of family, etc.). These activities help the child become aware that writing, like oral language, is a form of communication.

2. When reading a book or the child's words from language experience or dictation, point to the words as you read them to make sure the child is following along. This will help increase the child's awareness of the directionality of print.

3. Encourage the child to begin his own key vocabulary. (See the language experience section for more information.) Talking about the child's important words helps her to develop letter recognition and the concept that groups of letters make a word. Arranging the key words in sentences also helps the child to learn what a sentence is.

4. Encouraging children to draw or talk about a topic before writing (rehearsal) can provide them with ideas for the content of their writing.

5. After the child understands that he can use writing to express thoughts and becomes comfortable writing, you may begin to mention casually that leaving spaces between words makes it easier for the reader to understand the message. Later, you may want to draw the writer's attention to basic forms of punctuation such as periods, question and exclamation marks and to the use of capital letters. You can use books as well as language experience or dictation to point out these conventions of writing.

6. Recent research (Read, 1975) suggests that children go through developmental stages in learning to spell. Encouraging children to spell words as they think they should be spelled rather than focusing on conventional spelling seems to facilitate the writing process. Emphasizing correct spelling can discourage young children struggling to get their thoughts down on paper, thinking about spacing, and remembering to add punctuation. Children need to be encouraged about writing. Research (King and Rentel, 1981) indicates that some time during the second or third grade, most children learn to spell conventionally. Correct spelling, therefore, should not be a primary concern of the kindergarten teacher.

Most of our knowledge about young children's writing is relatively recent. Teachers may want to consult *The Beginnings of Writing* (Temple, Nathan, and Burris, 1982) for more information.

### Record Keeping

It is essential that the kindergarten teacher keep records of the students' developing literacy. Samples of their writing, lists of books read, as well as comments or anecdotal records of children's speaking, reading, and writing behavior can be helpful during parent conferences and when sharing information with principals or other school staff members. Records should be dated and placed in separate file folders for each child.

## View Beginning Readers as Emerging in Competence

Rather than perceiving beginning readers as incompetent and deficient, beginning teachers need to view beginning readers as *emerging* in competence. Beginning teachers should not expect all children to learn to read and write at the same time. When children are perceived as deficient, they sense it and begin to respond accordingly. Remember that children require a period of *several years* to become competent language users. We cannot expect all children to become fluent readers and writers during the first month, or even the first year, of school.

Beginning teachers need to assume a developmental perspective about children's so-called "mistakes" in speaking, reading, and writing. As I mentioned already in the evaluation section, such mistakes are natural, developmentally appropriate behaviors. Analzying such mistakes provides an insight into the students' language, reading, and writing development and helps the teacher to plan more appropriate learning experiences for young children.

## Reporting to Parents

Several considerations need to be kept in mind when making reports to parents. First of all, records and samples of the child's writing can be helpful in demonstrating her developing competence to parents. Teachers can also provide parents with ideas about how they can continue to encourage their children's development at home (e.g., reading to them every day, taking them to the library, providing paper and pencils for them, encouraging them to write letters to grandparents and cousins, writing notes or leaving messages on the refrigerator; one of my favorites is to put a note in my son's lunch box now and then saying "I love you, Jon," "Hope you have a good day!" or "Tonight we will have pizza!").

Parents may need to be informed about how children's reading and writing develop—that it takes time, just as learning to walk and talk did. This information can be shared with parents at conference time, at open houses, during PTA presentations, or through more informal approaches such as a classroom newsletter or a parents' bulletin board that displays information about young children's reading and writing. A good source of information for parents is Butler and Clay's book, *Reading Begins at Home* (1979). Also, refer to Chapter 22 of this book for techniques that involve parents with the development of their children's literacy skills at home.

## SUMMARY

Take another look at those questions you were asked at the beginning of this chapter. How do you feel now about teaching beginning readers? I hope you feel more secure, with just a healthy bit of anxiety remaining.

What do you know about beginning readers? I hope you know that most children come to school with some ideas about print. Although the children's abilities vary, they are all emerging in competence. They are already on their way to becoming literate when they come to school.

## REFERENCES

Ashton-Warner, S. *Teacher.* New York: Bantom Books, 1963.

Bettelheim, B. Learning to read, a primer for literacy. *Harpers,* 1978, **256,** 56–58.

Bissex, G. *Gnys at wrk: A child learns to write and read.* Cambridge, Mass.: Harvard University Press, 1980.

Butler, D., and Clay, D. *Reading begins at home.* Exeter, N.H.: Heinemann Educational Books, 1979.

Chomsky, C. Write now, read later. *Childhood Education,* 1971, **47,** 296–299.

Chomsky, C. After decoding: What? *Language Arts,* 1976, **53,** 288–296, 314.

Clark, M. *Young fluent readers.* Exeter, N.H.: Heinemann Educational Books, 1976.

Clay, M. *Reading: The patterning of complex behavior.* Exeter, N.H.: Heinemann Educational Books, 1972.

Donaldson, M. *Children's minds.* New York: W. W. Norton, 1979.

Durkin, D. *Children who read early.* New York: Teachers College Press, Columbia University, 1966.

Durkin, D. *Getting reading started.* Boston: Allyn and Bacon, 1982.

Elkind, D. *A sympathetic understanding of the child.* Boston: Allyn and Bacon, 1978.

Goodman, Y. The roots of literacy. In M. Douglas (Ed.), *Forty-fourth yearbook, the Claremont Reading Conference.* Claremont, Calif.: Claremont College Library, 1980.

Graves, D. *Writing: Teachers and children at work.* Exeter, N.H.: Heinemann Educational Books, 1982.

Harste, J., Burke, C., and Woodward, V. *Children, their language and world: Initial encounters with print.* Final Report (NIE-79-G-0132). Bloomington, Ind.: Indiana University Language Education Department, 1981.

Hersh, R., Paolitto, D., and Reimer, J. *Promoting moral growth from Piaget to Kohlberg.* New York: Longman, 1979.

Holdaway, D. *The foundations of literacy.* New York: Ashton Scholastic, 1979.

King, M., and Rentel, V. *How children learn to write: A longitudinal study.* Final Report (NIE-79-G-0137 and NIE-G-79-0039). Washington, D.C.: Department of Health and Human Services, National Institute of Education, June 1981.

Lee, D., and Allen, V. *Learning to read through experience.* New York: Meredith Corporation, 1963.

Martin, B., and Brogan, P. *Teachers guide, instant readers.* New York: Holt, Rinehart and Winston, 1972.

Piaget, J., and Inhelder, B. *The psychology of the child.* New York: Basic Books, 1969.

Price, E. How thirty-seven gifted children learned to read. *The Reading Teacher,* 1976, **30,** 44–48.

Read, C. *Children's categorizations of speech sounds in English.* Urbana, Ill.: National Council of Teachers of English, 1975.

Rhodes, L. K. I can read? Predictable books as resources for reading and writing instruction. *The Reading Teacher,* 1981, **35,** 511–518.

Temple, C., Nathan, R., and Burris, N. *The beginnings of writing.* Boston: Allyn and Bacon, 1982.

Vygotsky, L. *Mind in society.* (M. Cole, V. John-Steiner, S. Scribner, and E. Souberman, Eds. and Trans.) Cambridge, Mass.: Harvard University Press, 1978.

Wolfgang, C., and Freeman, E. Reading readiness: A Piagetian perspective. *The Ohio Reading Teacher,* 1977, **11,** 27–31.

## RECOMMENDED READINGS

Butler, D., and Clay, M. *Reading begins at home.* Exeter, N.H.: Heinemann Educational Books, 1979. This short paperback for parents provides information about the development of reading at home during the child's preschool years. Practical suggestions are provided for parents helping their children learn to read. This book and its information would be very helpful for teachers of young children to share with parents.

Donaldson, M. *Children's minds.* New York: W. W. Norton, 1979. On the book jacket Jerome Bruner says, "One of the most powerful, most wisely balanced and best informed books on the development of the child's mind to have appeared in twenty years. Its implications are enormous." Donaldson provides a thorough discussion about what teachers can do to help children in learning to read.

Holdaway, D. *The foundations of literacy.* New York: Ashton Scholastic, 1979. Holdaway's book should be in the library of every teacher. His discussion of literacy development before school is in itself worth the price of the book. He provides a very clear discussion of various approaches to teaching reading. Much of the book describes the shared book approach. Other chapters include discussions on creativity and developmental and diagnostic teaching as well as a penetrating discussion of the so-called back-to-basics movement.

Rhodes, L. K. I can read? Predictable books as resources for reading and writing. *The Reading Teacher,* 1981, **35,** 511–518. Rhodes's article describes the characteristics of predictable books and demonstrates how these books can be used as resources for reading and writing instruction. An extensive bibliography of predictable books is also included. All in all, it is an excellent source of information for teachers of young children.

Temple, C., Nathan, R., and Burris, N. *The beginnings of writing.* Boston: Allyn and Bacon, 1982. This book includes recent information about the development of young children's writing. Many worthwhile suggestions are provided for parents and teachers in helping young children become writers. This book is filled with delightful examples of children's writings. It is an important source in helping teachers to understand young children's writing and its relationship to reading.

# PART II

## Measuring and Assessing Reading Growth: Diagnosing Reading Ability to Improve Instruction

*Part II addresses the issue of how beginning teachers can effectively and efficiently assess students' reading ability so that appropriate instructional decisions can be made. Chapter 9 describes how teachers can use the cloze procedure, the informal reading inventory, and criterion-referenced tests to determine students' instructional reading levels and to acquire diagnostic information. Chapter 10 is a comprehensive discussion of how to interpret standardized reading test scores properly, and Chapters 11 and 12 build on this knowledge and present two alternate strategies that classroom teachers can use to make appropriate use of information from group, standardized reading test scores. Chapter 13 concludes part II with a discussion of how to prepare students for performance on standardized tests in light of the reality that standardized tests are here to stay and that important educational decisions are based on them.*

# CHAPTER 9

# Informal Diagnosis of Reading Abilities

Peggy E. Ransom
Ball State University
Muncie, Indiana

Del Patty
Southern Illinois University at Edwardsville

*Effective reading instruction is based on accurate assessment. Ideally, teachers teach what students need to learn, which is determined by the appropriate assessment of students' reading skills. In this chapter, Peggy Ransom and Del Patty discuss informal measures for assessing reading ability. "Informal" in this context means that the instruments are not standardized, norm-referenced tests, that is, that they do not have formal procedures for administration and scoring and do not report scores such as percentiles and stanines. Additionally, informal tests are often constructed by teachers rather than produced commercially. Ransom and Patty discuss three specific classes of informal measures appropriate for use in an elementary classroom by a beginning teacher: the cloze test, the informal reading inventory, and criterion-referenced tests made up by teachers. Any reading assessment instrument should lead to some form of instructional decision. The instructional decisions that these informal instruments help teachers to make are (1) the determination of students' instructional reading levels so that children can be assigned to basal readers or content textbooks of appropriate difficulty and (2) the identification of specific reading skill strengths and weaknesses so that teachers can provide appropriate corrective instruction when necessary.*

Although many fine commercial reading tests are available, teachers often make their best professional judgments through careful, structured observations of pupils and through the use of informal diagnostic procedures they make up themselves. It is commonly assumed that we teach best by identifying each pupil's exact needs and then choosing the most suitable materials and methods for teaching. In other words, ideally we become diagnostic teachers who determine students' instructional reading levels, match students to appropriate instructional reading materials, and identify deficiencies in specific skill areas and provide instruction in these needed skills. The purpose of this chapter is to describe the background and techniques necessary for using informal testing measures with students in the classroom. More specifically, the following questions will be answered by reading this chapter.

1. What are some informal reading measures?
2. How can these measures be used as diagnostic tools for teachers?
3. How will using these informal tests help teachers to improve reading instruction?
4. How does a teacher use informal diagnostic tools with students in the classroom?
5. How practical are the informal diagnostic measures?

This chapter introduces three teacher-made procedures for diagnosing pupils' reading patterns: (1) the cloze procedure, or cloze test, which requires students to fill in words deleted from a passage in order to determine students' instructional reading levels and assess general reading comprehension, (2) the informal reading inventory (IRI), which requires pupils to read passages of increasing difficulty in order to determine students' instructional reading levels and to identify specific reading strengths and weaknesses, and (3) teacher-made criterion-referenced tests (CRTs), which aid teachers in determining which students have mastered specific reading skills and which students are still in need of instruction.

## THE CLOZE TEST

A cloze test is an informal assessment measure that provides a global measure of reading comprehension. A cloze test requires a reader to fill in blanks in a passage through the use of context clues provided in the passage itself and through her prior knowledge of language and the world. For example, try to fill in the blanks in the following sample sentences.

Why did you choose ＿＿＿＿＿＿ teaching profession?

Was it ＿＿＿＿＿＿ you liked children? I ＿＿＿＿＿＿ it was not to get rich!

Did you insert the words *the, because,* and *hope* or some reasonable synonyms? If you did, you were using context clues and prior knowledge to make these insertions, which indicate that you comprehend the sentences.

Research on the cloze technique (Bormuth, 1967, 1968a; Rankin and Culhane, 1969) has established a relationship between the percentage of correct responses students make on a cloze test (like that above but much longer) and their performance on traditional multiple-choice tests assessing comprehension of the same passage (the greater the number of correct insertions, the more multiple-choice questions answered correctly). In addition, a relationship between scores on cloze tests and students' independent, instructional, and frustration reading levels has also been established (Rankin, 1971; Ransom, 1968). According to considerable evidence, therefore, the cloze test is a valid measure of reading comprehension, and it can be used (much like an informal reading inventory) to estimate students' independent, instructional, and frustration reading levels and thus to place students in basal readers or content area textbooks. The uses of the cloze test as an assessment tool are (1) to estimate students' independent, instructional, and frustration reading levels so that they may be placed in a basal reader series when appropriate, and (2) to determine how successfully students will be able to read and understand a particular content textbook for subjects such as science and social studies. A cloze *procedure* (but not a formal cloze *test*) is also very useful to a teacher as an instructional tool for teaching children to use context clues. The instructional use of the cloze procedure, however, need not follow the strict guidelines presented later for the construction of a cloze test. The instructional use of the cloze procedure can be much less formal, and the teacher can decide which words to delete, how many words to delete, or even what parts of words to delete. Chapter 1 includes several examples of the instructional use of cloze.

## Using a Cloze Test to Place Students in Basal Readers

Ideally, children should be assigned a basal reader at their *instructional reading level,* that is, a text that is neither so advanced that they have difficulty decoding many words and do not comprehend what they read (i.e., at their frustration level) nor so easy that they are not challenged by new words and readily comprehend all of what they read (i.e., at their independent level). A cloze test can be used to *estimate* students' instructional reading levels with respect to basal readers, that is, to guide a teacher in identifying the level of basal reader closest to a student's instructional reading level.

To construct a basal cloze test, a teacher needs to determine the levels of basal readers he will use for reading instruction. For example, a fourth-grade teacher might decide to place students in a level-$3^2$ basal (second book of third grade), a level-4 basal, or a level-5 basal. (Chances are, however, that some fourth-grade students would be reading at levels both above and below this range. Refer to Chapters 14 and 18 for suggestions on dealing with students at these extremes.) The cloze test, therefore, would consist of passages selected from basal levels $3^2$, 4, and 5. By having students complete a series of cloze tests at these various levels (i.e., read and fill in blanks) and then comparing students' scores to established criteria, the teacher would be able to estimate intelligently students' in-structional reading levels and assign children to basal reader texts.

### Constructing a Basal Cloze Test

Although there is no universal agreement about the exact procedures for constructing a cloze test, the following steps represent the most commonly accepted procedures.

1. Choose one or more samples from each basal level that are reasonably respre-sentative of the entire book. Although a basal cloze procedure can be based on a *single* excerpt from a book, logic tells us that two or three samples would be more reliable. Also, select samples that can be easily understood when excerpted from the book; that is, make sure that your cloze selections do not depend on prior selections or parts of selections for them to be understood. Usually, taking the beginning part of a basal story eliminates this problem.
2. Choose selections of between 250 and 300 words long. This ensures that enough deletions are possible, since a minimum of 50 deletions is necessary for an acceptable reliability level.

3. Leave the first sentence intact; that is, do not delete any words.
4. Then, starting with the second sentence, delete every *fifth* word, regardless of what it is. Insert blanks of identical width for every deleted word—10 to 15 typewriter spaces is usually adequate.
5. Continue deleting every fifth word through the end of the selection. Remember that a minimum of 50 deletions is necessary.

### Administering a Basal Cloze Test

One cloze test should be administered each day until all tests have been completed. This might require only three days if, for example, the fourth-grade teacher described above selected only one cloze passage for each of the three basal levels. More days will be needed when two or more samples from each text are used. The class should complete a brief practice cloze exercise before the first test is administered. Examples written on the chalkboard or a transparency would be sufficient to make sure that the students understood the task. The students should be directed to read through the passage and to try to "figure out what word will make sense in each blank and write that word in the blank." They should be given as much time as they need (30 minutes is usually adequate) to complete the cloze test.

### Scoring a Basal Cloze Test

Each cloze passage can be scored in the following manner.

1. Score only *exact* substitutions as correct. For example, if the deleted word were *automobile* and the student inserted *car,* the response would be considered incorrect. Do not penalize students for misspellings, however (as long as you can determine what the intended word is). *Do not* give credit for tense changes (e.g., *jumped* for *jump* or changes in inflection (e.g., *flowers* for *flower*). Although these guidelines may seem unfair, since many of the responses marked incorrect may seem to make sense, follow them strictly, for they are linked to the validating research. If the scoring procedures are altered, the results may become invalid.
2. Calculate the percentage of correct insertions. For example, if there are 50 blanks in a particular cloze test and a student correctly inserted 27 words, the percentage correct would be 54 percent (i.e., 27/50 = 54%).

### Preparing a Class Summary Chart and Interpreting Results

After all levels of cloze tests have been administered and scored, a class summary chart like the partial one reproduced in Figure 9.1 should be prepared, with the percentage scores inserted into the appropriate columns.

Independent, instructional, and frustration reading levels can be determined by referring to the following criteria taken from Bormuth (1968b):

58%–100%:   Independent reading level

44%–57%:   Instructional reading level

0%–43%:   Frustration reading level

| Student | Level 3[2] | | Level 4 | | Level 5 | |
|---|---|---|---|---|---|---|
| | Percentage Correct | Reading Level | Percentage Correct | Reading Level | Percentage Correct | Reading Level |
| Rachel A. | 80% | Indep. | 70% | Indep. | 55% | Instr. |
| Jonathan B. | 55% | Instr. | 41% | Frust. | 32% | Frust. |
| Kathleen B. | 65% | Indep. | 50% | Instr. | 45% | Instr. |
| Thomas B. | 60% | Indep. | 48% | Instr. | 40% | Frust. |
| Marla F. | 90% | Indep. | 68% | Indep. | 60% | Indep. |
| Eric F. | 47% | Instr. | 38% | Frust. | 35% | Frust. |
| Laura H. | 67% | Indep. | 52% | Instr. | 40% | Frust. |
| Jose J. | 42% | Frust. | 40% | Frust. | 22% | Frust. |
| Kim K. | 59% | Indep. | 51% | Instr. | 37% | Frust. |

Figure 9.1. A portion of a summary chart for a hypothetical fourth-grade class's performance on a basal cloze test.

Although other researchers (Rankin and Culhane, 1969; Ransom, 1968) have established slightly different criteria, Bormuth's values have been widely accepted and vary little from other cloze interpretive criteria.

The data obtained from a cloze test represent only an *estimate* of the students' instructional reading levels. When actually assigning students to basal readers, therefore, the teacher must consider factors other than the cloze test results. Informal observation of the students' reading ability, other reading test scores (e.g., informal reading inventory, standardized test results), and the students' actual performance in reading class should be considered when making group or material placements (or when revising them). (Refer to Chapter 14 for a more complete discussion of the issues involved in assigning students to basal readers.)

## Using a Cloze Test to Determine the Suitability of Content Textbooks

A second use of the cloze test is in determining how well students will be able to read and comprehend content area textbooks. For content cloze tests, the teacher selects one or more (more is better) selections from each content book to be evaluated. The test construction, administration, and scoring procedures outlined for basal tests in the preceding section apply also to content tests. A class summary chart similar to the basal summary chart is also constructed. An example is Figure 9.2. (If more than one cloze test passage is used for each textbook, the individual cloze test scores should be averaged and the average percentage correct inserted into the chart.) Bormuth's (1968b) criteria can then be used to determine independent, instructional, and frustration reading levels.

Through inspecting a summary chart like the one in Figure 9.2, several things can be learned. A teacher can identify those students for whom a particular textbook may be appropriate (usually students' performance at independent and instructional levels indicates

| Student | Social Studies | | Science | | Health and Safety | |
|---|---|---|---|---|---|---|
| | Percentage Correct | Reading Level | Percentage Correct | Reading Level | Percentage Correct | Reading Level |
| Marla B. | 80% | Indep. | 74% | Indep. | 54% | Instr. |
| Richard C. | 50% | Instr. | 52% | Instr. | 40% | Frust. |
| Stephanie D. | 40% | Frust. | 38% | Frust. | 30% | Frust. |
| Tanya H. | 66% | Indep. | 57% | Instr. | 45% | Instr. |
| Rachel J. | 43% | Frust. | 48% | Instr. | 38% | Frust. |
| Thomas M. | 47% | Instr. | 50% | Instr. | 47% | Instr. |
| Frank M. | 78% | Indep. | 80% | Indep. | 55% | Instr. |
| Deborah P. | 39% | Frust. | 37% | Frust. | 25% | Frust. |

Figure 9.2. A portion of a summary chart for a hypothetical sixth-grade class's performance on a content cloze test.

that the book tested is appropriate for classroom use) and those for whom it may be too difficult (i.e., at the frustration level). Also, a teacher can acquire a sense of the relative difficulty of a textbook. For example, from an examination of the chart in Figure 9.2, it appears that the health and safety textbook is more difficult than either the social studies or science text. Such interpretations should be made carefully, however, especially when only one cloze passage is taken from a textbook, because the passage selected may have been particularly "hard" and the findings may not generalize to the entire textbook.

For those students for whom a particular textbook falls at the frustration reading level, a teacher needs either to provide an alternate reading source (i.e., a different textbook or supplementary material) or to adapt the reading assignments in some fashion. (Refer to chapter 18 for suggestions in these areas.)

## THE INFORMAL READING INVENTORY

The informal reading inventory (IRI) is a one-to-one testing instrument used by classroom teachers to determine students' instructional reading levels and to acquire specific diagnostic information about students' decoding and comprehension abilities. An IRI consists of a series of graded passages—usually corresponding to a basal reader—and accompanying comprehension questions. After the appropriate entry level in the IRI has been determined (usually about two grade levels below grade placement), a student reads orally each graded passage, and the teacher records any oral reading errors, or miscues. This information provides the teacher with a measure of the student's word identification skill. The student is then asked to respond to questions that probe her comprehension of the passage. Some IRIs also include a second passage at the same level of difficulty that the student reads silently. The teacher then asks a second set of comprehension questions; these provide the teacher a measure of silent comprehension. The student then progresses to the next level in the IRI, and the process is repeated until the teacher determines that the student's frustration reading level has been reached.

Since IRIs typically are used to place students in basal readers (similar to the basal cloze test procedure), most current basal reader series include accompanying IRIs; that is, they identify passages from each level of basal reader (preprimer through grade eight) and supply corresponding written comprehension questions. Sometimes these IRIs are referred to as "placement tests," usually found in the teacher's edition.

A number of commercial IRIs that follow the same general format are also available. A typical commercial IRI includes an instruction manual, graded passages, teacher's worksheets, and reproducible forms for scoring. Most commercial IRIs also include a series of graded word lists that help the teacher determine the entry level in the IRI. Listed here are several commercial IRIs available for purchase.

## Commercial IRIs

Paul C. Burns and Betty D. Roe. *Informal reading assessment: Preprimer to twelfth grade.* Chicago: Rand McNally College Publishing Company, 1980.

Eldon E. Ekwall. *Ekwall reading inventory.* Boston: Allyn and Bacon, 1979.

Jerry L. Johns. *Basic reading inventory: Preprimer–grade eight.* (2nd ed.) Dubuque, Iowa: Kendall/Hunt, 1981.

Nicholas J. Silvaroli. *Classroom reading inventory.* (4th ed.) Dubuque, Iowa: William C. Brown, 1982.

Mary Lynn Woods and Alden J. Moe. *Analytical reading inventory.* Columbus, Ohio: Charles E. Merrill, 1977.

Using the IRIs provided with basal reading series saves the teacher time and effort. Although the basal IRIs vary in format from reading series to reading series, all provide valuable information and insight into the reading ability of students.

When the basal program being used includes no accompanying IRI, a reasonable alternative is a commercial IRI such as one of those listed above. The disadvantage of using such a commercial IRI is that it does not match exactly the basal reader into which the students are being placed; that is, although readability has been controlled for all passages in the IRI, the content, the form, and even the writing style may differ from those of the basal series to be used in the classroom. In other words, if the teacher's goal is to use an IRI to place students in basal readers, the teacher ideally should administer an IRI whose passages are taken directly from the basal series to be used.

For basal series that have no accompanying IRIs, a second alternative is for the teacher to construct an IRI himself. Although constructing the instrument is a time-consuming process, the teacher can use the instrument as long as he is using the basal program on which it is based.

### Constructing an Informal Reading Inventory

The steps involved in constructing an IRI for a basal reader series include the following.

1. Select passages about a fourth of the way through each basal reader volume to be included. (See the comment at the end of this section.) Primary selections (grades

one through three) should be about 75 to 125 words long; intermediate selections (grades four through six) and those from grade-seven and grade-eight texts should be about 150 to 250 words long. When selecting the passages, make sure that the portion of the text chosen makes sense when taken out of context (as when selecting cloze passages). For the silent reading section, select the part of the story that follows the oral reading section.

2. Since readability levels are controlled very carefully in basal readers, you can have a reasonable amount of confidence that the difficulty level of your IRI selections corresponds closely to the designated level of the text (e.g., fourth-grade text, fourth-grade readability). If you doubt this contention, however, use a readability formula to verify the difficulty level of the passages you selected. The Fry Readability Graph, reproduced in Chapter 16, is an appropriate readability formula to use for this purpose.

3. Develop comprehension questions for each oral and silent passage. Ideally, you should write *ten* questions: four at the literal level and three each at the inferential and interpretive (evaluation) levels. For passages below the second-grade level, however, it may not be possible to write ten questions. For these make sure that you write a *minimum* of *six* questions (two each at the literal, inferential, and interpretive levels) for every passage. Also, make sure that the questions you write are *passage dependent,* meaning that it is necessary for the student to read and comprehend the passage in order to answer the questions. A good way to evaluate your questions for passage dependency is to have someone try to answer them without having read the story. Those that are easily answered without reading the story should be discarded and substitute questions should be written.

4. Develop a brief "purpose for reading" statement for each passage. This statement gives the students using the IRI a little background before they read each passage. For example, a statement like the following would be sufficient: "In this story you will read about Max and Martha, who have just found a baby kangaroo in their backyard. Read to find out what they do with the kangaroo."

5. For each level of the IRI, mark the student textbook so that it is clear where the student is to begin reading and where she is to stop (pencil marks are acceptable). Make a photocopy of the passage for yourself, which you will use to follow along while the child is reading. Later, you will score the oral reading miscues on these pages. Prepare additional pages that contain the purpose for reading statements and corresponding comprehension questions to be asked. Allow enough room to write down the students' responses to the comprehension questions. It is also wise to indicate parenthetically each question's type (literal, inferential, or interpretive). You can use this information later when analyzing comprehension ability.

Although the process of constructing a good IRI is tedious, you may be able to reduce your work if you can anticipate the number of levels of IRI you will need. For example, if you are a fourth-grade teacher, you may only need to prepare IRI stories and questions for basal reader levels $3^1$, $3^2$, 4, 5, and 6. You may indeed have students who score outside this range, but if you do not intend to place students in these basal levels, preparing IRI passages for them is not sensible. In other words, it is not necessary to prepare a preprimer–grade-eight IRI if you will not assign students to basal texts across this entire range of levels.

## Administering an Informal Reading Inventory

The teacher's goal in administering an IRI is to acquire the best possible sample of pupils' reading performance. To obtain a representative sample of reading behavior, the teacher should adhere to the following steps when administering an IRI.

1. Select a quiet, comfortable location, free of distractions, for administering the IRI.
2. Begin the IRI at a level at which the students are likely to demonstrate independent reading ability. A good rule of thumb is to begin two grade levels below your best guess of the student's instructional level (which you can estimate from previous basal placements, other test scores, and informal observations).
3. Provide the purpose for reading statement and ask the student to read the passage orally.
4. While the pupil is reading, record any oral reading miscues on your copy of the passage. Use the markings explained in the key in Table 9.1 to record the miscues. Try to be as explicit as possible in recording deviations from the actual passage, because you will analyze these miscues later when you attempt to diagnose reading strengths and weaknesses. Also, tape-record the oral reading portions of the IRI. This will allow you to verify your coding of oral reading miscues later.
5. When the student has finished reading orally, have him close the book and respond to the comprehension questions. Record the student's responses on a comprehension question sheet.
6. Next, have the student read the silent passage at the same grade level and respond to the silent comprehension questions.
7. Repeat steps three through six for the increasingly more difficult passages. Continue until you have estimated that the student has reached the frustration level. Make sure you proceed far enough in the IRI. Sometimes a student will do poorly on one passage and then do dramatically better on the next, more difficult level. When a child has performed poorly on two successive passages, it is safe to assume that her frustration level has been reached.

## Scoring an Informal Reading Inventory

After the IRI data have been gathered, the oral reading miscues and comprehension questions are scored to determine the students' reading levels (independent, instructional, and frustration). The oral reading miscues are scored according to the number of scorable miscues and recordable miscues. (Refer again to Table 9.1.) The difference between these miscues should be noted. Scorable miscues are those oral reading errors that are formally counted as errors in calculating an oral reading score; recordable miscues are marked on the code sheet but are of lesser significance and are used only for the diagnostic interpretation of a student's oral reading behavior; *they are not used for calculating an oral reading score.* The comprehension questions are scored as correct or incorrect. When a student was partially correct in responding to a comprehension question, half credit can be awarded. A scoring sheet like the sample in Figure 9.3 should be used for each IRI passage administered.

## Table 9.1 Marking Oral Reading Miscues

| Scorable Reading Miscues | | | Recordable Reading Miscues | | |
|---|---|---|---|---|---|
| **Miscue** | **Explanation** | **Example** | **Miscue** | **Explanation** | **Example** |
| Mispronunciation | Mispronounces a nonword for one appearing in print. | selver<br>several | Corrected error | Misreads a word, repeats, and corrects. | was working C<br>was walking |
| Substitution | Pronounces another word in place of one in print. | final<br>finally | Repetition | Repeats a word already pronounced. | hospital<br>(repeated once or)<br>hospital<br>(repeated twice) |
| Pronunciation by examiner | Does not pronounce the word, but waits for the examiner to supply it. | P<br>ambulance | Hesitation | Pauses between words. | Walk /slowly<br>(five-second pause or)<br>Walk //slowly<br>(ten-second pause) |
| Omission | Does not pronounce the word, but reads on. | because | Punctuation | Disregards or misinterprets punctuation in print. | days, I |
| Transposition | Pronounces the actual words, but changes the order. | so badly | Proper names | Not computed; a word often unfamiliar to the reader. | Jasmine de Lei |
| Additions | Adds a word not appearing in print, perhaps to gain meaning. | then<br>and hurt | Dialect | Pronounces as in speech; not a reading error. | frum<br>from |

Practice in calculating IRI reading levels can be gained by scoring the responses shown in Figure 9.4, which shows a portion of an IRI passage. Referring to this passage, complete blanks on the scoring sheet Figure 9.3. You will need to determine which miscues are scorable and which are recordable by referring to Table 9.1. Placing checks in the left column for each scorable miscue may help you.

Compare your results to those found in Table 9.2. Were you accurate in determining the scorable and recordable miscues? Did you calculate the percentage of correctly pronounced words accurately? If you made errors, go back and see whether you can discover your mistakes.

Student's Name _____

Basal Level _____ Date _____

| Scorable Miscues | Recordable Miscues |
|---|---|
| Mispronunciations . . . . . . . . . . . . _____ | Corrected errors . . . . . . . . . . . . . . _____ |
| Substitutions . . . . . . . . . . . . . . . _____ | Repetitions . . . . . . . . . . . . . . . . . . _____ |
| Pronunciations by examiner . . . _____ | Hesitations . . . . . . . . . . . . . . . . . _____ |
| Omissions . . . . . . . . . . . . . . . . . _____ | Punctuation . . . . . . . . . . . . . . . . . _____ |
| Transpositions . . . . . . . . . . . . . . _____ | Proper names . . . . . . . . . . . . . . . _____ |
| Additions . . . . . . . . . . . . . . . . . . _____ | Dialect . . . . . . . . . . . . . . . . . . . . . _____ |

Total words in passage . . . . . . . . . . . . . . . . . . . . . . . . . . . . . . . . . . . . . . . _____

Total scorable miscues . . . . . . . . . . . . . . . . . . . . . . . . . . . . . . . . . . . . . . . . _____

Words correctly pronounced (total words – total scorable miscues) . . . . . . . . _____

Percentage of correctly pronounced words (words correctly
pronounced/total words in passage) . . . . . . . . . . . . . . . . . . . . . . . . . . . . . . . . _____

COMPREHENSION

|  | Oral | Silent |
|---|---|---|
| Literal comprehension errors . . . . . . . . . . . . . . . . . . . . . . . . . . . . . . . | _____ | _____ |
| Inferential comprehension errors . . . . . . . . . . . . . . . . . . . . . . . . . . . . | _____ | _____ |
| Interpretive comprehension errors . . . . . . . . . . . . . . . . . . . . . . . . . . . | _____ | _____ |
| Total comprehension errors . . . . . . . . . . . . . . . . . . . . . . . . . . . . . . . | _____ | _____ |
| Percentage of comprehension questions answered correctly (number of questions correct/ten) . . . . . . . . . . . . . . . . | _____ | _____ |

READING LEVEL _____

Figure 9.3. A sample IRI scoring sheet.

In determining a student's reading level for a given passage, both his performance on the oral reading portion (word recognition) and the comprehension portion of the IRI must be considered. For the purpose of the example in Figure 9.4, let us assume that the student correctly answered six of the ten oral comprehension questions and seven of the ten silent comprehension questions. The percentage of comprehension questions answered correctly working C

It was/winter and I was walking to school. I fell on the

then              P

ice and hurt my back. It hurt (so badly) I even cried, (because)

down C            thereby C

I just could not get up at all. A person nearby called the

P           nostald

ambulance which took me to the hospital. The X-rays showed

did

I sprained my back so I was/kept in the hospital three days. X

I began to walk slowly/after three days. After several weeks

selver

fihal   P    Prum d   accent

I finally recovered from the accident, but I do not like to

walk on ice/now!

Figure 9.4. A portion of an IRI code sheet.

### Table 9.2. Correct Scoring of Sample Passage

| Scorable Miscues | | Recordable Miscues | |
|---|---|---|---|
| Mispronunciations | 2 | Corrected errors | 3 |
| Substitutions | 2 | Repetitions | 7 |
| Pronounciations by examiner | 3 | Hesitations | 5 |
| Omissions | 2 | Punctuation | 1 |
| Transpositions | 1 | Proper name | 0 |
| Additions | 2 | Dialect | 1 |
| Total words in passage | | | 89 |
| Total scorable miscues | | | 12 |
| Words correctly pronounced | | | 77 |
| Percentage of correctly pronounced words | | | 87% |

entered on the IRI scoring sheet (Figure 9.3) would be 60 percent and 70 percent, respectively, for oral and silent comprehension. Thus, the word recognition and comprehension percentages for this student are 87 percent and 60/70 percent, respectively.

The reading level associated with these percentages is determined by referring to the commonly used Betts (1946) IRI criteria (Table 9.3). Note that the 87 percent word recognition and 60 percent/70 percent comprehension scores clearly place the student's performance on this passage in the frustration reading category. The IRI criteria in Table 9.3 are merely *guidelines* for evaluating a student's performance. They are not hard-and-fast standards. For example, if a child scored 92 percent on word recognition and 83 percent on comprehension, the teacher would be forced to decide whether that fell at the instructional or the frustration reading level. To do this, she considers the *quality* of the responses to the IRI. Were the oral reading errors miscues that dramatically affected the meaning, or were they merely "careless" errors? If they generally were careless errors, the teacher might

**Table 9.3. Criteria for Determining IRI Reading Levels**

| Book Level | Word Pronunciation | Comprehension | Interpretation |
|---|---|---|---|
| Independent | 99% or more | 90% or more | A book level at which a pupil can read without assistance from others; i.e., teacher, friends, parents, etc.; it is the difficulty level that may be used to select recreational materials |
| Instructional | 95% or more | 75% or more | A book level at which instruction should take place, with material neither too difficult nor too easy; students working at this level can be expected to make optimum achievement gains |
| Frustration | 94% or less | 74% or less | A book level at which material is too difficult; students forced to operate at this level do substantially less well in achievement than those taught at more suitable reading levels |

NOTE: The criteria are from Betts (1946) and are the criteria most frequently used for determining students' independent, instrucitonal, and frustration reading levels.

decide to consider this passage to be at the student's instructional level. If the miscues were more serious, she might consider it to be at the frustration level. The important point to remember is that the IRI criteria are only guidelines for determining students' reading levels. The quality of students' performances must be considered when reading levels are being established.

### Interpreting an Informal Reading Inventory

Some interpretation of results of an IRI occurs when the teacher determines instructional reading levels, but even more interpretation is needed when he tries to obtain specific diagnostic information about students' word recognition and comprehension abilities from their performance on an IRI. In other words, the teacher is not concerned with the numbers associated with a student's performance on an IRI (i.e., as when calculating the reading levels described in the preceding section); rather, she is interested in determining specific *diagnostic* information so that she can provide corrective instruction for students who demonstrate weaknesses.

Tables 9.4 and 9.5 provide interpretive guidelines that may be helpful in analyses of oral reading miscues on IRIs. What the teacher should look for when analyzing and reading miscues are patterns of responses. For example, if a student continually omitted or substituted basic sight words, he might need to work on sight vocabulary. If a student substituted many words that did not make sense (i.e., they were contextually inconsistent), she might not be reading for meaning and might need to work on developing her semantic cue system. If the teacher noted a pattern of mispronunciations of words with short vowels, instruction on short vowels should seem warranted. A good source for information on corrective activities for weaknesses identified through qualitative analysis of word recognition errors can be found in Chapter 1 of this text.

Patterns of errors in comprehension should be identified as well. Is a student continually missing only inferential comprehension questions? When this is the case, the teacher needs to provide additional instruction in this area. Error patterns occur in other comprehension areas as well. An IRI is primarily a teaching tool that the teacher must use

**Table 9.4. Interpretation of Scorable Reading Miscues**

| Miscue | Interpretation |
| --- | --- |
| *Mispronunciations:* Student actually pronounces a nonword in place of the word in text. | The pupil relies on phonic or other word identification clues to approximate the word in print, failing to label an actual word. Since he fails to use words from his oral language, we assume that he does not expect his reading to "make sense." If comprehension is the actual purpose of reading, this miscue pattern is the most serious; the reader uses neither word clues nor context to gain meaning. Frequent mispronunciations call for the development of more automatic word skills and greater attention to context. |
| *Substitutions:* Reader uses some other word in place of the word in print. | The reader may rely on minimal word clues (attention to word beginnings and endings, for example), without precise scrutiny, to choose a word that seems to fit. Substitutions may or may not change meaning but show disregard for the author's expression. Failure to attain "automaticity," or automatic decoding, may retard rate, fluency, and thus comprehension for many. Frequent use of substitutions, particularly when meaning is affected, warrants closer attention to text and to development of added word skills. |
| *Omissions:* Pupil misses or disregards a word part, whole word, or longer passage segment. | The student is unable to deal with unfamiliar words or word parts. Also, she may skip to retain comprehension. Frequent omissions show the need for added word skill instruction or greater attention to text. |
| *Pronunciations by examiner:* Reader waits for the teacher to provide the unknown word. | The pupil apparently cannot deal with the word. Neither decoding clues nor context seem to aid good word identification. Frequent patterns of words pronounced by the instructor show the need for additional word skill instruction. |
| *Additions:* Student adds a word which did not appear in the story. | The pupil may attempt to retain meaning by adding a word that the writer did not include. This disregard for text may or may not change meaning. If meaning is altered frequently, instruction to call the pupil's attention to additions is appropriate. |
| *Transpositions:* Child changes the word order or a part of the sentence. | The reader's shift in word order may result from rapid, inexact perception or may show an emphasis on meaning that disregards the text. Developing the pupil's awareness of the errors is probably the best prescription, if one is needed. |

## Table 9.5. Interpretation of Recordable Reading Miscues

| Miscue | Interpretation |
|---|---|
| *Corrected errors:* Reader mislabels the word or sentence segment, repeats and labels correctly. | The student is likely to use context, perhaps along with partial word clues, to reconsider text. There is a chance that this reader may not have developed word skills to "automaticity," which may reduce accuracy and rate, thus affecting comprehension. Very often, however, this student's pattern shows effective reading, with a healthy reliance on both word recognition skills and use of context. If the pattern occurs extensively, correction is warranted. |
| *Repetitions:* Pupil repeats a word or group of words, perhaps more than once. | The pupil often repeats words to stall for the time needed to clarify words or meaning. Habitual repetitions are not easily remediated, and they surely represent symptoms of decoding problems or content confusion. Promising prescriptions include adjusted content difficulty, emphasis on fluency, and development of new word skills. |
| *Hesitations:* Student pauses, losing fluency, between words. | The reader hesitates while decoding or searching for meaning. More careful analysis may reveal whether there is only a slight break in fluency or a habitual word-by-word reader is represented. Persistent hesitations surely reduce fluency, rate, and comprehension. Oftentimes, excessive hesitations show a heavy concept load in the story. Improved word skills, emphasis on fluency, or readjusted passage difficulty are promising prescriptions. |
| *Punctuation:* Reader disregards or misinterprets punctuation. | The student does not use punctuation, or in the search for meaning punctuation seems unimportant. A shift in intonation, often including a disregard of punctuation, may indicate a reinterpretation of the text in the reader's thinking. This shift may change the writer's intent. The standard prescription is to call the reader's attention to the pattern when comprehension is altered. |
| *Proper names:* Pupil miscalls a proper name; often he is unfamiliar with the word. | Many proper names are poorly identified through conventional word clue patterns, leaving the reader with no effective means of identification. Pupils know the function of such words but may not be able to deal with the actual words. |
| *Dialect:* Reader pronounces the word differently from standard speech. | While reading, the pupil may pronounce the miscue as she would pronounce it during conversation. The pattern does not represent a reading difficulty at all but may warrant additional language development, teaching standard speech along with the dialect. Dialect miscues rarely change meaning. |

wisely. If the teacher takes the time to administer IRIs to some or all of his students, he should take the added time necessary (1) to analyze the oral reading miscue patterns and comprehension errors and (2) to provide individual or group (several students may need the same skills) corrective instruction for students who demonstrate weaknesses in the areas identified.

### Alternatives to Using the Complete IRI

The IRI is a time-consuming instrument to use, a characteristic for which it has been justly criticized. Alternative informal assessment techniques, or modified IRIs, that can be considered include the following.

1. Identify only the instructional and frustration levels, omitting the independent level.
2. Use the finger-count method to locate the instructional level, sampling oral reading without checking comprehension. If the pupil makes about one scorable miscue in 20 words, the book is suitable; one miscue in 10 words and the book is too difficult; one miscue in 30 words and the book is too easy. This process may be employed during regular instruction.
3. Use a set of short, graded oral reading paragraphs (like those found in commercial IRIs). Ask pupils to read individually as you check scorable reading miscues to gain a tentative estimate of instructional level.
4. Prepare graded passages for pupils to read silently, and then have them complete the comprehension responses in a multiple-choice format. The highest graded passage level at which the pupil shows 75 percent comprehension represents her tentative instructional level.

The IRI is a valuable instrument to use with any student for whom the teacher needs a great deal of reading information. Because of the time involved, however, many teachers prefer to give a shortened, modified IRI, or a cloze test, to the majority of students. Becoming proficient with the IRI does, however, provide the classroom teacher with diagnostic proficiency.

## TEACHER-MADE CRITERION-REFERENCED TESTS

Criterion-referenced tests are diagnostic and prescriptive; that is, they tell the teacher what students can and cannot do and what should be taught next. A good criterion-referenced system, therefore, supports a highly personalized, or individualized, reading program (see Chapter 16), since a set of criterion-referenced reading tests helps teachers to determine whether the objectives of the individualized reading program are being met.

Criterion-referenced tests accompany some basal reader series. These tests are usually carefully constructed and provide comprehensive assessments of the skills taught in various units and at various levels of the basal program. Some school districts purchase program-external criterion-referenced testing programs. These commercially produced testing programs do not directly follow the basal reader, although they provide a systematic, comprehensive set of objectives and criterion-referenced tests. If the teacher wants to use a criterion-referenced system but does not have a commercial program available to him, he may choose to prepare his own tests.

Criterion-referenced tests measure students' ability to perform designated tasks; that is, they are a form of mastery test that indicates whether or not a student has mastered a particular skill. For example, a test for recognition of the letter *b* as a beginning sound would assess a student's ability only in this discrete area. By definition, a criterion-referenced test has an established *criterion*, or standard of performance, for mastery. When a 90 percent criterion seems appropriate for the letter-*b* test, then students must correctly respond to 90 percent or more of the items on that test. Examples of criterion-referenced test items and corresponding criterion levels follow.

*Main Idea (75 percent).* The student must answer correctly three out of four items like the following.

> Jeremy enjoys stamp collecting. He has many American stamps, as well as stamps from several other countries. Jeremy has collections of Boy Scout knives, rocks, and arrowheads, too.

The main idea of this paragraph is (a) stamp collecting, (b) all about Jeremy, (c) Jeremy's collections, (d) knives, rocks, and arrowheads.

*Initial M and D (75 percent).* The teacher pronounces 16 words in random order, 8 beginning with *m* and 8 beginning with *d*. Students write down the letter representing the beginning sound of each word. Students must correctly identify 6, 7, or 8 of both initial *m*s and initial *d*s.

*Sequence (80 percent).* The student describes accurately the sequence of events in four out of five consecutive third-grade basal stories.

In each of the above examples, specific tasks or structured processes are used to help the teacher determine whether a student has or has not attained mastery of the specified objective. Performance standards (criteria) have also been established to determine mastery. When the teacher decides to adopt a criterion-referenced program, she should keep many records of the students' performance (as in an individualized reading program). An example of a group profile for a series of skills assessed through criterion-referenced tests is reproduced in Figure 9.5. As you can see, extensive testing, scoring, and record keeping are necessary for such a system to be successful.

A few words of caution must accompany a discussion of criterion testing. Criterion-referenced tests assess reading subskills rather than reading itself. If you use a criterion-referenced program, you should not lose sight of the ultimate goal of reading instruction—fluent reading with skillful comprehension—since the mastery of a series of subskills does not necessarily result in the attainment of this goal. Also, mastery or nonmastery of a particular skill should be cautiously determined. Each skill should be sampled and tested more than once to provide enough information for accurately determining mastery or nonmastery.

## SUMMARY

The major goals of informal diagnostic testing are to identify the reading levels of students and to make better instructional decisions. For using informal tests, classroom teachers do not need special training. Since informal tests can be used throughout the year, they offer a great deal of evaluative flexibility to the beginning teacher. Informal measures help teachers make decisions about types and levels of materials to use with students. The informal procedures discussed in this chapter can be modified or simplified to meet the needs of students and teachers alike.

Any informal test is only as good as its construction and interpretation. Teachers should exercise caution when using informal tests, since they provide only an *isolated* view of a student's reading behavior. Any performance on an informal test yields a *single* sampling of the pupil's reading ability, and this sampling may or may not be adequate.

Careful and wise use of informal tests, however, provides valuable insights into students' reading ability.

The informal diagnostic instruments described in this chapter (i.e., the cloze test, IRI, and criterion-referenced test) are tools made by teachers that can be used in typical

**Teacher's Record**

Teacher _____

Level _____

| | Jason | Sarah | Melissa | Rich | Mark | Amy | Robin | Joe | John |
|---|---|---|---|---|---|---|---|---|---|
| **Reading Comprehension:** | | | | | | | | | |
| Identifying facts | X | ✶ | ✶ | X | X | X | ✶ | / | / |
| Determining sequence | / | ✶ | ✶ | ✶ | / | X | X | X | X |
| Identifying main idea | X | ✶ | / | ✶ | ✶ | X | ✶ | / | X |
| Using personal judgment | / | X | / | ✶ | ✶ | / | X | / | X |
| Identifying cause and effect | / | ✶ | / | ✶ | X | X | ✶ | X | X |
| Comparing details | X | ✶ | ✶ | ✶ | X | X | / | / | X |
| Solving problems | / | ✶ | / | ✶ | X | X | ✶ | X | X |
| **Language:** | | | | | | | | | |
| Arranging words and phrases to convey meaning | X | ✶ | ✶ | ✶ | ✶ | X | ✶ | / | X |
| Identifying meanings of prefixes, combining forms and root words | X | ✶ | ✶ | ✶ | X | / | ✶ | X | X |
| Understanding multiple meanings of words | / | ✶ | ✶ | X | X | / | ✶ | / | X |
| Reorganizing and using key words | / | ✶ | ✶ | ✶ | X | / | / | / | X |
| **Literature and the Writer's Craft:** | | | | | | | | | |
| Recognizing influence of point of view on story interpretation | X | ✶ | ✶ | ✶ | X | X | ✶ | / | X |
| Describing the poet's diction or choice of words | / | ✶ | X | ✶ | X | / | X | / | / |
| Recognizing conflict as the basis of plot development | / | ✶ | ✶ | ✶ | X | X | X | X | X |

KEY: Total Mastery ✶ ; Suitable X ; Reteach / .

Figure 9.5. A sample reading group profile based on criterion-referenced testing. (This example of unit record keeping was adapted from materials in *The Widening Path,* Allyn and Bacon Pathfinder Reading Program. [Boston: Allyn and Bacon, 1978, p. 2.])

classrooms. The informal measures can be used with a variety of classroom materials but perhaps are used most often with basal readers. Teachers who use them may become better observers and on-the-spot diagnosticians.

## REFERENCES

Betts, E. A. *Foundations of reading instruction.* New York: American Book Company, 1946.

Bormuth, J. R. Comparable cloze and multiple-choice comprehension test scores. *Journal of Reading,* 1967, **10,** 291–299.

Bormuth, J. R. Cloze test readability: Criterion reference scores. *Journal of Educational Measurement,* 1968, **5,** 189–196. (a)

Bormuth, J. R. The cloze readability procedure. In J. R. Bormuth (Ed.), *Readability in 1968.* Champaign, Ill.: National Council of Teachers of English, 1968. (b)

Rankin, E. F. Grade level interpretation of cloze readability scores. In F. Green (Ed.), *The right to participate.* Milwaukee, Wis.: National Reading Conference, 1971.

Rankin, E. F., and Culhane, J. W. Comparable cloze and multiple-choice comprehension test scores. *Journal of Reading,* 1969, **13,** 193–198.

Ransom, P. E. Determining reading levels of elementary school children by cloze testing. In J. A. Figurel (Ed.), *Forging ahead in reading.* Proceedings of the International Reading Association, Vol. 12, Pt. 1. Newark, Del.: International Reading Association, 1968.

## RECOMMENDED READINGS

Alexander, J. E., Breen, L. G., Davis, A. R., Donnelly, M. M., Heathington, B. S., Huff, P. E., Knight, L., Kolker, B., Tanner, N., Turner, T., and Wynn, S. *Teaching reading.* Boston: Little Brown and Company, 1979.

The second section of Chapter 16 describes specific applications of informal diagnosis to teaching strategies.

Betts, E. A. *Foundations of reading instruction.* New York: American Book Company, 1957.

Information about the preparation, administration, and use of the original IRI can be found in Chapter 21. Betts was the developer of the IRI concept.

Cheek, M. C., and Cheek, E. H. *Diagnostic-prescriptive reading instruction.* Dubuque, Iowa: William C. Brown, 1980.

The IRI, the cloze procedure, and criterion-referenced testing are presented on pp. 53 to 97.

Farr, R., and Roser, N. *Teaching a child to read.* New York: Harcourt Brace Jovanovich, 1979.

Chapter 9 shows ways of using objective data to organize classrooms.

Johns, J. L. *Assessing reading behavior: Informal reading inventories.* Newark, Del.: International Reading Association, 1977.

Current information about the preparation, administration, and use of IRIs is found in this volume.

Johnson, M. S., and Kress, R. A. *Informal reading inventories.* Newark, Del.: International Reading Association, 1965.

The conventional source book on IRIs and pupil assessment.

Jongsma, E. *The cloze procedure as a teaching technique.* Newark, Del.: International Reading Association, 1971.

Literature about the cloze procedure as a teaching tool is presented.

McKenna, M. C., and Robinson, R. D. (Eds.) *An introduction to the cloze procedure.* Newark, Del.: International Reading Association, 1980.

McKenna and Robinson's book describes the development and use of the cloze procedure for diagnosis and instruction.

Patty, D. Evaluating children's reading abilities. In L. Barney (Ed.), *Building reading power.* Dubuque, Iowa: Kendall/Hunt, 1969, pp. 143–201.

This publication describes the teacher's use of a practical review of the IRI to determine student reading levels; practices are included.

Pikulski, J. J., and Shanahan, T. (Eds.) *Approaches to the informal evaluation of reading.* Newark, Del.: International Reading Association, 1982.
  An up-to-date description of cloze procedures, IRIs, and other informal diagnostic tools can be found in this volume.
Ransom, P. E. Diagnosing reading levels with the cloze test. *Reading Newsletter*, November 1981, **13**, 3–4.
  Ransom describes the preparation, administration, and scoring of the cloze test and ties the cloze to teaching procedures.
Thomas, K. J. Instructional application of the cloze technique. *Reading World*, October 1978, **18**, 1–4.
  Practical applications of the cloze are placed in classroom settings.
Wallen, C. J. *Competency in teaching reading.* (2nd ed.) Chicago: Science Research Associates, 1981.
  The final chapter relates criterion-referenced tests to classroom organization.

# CHAPTER 10

# Standardized Reading Test Scores and Teachers

James F. Baumann
Purdue University
West Lafayette, Indiana

*Chapter 9 discussed the construction, administration, scoring, and interpretation of informal reading assessment measures. In this chapter, standardized, norm-referenced tests are discussed—tests that are commercially produced, possess uniform procedures for administration and scoring, and compare students' performance to one another by way of norms. The use of standardized, norm-referenced tests is widespread, and there is little likelihood that their use will diminish. It is important, therefore, for beginning teachers to be knowledgeable about how to interpret the scores obtained from such tests. In this chapter, James Baumann discusses the three scores most commonly obtained from standardized, norm-referenced reading tests: grade equivalency, percentile, and stanine scores. For each score, he provides a description of how the score is derived (that is, how the norms were constructed) and how the score is properly interpreted. The information contained in this chapter should help beginning teachers to understand standardized reading test scores so that the information they convey can be used properly. A clear understanding of these test scores should give new teachers confidence when they interpret standardized reading test scores for parents.*

Test yourself.[1] See how many of the following questions about standardized reading achievement test scores you can answer correctly. (See pages 151–152 for the answers.)

1.  What is a norm-referenced test?
2.  What does a percentile score of 88 mean?

[1]Portions of this chapter were adapted from the article "Understanding standardized reading achievement test scores," by James F. Baumann and Jennifer A. Stevenson, which appeared in *The Reading Teacher*, 1982, **35**, 648–654.

3.  If a fifth-grade student obtained a grade equivalency score of 3.8 on a group reading achievement test, how would you interpret this score for a parent?
4.  What is a "higher" score, a percentile score of 90, or a stanine score of 9?
5.  If a student in your third-grade class obtained grade equivalency scores of 4.8 in vocabulary and 4.4 in comprehension on a reading achievement test, could you assume that this student is "better" in vocabulary than comprehension?
6.  If a fifth-grader obtained a percentile score of 58 in reading comprehension and the next year obtained a percentile score of 55 in reading comprehension, should you assume that this student's comprehension ability has diminished?
7.  When a parent of one of your third-graders asks the following question, how should you respond? "Tony has a grade equivalency score of 5.8 in reading, and you have him working in a third-grade-level basal reader. Since he is reading at the fifth-grade level, why don't you put him in a fifth-grade reader?"

How well did you do? Were there some (many?) questions you failed to answer correctly? As an elementary teacher you will encounter numerous standardized, norm-referenced tests, many of which will be reading tests. In all probability, for example, your students will be required to take an achievement test battery annually (e.g., California Achievement Test, 1977; Iowa Tests of Basic Skills, 1973; Metropolitan Achievement Test, 1978; Stanford Achievement Test, 1978), and one or more of the subtests will be reading tests. Your district may also administer a group diagnostic reading test (e.g., Stanford Diagnostic Reading Test, 1976). Surely, in addition, some of your students will have taken an individual diagnostic reading test (e.g., Durrell Analysis of Reading Difficulty, 1980; Spache Diagnostic Reading Scales, 1972), administered by a reading specialist or diagnostician.

All of these tests report a variety of test scores. You, as a professional teacher, need to understand clearly what these reading test scores mean and what they do not mean. This knowledge enables you to make accurate educational decisions about your students' reading progress, for example, decisions about placing students in reading groups, determining which students may require further testing, and so forth. Additionally, you must be able to interpret test scores for parents when they inquire about their daughter or son's performance on a particular test.

It is the purpose of this chapter to inform you about the proper interpretation of test scores reported from standardized, norm-referenced reading achievement tests. First, a definition of a standardized, norm-referenced test will be given; then, a discussion of the three most commonly-reported test scores (grade equivalents, percentiles, and stanines) will follow.

## A STANDARDIZED, NORM-REFERENCED READING TEST: WHAT IS IT?

Many reading tests are administered to students. Some are standardized; others are not. Some are norm referenced; some are not. What distinguishes a standardized, norm-referenced reading test from other tests? First, the word *standardized* means that all test procedures are the same for all test takers. That is, all students use the same test materials (test books, answer sheets, pencils), all students receive the same directions, everyone has the same amount of time to complete the test, and all tests are scored in the same manner.

Thus, a standardized reading test is a formal, published test, not an informal, teacher-made instrument such as an informal reading inventory.

A standardized test, however, is not necessarily a norm-referenced test. A *norm-referenced* test compares students' performances to one another—individual students to one another (Rita to Marie), individuals to groups (Rita to her class or district or to the entire country), or groups of students to one another (entire classes, schools, or districts compared to one another or to a national sample). A norm-referenced test should be contrasted to a *criterion-referenced* test, which compares students' performances to a specific standard of performance, or criterion. For example, if a teacher constructed a basic sight vocabulary test and determined that students must correctly read 90 percent of the words to demonstrate mastery, the student would be compared to a specific standard, not to other students. Criterion-referenced tests can also be formal, published tests, such as minimum competency tests or mastery tests that accompany basal readers. Since this chapter deals only with norm-referenced tests, however, no further discussion of criterion-referenced tests will be offered. Simply remember that criterion-referenced tests are mastery-type tests that determine whether or not a student has learned some specific skills; thus, the comparison is made between the student and the skill, not between students.[2]

To make accurate comparisons among and between students, one must use some form of derived score. A *derived score* is a converted raw score, which is simply the number correct on the test. The derived scores that will be discussed in this chapter are grade equivalency scores, percentile scores, and stanine scores. Each of these scores is based on separate tables of norms. *Norms* are sets of statistics that indicate students' actual performance on tests. When a test publisher develops a new, norm-referenced test, the test is administered to many thousands of students across the country. Based on their performance, these sets of statistics, or norms, are developed so that the performance of future test takers can be compared to the norm group. In other words, the norms enable a teacher to determine how a student's performance compares to "the national average."

In summary, a standardized, norm-referenced reading test is an instrument prepared and distributed by a test publisher. In addition, the test has uniform procedures for administration and scoring (i.e., it is "standardized"), and tables of norms, and scores based on these norms, can be used to determine how well a student performed in relation to the norm group. Since grade equivalents, percentiles, and stanines are based on different sets of norms, each of these scores has a different interpretation. The following sections describe how these scores are derived and how they are properly interpreted.

## GRADE EQUIVALENCY SCORES

Grade equivalency scores provide information about children's reading achievement compared to students at various grade levels. A grade equivalency score consists of two

---

[2]Although technically a standardized test is not necessarily norm referenced (i.e., comparing students to one another through the use of norm tables), *most* standardized tests are norm referenced. Consequently, many persons assume that all standardized tests (i.e., tests with standard procedures for administration and scoring) also possess norms. This is not always the case, however. For example, many states have adopted minimum compentency tests, which are standardized instruments. Competency tests, however, are mastery tests, since students' achievement is compared to the specified minimum compentencies. Hence, such tests are not norm referenced (i.e, they do not possess norms) but are instead criterion referenced. Be aware, therefore, that not all fancy published-and-packaged, standardized reading tests are necessarily norm-referenced instruments.

digits separated by a decimal point. The first digit represents the grade level, and the second digit indicates the month in school. A grade equivalency score of 1.8, for example, means first grade, eighth month; 6.2 means sixth grade, second month. The year digit ranges from zero (kindergarten, frequently represented by K) to twelfth grade and sometimes beyond. The month digit ranges from 0 to 9, which corresponds to September through June on most school calendars. The proper interpretation of a student's grade equivalency score of 4.6 on a comprehension subtest would be that she performed as well on that test as did the average student in the sixth month of fourth grade.

To understand some of the limitations of grade equivalency scores, one must understand how the norms for these scores are constructed. To develop these norms, test publishers administer tests to large groups of students at several grade levels. If grade equivalency norms for a fourth-grade comprehension test were to be developed, for example, the test would be administered not only to groups of fourth-graders but also to groups of third- and fifth-graders. If this were done in September (i.e., the .0 month) and if the mean (average) raw score for the fourth-graders in the norm group were 30, a grade equivalency score of 4.0 would be assigned to a raw score of 30. If mean raw scores for the third- and fifth-graders were 24 and 35, respectively, grade equivalency scores of 3.0 and 5.0 would be assigned to those raw scores. (See Figure 10.1.)

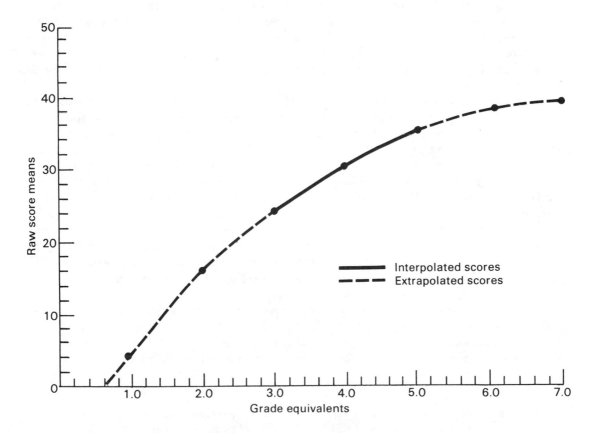

Figure 10.1. An example of interpolated and extrapolated grade equivalency scores.

How are grade equivalency scores determined for raw scores that fall between scores obtained from actual test results—scores that fall between 24 and 30 and between 30 and 35 in the preceding example? Ideally, test publishers would administer tests to different norm groups each month of the school year, thus establishing precise, month-by-month mean raw scores and corresponding grade equivalency scores.[3] Since this procedure is costly and time-consuming, intervening scores are determined by interpolation. *Interpolation* is a procedure whereby the difference in average raw scores obtained from the norm groups (who were tested during only one particular month of the school year) are divided into tenths, and the intervening grade equivalency scores are determined by being plotted against this curve. As shown in Figure 10.1, a raw score of 28 converts to a grade equivalency score of 3.6, 34 converts to 4.8, and so forth.

Grade equivalency scores above or below the grades in the norming population, however, cannot be interpolated. To obtain grade equivalency scores outside this range, test publishers use the process of extrapolation. *Extrapolation* involves projecting the average performance of students at grade levels that were tested to students at grade levels that were not tested. Essentially, this involves extending the interpolated curve. Thus, for the data presented in Figure 10.1, a raw score of 17 would convert to a grade equivalency score of 2.2, 39 would convert to 6.3, and so forth.

The advantage of grade equivalency scores is that they provide a concrete referent (years and months) for comparing students' reading achievement. For scores that fall within a grade level or two of a student's actual grade placement, grade equivalency scores are also reasonably accurate and useful for making comparisons. Several characteristics of grade equivalency scores, however, limit their accuracy and make them prone to misinterpretation.

First, the processes of interpolation and extrapolation involve guesswork. The assumption underyling interpolated scores is that progress occurs throughout the school year at a constant rate; that is, the amount of gain is the same from one month to the next, since an entire year's growth is equally divided into ten months. This assumption is questionable, however, for growth may not occur at a constant rate throughout the school year. This is especially evident when one compares the learning that takes place in a holiday month such as December to another less disruptive month such as October or February.

Extrapolated scores must be viewed even more skeptically. Although these extreme grade equivalency scores may indeed indicate "very high" or "very low" achievement, the actual grade-level designation is only an estimate, since the scores are not established by empirical data. In other words, extrapolated scores are based on mathematical projections, not on actual test results obtained from students.

A second limitation of grade equivalency scores is that they are not directly comparable across tests or subtests. A student who obtained a grade equivalency score of 3.2 on a comprehension subtest and a 2.8 on a vocabulary subtest, for example, may actually be achieving at a higher level in vocabulary than in comprehension. Such a paradox can result

---

[3]In fact, some test publishers administer their tests to separate norm groups at two different times of year, once in the fall and once in the spring. Although this second data source reduces some of the difficulties associated with grade equivalency scores, it by no means eliminates the limitations imposed by interpolation and extrapolation.

from the processes of interpolation and extrapolation, although this situation is more likely to occur for very high or very low grade equivalency scores. Comparisons among or between grade equivalency scores, therefore, are appropriate only within an individual subtest, not across tests or subtests.

A third problem with grade equivalency scores is that they are not uniformly spaced throughout the scale. In terms of raw score points, a "year of growth" may be different at various points on the grade equivalency scale. For example, Figure 10.1 shows that approximately 12 raw score points separate 1.0 and 2.0, whereas only 6 raw score points separate 3.0 and 4.0 and 3 points separate 6.0 and 7.0. Thus, a raw-score difference of several points may represent a trivial amount of achievement at one portion of the scale but a significant amount at another portion of the scale.

Finally, perhaps the greatest limitation of grade equivalency scores is that they are prone to misinterpretation in several ways. Assume, for example, that a second-grader obtained a grade equivalency score of 4.8 on a reading vocabulary test. The proper interpretation of this score is that this second-grader did as well on this test as did the average child who completed eight months of fourth grade. Although this score indicates that the student has a very good reading vocabulary, it says nothing about the content of the reading curriculum; that is, it does not necessarily mean that this second-grader should be placed in fourth-grade reading materials. The student, though very proficient in reading vocabulary, may not possess a number of reading skills that would be necessary for success in a fourth-grade reading program. Thus, it would be an oversimplification and misuse of grade equivalency scores to state that this student "is reading at the fourth-grade level."

Grade equivalency scores are also commonly misinterpreted by those who believe them to represent a standard of performance. It is not uncommon to hear a parent or teacher say, "We need to get all our students reading at or above grade level." Although it is admirable to promote greater achievement, which can be evidenced by increased standardized test scores, it is theoretically impossible to have all students "reading above grade level" when grade equivalency scores are used to determine achievement. Grade equivalency scores are based upon average performances. By definition, therefore, half of the students within the norm groups were above grade level, and half were below grade level. If the test norms are current and representative of the students who took the test, one should expect a reasonable proportion of students within a typical class, school, or district to fall both above and below their grade-level designations.

## PERCENTILE SCORES

As noted above, grade equivalency norms are constructed by testing children at several grade levels. Percentile score norms, however, are developed through examinations of students' performances only within a single grade level. For example, the norming population for a second-grade word identification test would consist only of second-graders. Thus, percentile scores indicate relative performance within a particular grade level, but not across grade levels.

Test publishers develop percentile norms in the following manner. After a test has been administered to the norm group, all raw scores are plotted on a frequency diagram. (See Fig. 10.2.) Since most academic achievement data are normally distributed, the graph typically results in a bell-shaped curve. Percentile scores are based on percentages and

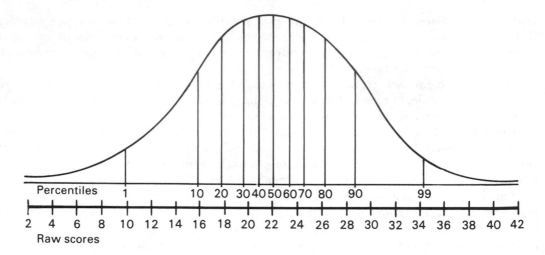

Figure 10.2. The construction of percentile norms.

range from 1 to 99, with 50 being the middle (median) score. Percentiles are constructed by simply segmenting the raw-score distribution into hundredths.

Since percentile scores only compare students within a single grade level, their interpretation is straightforward and intuitively simple: A percentile score represents the percentage of scores equal to or lower than that particular score. For example, if a second-grader obtained a percentile score of 45 on a word identification test, the proper interpretation of that score would be that the student scored as well or better than 45 percent of the second-graders in the norming population (or, conversely, lower than 55 percent of the norm group).

An advantage of percentile scores not shared by grade equivalency scores is that they can be directly compared across subtests or entire tests. A percentile score of 45 is interpreted the same way whether it is from a standardized word indentification test, a comprehension test, an IQ test, or a reading readiness test—in all cases, the student scored as well as or better than 45 percent of the students in the norm group. It is appropriate to state, therefore, that Michael is better in word identification than reading comprehension if his percentile scores are 60 and 45, respectively.

One limitation of percentile scores, however, is that the relationship between the percentile units and the corresponding raw score points is not constant. For example, in Figure 10.2, the difference between the percentiles of 50 and 60 corresponds to about 1.5 raw score points, whereas the difference between the 80th and 90th percentiles represents about 3 raw score points and the difference between the 89th and 99th percentiles corresponds to about 6 raw score points. Percentiles are systematically unequal; they "bunch up" in the middle and "spread out" at the extremes. This occurrence must be considered when interpreting percentile scores. If one student's percentile scores for a reading vocabulary and reading comprehension subtest were 50 and 58, respectively, the teacher might infer that the student was slightly better in comprehension than in vocabulary. However, if a second student's percentile scores were 90 and 98 for the same subtests, the second 8-point percentile difference should be viewed as being more impressive, since it would correspond to a greater raw-score difference.

A second potential limitation of percentile scores is the fact that they can give a false impression of precision. If a student's fourth-grade reading comprehension percentile score were 57 and his fifth-grade score 53, a teacher or parent might be concerned that this student's comprehension ability has diminished. All achievement tests, however, have some built-in error, which is formally referred to as the *standard error of measurement*. A 4-point percentile difference, in most instances, therefore, would not indicate an educationally significant difference. In fact, many standardized, norm-referenced tests report percentile bands. A *percentile band* takes into account this error factor and indicates a range of percentile scores. If a reading test reported percentiles as percentile bands, a range of scores would be indicated, for example 48 to 55, and such a student's "true" score would fall somewhere between the 48th and 55th percentiles.

## STANINE SCORES

A stanine is a form of *standard score*. All standard scores (e.g., stanines, Z scores, T scores, IQ scores, college board scores), like percentiles, are based on norm groups for specific age or grade levels; that is, comparisons are made only to students of the same age or grade. A stanine, in fact, is a form of converted percentile in which the tendency to "bunch up" in the middle and "spread out" at the extremes is eliminated. This is accomplished through the use of a standard measure of spread (the standard deviation; hence, the term "standard" score) on which increments are based.

The stanine is the most commonly reported standard score for reading achievement tests. The word *stanine* comes from "standard nine-point scale." Thus, stanines are single digits that range from 1 to 9. The middle stanine is 5, and it brackets the 50th percentile. Stanines 6, 7, 8, and 9 indicate increasingly better performance, and stanines 4, 3, 2, and 1 represent decreasing performance.

Figure 10.3 shows the same raw-score distribution as Figure 10.2, but here the units are stanines. Note that, with the exception of the first and ninth stanines, all stanines are the same width—about 2.5 raw score points in this example. (Technically, each stanine is one half a standard deviation in width.) Thus, unlike differences between percentiles, differences between stanines have the same meaning (in terms of raw score points) regardless of their position on the scale. Because raw scores and stanines are equated, however, one finds different percentages of scores within each stanine. For example, a full 20 percent of the scores falls within the fifth stanine, but only 7 percent of the scores falls within either the second or eighth stanines. Thus, for a "typical" class of students, one could expect about 50 percent of the students to achieve stanine scores of 4, 5, and 6, and one could expect the other half of the students to be roughly equally divided between the bottom three and top three stanines.

Using stanine scores has several advantages. They are easily interpretable, since each is only a single digit; they can be directly compared across tests and subtests (like percentiles); and they are evenly "spread-out" with respect to raw scores. A potential disadvantage of stanines is that they are rather gross measures. If a student obtained a fifth-stanine score on a vocabulary subtest, her exact percentile score could range from 40

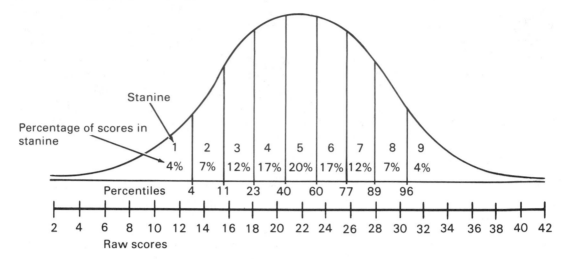

Figure 10.3. The construction of stanine norms.

to 60, a rather large range. So, although stanines do not give a false impression of precision as percentiles do, they may mask some information, because there are only nine different scores that can be achieved.

## SUMMARY

The purpose of this chapter was to describe how the three scores most commonly obtained from standardized, norm-referenced reading achievement tests are derived and to explain their proper interpretation. Each of the scores discussed—grade equivalency, percentile, and stanine—has strengths, and each has limitations. Of the three scores, probably either percentile or stanine scores are most useful to teachers. Either of these scores can be used effectively to make educational decisions concerning the student's reading program. Grade equivalency scores must be used with caution. Although these scores can be informative and useful when they are understood and used properly, they offer little advantage over the more flexible percentile and stanine scores. In addition, because grade equivalency scores are so susceptible to misinterpretation and misunderstanding, the classroom teacher is better off disregarding them totally.[4]

Understand, however, that a proper understanding and interpretation of standardized test scores does not guarantee appropriate use of the tests themselves. Many other

[4]In fact, the major professional organization of reading educators, the International Reading Association, has recommended that the use of grade equivalency scores be discontinued for these same reasons. In April 1982, the IRA Delegates Assembly adopted the following resolution:

RESOLVED, that the International Reading Association strongly advocates that those who administer standardized tests abandon the practice of using grade equivalents to report performance of either individuals or groups of test-takers, and be it further

RESOLVED, that the president or executive director of the Association write to test publishers urging them to eliminate grade equivalents from their tests.

concerns beyond proper score interpretation are related to the use of norm-referenced tests. One such concern is that the results of survey, standardized achievement tests cannot, and should not, be used to diagnose a student's specific instructional needs. For example, if a fifth-grade student performed very poorly (ninth percentile, second stanine) on the reading comprehension subtest of a survey achievement test, a teacher would be unable to make specific diagnostic analyses. All the test score indicates is that this student did poorly when compared to his peers. The teacher cannot determine from the test score which specific comprehension skills are weak—literal comprehension, inferential comprehension, main-idea comprehension, sequence, and so forth.

How can the classroom teacher make appropriate use of survey, standardized reading tests? Since these tests only supply information about students' general levels of achievement in reading, only preliminary screening decisions are justified. Some examples include decisions that involve identifying students for further, in-depth diagnostic evaluation. Refer to Chapter 11 of this text for a complete description of a procedure that can be employed to get the most (and appropriate) use of results from these tests.

Other areas of concern about standardized, norm-referenced reading achievement tests involve issues such as content validity (does the test measure what is being taught?); construct validity (does the test measure what it says it measures?); clarity of directions for both students and teachers; potential problems with racial, sexual, and cultural biases; and technical concerns such as the representativeness of students in the norming population, the recency of norms (are they current?), and test reliability. These issues need not be of concern to the classroom teacher; however, a teacher serving on a school district test-selection committee would need further knowledge in these areas. Refer to the Recommended Readings at the end of this chapter for sources that contain information.

In conclusion, there is nothing mystical about test scores from standardized, norm-referenced tests. Each score provides a limited but potentially useful bit of information about a student's test performance and reading achievement. With a proper understanding of the appropriate interpretation and use of each test score, the classroom teacher can intelligently evaluate her students' performance and make sensible instructional decisions. In the hands of the uninformed, however, these same test scores can be misunderstood and abused.

## ANSWER KEY

1. A norm-referenced test is an instrument that compares an individual's performance to that of a larger group of persons who previously took the test. Thus, a norm-referenced test enables one to determine whether a person's performance is "average," "above average," or "below average" with respect to the larger (norm) group.

2. A percentile score of 88 means that the person who achieved this score performed as well as or better than 88 percent of the persons within the norming population for that test. Alternately, it means that only 12 percent of the persons in the norm group outperformed this person on the test.

3. A score of 3.8 means that this student performed as well on this test as did the

average third-grade student who completed eight months of third grade.

4. A stanine score of 9 is higher, because the 9th stanine corresponds to the 96th percentile and above.

5. Not necessarily so. Because of the manner in which grade equivalency scores are constructed, comparisons across different tests and subtests are technically not permissible. Thus, it may be that a grade equivalency score of 4.4 in comprehension actually represents a level of achievement greater than that indicated by a grade equivalency score of 4.8 in vocabulary.

6. Again, not necessarily so. All tests have some built-in error, which is referred to as the standard error of measurement. Thus, a 3-point percentile difference may be within this margin of error and may not represent an educationally significant difference.

7. The grade equivalency score of 5.8 indicates a high level of reading achievement, but it does not necessarily mean that this student is "reading at the fifth-grade level." This score is based on a third-grade test, which primarily assesses third-grade reading material. The 5.8 score indicates that this third-grade student performed as well as one would expect a student at the end of fifth grade to perform. Since this conclusion is based on a third-grade test, however, it is inaccurate to assume that this student would automatically be able to read at a fifth-grade level and compete with fifth-grade students.

## REFERENCES

*California achievement test.* Monterey, Calif.: CTB/McGraw-Hill, 1977.
*Durrell analysis of reading difficulty: Revised.* New York: Psychological Corporation, 1980.
*Iowa tests of basic skills.* Boston: Houghton Mifflin, 1973.
*Metropolitan achievement test.* New York: Psychological Corporation, 1978.
*Spache diagnostic reading scales.* Monterey, Calif.: CTB/McGraw-Hill, 1972.
*Stanford achievement test.* New York: Psychological Corporation, 1978.
*Stanford diagnostic reading test.* New York: Psychological Corporation, 1976.

## RECOMMENDED READINGS

Blanton, W. E., Farr, R., and Tuinman, J. J. (Eds.) *Measuring reading performance.* Newark, Del.: International Reading Association, 1974.
This volume includes a discussion of issues related to reading tests.
Farr, R. *Reading: What can be measured?* Newark, Del.: International Reading Association, 1969.
A number of published standardized reading tests are described and evaluated.
Mehrens, W. A., and Lehmann, I. J. *Measurement and evaluation in education and psychology.* New York: Holt, Rinehart and Winston, 1973.
This text covers the use of measurement and evaluation in the areas of education and psychology.
Schreiner, R. (Ed.) *Reading tests and teachers: A practical guide.* Newark, Del.: International Reading Association, 1979.
Issues related to reading tests are discussed.
*Standards for educational and psychological tests.* Washington, D.C.: American Psychological Association, 1974.
This reference book is a comprehensive and technical analysis of selecting and constructing educational or psychological tests.

Stanley, J. C., and Hopkins, K. D. *Educational and psychological measurement and evaluation.* Englewood Cliffs, N.J.: Prentice-Hall, 1972.

As the title implies, this is a textbook on measurement and evaluation in education and psychology.

Thorndike, R. L., and Hagen, E. *Measurement and evaluation in psychology and education.* (4th ed.) New York: John Wiley and Sons, 1977.

This is still another textbook on the topic of measurement and evaluation as pertinent to psychology and education.

# CHAPTER 11

# Using Standardized Reading Test Scores to Make Instructional Decisions

Jennifer A. Stevenson
Scott, Foresman and Company
Glenview, Illinois

James F. Baumann
Purdue University
West Lafayette, Indiana

*Chapter 10 presented a thorough discussion of how to interpret scores obtained from standardized, norm-referenced reading tests. A knowledge of proper score interpretation is necessary for test information to be used wisely. Unfortunately, this knowledge does not guarantee that the test data will be used correctly, that is, that an appropriate instructional decision will be made. Too frequently, results from standardized reading tests are filed away in students' cumulative folders and never contribute to instructional decision making; or more seriously, the information the results convey is misunderstood and incorrect instructional decisions are made. In this chapter, Jennifer Stevenson and James Baumann describe a procedure whereby test score data from group, standardized reading achievement tests can be used by the classroom teacher. Given the understanding that survey reading tests provide only global, comparative information about students' reading performance, the procedure Stevenson and Baumann present enables a teacher to examine test scores in relation to other pieces of information about each student and to make preliminary screening decisions about placing students in reading groups and instructional materials.*

Why do schools teach reading?[1] Why do schools test reading? Why should one talk about the testing and teaching of reading together? The major purpose of reading instruction is to help students to develop those skills and abilities that will enable them to become competent readers. In order to determine whether instruction and learning are proceeding well, teachers and schools must periodically assess reading progress. Assess-

---

[1]Portions of this chapter were adapted from the article "Using scores from standardized reading achievement tests," by James F. Baumann and Jennifer A. Stevenson, which appeared in *The Reading Teacher*, 1982, **35**, 528–532.

ment of students' reading progress provides information about whether the current instructional program should be continued as it is or whether it should be changed. That is, if students are doing well, then the present method of instruction and the materials that are being used are probably doing the job; if students are not doing well, then perhaps other methods and materials ought to be considered. In other words, the purpose of testing is to gain information about teaching and learning; the purpose of assessment is to lead to instructional decisions. In fact, as Pearson and Johnson (1978, p. 200) have stated, "If testing does not lead to decision making, it has served no purpose."

There are a number of ways in which teachers can assess reading progress. They can informally note individual students' daily work in the regular classroom situation; they can administer individual or group informal reading inventories; they can give teacher-made or commercial criterion-referenced tests; they can administer individual or group standardized diagnostic or survey reading achievement tests. Each of these kinds of assessment provides different information about reading progress, but no matter what kind of assessment device is used, several points should be kept in mind. First, if tests are to be given, it is important that the resulting information be used and not simply filed away. Second, if the information is to be properly used, it is important that teachers understand the correct interpretation of the scores from each particular kind of test. Third, all available assessment information ought to be considered concurrently; that is, instructional decisions should be based on a knowledge of student behavior in a variety of reading situations rather than on just one—possibly isolated and atypical—instance.

The purpose of this chapter is to describe a procedure that considers the three points above and uses the information obtained from one kind of assessment: a group, standardized survey reading achievement test. This procedure allows a teacher to examine scores from survey reading achievement tests and to use the scores appropriately to make decisions about a reading program for individual students within the classroom.

## SCOPE OF SURVEY, STANDARDIZED READING ACHIEVEMENT TESTS

Survey, standardized reading achievement tests are usually subtests within general educational achievement test batteries. For example, a general standardized achievement test, such as the Iowa Tests of Basic Skills (1978) or the Metropolitan Achievement Test (1978), may include several reading subtests, such as reading comprehension or reading vocabulary. General standardized achievement tests are widely administered in schools today; sometimes the results are considered seriously, and sometimes they are merely recorded and filed away. How can the results of such tests be best used? To answer that question, one must understand the nature, scope, and intent of these survey batteries.

Standardized tests, and the reading subtests within general survey achievement tests, are norm referenced and are, therefore, tests that compare performance among and between individual students and groups of students. The purpose of a norm-referenced test (see Chapter 10) is to provide information about students' performance in relation to the performance of other students of like age or grade. (The purpose is not, as with a criterion-referenced test, to compare students' performance against an established standard or criterion.) These standardized comparisons of students' reading achievement are generally most interesting to administrators (and parents, when the results are to be printed in the local newspaper) who wish to determine how achievement within or between particular classes, schools, or districts compares to national norms.

A second point important to an understanding of survey achievement tests is that individual students' scores indicate only a global measure of achievement; in other words, the scores do *not* provide diagnostic information about specific strengths and weaknesses. Survey tests are meant to be just that—brief surveys of achievement. Thus, the scope of such tests is limited, since the content included in the test for each instructional area is merely sampled, not comprehensively tested. For example, a student's score on a reading comprehension subtest provides information about that student's general level of reading achievement, but it provides no information about specific skills, such as literal or inferential comprehension, main idea–detail comprehension, or comprehension of sequence or causal relationships. Diagnostic information about students' achievement in such subskill areas could be obtained only from tests that contained many more items per skill. Survey tests, however, are not designed to provide such detailed information, and therefore, teachers should not attempt to find diagnostic information within these scores.

A third consideration important to understanding standardized tests is the correct interpretation of the scores. At least three kinds of scores are usually included in the results of such tests: grade equivalency scores, percentile scores, and stanine scores. Unfortunately, these scores are frequently misunderstood. Chapter 10 includes a full description of the manner in which these scores are constructed and of how they should be interpreted. We will assume that you have read the previous chapter and understand the proper interpretation of these scores. For the procedure that follows, we recommend that you ignore grade equivalency scores and focus instead on either percentile or stanine scores, because both percentile and stanine scores are relatively easy to interpret and both are directly comparable across subtests. The latter factor is critical to the use of the procedure we will describe.

## A PROCEDURE FOR THE SENSIBLE
## USE OF STANDARDIZED TEST SCORES

Consider the above discussion of assessment and standardized tests, and then consider how standardized test scores can be appropriately used to make instructional decisions within the classroom. Keep the following points in mind: (1) Standardized tests, which represent only one measure of reading achievement, are widely administered, and the results are readily available to classroom teachers. (2) Standardized test scores are most useful for making comparisons of reading progress among and between individuals or groups of students. (3) When individual scores are examined, they should be considered as a global measure of achievement, since they do not provide diagnostic information about specific strengths and weaknesses. (4) The most straightforward and useful kinds of standardized test scores are percentile or stanine scores. (5) Any one index of reading achievement ought to be considered in conjunction with all other available measures of reading progress so that instructional decisions can be based on a combination of information from a variety of reading situations; it is possible that any one index, taken alone, may provide either incomplete or erroneous information.

Considering these points, we recommend the following procedure. Teachers can justifiably use standardized test scores as one means of making preliminary screening decisions within the classroom. Specifically, two types of decisions are appropriate. Teachers can use these test scores to evaluate students' placement in reading groups and materials, and teachers can use these scores to identify children for further, in-depth diagnostic evaluation.

To use standardized test data sensibly in making either of these decisions, the reading score should be interpreted in concert with at least three other pieces of information about each student: (1) some measure of a student's academic potential (IQ), (2) a student's ability to perform in a group, standardized testing situation, and (3) a student's current placement and progress in the reading program.

Teachers should be aware of the many limitations and abuses of intelligence tests (cf. Houts, 1977). It is helpful, however, to consider a student's potential for reading progress and to relate that estimate to actual progress. Current intelligence (IQ) or aptitude test scores may be useful for making that comparison.

Not all children perform well in a group, standardized testing situation. Some students may not understand the directions, either those written in the test booklet or those given verbally by the teacher. Other students may not understand how to mark a separate answer sheet or how to coordinate the items on the answer sheet with the items in the test booklet. Others may not attend to the task and may fill in the answer sheet randomly, with no attempt to discern the correct responses. Because a variety of such factors can affect test performance, the classroom teacher must observe students during testing in order to identify those who are unable or unwilling to do their best. We recommend that teachers take notes during testing sessions and look through test books after testing to identify students for whom the test results may be invalid. (See Chapter 13 for a complete discussion of test-taking skills.)

A reading test score should be interpreted in relation to how well or poorly a student is performing in class. For example, test information may indicate that a student is performing as well as can be expected or that she needs to be challenged more or that the reading materials are too difficult.

On the basis of such information, teachers can make instructional decisions about students' reading programs and materials. After considering a standardized reading test score in conjunction with these three other kinds of information, a teacher may conclude (1) that a student's present program should be maintained, (2) that it should be altered, or (3) that more information should be gathered before a decision is made.

The following procedure may be used to organize all of the information and then to make an instructional decision. After the standardized achievement test scores have been obtained, the teacher constructs a summary table that includes the reading subtest score(s), an IQ or aptitude test score (if available), an indication of test-taking ability, and information regarding current placement and progress in the classroom reading program. As noted earlier, only percentile or stanine scores (*not* grade equivalency scores) from the reading and IQ tests should be included in this summary table, since only these scores are directly comparable across the two kinds of tests—reading achievement and academic potential.

## AN EXAMPLE

The composite summary chart might look like that shown in Table 11.1, which presents the information for part of a hypothetical third-grade class. Let us assume that

**Table 11.1. Summary Chart for a Hypothetical Third-Grade Class**

| Name | Reading Score | Aptitude Score | Testing Ability | Reading Program Placement | Reading Program Progress | Instructional Decision |
|---|---|---|---|---|---|---|
| José | 53 | 55 | Adequate | Level-3 basal | Sure and steady; a good, average student | Maintain current placement and program |
| Rachel | 98 | 97 | Excellent | Level-4 basal | Extraordinary; the very best reader | Administer an IRI to determine instructional level; develop individualized activities; pursue gifted and talented placement |
| Emily | 25 | 60 | Very poor; did not pay close attention | Level-3 basal | Very good; steady progress | Invalid reading test; maintain current placement; conduct individual reading test |
| Thomas | 35 | 82 | No problems detected | Level-3 basal | Struggling but seems to have the ability | Discuss concern with principal and parents; possible multidisciplinary team evaluation |
| Rita | 48 | 55 | Good | Level-4 basal | Tries hard but is having difficulty | Consider a trial period in the level-3 reader; reading materials may be too difficult |
| Eric | 28 | 33 | Adequate | Level-2 basal | Good; slow but steady progress | Maintain current placement and program; watch carefully |

this particular test battery reported only a single reading test score. If two subtest scores, such as vocabulary and comprehension, are available, those should both be included. The reading scores and aptitude scores in Table 11.1 are reported as percentiles. (If you are unsure of the meaning of percentile scores, review that information in Chapter 10 before examining Table 11.1.) Assume, also, that the teacher has the reading class organized into "low," "middle," and "high" groups who work in second-, third-, and fourth-grade basal readers, respectively. Then, the instructional decision-making procedure for the six students shown in Table 11.1 might proceed as follows.

Consider the array of data for José. Both his reading score and IQ score are within the average range. His teacher detected no problems in José's ability to handle the group-testing situation, and he is making good, steady progress in the third-grade-level reader. As a result, the instructional decision is to maintain his current placement and reading instructional program. Although such a "decision" may not seem to be an instructional decision at all, the information has confirmed that José's reading program is successful and is accommodating his needs.

Rachel's reading test score indicates very high reading achievement (98th percentile), and in light of her apparently high level of aptitude (IQ score at the 97th percentile), this accelerated performance is expected. The classroom teacher recognized Rachel's potential and placed her in an advanced reading group, within which Rachel has distinguished herself as the best student. Yet, in spite of her advanced placement, the test results, along with her current level of performance, suggest that perhaps Rachel is not being challenged enough. The teacher has decided to use an informal reading inventory to determine Rachel's instructional reading level and to involve her in some special individualized reading activities. The teacher may also have Rachel formally evaluated for inclusion in a program for the gifted and talented.

In examining Emily's 25th-percentile reading test score relative to her apparent aptitude (60th percentile), one might jump to the conclusion that Emily has a definite reading problem or perhaps a specific "learning disability." According to the teacher's notes, however, Emily was one of those students who was unable to handle the group-testing situation. For whatever reason, she did not attend to the task but instead made an attractive pattern of dots on the answer sheet. Consequently, her reading test score is invalid and should not be used for decision making. If the teacher were concerned about a possible discrepancy between reading achievement and ability (although Emily's class performance seems consistent with her apparent aptitude), additional, individual testing would be necessary—perhaps with an individual, standardized diagnostic reading test or an informal reading inventory.

Like Emily's scores, Thomas's scores indicate an apparent gap between his reading achievement and his intellectual capacity (35th and 82nd percentiles, respectively). Since he seemed to handle the testing situation adequately, some concern about his current low level of reading achievement may be justified. Before considering Thomas a candidate for a learning disabilities class, however, a further, in-depth evaluation of his reading ability and intelligence should be performed. Individual testing may reveal that the IQ score overestimated his aptitude or that the reading score underestimated his reading achievement or that both measures were invalid. Certainly, here is a student to consider for further evaluation. A formal multidisciplinary team evaluation may be appropriate, especially if similar patterns exist in other academic areas.

Rita's reading and aptitude test scores (48th and 55th percentiles, respectively) are both within the average range, but she is currently placed in the highest reading group. Since she is having difficulty competing with others in this group, the reading test score confirms what the teacher has suspected: Rita is placed in materials too difficult for her. The teacher may decide to confer with the principal, Rita's parents, and Rita herself, and then give Rita a trial period in less difficult reading materials.

Eric's test scores indicate that his progress in reading (28th percentile) is commensurate with his general ability (33rd percentile), and his reading class performance is consistent with this analysis. In effect, Eric's profile differs little from José's, save for Eric's lower level of achievement. Eric's progress should be monitored closely, and he should be given every opportunity to improve his reading ability as much as possible. To become overly anxious or concerned about Eric's "below-grade-level" performance, however, would be unwarranted, for his achievement appears consistent with his ability.

## DISCUSSION

The examples in Table 11.1 represent just a few of the many possible patterns of data and corresponding instructional decisions. In reality, most decisions made for any given class (like the decisions for José and Eric) will confirm that the classroom teacher's estimations of the children's instructional reading levels have been accurate and that he has designed an appropriate reading program. Although this information may not have any direct impact on the reading program for these students, it is valuable, because it gives a teacher assurance that she is providing adequate reading instruction. A teacher may also learn that there are one or two students in the class (like Emily) who do not test well in a group setting. This knowledge, too, is valuable, since it will prevent the misuse of invalid test results, which otherwise might have led to erroneous instructional decisions. Finally, this procedure may help a teacher to identify those students who are in need of further evaluation and of a possible change in their present instructional program.

## A PRACTICE EXERCISE

Now, try this procedure yourself. Consider the explanation and examples of the procedure described above. Then, look at Table 11.2. It presents a partial composite summary chart for six additional students in the hypothetical third-grade class. The table shows a summary of these six students' reading test scores, aptitude test scores, test-taking abilities and current reading program placement and progress. What is not shown in Table 11.2 is the instructional decision made for each student that might result from consideration of the information shown. In order to practice the procedure described above, examine the information shown, make your decision for each student, and then check the answer key at the end of the chapter to note how your decision may correspond to ours or differ from it.

## SUMMARY

This procedure, although far from infallible, is one method of using standardized test data to make instructional decisions within the classroom. The procedure takes account of

**Table 11.2 Partial Summary Chart for a Hypothetical Third-Grade Class**

| Name | Reading Score | Aptitude Score | Testing Ability | Reading Program | | Instructional Decision |
|------|------|------|------|------|------|------|
| | | | | Placement | Progress | |
| Christine | 59 | 57 | Very good | Level-2 basal | Excellent | |
| Nathan | 25 | 50 | Very poor; did not pay close attention | Level-2 basal | Struggling; little effort | |
| Sarah | 55 | 35 | Good concentration | Level-3 basal | Average; steady progress | |
| Robert | 73 | 70 | Excellent | Level-4 basal | Very good | |
| Tina | 35 | 40 | Very poor; did not pay close attention | Level-2 basal | Superior; top of the reading group | |
| Danny | 25 | 35 | Very poor attention | Level-1 basal | Very poor | |

the facts that (1) standardized test data are readily available to the classroom teacher, (2) test data ought to be sensibly used, rather than misused or unused, (3) individual scores on standardized survey tests should be used to make only preliminary screening decisions, and (4) instructional decisions ought to be based on an analysis of information from a variety of assessment indexes. We hope that you will consider using this procedure and that you will find it helpful in your teaching.

## ANSWER KEY

*Christine.* Christine's reading and aptitude scores both indicate that she should be reading at grade level; however, she is presently placed in a below-grade-level basal reader, in which she is making excellent progress. She may be misplaced at the moment. Give her a chance to try a level-3 basal reader, and monitor her progress carefully.

*Nathan.* Nathan's aptitude score indicates that he may be able to do better than he currently is doing within the class. His reading score is low, but he did not attend to the test, and he makes little effort during classroom instruction. Possibly, Nathan's progress is slow because of poor motivation. Consider giving Nathan more individual help and encouragement, either within the classroom or outside the classroom with a reading specialist. For now, maintain his present placement in a level-2 basal reader, but watch for reading improvement as he is given more individualized instruction.

*Sarah.* Almost all of the information in Sarah's chart indicates that her present instructional program is proceeding well. Her aptitude score, however, is somewhat lower than one might expect. Possibly that score is erroneous for some reason, or possibly she tries hard and is doing better than one would predict. In either case, the decision should be to maintain her present program.

*Robert.* All of the information shown in Robert's chart points to one conclusion: He is a bright, motivated, good reader, and his current instructional program is proceeding well. His present reading program should be maintained as it is.

*Tina.* Both of Tina's test scores are below average, and she is presently placed in a below-average level-2 basal reader. She is making superior progress at that level, however, and she may be able to do even better. It appears that her test-taking ability is poor, and it may be that poor attention has affected both test scores so that neither the reading nor the aptitude score is an accurate estimate. More information should be gathered. Consider administering an informal reading inventory to help determine whether Tina is well placed in her present reading program or should be given a trial period in a higher, level-3 basal reader.

*Danny.* All of the information in Danny's chart shows him to be a very poor reader. Considering the severity of this student's reading problem, one should determine whether his needs are being adequately met within a classroom instructional program. If Danny has not been given individualized help with reading and if the services of a specialist or tutor are available, he should be given extra, remedial help outside of the classroom.

## REFERENCES

Houts, P. L. *The myth of measurability.* New York: Hart, 1977.
*Iowa tests of basic skills.* Boston: Houghton Mifflin, 1978.
*Metropolitan achievement test.* New York: Psychological Corporation, 1978.
Pearson, P. D., and Johnson, D. D. *Teaching reading comprehension.* New York: Holt, Rinehart and Winston, 1978.

## RECOMMENDED READINGS

Blanton, W. E., Farr, R., and Tuinman, J. J. (Eds.) *Measuring reading performance.* Newark, Del.: International Reading Association, 1974.
This volume includes a discussion of issues related to reading tests.
Farr, R. *Reading: What can be measured?* Newark, Del.: International Reading Association, 1969.
Issues related to reading tests are discussed.
Farr, R., and Anastasiow, N. *Tests of reading readiness and achievement: A review and evaluation.* Newark, Del.: International Reading Association, 1969.
A number of published standardized reading tests are described and evaluated.
MacGinitie, W. H. (Ed.) *Assessment problems in reading.* Newark, Del.: International Reading Association, 1973.
This volume includes a discussion of issues related to reading tests.
Pikulski, J. P., and Shanahan, T. (Eds.) *Approaches to the informal evaluation of reading.* Newark, Del.: International Reading Association, 1982.
A considerable range of informal procedures for evaluating and diagnosing reading progress is described.
Schell, L. M. (Ed.) *Diagnostic and criterion-referenced reading tests: Review and evaluation.* Newark, Del.: International Reading Association, 1981.
Schell's volume includes a review and an evaluation of a number of published diagnostic and criterion-referenced reading tests.
Schreiner, R. (Ed.) *Reading tests and teachers: A practical guide.* Newark, Del.: International Reading Association, 1979.
Issues related to reading tests are discussed.

# CHAPTER 12

# Using Scattergrams to Organize the Reading Program

Carol J. Hopkins
Purdue University
West Lafayette, Indiana

*Chapter 11 described a procedure that enables a teacher to use standardized reading test score data to make appropriate instructional decisions. In this chapter, Carol Hopkins presents another technique classroom teachers can use when they receive the computer printout list of their students' reading test scores. The procedure Hopkins discusses involves the use of scattergrams, which are graphic comparisons of two sets of test scores. The construction of a reading scattergram involves a simple exercise in coordinate geometry in which a reading achievement test score for each student is plotted against a measure of academic potential—an IQ or a listening comprehension test score. By examining how well a student's current level of achievement (as measured by the reading test score) compares to the estimate of academic potential (IQ or listening comprehension score), a teacher can make some preliminary decisions about the student's ability to perform up to his academic potential. In addition, a teacher can use the array of points on the scattergram to cluster together students of similar achievement and potential for reading instruction.*

Several weeks after administering standardized achievement tests to her class, Ms. Morgan received a computer printout listing her students' scores. Beside each child's name was a series of numbers that included raw scores, grade equivalency scores, percentile ranks, and stanine scores for each of the subtests. Ms. Morgan must then begin to interpret these data, for testing will have served no useful purpose if the students' scores are merely recorded in a cumulative record filed in the school's main office.

On an individual basis, Ms. Morgan can evaluate each student's test scores in relation to her expectations based on each student's potential and daily classroom performance.

Synthesizing this information for all of her students into a single manageable set of data that can be used to make valid instructional decisions about grouping and pacing students or selecting materials may prove to be difficult, since she must keep so many different variables in mind.

The purpose of this chapter is to describe the use of scattergrams, a procedure that can be used to compare simultaneously a group of students' performances on two different measures. On completion of this chapter, the reader should be able to construct and interpret a scattergram.

## WHAT IS A SCATTERGRAM?

A scattergram, sometimes referred to as a scatter diagram or scatterplot, is a graphic comparison of any two sets of scores for a group of students. This plotting of scores illustrates to what extent those students who scored well on one measure also scored well on the other or, conversely, the extent to which students who scored poorly on one measure also scored poorly on the other. By examining a scattergram, we can also determine discrepancies in student performance that result in noticeably higher or lower scores on one of the two measures.

## FEATURES OF A SCATTERGRAM

Let us examine the scattergram in Figure 12.1 to identify the types of information it contains. Notice that the scattergram is constructed on a grid, such as graph paper. In this example, each letter represents an individual student whose placement on the grid is determined by locating his reading comprehension score on the horizontal axis, locating his intelligence test (IQ) score on the vertical axis, and moving along imaginary lines to the point at which the lines intersect. For example, student A scored at the 78th percentile on the reading comprehension subtest and at the 74th percentile on the IQ test. (Refer to the discussion of percentiles in Chapter 10 if you are not sure how to interpret them.) A score at the 50th percentile on the reading comprehension subtest and the 45th percentile on the IQ test resulted in student B's placement on the grid. By studying this sample scattergram, you should be able to determine the reading and IQ percentile scores of the other students in this class.

The horizontal and vertical broken lines crossing the grid represent the class mean (i.e., average score) for each of the measures being plotted. Note that the horizontal broken line represents the mean percentile score for this class of students on the IQ test and that the vertical broken line represents the mean percentile for the same class on the reading comprehension subtest. The locations of individual students can be described by identifying the appropriate quarter, or quadrant, of the grid for each.

## CONSTRUCTING A SCATTERGRAM

To construct a scattergram, you must first decide which scores you want to plot in order to examine their relationship to one another. Scattergrams are most often constructed on the basis of a measure of achievement and a measure of potential for each student in the class. Achievement scores in a given subject area are readily obtained directly from standardized achievement test results. IQ test scores from a standardized

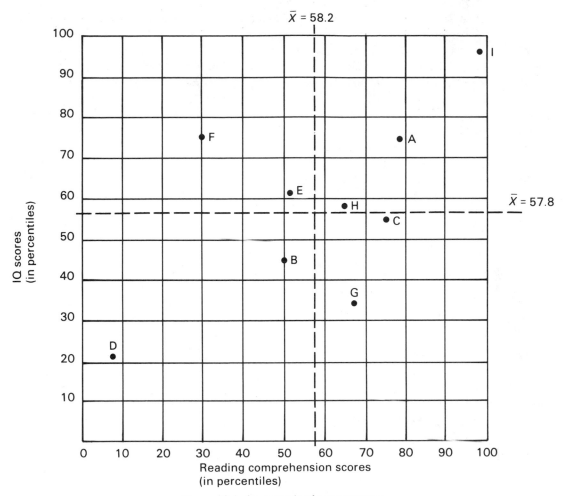

Figure 12.1. An example of a scattergram.

intelligence test or listening comprehension subtest scores from a standardized achievement test can be used as a measure of potential.

In the preceding example (Figure 12.1), IQ scores were used as a measure of academic potential, since they provide an index of what a student is capable of learning. (However, be aware of the limitations and frequent criticisms of intelligence tests; cf. Houts, 1977.) Listening comprehension subtest scores (e.g., the listening comprehension subtest from the Iowa Tests of Basic Skills, 1973) could also be used as a measure of potential, as could general academic aptitude, because they are dependent on verbal ability and comprehension; yet they are independent of the mechanics of reading, since the test is administered orally.

Once the decision about which sets of scores to plot has been made, the form of the scores to be used must be determined. Most test publishers report results in several different forms, including raw scores, grade equivalency scores, stanine scores, and percentile ranks. In making comparisons between two measures on a scattergram, the use of raw scores (the number of items answered correctly on a test) is inappropriate, because not all tests contain the same number of items. Grade equivalency scores are also inappropriate, since the statistical manipulations performed to derive these scores do not lend themselves to comparisons across subtests. Using stanine scores on a scattergram also presents problems because of the wide range of scores represented by each stanine. Thus, the most appropriate scores to use for constructing a scattergram are percentiles, for they permit legitimate and informative comparisons across subtests. (Refer to Chapter 10 for an in-depth discussion of test scores.)

Once the measures to be plotted and the appropriate scores to be used have been decided upon, the next step is to prepare the grid by dividing it into even increments that will allow you to accommodate all scores. Since percentile scores range from 1 to 99, it works best to divide the grid into ten vertical and ten horizontal sections that cover the range from 0 to 100. Each horizontal and vertical box on the grid represents a range of 10 points. (See Figure 12.1.)

Plotting the scores for each student on the prepared grid is an uncomplicated procedure, which is accomplished by locating one of the scores on the horizontal scale, locating the other score on the vertical scale, moving along imaginary horizontal and vertical lines, and placing the student's identification number or letter on the point at which these lines intersect.

The final step in constructing a scattergram is calculating and plotting the class average, or mean, for each set of scores, so that we have a basis for the comparison of reading comprehension and IQ percentile scores when we interpret the scattergram results. The mean is computed by adding all students' scores for each measure and then dividing this total by the number of students taking the test. The class means are indicated by plotting horizontal and vertical broken lines on the grid.

Using the hypothetical sets of percentile scores (Table 12.1) obtained by 24 second-grade students on the reading comprehension subtest of the Stanford Achievement Test (1973) and the Otis-Lennon School Ability Test (1967) (an IQ test), construct a scattergram on the grid provided in Figure 12.2.

## INTERPRETING SCATTERGRAM RESULTS

Just as there is no value in administering tests and doing nothing with the scores but recording them, no benefit can be gained from constructing a scattergram and not interpreting the results. The following discussion is based on the scattergram you constructed from the data in Table 12.1. If you have plotted the scores correctly, your scattergram should look like the one in Figure 12.3.

Earlier in this chapter, it was stated that a scattergram helps one visualize the performance of a group of students in relation to their potential. If all students were performing at a level that closely approximated their potential, parents, teachers, and administrators would be pleased. Discrepancies in student performance do occur and should be noted (especially instances in which achievement is significantly low compared to potential), and steps should be taken to resolve them. On the Figure 12.3 scattergram, if all students were reading up to their measured potential, all points would fall along a diagonal line drawn from the lower-left-hand corner to the upper-right-hand corner of the

### Table 12.1. Data for Constructing a Sample Scattergram

| Student | Reading Comprehension Percentile | IQ Percentile |
|---------|----------------------------------|---------------|
| A | 72 | 87 |
| B | 54 | 59 |
| C | 87 | 78 |
| D | 99 | 99 |
| E | 61 | 62 |
| F | 45 | 81 |
| G | 36 | 31 |
| H | 71 | 76 |
| I | 66 | 42 |
| J | 31 | 79 |
| K | 98 | 96 |
| L | 18 | 67 |
| M | 30 | 26 |
| N | 93 | 84 |
| O | 75 | 70 |
| P | 32 | 37 |
| Q | 96 | 90 |
| R | 51 | 54 |
| S | 63 | 53 |
| T | 19 | 15 |
| U | 70 | 58 |
| V | 28 | 50 |
| W | 79 | 48 |
| X | 40 | 43 |

grid through the intersection of the class means; that is, each student's reading comprehension and IQ percentile scores would be equal or nearly equal. Looking at the grid, we see that, though the points for many students are concentrated on or near this diagonal line, some are not. Because of a factor known as the "standard error of measurement" (defined in Chapter 10), we accept scores located near the line as being close enough to indicate performance commensurate with ability. This area is marked by a diagonal band on the grid encompassing approximately ten percentile points on either side of the diagonal.

### Students Along the Diagonal Line

Let us begin our discussion by looking only at the students whose scores fall within the diagonal band and try to make some decisions about grouping for instruction. All of the students appear to be working up to their potential (i.e., their achievement and potential are consistent with one another). If we were organizing our students within the common framework of a three-reading-group classroom, students T, M, G, X, and P at the lower end of this diagonal band would probably be placed in our low group, perhaps in a 2.1-level basal reader. They are working up to their potential but below the average performance of students in this class. Students in this group might benefit from instruction conducted at a slower pace than that received by the other reading groups. The teacher might also find it

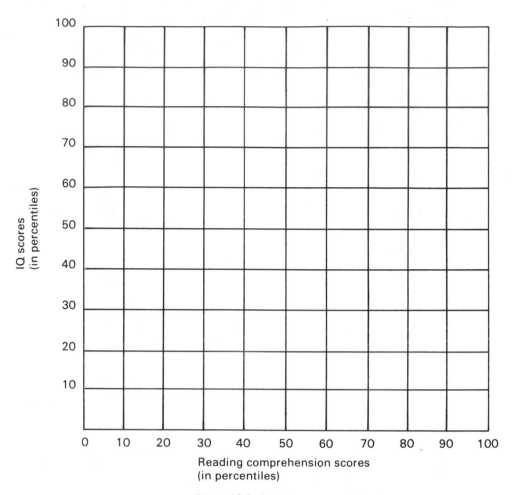

Figure 12.2. A scattergram worksheet.

helpful to use supplemental instructional materials, such as the Specific Skill Series (1976) or the New Practice Readers (1978), to provide additional reinforcement and practice on skills being taught.

Next, let us consider the students we would probably place in the average group in our three-reading-group classroom. On the scattergram, these students' scores are located near the middle of the diagonal band, close to the point at which the class means intersect. In this example, students R, B, E, S, U, O, and H would be placed in this group and might be assigned to a 2.2-level basal reader. Typically, this area of the grid contains the largest concentration of scores. The program for these students is of a developmental nature; they are usually able to assimilate and apply newly introduced reading skills without the need for reteaching or additional practice in supplementary instructional materials.

Students D, Q, N, C, and K, whose scores fall near the top of the diagonal band on the scattergram, would be candidates for the highest reading group, perhaps one using a 3.1-reader, or for an individualized program based on self-selection and self-pacing. The

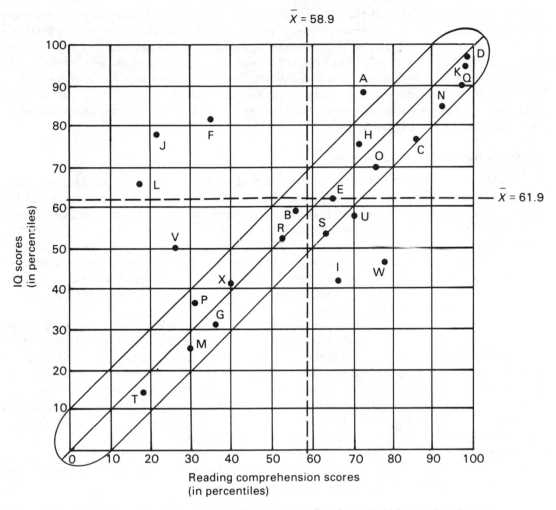

Figure 12.3. A reading comprehension-IQ scattergram for a hypothetical second-grade class.

reading performance of these students surpasses that of the average second-grader in this class. Many of these students have no problem applying decoding skills, comprehend well, and are able to go beyond the instructional materials in the classroom reading series.

Just where the divisions that separate the low, middle, and top groups within the diagonal band should be located is best determined by examining the clusters of scores on the scattergram, by considering the classroom teacher's observations of daily reading performance, and by using any other evaluative information available. Informal reading inventories and students' placement tests that accompany some reading series provide such additional information.

How would the students who fall outside the diagonal band on the scattergram fit into the classroom reading program? Before addressing this issue, I would like to recommend that in cases in which there are large discrepancies in performance and potential you consider the possibility that the student was ill on the test day, that answer sheets were improperly coded, or that the student misunderstood the directions as possible explanations for poor performance. If any of these reasons appears to be the cause of low achievement scores, the test results should be considered invalid, and an appropriate notation should be made in the child's cumulative record. Assuming, however, that there has been no error in scoring the test results for the students on our grid, let us proceed to examining the relationship of these students' potential and achievement for the portions above and below the diagonal line on the scattergram.

## Students Above the Diagonal Line

All students represented on the scattergram above the diagonal have IQ scores higher than their comprehension scores; that is, if you have confidence in the accuracy of the scores, you can assume that these students are "underachievers." Students such as student A are reading well above the average students in the class but could probably be reading even better. Since student A could be placed in the middle or high group, the teacher's observations or insights about why this child is not reaching her expected level of performance should be the deciding factor. Perhaps the problem is one of motivation. Perhaps there is some skill area that needs to be strengthened in order for the child to reach her maximum potential.

Students L, F, V, and J whose scores fall above the diagonal line on the scattergram also exhibit discrepancy between their reading performance and their potential. That is, these students' IQ scores are significantly higher than their corresponding reading comprehension scores. If the comprehension scores are typical of their daily classroom performances, these students may be candidates for corrective or remedial instruction. They may need intensive one-to-one instruction to overcome deficiencies that may be a result of poor teaching, the use of inappropriate instructional materials, or excessive school absences during critical periods of instruction. In a few cases, the possibility of a learning disability might also be considered. The teacher clearly needs to consider a number of factors to arrive at the best instructional placement for these students. Further diagnostic information is likely to be needed to help make these determinations.

## Students Below the Diagonal Line

The final group of students to be considered are those whose scores fall below the diagonal band. For all of these students, their achievement as measured by the standardized test is greater than their measured potential—perhaps an impossible situation, but one sometimes referred to as "overachievement." Again, one of the first questions a teacher must ask himself about these students is whether each child's measured potential seems to be in line with the teacher's daily observations. If the measured potentials of the students seem reasonable, the students' above-average reading performance on this test could be explained by lucky guessing. A more likely explanation of this discrepancy, however, would be that students such as I and W exhibit great perseverance in reading tasks and so are able to eliminate some of the possible answer choices for the test items and to make good guesses on the rest. These children probably are operating at or near their frustration level on the reading achievement test, a situation that results in an overestimate of their reading ability. When making instructional decisions about placement and pacing, the teacher should proceed cautiously. In most cases, placing such students in the lower group, with the option of promoting them to a higher group if their performance warrants it, would be much better than placing them in a higher group, where they might experience unnecessary difficulty and eventually face reassignment to a lower group.

## SUMMARY

Constructing a scattergram is a procedure that can help the teacher to interpret test performance and organize her classroom reading program. It allows the teacher to examine her students' performance in relation to their potential on an individual basis and, more important, as part of an entire class. Scattergrams allow the teacher to examine two sets of scores simultaneously, so that more than one factor can be used to determine student placement. The use of scattergrams should not be the *sole basis* for making instructional decisions, but coupled with daily classroom observations of student performance, it can be used to help the teacher make instructional decisions about the placement of students in reading groups, the pacing of instruction within the groups, and the possible need for additional or alternative instructional materials.

## REFERENCES

Houts, P. L. (Ed.) *The myth of measurability.* New York: Hart, 1977.
*Iowa tests of basic skills.* Boston: Houghton Mifflin, 1973.
*New practice readers.* New York: Webster Division, McGraw-Hill, 1978.
*Otis-Lennon school ability test.* New York: Psychological Corporation, 1967.
*Specific skill series.* Baldwin, N.Y.: Barnell Loft, 1976.
*Stanford achievement test.* New York: Psychological Corporation, 1973.

## RECOMMENDED READINGS

Dechant, E. V. *Diagnosis and remediation of reading disabilities.* Englewood Cliffs, N.J.: Prentice-Hall, 1981, pp. 20–23.
   Scattergram analysis on the basis of reading and IQ scores from a sixth-grade class is discussed in one chapter. An interpretation of the resulting pupil placement is included.
Green, B. F. A primer of testing. *American Psychologist,* 1981 **36**, 1001–1011.
   This discussion of test theory includes basic statistical concepts, principles of test construction and item analysis, and procedures for working with raw test data.
Schreiner, R. (Ed.) *Reading tests and teachers: A practical guide.* Newark, Del.: International Reading Association, 1979.
   Practical discussions of test selection, development of valid and reliable classroom tests, and use of test results as resources for instructional planning are discussed.

# CHAPTER 13

# Preparing Students for Test Performance

Anne Chartrand Hess
State of Alabama Department of Education
Montgomery

*Like Chapters 10, 11, and 12, the final chapter in Part II discusses standardized reading achievement tests. Rather than providing the reader with a description of standardized reading test scores or a procedure for using them, however, this chapter considers the issue of how to prepare students to perform their best on standardized reading achievement tests. The emphasis of this chapter is not to debate the appropriateness or usefulness of standardized testing; Anne Chartrand Hess acknowledges that standardized, norm-referenced, and criterion-referenced tests are here to stay, that the decisions resulting from these tests have a profound influence on students' subsequent education, and that perhaps the best service we can offer children is to prepare them to perform at their highest possible level on these tests. This chapter offers three sets of specific techniques and strategies that beginning teachers can use to help students perform better on standardized reading tests: (1) how teachers can acquaint themselves and their students with tests, (2) how they can directly teach test-taking skills, and (3) how they can adapt instruction to improve students' test-taking performance.*

We have become a test-conscious nation. Legislators, school administrators, parents, and university professors are demanding improved performance in our schools. Virtually every state in our nation is involved in some type of standardized, criterion-referenced, norm-referenced, or competency testing program. Right or wrong, the test results are used to make significant educational decisions about students' competency levels, grades, and graduation from or admission to schools.

Since standardized tests are here to stay and since the decisions that are based on them are often profound, it is only sensible that educators help students to perform their best on these tests. The purpose of this chapter, therefore, is not to deal with the controversial discussion of the merits of testing or the appropriateness of specific tests; its purpose is to provide teachers with practical suggestions and strategies to consider and use in helping students take standardized tests. Too often, we end up testing students on how well they can take a test instead of determining whether they understand the materials and skills being tested. The emphasis in test-taking skills should be on obtaining accurate results so that valid instructional decisions can be made for the students. Within this chapter you will find specific techniques and varied learning activities that can help students perform better on tests. Specifically, three sets of procedures and strategies are discussed: (1) how to acquaint yourself and your students with tests, (2) how to teach test-taking strategies directly, and (3) how to adapt your instruction to improve your students' test-taking performance.

## ACQUAINTING TEACHERS AND STUDENTS WITH TESTS

### Study the Test Manual

Thoroughly acquainting yourself with the test and the examiner's manual *before* testing is one of the most important things you can do to help your students do as well as they can on a test. You must understand the test format and how it is to be administered if you are to eliminate any confusion on the students' part. This sounds like common sense, and it is, but many teachers are rushed before testing and assume that they can simply read the manual as they administer the test. More often than not, however, unprepared teachers end up stumbling with directions and thus confusing students. This situation can hinder a child's performance, especially when she is anxious about taking tests in the first place. Rule number one should be: *Study the examiner's manual* before *testing!*

By becoming thoroughly familiar with the examiner's manual, you can understand how that particular test gives instructions. The instructions you are to read directly to students may have been set in bold print or italics, underlined, or shaded. You may be instructed to "demonstrate" or "hold up student booklet." A prior reading of the manual is the only way to know what to do and what you need to have on hand. By reading the manual, you also become aware of the time required for testing so that you can schedule adequate testing periods. A student should not sense unreasonable pressure because you failed to schedule portions of the test appropriately. Allowing ample time for distribution and collection of materials, setting the tone, and giving directions is also important. Providing enough time for taking tests helps reduce the students' anxiety. Saying "Hurry up, we've got to start this test immediately, we're running late" may be just enough to give a student "test fright."

The examiner's manual provides all the information required when used properly. It lists the materials needed by the examiner and the students. The manual also describes the information to be given to the students about how to correct mistakes, what page numbers to turn to, and what the test is about.

Students should be informed before testing begins about the kind of test they are taking, the time required for testing, the breaks they are allowed, and the rules they must follow. They have a right to know how the test is administered. Will you be reading the directions to them, or will they be expected to read all the directions themselves? You must impress upon them the necessity of following all the directions exactly.

## Be Aware of Different Test Formats

Two different test formats are used in elementary schools: a consumable booklet format or a separate answer sheet format. Because most standardized tests are now machine scored, it is critical that students mark their answers properly. The consumable booklet format is usually used in primary grades. The students are allowed to answer directly on their test booklets, and the booklets themselves are scored. Either the examiner's manual shows an example or the student's booklet demonstrates how the students are to mark their answers. You should find out before testing whether the students should shade in a circle or an oval or fill in the space between two slashes to mark their answers. Are the answer blanks above, below, or beside the answer choices? Unfamiliar answering schemes can be very confusing to primary-grade students.

Beginning in about the third or fourth grade, students are required to use a separate answer sheet. They are given a test booklet that contains the questions and answer choices and another sheet on which they are to mark their answers. This system involves an entirely new skill that can be threatening and confusing. A student who is unaccustomed to answering on a separate sheet may well score lower on the test just because of the unfamiliarity of the format. He may be competent in a skill and still fail to transfer the answer properly. Since so many potential problems arise in having students mark answers for machine-scored standardized tests, we should probably make rule number two: *Give plenty of practice on how to mark answers.*

## Practice Marking Answers

Both the consumable-booklet and separate-answer-sheet formats often provide practice tests. Although these are tremendously helpful, some students require more practice than just those few examples on the day of the test. If you know how a test is to be marked, give your students practice in that exact format several times throughout the year. Then, when it comes time to administer the actual test, your students will not be afraid of the method for answering questions, especially if they must contend with a separate answer sheet.

Think back. Chances are you can remember marking a wrong answer because you were on the wrong line of the answer sheet or because you began marking the bubbles going across the page only to notice a few items later that you should have been going down the page! Erasing frantically is the only recourse, and because of the time limit, you feel anxious throughout the rest of the test. Imagine, then, how an eight- or nine-year-old must feel when she has never seen a machine-scored test booklet or answer sheet before the day of testing.

Do your class a favor. Look at the answer booklet or answer sheet they will be using. Determine how your students will be required to mark the answers. Do the numbers of the items go across the page or down the page?

1. (A) (B) (C) (D)    2. (A) (B) (C) (D)    1. (A) (B) (C) (D)
                                            2. (A) (B) (C) (D)

Will your students have to fill in circles (A), ovals (A), or railroad tracks |A|? How are the answers labeled? Here are a few examples from different tests.

1. Ⓐ Ⓑ Ⓒ Ⓓ    A  B  C  D  is  used  for  every  question.
2. Ⓐ Ⓑ Ⓒ Ⓓ

1. |1| |2| |3| |4|    Numbers are occasionally used and can be confused with the
2. |1| |2| |3| |4|    number of the question.

1. Ⓐ Ⓑ Ⓒ Ⓓ    This sequence is repeated throughout the test.
2. Ⓔ Ⓕ Ⓖ Ⓗ

1. Ⓐ Ⓑ Ⓒ Ⓓ    This is a common format. Notice that the letters E and I are
2. Ⓕ Ⓖ Ⓗ Ⓙ    missing. You may want to point that out to your students,
                 since someone is bound to ask about it.

Some tests vary the number of answer choices from section to section. A student may have to choose the correct answer from options A, B, C, D, then from A, B, C, D, E, and change again to choose from A, B, C. If the number of answer options varies, warn your students. It is also worth your time to point out the option "none of these" or "none" when you know that they will encounter it as a possible choice. To familiarize your students with this option, use these terms as a choice on your own teacher-made tests occasionally.

The answer-sheet format involves another problem. Very often, information about the student must be filled in before testing. Sometimes, the teachers do this themselves. If, however, you require your students to fill in this information, be sure to give them all the assistance they need. It is not unusual for students to become so upset with mistakes that they have made while filling in bubbles showing names and dates that they become apprehensive about the rest of the test. Do everything you can to prepare your students for handling the mechanics of taking the test. Then, they can spend their test time answering the questions rather than contemplating the marking procedure and erasing mistakes.

## TEACHING TEST-TAKING STRATEGIES

### Teach Testing Vocabulary

An important factor in effectively dealing with tests is being familiar with the vocabulary. A student may be a good reader and talented in the skill area a reading test assesses, but if he is not familiar with the terms used in test directions or questions, he may perform poorly on the test. Let us make rule number three, therefore: *Familiarize your students with vocabulary commonly used in test directions.* Familiarity with testing vocabulary also helps them deal with regular classroom worksheets and assignments more independently. Students are famous for having trouble following directions. They need *instruction* and *practice* in this skill.

The following list contains some of the most commonly used words and phrases in reading tests. If students have difficulty either reading or understanding these words, they probably will have trouble answering questions that use these terms and phrases.

| *Direction Terms* | *Reading Skill Terms* | *Answer Selection Terms* |
|---|---|---|
| Mark | Opposite | Different |
| Circle | Opinion | Best |
| Underlined | Fact | Correct |
| Choose | Blends | Right |
| Find | Vowels | Wrong |
| Pick | First | Section |
| Look | Second | Oval |
| Listen | Third | Space |
| Key word | Fourth | None of the above |
| Definition | Last | I don't know |
| Sample | Compound words | All of the above |
| Who | Contraction | The story does not say |
| What | Root word | Go on to the next page |
| Where | Base word | Stop |
| When | Beginning | Wait for directions |
| Why | Ending | |
| How | Synonym | |
| Paragraph | Antonym | |
| Passage | Main idea | |
| Phrase | Same | |

Notice that some of the words and phrases deal with directions. These key words tell the students what they are required to do on certain items or at certain points of the test. Other words have to do with reading skill terminology. The students may be asked to "find the compound word." If, however, they are unfamiliar with the word *compound,* they are likely to answer those items incorrectly even when they understand the concept.

Take time to notice the terminology that is used in any test you will administer. Some confusion may arise when the test asks the students to "choose the base word" if you have been teaching about "root words" all year. Some tests ask about words that "mean the same" or "mean the opposite," while other tests direct the student to find the "synonym" or "antonym." Again, students may possess the relevant skills but respond incorrectly because they are unfamiliar with the terminology used in the test.

Many times students are asked questions about specific sentences or paragraphs that are numbered or lettered. If they have trouble with the concept of first, second, and third or if they do not know how to count paragraphs or sentences, they will have difficulty answering the question.

What are your students asked to fill in: the "space," the "oval," the "bubble," the "circle"? Make sure they are familiar with the particular term that is used. Standardized tests are timed; therefore, time lost in trying to decipher the directions may hinder a child's performance.

You should point out to your students the difference between choosing the "correct" answer and choosing the "best" answer. The term "correct" indicates that there is one somewhat obvious correct answer; asking for the "best" answer indicates a more subtle distinction between correct and incorrect answers. "Best" answer items may have other options that may seem correct, so the student must be careful to decide on the most appropriate one. Especially in the upper elementary grades, students often quickly mark the first option they read that may be correct. Teach them not to jump to conclusions and to consider all options.

Certain phrases that are sometimes used as answer choices have been included on the vocabulary list. "None of the above," "all of the above," and "the story does not say" used as options can make an item more difficult for the student. If a test you are to administer does include this type of question, it is worth your time to acquaint your students with these choices. Once again, warn your students about marking an answer before they have read all of the answer choices.

## Use a Marker

The potential problems in having students mark their answers on a separate sheet have already been discussed. One suggested strategy to help students cope with this problem is to let them use a marker to keep their place on the answer sheet. Just as you should have your students practice answering on a separate sheet many times before the actual test, you also should give them practice using a marker. You may want to pass out pieces of construction paper, approximately one by six inches in size, and to direct your students to keep the marker under the row of answer spaces on which they are working. Index cards could also be used. Accidentally marking the wrong space on the wrong line is easy to do, and the following answer spaces then are also marked incorrectly. Having your students use a marker may prevent errors and increase a student's total score on the test.

## Help With Timing

Most tests are timed as a part of the standardization. You may have experienced momentary panic when a test administrator says "Go" and you hear the clock ticking like a time bomb. It is helpful to have your students become accustomed to being timed *before* they take the test. Hand out a set of instructions and allow the students a certain amount of time to read them. Then, give them a specific number of minutes to complete a problem or a worksheet. You may be surprised to see how well students perform a task when they only have a certain amount of time.

Allow different amounts of time for different tasks. This helps your students get a better idea of the concept of time. Some students have no understanding of the difference between 5 minutes and 30 minutes. Your primary goal should be to help students learn to pace themselves within time frames while you eliminate the tenseness caused by the ticking clock.

## Check Answers

One other suggestion that may help students to improve their scores is to teach students how to check their answers after completing a section of the test. Students are usually instructed to check their work, but very few students take advantage of this advice.

First, students must have experience in *proofreading*. Ask your students at the end of an assignment to take five minutes to find mistakes on their papers. Then, during practice testing sessions, encourage them to check their work after completing the test. They should understand that when they have time left during a testing period, they may go back over the section on which they were working to check their answers. Students should also get in the habit of checking their marks on the answer spaces. Are the spaces filled in appropriately? Are there any stray marks? If time permits, students should learn to sample their answers randomly. They can choose a question, answer it again, and check to make sure they marked the answer in the appropriate space. Occasionally, this second check reveals that a student answered on the wrong line or space. When an error is corrected, the time has been well spent.

## ADAPTING INSTRUCTIONAL ACTIVITIES FOR TEST-TAKING IMPROVEMENT

Sometimes a child is penalized on a test because of the format of the test items themselves. A teacher might consider a student to be reasonably competent in a specific skill only to have test results report "nonmastery." Occasionally, this unexpected poor performance can be attributed to the child's unfamiliarity with the way a skill is tested. She either answers items incorrectly or not at all.

Here is an example of this problem. All year the teacher has worked on consonant blends. She has taught many lessons and administered numerous worksheets. The student was always told to "circle the blend in each word" or to "circle the word next to the picture that has the same beginning sound as the picture." Test day arrives and the student is then told to "mark the oval next to the word that has the same beginning sound as the word I say." This direction thoroughly confuses the child, and she ends up doing very poorly on a skill she actually knows well.

The point is that teachers can get into a habit of teaching, practicing, and checking a skill in one specific way, especially when the teacher uses ready-made worksheets. Then, when the same skill is tested in a different manner, students become confused and may not know how to deal with the format of the item.

This is another reason why teachers should be familiar with the tests they administer. *I am in no way suggesting that you practice actual test items with students,* but it is difficult, and perhaps unfair, for children to be tested auditorally when they have experienced nothing but worksheets with pictures. The idea is to give the students enough *different* activities practicing a skill that they are able to cope with various types of item formats. Rule number four, therefore, is: *Vary classroom skill activities.*

Primary-level reading tests frequently include items that assess phonic and structural analysis. Teachers need to allow their students practice with these skills in many different ways. Then, no matter what a test item requires, they can understand what they are to do.

Figure 13.1 exemplifies several formats for testing initial consonants and blends. If your students are familiar with only one format, they may be unable to cope with other test formats. Rather than just giving one worksheet that practices or checks a skill in only one manner, administer a variety of worksheets that employ several item formats. The more varied practice provided, the more familiar students become with different methods of testing a skill.

Do not forget the auditory testing method. Many tests require students to listen to a word dictated by the examiner and then to mark the word that has the same beginning or ending sound as the word that was spoken. For students to be successful, they must listen

Vary the tasks that the children must perform. Develop worksheets that present a skill in a variety of formats. Vary the difficulty level.

## Format A

Look at the picture. Mark the letter that is missing.

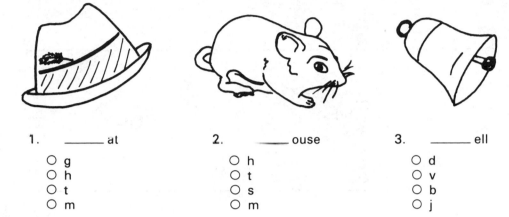

| 1. _____ at | 2. _____ ouse | 3. _____ ell |
|---|---|---|
| ◯ g | ◯ h | ◯ d |
| ◯ h | ◯ t | ◯ v |
| ◯ t | ◯ s | ◯ b |
| ◯ m | ◯ m | ◯ j |

## Format B

1. Underline the beginning sound.

football

2. Fill in the beginning sound.

_____ ootball

Figure 13.1. A variety of formats for testing initial consonants and blends.

## Format C

Fill in the missing letter.

1. _____ ose

- ○ j
- ○ n
- ○ g
- ○ b

2. _____ ookie

- ○ c
- ○ d
- ○ m
- ○ t

## Format D

Mark the letter that will go in the box to make a word.

1. ☐able

- A. b
- B. z
- C. d
- D. t

2. ☐irl

- A. t
- B. g
- C. s
- D. m

## Format E

Mark the *word* on your paper that begins with the same sound as the word I say, "Mat." (Answer choices are given on the children's papers.)

## Format F

Mark the *picture* on your paper that begins with the same sound as the word I say.

## Format G

Circle the blend in each word.

1. flower        2. blue        3. slip

## Format H

Find the group of letters that will go in the box to make a word.

1. ☐ake

- ○ bl
- ○ sn
- ○ sw
- ○ gl

2. sh☐

- ○ ird
- ○ ing
- ○ an
- ○ op

3. ☐ow

- ○ thr
- ○ scr
- ○ skw
- ○ th

## Format I

Fill in the letters to make a word for the picture.

_____ ower

**Figure 13.1** *(continued)*

## Format J

Fill in the space that goes with the word that begins with the same sound as the word I say, "Swing."

(Children's papers should have either the answers to mark on their papers or the letters next to the answers if they are practicing with separate answer sheets.)

| | |
|---|---|
| ○ street | A. street |
| ○ stop | B. stop |
| ○ sweet | C. sweet |
| ○ show | D. show |

## Format K

Underline the blend in each word.

1. flower
2. stop
3. blew

**Figure 13.1** *(continued)*

carefully, and the examiner must speak clearly. If students have had only worksheet experience, the auditory method may cause problems. Practice this technique with your class, also.

A note of caution should be added here. *These suggestions are not meant to condone the overuse of worksheets.* Some worksheets, however, are used in every classroom, and you should look at them, determine whether they serve a useful purpose, and then vary them to provide several different types of experiences.

For the reasons stated above, it is important to get your students accustomed to varied test formats. The following are a few examples of different ways of dealing with a few selected reading skills.

### Compound Words

1. Matching

air     room
base     plane
store     ball

2. Which of the following words is a compound word?

   a. remember
   b. toothpaste
   c. bicycle
   d. selfish

Choose the word that when added to the first word will make another word.

3. <u>foot</u>      toe      shoe      step      let
            ○      ○      ○     ○

## Vowels

Mark the word that has the same vowel sound as the vowel sound in the word I say. (Teacher says "Close.")

1. (A)  cloth
   (B)  slow
   (C)  top
   (D)  cook

Mark the word that has the same vowel sound as the underlined word.

2. <u>cat</u>
    (1) . dark
    (2)  date
    (3)  sad
    (4)  said

Choose the word that has the same vowel sound as the underlined part of the key word.

3. t<u>ur</u>n      tune      s<u>o</u>n      learn      r<u>u</u>n
           ○      ○     ○     ○

## Comprehension

To test comprehension, most reading tests require students to read a story or passage and then answer a series of questions that assess comprehension subskills, such as main idea, details, sequence, cause and effect, conclusions, inference, and the like. You can help your students to answer these questions by getting them in the habit of reading the questions *before* they read the story. When your students understand that they must read a story or passage and then answer questions, train them to skip down and read all the questions before reading the story. This gives them a purpose for reading and makes them focus their comprehension on answering the questions. You should emphasize that they should read the entire passage, however, so that they do not miss important details.

## Vocabulary, Context Clues, Multimeaning Words

Tests that measure reading vocabulary, context clues, and multimeaning words are, in many cases, indistinguishable from one another, for all measure the students' knowledge of word meanings. Nevertheless, word meanings are tested in a variety of ways. A few examples of various ways to practice or assess these skills include the following.

Read the underlined word. A meaning of that word is written beside it. Then read the sentences and choose the one that uses that meaning.

<u>ring</u>:   a band around a finger.
a.   The boxers entered the ring.
b.   Clean the ring out of the bathtub.
c.   Her ring was made of gold.

Choose the correct word to go in the blank.

The barber _____ John's hair with scissors.

○ hit
○ laughed
○ cut
○ grew

Some tests check vocabulary by having the examiner read a sentence aloud while the student chooses the word that completes the sentence. The student sees only four or five word choices. You could practice this activity during reading lessons every now and then. For example, the teacher reads the sentence "You would ask a doctor about a _____" aloud, and the students mark one of the following words on their papers or answer sheets.

1. Disaster
2. Disease
3. Plant
4. Planet

Listening plays an important role in this kind of test. Practice with your students if this format is used in the test administered in your school.

## Language

Separating reading from language is difficult. Often, students must take a language portion of a standardized test after taking the reading section. It is recommended, therefore, that teachers deal with this part of the test in the same manner as the reading test.

Look at the language test for format. There are several ways of testing spelling, for instance. You may be certain that your students know how to spell *butter*, but when they see the word spelled four different ways on the test, they may become confused. Suddenly, more than one spelling looks correct to the students.

○ buttar
○ butter
○ buttur
○ buter

If spelling is to be tested this way, it may help your students to let them become accustomed to having to choose a correctly spelled word from other incorrect spellings. Other examples of spelling activities follow.

Mark the word spelled incorrectly.
The stars are butiful tonight.   None
Which house <u>burnned</u> down?   Right   Wrong
<u>Woud</u> you <u>answer</u> the <u>door</u>?   None   a b c d
   a         b         c         d   ○○○○

Find the word that is misspelled.
1. he doesn't <u>know</u>    3. <u>mail</u> the letter
2. <u>reed</u> the book      4. <u>here</u> it is
① ② ③ ④

One last recommendation that will assist students in all tests, but especially in language tests, is for you to help your students constantly in the practice of *proofreading*. A good part of any language test involves finding an error or reading sentences to determine punctuation and capitalization. Proofreading is involved in spelling portions of the test, also. Unfortunately, very little time is spent instructing students in proofreading skills. Yet, this is the predominant skill required in language mechanics tests.

Have your students practice finding errors in punctuation and spelling. Provide students sentences that have no punctuation or capitalization and require your students to add them. When you find errors in a paper a student has written, write the number of errors you found at the top of the page, and let him go back and find the mistakes.

It is difficult to read a sentence with little letters or circles below it, find the mistake, and then mark it on another answer sheet. For example:

What punctuation is needed?

John pick up the papers, please.

| . | ? | " | , | none |
|---|---|---|---|------|
| a | b | c | d | e    |

Where is the error?

"Go now, John said, "before it's too late."
A     B      C       D

Which part of the sentence needs a capital letter?

Our church / took the senior citizens / on a trip / to ashville.   none
f        g        h     j     k

These are only a few examples of how crucial proofreading is in a standardized test. Students do not actually write sentences or paragraphs, and, therefore, punctuation, capitalization, and spelling must be tested objectively. They must "find errors." Good teaching includes instruction in proofreading. Such instruction assists not only test skills but classroom assignments as well.

## SUMMARY

*It must be emphasized again that this chapter in no way suggests teaching actual test items.* It does suggest, however, that students have a right to be comfortable with formats so that test results provide valid information about students' knowledge of skills. An enormous amount of money is spent each year in the United States on administering standardized tests. Yet, very little is done to assist teachers in helping their students become test-wise, although test-wise-ness is a variable that can indeed influence test scores.

There are several general techniques that can help a student take tests. One is to encourage a positive attitude. The students and their parents should be aware of the why, when, and what of all testing. Eliminating or reducing anxiety *before* the test pays off *during* the test. The environment should be as comfortable as possible during testing. Appropriate seating arrangements, good ventilation, and a sign on the door should all be taken care of prior to testing.

One primary purpose for administering reading and language tests in the elementary grades is to provide teachers with information on which to base sound instructional decisions. We truly want to know in which areas students need assistance. For this reason, we want the test results to be as accurate and revealing as possible. The four rules presented in this chapter can help provide such information and avoid penalizing unnecessarily the student who has not had much experience in taking standardized tests.

Remember to (1) study the examiner's manual *before* testing, (2) give plenty of practice on how to mark answers (especially on separate sheets), (3) familiarize your students with vocabulary commonly used in test directions, and (4) vary classroom activities to accommodate many methods of practicing and assessing skills.

Helping your students with timing, self-pacing, checking answers, and carefully following directions all should be incorporated into everyday classroom activities. Everything possible should be done to help students to perform as well as they can on a test. The goal is not to overdose on test taking but to make the inevitable test taking as fair as possible to all students.

## RECOMMENDED READINGS

Relatively little has been written on the subject of preparing students for test performance, especially students at the elementary level. The following is a list of books and articles that deal with the subject of test-wise-ness. Some of them are geared toward older students, but the general information is valuable to all teachers helping students with testing situations.

### Books

Alford, R. L. *Tips on testing: Strategies for test taking.* Washington, D.C.: University Press of America, 1979.

Dobbin, J. E. *How to take a test.* Princeton, N.J.: Educational Testing Service, 1981.

Feder, B. *The complete guide to taking tests.* Englewood Cliffs, N.J.: Prentice-Hall, 1979.

Gifford, C. S., and Fluitt, J. L. *Test-taking made easier.* Danville, Ill.: Interstate Printers and Publishers, 1981.

Millman, J., and Pauk, W. *How to take tests.* New York: McGraw-Hill, 1969.

Smith, C., and Elliot, P. *How to improve your score on reading competency tests.* New York: Macmillan, 1981.

### Articles

Downey, G. W. Is it time we started teaching children how to take tests? *The American School Board Journal,* 1977, **164**(1), 27–31.

Fluitt, J. L., and Gifford, C. S. Who's teaching teachers how to teach test-wiseness? *Contemporary Education,* 1980, **51**(3), 152–154.

Gifford, C. S., and Fluitt, J. L. Test-taking skills and test-wiseness. *The Clearing House,* 1978, **52**(2), 53–55.

Gifford, C. S., and Fluitt, J. L. How to make your students test-wise. *The American School Board Journal,* 1980, **167**(10), 29, 40.

Gifford, C. S., and Gifford, J. W. Teaching test-wiseness to insure fair test results. *Wisconsin State Reading Association Journal,* 1980, **25**(1), 4–6.

Weaver, G. C. Teaching children how to take standardized tests. *Measurement and Evaluation in Guidance,* 1979, **12**(2), 121–124.

## RESOURCES

The following resources are designed for classroom use in preparing for testing. Their format should be examined by the teacher to determine whether it is relevant to the testing program used by the school.

### Slide-Cassettes

Educational Testing Service, *A Little Anxiety: Test-Taking Skills.*

### Spirit Masters (Grade Levels)

Instructo and McGraw-Hill, *Building Test-Taking Skills in Language Arts.*

### Spirit Masters and Teacher's Guides with Activities (Correlated to Various Test Series— CTBS, CAT, MAT, SRA, STEP, and others)

Educational Solutions, *Mini-Tests.*

### Spirit Masters and Transparencies

Scholastic Book Services, *Scope Visuals 25: Improving Test Scores.*

### Teaching Kits (Grades Two Through Five)

Arista, *Test-Taking and Relaxing.* (Filmstrip, cassette, teacher's handbook, activity books.)

### Test Booklet Format

Random House, *Scoring High in Reading.*

# PART III

# Organizing and Managing a Reading Program:
## Some Plans That Work

*Part III is concerned with organizing and managing a reading program, an area of great interest and concern for beginning teachers. Chapters 14 and 15 deal with basal readers: Chapter 14 presents three grouping plans for basal reader instruction, and Chapter 15 provides suggestions to help beginning teachers administer effective skill instruction when using basal readers. A detailed account of how to develop and implement an individualized reading program is presented in Chapter 16. The complex problem of managing a classroom reading program is addressed in Chapter 17, and suggestions to help beginning teachers to organize their time and reading materials and to control and discipline children are also included. Chapter 18 provides beginning teachers with many ideas about dealing with poor readers in the regular classroom: how to adapt basal reader instruction for them and how to help them read and learn from content area textbooks. Chapter 19 concludes Part III with information about the use of microcomputers in reading instruction: what they are, what their advantages and limitations are, and what factors should be considered in evaluating and selecting computer software and hardware.*

# CHAPTER 14

# Grouping Plans for Basal Reader Instruction

John W. Miller
Wichita State University
Wichita, Kansas

*Basal readers have been regularly criticized on a number of counts. For example: they contain boring, un–true-to-life content; they promote the use of rigid grouping and tracking; they require children to complete all accompanying skill and workbook pages; they further stereotypes of sexes, races, age-groups, and handicapped persons; they contain unnatural sentence patterns; they do not actually teach reading skills; they do not provide for different learning styles. This much-maligned instructional tool, however, pervades reading instruction, for the majority of elementary teachers and students use basal readers in some fashion. When one analyzes the common criticisms of basal readers, it becomes apparent that most of the professed shortcomings are not limitations of the materials themselves but of the manner in which they are used. In this chapter, John Miller addresses one of the greatest problems facing a beginning teacher who uses basal readers—how to organize basal groups. Miller argues that grouping students for basal reading instruction, though not without potential problems, is sensible, efficient, and effective, especially for beginning teachers. He then describes three different ways in which students can be grouped for basal instruction: ability-level, skill development, and interest groups. In addition to detailed explanations for forming these groups, Miller provides a case study that affords the reader an opportunity to examine information about a class of children and then form ability-level, skill development, and interest basal groups.*

The purpose of this chapter is to familiarize the beginning teacher with different grouping procedures that can be used for basal reading instruction. Specifically, the rationale, advantages, and disadvantages for using ability-level groups, skill development groups, and interest groups will be discussed. After you have gained a background in these three grouping techniques and some understanding about the way these groups are formed, you will participate in a case study simulation. In this exercise, you will examine data from a class and work through different problems in grouping the class in different ways.

## OF BASEBALL AND BASAL READERS: AN ALLEGORY

The problems confronting a teacher using a grouping plan for reading instruction are similar to these problems encountered by a professional baseball team in the acquisition and development of new players. When a baseball team signs a contract with a new player, the team has high expectations for the player. The team manager expects that the player will someday be a highly productive "star." The player also holds high expectations, although in practice both the team manager and the player recognize that not everyone will become a major league star. At the onset, however, expectations are high for all players.

Rarely does one of the players start on the major league team and instantly become a superstar. Instead, players go through a development and training process that improves their skills so that they become more proficient. To promote growth in their players' baseball skills, management assigns players to different levels for competition and instruction. Remember that the expectations on both the part of the players and the team are uniformly high for all players, but the team management recognizes that players who have been signed to contracts have different levels of skills. Some players are better than others when they are signed. This does *not* mean, however, that certain players will always be better than others; rather, it merely means that, when players begin their professional baseball careers, they have different ability levels.

Why do these differences exist? There are many reasons. Some players may have received large amounts of training when they were young through participation in formal programs (e.g., Little League) or because their parents had particular expertise and were willing to work with them. They may differ because of various physical attributes. Some players may simply be bigger or stronger or faster than others. They may be different because of their willingness to work; that is, some players have greater abilities because they practice more. All of these factors, and many others, contribute to the various levels of *entry behavior*. Nevertheless, expectations for improvement in all players exist.

Because of these differences in levels of entry behavior, the players benefit from differerent types of instruction and from playing against players at roughly their own ability level. To account for this situation, the professional baseball team has a number of different levels of competition to which they can assign players. Some new players who need a large amount of training may be assigned initially to a rookie-league team for which the instructional component is basic. Other players who are slightly more sophisticated in their skills and abilities may be assigned to what is known as the lower minor leagues: an intermediate level of competition. Other players who have achieved a high degree of sophistication prior to signing their contracts may be assigned to the high-level minor leagues. Occasionally, a player may be assigned directly to the major league roster. In any event, these placements are based on careful scouting reports developed prior to the player's signing with the team and on observations made during spring training.

Even with all these sophisticated analyses of players' talents, some players may be misplaced. Some may be placed too high in the system, where they become discouraged because they are unable to compete with other players on an equal basis. Hence, they begin to question their own ability. The instruction available to them is often at too high a level of sophistication. They need more basic development of their skills. Other players may be misplaced by being located too low in the system. They also become discouraged. They feel that they are not making rapid enough progress. They see that they are more talented than their teammates and wonder why they have been placed in a lower league. They often become discontented and cause trouble. The instruction that they receive is inadequate for their level of sophistication. They need to work on polishing more-advanced skills rather than the ones taught in the lower leagues.

## WHY GROUP STUDENTS FOR READING INSTRUCTION?

The grouping and placement issues in the development of baseball players are similar to the problems encountered in the development of competent readers. A teacher confronted by a new group of students at the beginning of a school year has high expectations for all students. Nevertheless, he should recognize that his students are bound to display different entry behaviors in reading.

Why do students' reading ability levels vary? Some have received extensive practice at home with parents who have spent time reading to them or listening to them read. Other students simply have higher cognitive skills and are more adept at the intellectual processes involved in reading. Other students put forth more effort to learn to read and thus become better readers. For these reasons, and many others, differences in students' abilities always exist.

Because of their differences, students benefit from various types of instruction and benefit from being placed in groups of children with roughly equal needs. Teachers, at the beginning of the year, try to assess their students' reading ability levels, skill needs, and areas of interest in order to assign them properly to instructional groups. Utilizing a number of different assessment devices, including formal and informal tests, observations, and previous teachers' experiences (see Part II), the teacher makes these decisions.

Inevitably, nevertheless, some students are incorrectly placed. Some are overplaced, or put into groups in which the material is too challenging. Often, such students become discouraged, because the material is too difficult (Arnold and Sherry, 1975). The instructional level is more sophisticated than their current level of reading performance. Underplacement, or putting students of higher ability levels into groups working with lower difficulty materials, can also cause discouragement and boredom and result in a lack of appropriate instruction (Rubin, 1975).

Natural differences exist among the abilities of readers as they do among the talents of baseball players. Teachers try to recognize these differences, identify the differences accurately, and then place students for instruction in groups that best accommodate the students' needs. Grouping for reading instruction using basal readers is a form of planning used by the teacher prior to instruction (Barr, 1975). The planning is done with two basic purposes in mind. First, grouping for basal reader instruction narrows the range of reading abilities within a group of students. In other words, it reduces the differences among members within a group so that the teacher can more efficiently and effectively manage instruction. Second, grouping allows students to maintain longer periods of sustained effort, because they work in a smaller group setting with students who have similar needs.

## DIFFERENT KINDS OF READING GROUPS

Children entering school are characterized by a wide range of abilities. As educators begin to prepare students for reading instruction through reading readiness programs in kindergarten, these differences begin to emerge. As students enter first grade and begin formal reading instruction, these differences become more apparent and begin to grow. As students develop throughout first grade and the remaining elementary school years, the range of reading abilities increases further. In addition, students develop different strengths and weaknesses in specific reading skills, and they develop many various interests. In other words, students become more divergent in their general reading ability levels, their specific skill needs, and their reading interests.

Since students differ in these three ways—in ability, skill, and interest—three different methods of grouping students for instruction in basal readers are possible. They can be grouped according to (1) general reading ability level, (2) specific reading skills, or (3) special reading interests. The purpose of grouping students for instruction is to place students together on the basis of common needs. Teachers who plan to arrange groups according to general reading ability, therefore, should narrow the range of reading levels in any one group. Teachers who wish to instruct in skill-need groups should narrow the range of skill needs in any one group, and teachers who want to teach on the basis of the interests of students should narrow the types and range of interest within any one group. The next three sections describe how to form, organize, and teach ability-level, skill development, and interest reading groups.

### Ability-Level Groups

Grouping students according to their general reading ability level is far and away the most common form of grouping used for basal reader instruction in classrooms. This is true for a number of reasons, but mainly because basal reader programs themselves are organized into books that are created for specific reading ability levels. Most basal reader programs include 13 or 14 different difficulty levels (i.e., readability levels, "grade" levels) of material organized for students from kindergarten through the eighth grade. Generally, the reading readiness program is one level and the first grade is comprised of five or six levels that include the preprimers, primers, and first reader. The second and third grades include two levels each, and the fourth through eighth grades usually each have a single basal textbook. After determining the instructional reading level of all students in a class, a teacher can group students according to their reading ability levels and assign each group materials from the corresponding level of the basal reader program.

Typically, classroom teachers have found that three or four groups seem to be optimal for classroom instruction. Having fewer than three groups makes it difficult to match the appropriate difficulty level of basal reader to the students. For example, in a classroom in which all students are taught at one ability level, too many students would be working on materials that are either too easy or too difficult for them to profit from the instruction. In classrooms where more than four different ability-level groups are formed, the teachers' time for direct instruction is often so limited that she is unable to provide enough direct instruction for each group (Brophy and Evertson, 1976). Most teachers seem to find that using three or four ability groups is reasonably manageable. If there were considerably more than three different ability clusters of students within a classroom, the teacher would reconsider and examine how a wider range of differences and abilities could be accommodated in the grouping procedure.

One question you should be asking yourself at this point is how we assess the ability level of students to place them into these various ability-level groups. The best assessment is done through using a wide range of collected information in combination with one's own judgment to formulate grouping patterns. Some of the data that should be considered in making decisions on grouping come from standardized tests, end-of-level tests available from the basal reader's publisher, previous teachers' grade-level placements, informal teachers' assessments, and other observations. Appropriate procedures for determining students' instructional reading levels are discussed in Part II of this book; please refer to those chapters for specific procedures. Do remember, however, that you must be flexible in forming ability groups. Occasionally, students' instructional reading levels are determined incorrectly and students will need to be moved to other ability groups. The teacher should plan for this inevitability by not expecting his ability groups to remain static. He must be ready to make changes when they become necessary.

The placement of students in basal reader ability groups has two particular advantages. First, the teacher can be reasonably confident that students are receiving instruction in materials at or near their instructional reading levels. Second, since students are placed in a limited number of groups, the teacher is able to provide adequate amounts of direct instruction in specific reading skills.

Disadvantages are also associated with ability-level basal reading groups. First, groups often tend to become rigidly structured. Too frequently, ability-level groups are formed at the beginning of the year and remain unchanged throughout the school year. Not all students progress at the same rate. Some students' reading abilities develop at a rate slower or faster than the "norm" for their group. Consequently, some students may need to be moved to more challenging or less challenging groups. Second, students working in ability groups do not benefit from the variety of contributions offered by other students in their class. During reading instruction, they have the opportunity to interact only with students who are at their own reading level. Students in ability-level reading groups are not exposed to the ideas and insights of students in "higher" or "lower" reading groups, and students in "low" groups cannot observe fluent readers from more capable reading groups.

## Skill Development Groups

Even when students have been placed in ability-level groups according to their general reading ability, their specific skill needs in certain areas of reading instruction may not be met by ability-level grouping. The exercises associated with the stories in basal readers do not always identify skills that are necessary and appropriate for all students. By grouping students around basic skill needs and forming skill development groups, teachers can better account for individual differences.

Grouping based on skill deficiencies or skill needs generally begins with a scope and sequence of specific skills. Logically, this would be the scope and sequence of skills that are presented in the basal reading series. Every basal reading program has a scope and sequence chart that identifies the levels, and pages within those levels, at which every skill in the program is taught. This chart, or a portion of it, can usually be found in the teacher's edition of the basal reader. The chart arranges skills by difficulty level within the various skill areas—word identification, comprehension, study skills, and so on. In skill development groups, students work on deficient reading skills, starting with their most basic deficiences. Since a tremendous number of skills are to be learned, skill groups are widely diverse.

Once the scope and sequence of the skills to be taught are identified, the teacher must then assess each student's degree of competence in those identified skills. (Again, refer to Part II of this text.) After students have been identified as proficient or deficient in each of the individual skill areas, the teacher forms as many skill groups as she can manage. As with ability groups, a good rule of thumb is to have three or four groups. In some classrooms, this means that skill groups are formed for the instruction of very distinct and specific individual skills, such as differentiating and using the long *a* sound in words following the $c\bar{v}c\acute{e}$ principle. In other classrooms, teachers may decide to group for skill instruction based on broader skill clusters, such as deficiencies in the general area of long vowel sounds.

In either case, once these groups have been formed, they last until the students within the groups have mastered the skill for which the groups were formed. Skill development groups are formed, instruction occurs, learning is assessed, and the groups are disbanded as needs dictate. Consequently, one of the crucial issues in managing skill instruction groups for basal reader instruction lies in the teacher's ability to *pace* the skill development groups. When the teacher has formed four groups for skill instruction around specific skill needs, it is important that students within these groups accomplish their goals at about the same time. This is necessary if the teacher wishes to disband the groups and reform new ones based on other needs. If, for example, group A was formed to work on the comprehension skill of sequencing three events and it finished before the other groups, students from group A could not be regrouped with students from other groups, because the other students would not be ready to move on. Since all the students in group A probably would not require instruction in the next skill to be taught, group A must either wait for the others or be split into new groups based on other skill needs. Although this situation is not necessarily inappropriate, the beginning teacher may find it difficult to manage so many skill groups within one classroom. It is, therefore, usually better if the groups can be paced with enrichment and reinforcement activities so that they are terminated at the same time. The reformation of groups can then proceed in an orderly fashion.

Specific skill groups have a number of advantages. The use of skill development groups provides students instruction in skills each student specifically needs. Since specific skill group instruction is based on the basal reader's scope and sequence, a teacher can be confident that students are receiving instruction in appropriate skills and that such instruction is consistent with the adopted basal program. Also, the continual reformation of skill groups avoids the rigidness sometimes associated with ability groups. Often, it makes instruction more interesting to children. Finally, skill development grouping does not have to be the *only* technique used in the classroom. It may be best used in conjunction with ability groups or interest groups.

Several potential disadvantages are associated with skill development groups, however. First, managing skill groups when groups are not formed and terminated at the same time becomes very difficult. Second, grouping for skill instruction requires a thorough assessment of students' skill needs, and this is a time-consuming task. Also, teachers and students may become so involved with specific reading subskills that they lose sight of the more global goal of reading—acquiring meaning from print.

### Interest Groups

Grouping students by their interest in various topics is different from grouping children according to ability or skill need. Grouping students by ability levels assumes that the students will fit automatically into a sequence of basal reader material because of their general reading ability levels. When students are grouped on the basis of specific skill needs, their placement into the basal program is largely determined by the point in the scope and sequence of skills at which the students are ready to begin instruction. Placing students into groups based on their various interests, however, is a quite different process. It presents different problems in terms of basal reader instruction and requires the use of much more material than just the basal reader. The teacher must also utilize different assessment procedures for this grouping technique.

Teaching through interest groups makes it somewhat more difficult to use the basal reader, but an interest-oriented approach is possible, as noted by Quandt (1977).

> Developing a humanistic [i.e., interest-oriented] reading program when basal readers are the instructional materials, then, is quite possible. It cannot be done without a good deal of teacher effort, and it cannot be done without rearranging some of the basal's philosophy, but it can be done. By changing some of the instructional techniques . . . a [basal] program can meet the needs of the total child (pp. 192–193).

Grouping students by their interests assumes that the advantages in grouping students by ability levels are supplanted by the benefits of having students pursue their individual interests. This means that a good deal of the reading material used for interest-group instruction comes from sources other than basal readers. Stories from the basal reader may be used as a departure point, but other reading resources must be added. If a group of children expressed a specific interest after reading a basal story, a group related to the particular topic could be formed.

Generally, the interest groups that are formed are built around some purpose as well as a given topic. For example, if an interest group were formed around the topic of farming, the students should be required to use the information that they gained through reading to complete some group project or activity. For example, they could build a model farm or write a handbook of information about farming to read to the rest of the class before a field trip to a farm.

In addition to having to identify a wide range of reading interests and accumulate many resources, the teacher who implements interest grouping must also consider different methods of assessment. In ability-group assessment, the teacher must determine the students' general reading levels. In skill grouping, the students' specific skill deficiencies must be identified. In interest grouping, the teacher must discover topics about which the children *want* to read. It is often wise in this assessment to begin with a limited number of topics from which the children may choose. If the range of topics were not narrowed, students might identify an area in which they were interested but on which there would be very little material to read. If a second-grade group identified professional football as a topic of interest, it might be difficult to provide information at their reading level. It is a good idea, therefore, to narrow the range of possible topics to include only those for which the teacher has adequate reading materials.

Students' interests can be determined in several ways. Informally observing the books students select themselves is the easiest way to determine interests. Keeping notes about stories in which some children seem to be especially interested is also helpful. Such anecdotal records or notes can be based on specific stories from the basal reader. The teacher can also use a more formal interest inventory. (An example of such an inventory can be found in Chapter 20 of this book.) After their interests have been identified, students who have common interests can be grouped together.

There are several advantages in the use of interest groups. Interest groups can be highly motivating for students. Also, when children are using reading as a tool to enable them to complete activities in which they are interested, students are more likely to develop positive attitudes toward reading. Another advantage of this approach is that teachers are not forced to try to *create* interest. Rather, they find the students' interests and capitalize on them. Also, interest grouping allows children to work in groups with their friends.

Shortcomings in the use of interest grouping also exist. First, interest groups should not be the *only* organizational structure for teaching reading. Too many problems are associated with finding a way to teach needed skills and with providing a range of reading materials appropriate to the reading abilities of the students if *all* instruction centers around interest groups. Interest groups should not be the primary grouping plan. Within the basal reader model, however, this grouping approach may be used effectively as a *supplement*, or a change of pace, to ability grouping or skill grouping. (Refer to Chapters 16, 17, and 18 for additional information about teaching reading from a student interest perspective.)

## A CASE STUDY

Figure 14.1 presents data for a third-grade class. It is late August, and the school year is just beginning. You are the teacher of this class. Assume that the data have just been collected and organized onto this single class-profile sheet. As you work through this case study, you will be asked to try a number of different grouping plans. Your plans should take into account as much of the information provided as possible. At the end of this chapter, solutions to the questions posed in the grouping problems are provided. These are not necessarily the only correct alternatives; they are merely possible solutions to the grouping problems.

Try to keep track of your thoughts as you solve these grouping problems. You may raise as many questions as you find solutions. Remember these questions, for you may want to discuss your questions and the steps you followed with your instructor and classmates after you have completed this activity.

| Name | 1. ITBS comprehension | 2. ITBS vocabulary | 3. Previous level completed | 4. P—single consonants | 5. P—consonant blends | 6. P—short vowels | 7. P—long vowels | 8. P—consonant digraphs | 9. P—syllabication, blending, accents | 10. SA—variants | 11. SA—prefixes | 12. SA—suffixes | 13. SA—compounds | 14. Comprehension—literal | 15. Comprehension—inferential | 16. Comprehension—critical | 17. Comprehension—meaning vocabulary | 18. Works in group | 19. Shows leadership | 20. Area A—science | 21. Area B—pets and animals | 22. Area C—sports | 23. Area D—mysteries | 24. Area E—airplanes |
|---|---|---|---|---|---|---|---|---|---|---|---|---|---|---|---|---|---|---|---|---|---|---|---|---|
| 1. Dorris | 1.9 | 2.2 | $2^1$ | + | + | + | + | − | − | + | + | + | + | S | S | S | S | − | − | | 1 | 2 | | |
| 2. Evans | 5.0 | 4.2 | $3^2$ | + | + | + | + | + | + | + | + | + | + | S | S | S | S | + | − | 2 | | | | 1 |
| 3. Franks | 1.2 | 2.4 | 1 | − | + | + | − | − | − | + | + | − | − | S | W | W | W | + | + | 2 | 1 | | | |
| 4. Jones | 1.9 | 2.1 | $2^1$ | + | + | + | − | − | + | + | + | − | + | S | S | S | W | + | − | 2 | | | 1 | |
| 5. Lowe | 2.3 | 2.3 | $2^2$ | + | + | + | − | + | − | + | + | + | − | S | S | W | S | + | − | | 1 | 2 | | |
| 6. Matthews | 2.1 | 2.5 | $2^2$ | + | + | − | + | + | + | + | + | − | − | W | W | W | W | + | + | | 2 | 1 | | |
| 7. Morrison | 1.4 | 1.6 | 1 | − | − | − | − | − | − | − | − | − | + | S | W | W | S | − | − | | | 2 | 1 | |
| 8. Noland | 5.9 | 5.0 | $3^2$ | + | + | + | + | + | + | + | + | + | + | S | S | S | S | + | + | 1 | | | 2 | |
| 9. Parks | 3.2 | 3.1 | $2^2$ | + | + | − | + | + | − | + | − | + | + | W | W | W | W | + | − | | 1 | | 2 | |
| 10. Poole | 2.6 | 2.8 | $2^2$ | + | + | − | + | + | − | + | − | + | + | S | S | W | S | + | − | | 1 | 2 | | |
| 11. Porter | 1.4 | 1.5 | $2^1$ | + | − | + | + | − | − | + | + | + | + | S | S | W | S | + | − | | 1 | 2 | | |
| 12. Ray | 2.6 | 3.5 | $2^2$ | + | − | + | + | − | − | − | − | − | + | S | W | W | W | + | − | | 1 | | 2 | |
| 13. Reeves | 6.2 | 6.4 | $3^2$ | + | + | + | + | + | − | + | + | + | + | S | S | W | S | + | + | | 1 | | | 2 |
| 14. Ross | 2.3 | 2.1 | $2^1$ | + | + | − | − | − | − | + | + | − | + | S | W | W | W | + | + | 2 | | | | 1 |
| 15. Rothe | 2.8 | 2.3 | $2^2$ | + | + | + | − | − | − | + | + | + | + | S | S | S | S | − | − | | 1 | | 2 | |
| 16. Silman | 1.9 | 2.2 | $2^1$ | + | − | + | + | − | − | + | + | + | + | S | S | W | S | + | + | | 1 | | 2 | |
| 17. Spencer | 4.6 | 4.8 | $3^2$ | + | + | + | + | − | − | + | + | + | + | S | S | S | S | − | − | 2 | 1 | | | |
| 18. Sutton | 3.6 | 2.9 | $2^2$ | − | − | − | + | − | − | + | + | + | + | W | W | W | S | + | + | 2 | | 1 | | |
| 19. Swank | 3.8 | 4.2 | $3^2$ | + | + | + | + | − | − | + | − | + | + | S | W | W | W | − | + | 1 | | 2 | | |
| 20. Todd | 4.9 | 4.3 | $3^2$ | + | + | + | + | − | − | + | − | + | + | S | S | W | S | − | − | | | 2 | 1 | |
| 21. Towers | 5.6 | 5.8 | $3^2$ | + | + | + | + | − | − | + | − | − | + | S | W | W | S | + | + | 1 | 2 | | | |
| 22. Wagle | 2.3 | 2.5 | $2^2$ | + | + | + | + | + | − | + | − | − | − | S | S | W | S | + | + | | 1 | | 2 | |

Figure 14.1. A class data sheet for a third-grade class.

## Ability-Level Groups

To form ability-level groups for this third-grade class, three sets of data from columns one, two, and three of Figure 14.1 need to be considered. Scores in columns 1 and 2 are grade equivalency scores (see Chapter 10 for a proper interpretation of these scores) from the Iowa Tests of Basic Skills (ITBS), which is a standardized achievement test. Column 1 lists ITBS comprehension subtest scores, and column 2 lists scores derived from the ITBS vocabulary subtest. Column 3 indicates the last basal reader level completed in second grade. This information was supplied by the previous teacher. Note that the levels in column 3 indicate the grade-level designation of the basal reader. For example, Dorris completed the first second-grade reader ($2^1$), Evans completed the second third-grade reader ($3^2$), Franks completed the first-grade reader (1), and so forth.

"Grade level" for the beginning third grade is generally considered to be the first third-grade reader, the level-$3^1$ basal reader. As the teacher, you need to place the students in ability-level groups for instruction. It is important for you to match the students with reading materials that are neither too difficult nor too easy for them.

Your task is to form three reading groups based on the information contained in columns 1, 2, and 3 of Figure 14.1, in other words, to establish "high," "middle," and "low" reading groups. Also, you are to decide which level of basal reader is appropriate for each group. Be prepared to make some compromises, however, for every student will not neatly "fit" into one of these groups. Take your time and work carefully; then, refer to the solution for ability-level groups and the accompanying discussion at the end of this chapter.

## Skill Development Groups

The skills identified for the purpose of this case study include phonic skills, structural analysis skills, and comprehension skills. Assessments of the students' skill levels can be found in columns 4 through 17 in Figure 14.1. Columns 4 through 9 deal with phonic skills, columns 10 through 13 deal with structural analysis skills, and columns 14 through 17 deal with comprehension. The abbreviation $P$ signifies phonic skills, and the abbreviation $SA$ signifies structural analysis skills. A plus sign in columns 4 through 13 indicates that the teacher has determined that the student has mastered that phonic or structural analysis skill. A minus sign means that the student is deficient in that particular skill. Since the concept of "mastery" does not logically apply to comprehension (e.g., does one ever master critical reading?), you will find either an $S$, which indicates strength, or a $W$, which indicates weakness, in columns 14 through 17. Note that for the purpose of this case study the scope and sequence chart for these skills is limited when compared to the basal reader scope and sequence chart, which would be much more detailed.

First, examine columns 4 through 13, the phonic and structural analysis skills, and place each student in a group that corresponds to the deficient skill with the lowest number. For example, Dorris would belong in a consonant digraph group, Evans in an enrichment group (since she has mastered all skills), Franks in the single consonant group, and so on. When you have finished, look at the solutions for the skill development groups at the end of this chapter.

### Interest Groups

The data used to organize interest groups come from columns 18 through 24. Column 18 indicates whether the child works well in a group. A plus indicates that the student does, and a minus indicates that the student does not. Column 19 indicates whether or not a child demonstrates leadership skills. Columns 20 through 24 indicate reading interest areas. This information was obtained by having each student select a first and second choice from the general interest areas listed below. Each child's first choice is indicated under the appropriate row with a numeral 1, and the second choice is indicated with a 2. The topics were science, pets and animals, sports, mysteries, and airplanes.

Your job is to group the students in this class on the basis of their first interests. When you have done this, look at the solutions for interest groups at the end of this chapter.

## SUMMARY

Grouping for basal reader instruction is a form of preteaching planning used to limit the range of students' reading abilities, skills, or interests. This can be accomplished in many different ways. Three of the most common methods of grouping include ability-level groups, skill development groups, and interest groups. All of these patterns have strengths and weaknesses, and no one technique is superior to the others. They can also be used either in unison or alternately in a classroom. Some of the most effective teachers use all three grouping patterns at different times and in different combinations during the school year.

## SOLUTIONS

### Ability-Level Groups

Table 14.1 illustrates one possible solution to your problem. Three groups labeled "below level," "on level," and "above level" have been formed. The basal readers assigned to these groups are the level-$2^2$, level-$3^1$, and level-4 readers, respectively. Also note that following each student's name is the last basal reader completed in second grade.

#### Table 14.1. One Solution to the Ability-Level Grouping Problem

| Below Level (level-$2^2$ basal) | On Level (level-$3^1$ basal) | Above Level (level-4 basal) |
|---|---|---|
| Dorris ($2^1$) | Lowe ($2^2$) | Evans ($3^2$) |
| Franks (1) | Matthews ($2^2$) | Noland ($3^2$) |
| Jones ($2^1$) | Parks ($2^2$) | Reeves ($3^2$) |
| Morrison (1) | Poole ($2^2$) | Spencer ($3^2$) |
| Porter ($2^1$) | Ray ($2^2$) | Swank ($3^2$) |
| Ross ($2^1$) | Rothe ($2^2$) | Todd ($3^2$) |
| Silman ($2^1$) | Sutton ($2^2$) | Towers ($3^2$) |
| | Wagle ($2^2$) | |

Do you agree with these groupings? As previously stated, not all solutions are "neat." Students Franks and Morrison, for example, may find the $2^2$-level basal too difficult. As a result, you may need to form a separate (fourth) group for these two students.

Although it was easy enough to place all the students who completed the $2^2$ book in the second grade "on level" group and all the students who completed the $3^2$ book in your "above level" group, some of these placements may be inappropriate. For example, student Lowe, who only achieved grade equivalency scores of 2.3 on the ITBS, may find the $3^1$ basal reader too difficult. Conversely, student Reeves, who attained grade equivalency scores of 6.2 and 6.4, may find the level-4 reader not challenging enough.

You can only make your best professional judgments when assigning students to ability groups for basal instruction, and you will inevitably misplace some students. By continually evaluating your students' progress and placements (and perhaps administering a number of informal reading inventories to obtain more accurate estimates of your students' instructional reading levels; see Chapter 9), you would recognize these misplacements and appropriately move students to other groups. If you found yourself at the middle of the school year and you had *not* adjusted your reading groups, it would be time to reexamine your students' placements and their performance.

### Skill Development Groups

Did you identify six skill need groups and one advanced group with no particular needs? Your groups should look like Table 14.2.

You now have seven groups with which to work. This may be too many groups for you to manage successfully in your classroom. Also, remember that groups formed for a single need do not last very long. Let us try to work with a larger cluster of skills. What are your alternatives? First, try combining the existing groups into larger skill clusters. For

**Table 14.2. One Solution to the Skill Development Grouping Problem**

| Single Consonants | Consonant Blends | Short Vowels |
| --- | --- | --- |
| Franks | Porter | Matthews |
| Morrison | Ray | Parks |
| Sutton | Silman | Poole |
| | | Ross |

| Long Vowels | Consonant Digraphs | Syllabication |
| --- | --- | --- |
| Lowe | Dorris | Wagle |
| Jones | Spencer | Reeves |
| Rothe | Swank | |
| | Todd | |
| | Towers | |

| No Specific Needs | | |
| --- | --- | --- |
| Evans | | |
| Noland | | |

example, try clustering together all students who need work on consonants (columns 4, 5, and 8) and vowels (columns 6 and 7). Try this, and then continue reading.

Do your groups now look something like Table 14.3?

You now have only four groups with which to work, although it will be necessary to differentiate instruction within these groups, since some students need to practice different subskills.

Another possible solution is to group students into one of the three major skill areas; that is, to form a phonics group, a structural analysis group, and a comprehension group. Try this, and see what kinds of groups you come up with. Again, do this before reading any further.

When you tried regrouping based on the three general areas of need, you had more decisions to make. For each child you had to determine the *greatest* area of need. That process was somewhat arbitrary for some students. Do your groups look something like those in Table 14.4?

As you made these decisions did you notice that some students have strengths and weaknesses in every area (e.g., Franks) and that other students have major deficiencies in

**Table 14.3. Another Solution to the Skill Development Grouping Problem**

| Consonants | Vowels | Syllabication | No Specific Needs |
|---|---|---|---|
| Franks | Matthews | Wagle | Evans |
| Morrison | Parks | Reeves | Noland |
| Sutton | Poole | | |
| Porter | Ross | | |
| Ray | Lowe | | |
| Silman | Jones | | |
| Dorris | Rothe | | |
| Spencer | | | |
| Swank | | | |
| Todd | | | |
| Towers | | | |

**Table 14.4. Another Solution to the Skill Development Grouping Problem**

| Phonics | Structural | Comprehension | No Specific Needs |
|---|---|---|---|
| Dorris | Ray | Franks | Evans |
| Jones | Wagle | Matthews | Noland |
| Lowe | | Parks | |
| Morrison | | Reeves | |
| Poole | | Swank | |
| Porter | | Towers | |
| Ross | | | |
| Rothe | | | |
| Silman | | | |
| Spencer | | | |
| Sutton | | | |
| Todd | | | |

every area (e.g., Morrison) while others seem to have skills well beyond what their general reading ability levels would indicate (e.g., Dorris)? Some students even seem to have overall ability higher than their skills would indicate (e.g., Swank). These are all issues you need to consider when grouping for skill instruction.

## Interest Groups

If you simply placed students by their first interest choice, you should have created the groups listed in Table 14.5.

Although you have given students their first choices, you have five groups with which to work, which may be too many. In addition, the groups are unequal in size, which could make them difficult to teach (have you ever taught a "group" of two?). To make your interest grouping more manageable, reassign some students to equalize the group sizes. To do this, you will need to assign some students according to their second choices. Also, try to account for socialization skill (columns 18 and 19) when forming these new groups. Make new groups, and then continue reading. (Hint: try making three groups.)

Does your new set of groups look something like Table 14.6?

#### Table 14.5. One Solution to the Interest Grouping Problem

| Science | Pets and Animals | Sports | Mysteries | Airplanes |
|---------|------------------|--------|-----------|-----------|
| Noland | Dorris | Matthews | Jones | Evans |
| Swank | Franks | Sutton | Morrison | Ross |
| Towers | Lowe | Todd | | |
| | Parks | | | |
| | Poole | | | |
| | Porter | | | |
| | Ray | | | |
| | Reeves | | | |
| | Rothe | | | |
| | Silman | | | |
| | Spencer | | | |
| | Wagle | | | |

#### Table 14.6. Another Solution to the Interest Grouping Problem

| Science | Pets and Animals | Sports |
|---------|------------------|--------|
| Evans | Dorris | Matthews |
| Jones | Franks | Morrison |
| Noland | Lowe | Park |
| Ross | Poole | Porter |
| Spencer | Ray | Sutton |
| Swank | Reeves | Todd |
| Towers | Rothe | |
| | Silman | |
| | Wagle | |

If it does, or if you made some similar arrangement, you now have manageable interest groups that have the following advantages.

1. All students are in their first- or second-choice group.
2. There are only three groups to manage, instead of five.
3. Each group includes two of the six children who have difficulty working within a group.
4. Each group has two or more students with leadership skills, but no group has all leaders in it.
5. The smallest group includes more than 25 percent of the class, and the largest group includes fewer than 50 percent of the class.
6. Only seven children had to be moved from groups of their first to their second choice to form these new groups.

## REFERENCES

Arnold, R., and Sherry, N. A comparison of the reading levels of disabled readers with assigned textbooks. *Reading Improvement*, 1975, **12**, 207–211.

Barr, R. How children are taught to read: Grouping and pacing. *School Review*, 1975, **83**, 479–498.

Brophy, J., and Evertson, C. *Learning from teaching: A developmental perspective.* Boston: Allyn and Bacon, 1976.

Quandt, I. *Teaching reading: A human process.* Chicago: Rand McNally, 1977.

Rubin, R. Reading ability and assigned materials: Accommodation for the slow but not the accelerated. *The Elementary School Journal*, 1975, **75**, 373–377.

## RECOMMENDED READINGS

Anderson, L., Evertson, C., and Brophy, J. An experimental study of effective teaching in first grade reading groups. *The Elementary School Journal*, 1979, **79**, 193–223.

The results of an experimental study translating research findings into classroom practice are reported in this article. The effectiveness and efficiency of instructional techniques in the daily classroom routine are studied in first-grade reading group settings.

Dalhoff, V. *Ability grouping, content validity, and curriculum process analysis.* New York: Teachers College Press, Columbia University, 1971.

This book shows that the performance of a group working on any specific study topic may influence the teacher's ability to pace the instruction. The composition of instructional groups and classes and their homogeneity in ability may determine their pacing by the teacher.

Fitzgerald, G. Why kids can read the book but not the workbook. *The Reading Teacher*, 1979, **32**, 930–932.

Fitzgerald deals with the problems and implications of workbook reading levels higher than the reading level of their accompanying basal reader. Studies indicate that third-, fourth-, and fifth-grade workbooks would be difficult for students to use independently.

Guthrie, J. Grouping for reading. *The Reading Teacher*, 1979, **32**, 500–501.

The author's views on research in the effectiveness of grouping patterns are discussed.

Opinions indicate a number of outside variables that may influence reading ability. Grouping by individual ability, social implications, peer groups, friendships, and so on all have an effect on a reader's achievement and ability to learn.

Helton, G., Morrow, H., and Yates, J. Grouping for reading instruction 1965, 1975, 1985. *The Reading Teacher*, 1977, **31**, 28–33.

This article compares the grouping for instruction patterns of 1965 to those of 1975. It is concluded that in the future grouping may be flexible enough to allow teachers to select students, teaching methods, and instructional materials appropriate for the task.

Swaby, B. Varying the ways you teach reading with basal stories. *The Reading Teacher*, 1977, **31**, 28–33.

The many methods in which a reading instructor can add variety to teaching concepts, improve reading skills, and evoke thinking among her students by means of basal stories, are discussed. It is suggested that teaching strategies should consist of more than just opening the book and reading; they should allow the students to participate.

Taubenheim, B., and Christensen, J. Let's shoot "cock robin"!: Alternatives to "round robin" reading. *Language Arts*, 1978, **55**, 975–977.

The article focuses on "round-robin" reading in today's classroom and discusses more effective and enjoyable alternatives.

# CHAPTER 15

# Using Basal Readers for Skill Development

Patricia Shelton Koppman
San Diego, California

*In response to the criticism that basal readers promote tracking and rigid groupings, several alternate and flexible strategies for grouping students for basal instruction were discussed in Chapter 14. Another common criticism of basal readers is that they do not teach reading skills; instead, they merely provide practice and reinforcement of reading skills. In this chapter, Patricia Shelton Koppman discusses this criticism of basal readers and suggests ways beginning teachers can use basal readers more effectively for skill instruction. After describing the components of basal readers, Koppman presents an eight-step strategy for basal reader skill instruction: (1) identify the objective, (2) develop the instructional activity, (3) communicate the skill objective to the students, (4) directly teach the reading skill, (5) provide independent practice, (6) correct students' work, (7) enrich, reteach, or reinforce skills, and (8) evaluate what has been taught. Basal readers have great potential for developing children's reading skills. Application of the strategy presented in this chapter should help beginning teachers to provide effective skill instruction.*

Educators have been quick to criticize basal readers (Durkin, 1976). Over 80 percent of the teachers in the United States, however, use some form of basal program in their classrooms (Spache and Spache, 1977). Perhaps rather than being critical, educators should attempt to help teachers to use this educational tool effectively. How much do you really know about basals? Will you be able to use them appropriately and effectively? In this chapter, we will explore each part of a basal program, its intended use, and productive, effective ways you can use basal readers in your classroom for skill development instruction.

# BASAL READERS: A DEFINITION

What is a basal reading program? "Well, it's the reading book and workbook students use every day." Was that your answer? If it was, we need to look farther into the definition and purpose of basal readers. In the *Dictionary of Reading* (Harris and Hodges, 1981), published by the International Reading Association, a "basal reading program" is defined as "a comprehensive, integrated set of books, workbooks, teachers' manuals and other materials for developmental reading instruction." In other words, a basal reading program is a sequential set of instructional materials for supporting a continuous reading program in the elementary or middle school.

# HOW BASAL READERS ARE SELECTED

Some districts select a single basal program, and all teachers use the same reading series. Other districts allow teachers to select the basal series of their choice. In such situations, several programs are being used within a single building or classroom. Other school districts employ a procedure, known as "multiple adoption," in which two or more series are selected by the district and teachers choose from those the series they prefer to teach.

During the 1960s and 1970s, schools experienced a period of experimentation and innovation. During those years, the trend was for many teachers to use various programs and methods. The 1980s have seen a trend toward the return of "basic" education. As a part of this trend, more single adoptions of basal series within school districts are evident. The era of accountability has helped bring about this trend. Since districts are to be held accountable by parents, school boards, and legislators, district administrators feel the need to maintain more control and structure. Having one basal reader series in use throughout a district allows for more control and structure. For this reason, a beginning teacher can expect to teach from one required basal reader program. The challenge is to use the prescribed basal program in the most effective way. Before we discuss effective uses of basals, however, let us closely examine the components of a basal program.

# COMPONENTS OF A BASAL PROGRAM

## Scope and Sequence

If you were asked to name the major components of a basal reading program, what would your answer include? Was the scope and sequence chart on your list? Have you ever wondered why programs have such elaborate scope and sequence charts but why these charts are so seldom used? The scope and sequence chart is the road map of the basal reading program that guides teachers carefully to their desired destinations. It is vital that the teacher thoroughly examine the skills within the basal program to be taught. This preparation gives the teacher some insight into the skills presented, reviewed, and evaluated and into when mastery can be expected.

## Teacher's Manual

What do you think the most important component of a basal program is? Did you answer the teacher's manual? Some educators may disagree, but it is apparent that the teacher's manual is the part of the basal program most relevant to the teacher's success, since it describes the program's goals and strategies for obtaining those goals.

The teacher's manual guides the systematic teaching of the skills listed on the scope and sequence chart. It enables the teacher to present and teach skills at appropriate levels and to review them in subsequent units and levels until mastery is achieved.

The teacher's manual is *not* to be used verbatim, as though it were divinely inspired. Rather, it is to be used as an instructional guide. The teacher's manual is a tool that helps its user to attain the final goal—skilled, fluent reading. The teacher's task is to modify and adapt this tool to meet the needs of a specific group of students.

### Student's Text

Next to the teacher's manual, the student's text is the most important part of a basal program. The textbook is a carefully constructed anthology of literature that controls for vocabulary and readability. Most basal texts include poetry and prose, fiction and nonfiction, as well as factual, fantasy, and realistic selections. Since many of the selections are excerpts from children's literature, children can find the original sources in libraries; this encourages students to bridge the gap from their reading textbooks to full-length books. The text usually includes an outstanding collection of artwork as well, which brings even more enjoyment and interest to the child.

### Basal Workbook

How vital is the workbook to the basal program? It can be extremely vital when it is used appropriately and for its intended purpose. If workbook pages are assigned because "this page comes next" or "this is the seatwork for today," then workbooks are being misused. A workbook's purpose is to provide *practice* in a particular skill that *has previously been taught by the teacher.* The assignment should be, not the *next page* necessarily, but the page that correlates with the skill just taught by the teacher. The student is provided with practice in the skill that was taught. The workbook exercises also provide the teacher feedback concerning whether the students understood and learned the skill taught.

To summarize, then, the core components of a basal reading program, as we have discussed them, include (1) the scope and sequence chart, (2) the teacher's manual, (3) the student's textbook, and (4) the workbook. You may notice that many other components of basal programs are not included in this list. In our discussion, we will concentrate on the use of the core components only, since reading can be taught, and taught well, with these core materials. Supplementary materials extend and enrich the reading experiences of students, but they are not essential for *effective* basal instruction.

## STRATEGY FOR EFFECTIVE SKILL INSTRUCTION USING BASAL READERS

Singer (1977) suggested that a competent teaching staff equipped with a program of continuous progress is the key to successful reading instruction in schools. With this in mind, let us move on to strategies for increasing your competence in using basal readers. For the purposes of this chapter, only basal reader *skill instruction* will be discussed. Other facets—such as prereading activities, guided reading of stories, and supplemental and enrichment activities—will not be directly discussed. The greatest problem beginning teachers face when using basals, however, is providing effective skill instruction; therefore, an appropriate strategy for skill development instruction is presented in detail. Figure 15.1 illustrates an eight-step strategy for teaching reading skills in basal programs. The following sections describe these eight steps in detail.

### Identify Your Objective

Every teacher's manual lists an objective for every skill development lesson. In the *Dictionary of Reading* (Harris and Hodges, 1981), "objective" is defined as "a target toward which instruction is specifically directed." In other words, each skill development lesson specifies your instructional goal, your "target." Logically, therefore, you should initiate your lesson by identifying your instructional objective before proceeding further. Read the objective and then develop your lesson to teach toward mastery of the specified skill.

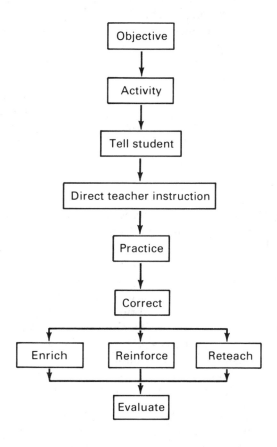

Figure 15.1. A model for skill instruction using basal readers.

## Develop the Instructional Activity

Once the objective for the lesson has been determined, you are ready to move on to step two: developing an instructional activity for teaching the objective. Investigate first the activities suggested in the manual. At times, there is more than one activity from which to choose. Again, it is you, *the teacher,* who is responsible for choosing the most appropriate activity on the basis of your students' needs. Some students respond better to paper-and-pencil–type activities; others seem to gain more from discussion. All students, however, benefit most from direct teacher instruction, that is, from your formally showing, modeling, telling, demonstrating, *teaching* the skill. If little direct instruction of the skill is dictated in the teacher's manual, you need to embellish or extend the lesson. Not surprisingly, students tend to learn those things that they are taught directly.

## Tell Your Students What They Will Learn

The next step is to tell the students your objective for the lesson. Too frequently, we leave children in the dark; that is, we teach a lesson to a reading group, but the students never recognize the purpose of the activities. By knowing what a lesson is about, the students can focus more clearly on the objective and, hence, better master the skill. As adults, we follow agendas at meetings, programs at conferences and concerts, as well as itineraries for trips. Why? Because we can participate more effectively and acquire more information when we know "where we are going." Let your students know where they are going—tell them what they are learning.

Depending on the age-group and sophistication of your students, you may have to restate the objective in more understandable terms. It would not help a student to know that the lesson deals with sequence if she did not understand what "sequence" means. Rephrasing the objective as "putting things in order" might be a more understandable way to state this objective.

## Administer Direct Teacher Instruction

Direct teacher instruction is not only the next step, it is the most integral part of the instructional strategy. Using an activity that you have selected from the basal reader or one you have developed for presenting the skill, you directly teach the skill identified; that is, you administer instruction, not merely assign seatwork, give tests, or play games.

Direct teacher instruction does not necessarily mean lecturing; it means actively involving students in learning. In many situations, teachers involve only the students who raise their hands or only the children called on for answers. "Every child response" is a more appropriate goal for students in the teaching and learning processes; that is, you should actively involve children as much as possible in the teaching and learning situation. To involve every child, try using one of the following techniques.

### Mini-Chalkboards

Mini-chalkboards can be constructed from discarded classroom chalkboards. Have the boards cut into 9-by-12-inch pieces, one for each student in the reading group. If old chalkboards are not available, you can make your own mini-chalkboards with spray-on chalkboard paint purchased from a local paint store. Approximately six layers of paint are sprayed onto 9-by-12-inch sheets of masonite board or thick cardboard. After the final coat of paint is dry, rub chalk dust over the boards so that they will not be scratched the first time they are used. Supply each student in the group with a container in which they can keep a piece of chalk and some type of eraser (old stockings and washcloths work well). All students can respond on their individual chalkboards as the teacher directs the learning activity.

## Multiresponse Boards

Multiresponse boards are pieces of tagboard, cardboard, or heavy construction paper on which students write responses during direct teacher instruction. Figure 15.2 shows an example of a multiresponse board that could be used for the teaching of initial consonants. Students use a clothespin or hair clip to indicate their answers. When you ask for a response, for example, "Please find the beginning sound you hear in the word *rain*," every student can be involved and simultaneously respond. If a student selected an incorrect consonant, you could immediately recognize the incorrect response and provide further teaching.

## Skill Cards

Skill cards are made on ditto masters or spirit masters. Placed on the master are the materials to be taught, such as vocabulary words, phonic elements, words and definitions, spelling words, and even math problems. If the objective were prefixes, for example, the master might look like Figure 15.3. A second skill card would have root words that could be matched with the prefixes.

Skill cards should be duplicated so that each child has a copy. The children cut apart their skill cards, making them into small flash cards. As you proceed with the teaching of the skill, every student can participate. After instruction, the flash cards are stored in plastic bags, envelopes, or folders for future use and review.

## Provide Independent Practice

By this stage, you have provided direct instruction by using suggested activities from the teacher's manual or activities you yourself selected that were aimed toward involving

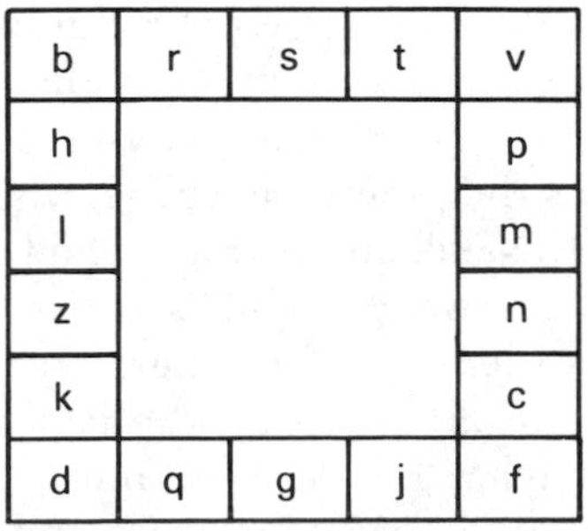

Figure 15.2. A sample multiresponse board with initial consonants.

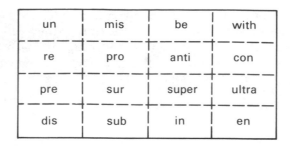

| un | mis | be | with |
|---|---|---|---|
| re | pro | anti | con |
| pre | sur | super | ultra |
| dis | sub | in | en |

Figure 15.3. A sample skill card with prefixes.

every student in the reading group. What is needed next is an opportunity for students to practice their newly acquired skills. Practice is the act of doing, repeatedly performing a skill in order to acquire mastery of that skill.

The workbook is designed as the source of practice exercises in basal reading programs. The appropriate use of workbook pages, however, requires that students understand the exercises and perform them correctly. You should not only give explicit directions for doing the page or pages but also make certain that students realize that what they are practicing is the skill previously taught. Also, be sure that the workbook pages assigned contain activities that practice the skill that was taught. In some instances, seeing the correlation between the skill taught and the practice sheet or activity suggested becomes difficult. When this is the case, find another practice activity in another source or develop a reinforcement activity yourself. Do not waste students' time on irrelevant material. Also, be aware that practice does not always have to include paper-and-pencil activities. For some groups, other types of practice such as learning centers, games, discussions, writing exercises, art, or additional readings may provide more beneficial practice. Here again, your own good judgment is the best guide.

### Correct Students' Work

Some teachers do not provide for student practice because "that's just too many papers to correct." Why should you take home workbooks and spend hours correcting them? Is your answer that you feel parents expect or want to know how the child is doing? If you are using workbook pages only as reports for parents, then you are misusing this material, for the primary purpose of any reinforcement activity is to practice a previously taught skill. After the student completes the practice exercise, why not correct the work *with* him? Then, you are there to reteach the skill and help the child understand his errors.

If red check marks are placed on the child's paper and no explanation or help is provided, the child has no way of learning from her errors. As an alternative to marking incorrect answers, try putting check marks on the paper for *correct* answers. From this system the student learns first what he *does know* and gains an immediate boost in self-confidence. Also, allowing the child to erase errors and make corrections can be constructive. Self-correction then becomes a part of the learning process. Self-correction should be done under your supervision so that further clarification or instruction can be provided. Giving the students the teacher's guide or an answer page to correct their own work does not provide the needed feedback.

### Enrich, Reteach, or Reinforce Skills

At this point, you must make more decisions, instructional decisions based on the practice results for each student. Student responses signal the next step: enrichment, reteaching, or reinforcement.

#### Enrichment

When students have performed satisfactorily on the practice material or activity, enrichment should be provided. "Enrich" means to make more productive. The ultimate goal of instruction is to provide students with the opportunity not only to learn new skills but also to use those skills productively in everyday activities. Enrichment activities should attempt to relate skills to everyday situations. If the skill of using certain prefixes had been taught and mastered, for example, students might start a prefix notebook, collecting as many words as possible with each of the prefixes they learned. Encourage students to use newspapers, advertisements, conversations, television shows, and radio programs as sources for their words.

#### Reteaching

When students have had difficulty performing the practice task, the need for additional instruction is indicated. Perhaps at this point you might change the mode of presentation—auditory to visual, visual to kinesthetic—but in some way you should reteach the original objective. Teacher's manuals generally include more than one activity for presenting any one skill. The reteaching phase is the time to look for additional teaching suggestions.

#### Reinforcement

The reinforcement of skills many times is ignored. Just because a person learns something, there is no guarantee that what is learned will be retained. If you learn to sew but never sew, you will not become a seamstress. If you learn to drive but never drive, your skills will soon be forgotten. "Reinforcement" means to give new force in order to strengthen. Therefore, provide supplementary activities that require students to strengthen and maintain the skills they have learned.

### Evaluate What You Have Taught

The final step is evaluation. All along you will have been doing informal evaluation, which can be very beneficial. In addition, most basal reading programs have unit-end and level-end criterion-referenced tests designed for evaluating the mastery of skills that have been taught. After checking once again the objective of your lesson, determine whether there is a test for that particular skill. Make sure that the test tests the skill taught. Make sure also that students understand the test's directions. (See Chapter 13.) Attempt to relieve their test-taking anxiety by assuring them that testing is only one way of learning how they are doing so that you can help them learn better.

## SUMMARY

By now it should be obvious that we have just walked through a lesson plan. Figure 15.1 schematically shows the procedure that can be used for every skill you determine important enough to teach to your students. If something is worth teaching, it is worth teaching well.

You may be asked why time has not been spent discussing the student's textbook, the reading of the stories, and oral and silent reading. I have deliberately attempted to separate story development from skill development. Skill development can be considered the learning "how to read" portion of the lesson, and the story development should be considered the "want to read" portion. Certainly, "wanting to read" is just as important as "knowing how to read." You are referred to Part IV of this book for specific suggestions about motivating your students to read. It is hoped that the preceding skill development strategy provides you with a structure for teaching your students the equally important task of learning "how to read."

## REFERENCES

Durkin, D. *Teaching young children to read.* Boston: Allyn and Bacon, 1976.

Harris, J., and Hodges, R. (Eds.) *Dictionary of reading and related terms.* Newark, Del.: International Reading Association, 1981.

Singer, H. Resolving curricular conflicts in the 1970s: Modifying the hypothesis, it's the teacher who makes the difference in reading achievement. *Language Arts*, 1977, **54**, 158–163.

Spache, G. D., and Spache, E. B. *Reading in the elementary school.* (4th ed.) Boston: Allyn and Bacon, 1977.

## RECOMMENDED READINGS

Criscuolo, N.P. Mag bags, peg sheds, crafty crannies, and reading. *Reading Teacher*, 1976, **29**, 376–378.

Criscuolo's article reminds us to look at how reading is being taught in many classrooms, but then gives suggestions for providing clever learning centers.

Durkin, D. *Teaching them to read.* Boston: Allyn and Bacon, 1978.

An entire chapter on basal readers and other commercial materials is included. Questions concerning both the negative and positive elements of basal programs are discussed.

Farr, R., and Roser, N. *Teaching a child to read.* New York: Harcourt Brace Jovanovich, 1979.

As a part of one chapter entitled "Programs for Teaching Reading," the basal reading program is discussed. A chart lists level designations for major programs on the market in 1979.

Spache, G. D., and Spache, E. B. *Reading in the elementary school.* (4th ed.) Boston: Allyn and Bacon, 1977.

This book is divided into three parts, one of which deals with the various reading practices currently in use. One of the approaches discussed is the basal reader approach.

# CHAPTER 16

# Developing and Implementing an Individualized Program of Reading Instruction

Edwina Battle-Vold
Indiana University of Pennsylvania
Indiana, Pennsylvania

*Basal readers offer beginning teachers a structure for teaching reading and a variety of prepared materials and instructional strategies. It is sensible, therefore, for beginning teachers to use basal readers in some fashion, and Chapters 14 and 15 have described how beginning teachers can make wise use of basal readers. Other approaches to reading instruction exist, however, and an individualized program of reading instruction is a viable alternative to a basal program, or an eclectic counterpart (i.e., one to be used in conjunction with them). In this chapter, Edwina Battle-Vold describes how a beginning teacher can develop and implement an individualized reading program. Since an individualized reading program is not for everyone, Battle-Vold begins by defining what such programs entail and discussing the characteristics teachers need to succeed in using an individualized reading program. She then presents a step-by-step description of how beginning teachers can prepare themselves and their classrooms to initiate either a completely individualized reading program or some modification of it. A sample time schedule for an individualized reading program and a detailed description of what the first week of an individualized reading program might be like conclude the chapter.*

What do you know about individualized programs for reading instruction? In your methods courses, you have probably read about this reading approach along with several other methods, such as the language experience or basal reader approach. As you may have observed in elementary school classrooms, many possible variations of the individualized reading approach can be used. Whatever your source of knowledge about

individualized programs of reading instruction, use the space below to jot down your definition. An individualized program of reading instruction is: _____
_____
_____
_____

Did you include in your definition the idea that the individualized reading approach attempts to deal with individual differences by designing reading instruction on a one-to-one basis? Did you include the principles upon which the individualized program of reading instruction approach is based, such as self-selection and self-pacing? Did you describe activities that take place in an individualized program of reading instruction in which teachers and students play active roles, such as individual conferences, skill development, and record keeping for evaluative purposes? Compare your definition of this reading approach with those of your classmates. You will probably find as many different definitions as there are persons willing to offer a definition of individualized reading.

Though the individualized program of reading instruction may mean different things to different people, for the purposes of this chapter, it is defined as follows: "individualized reading" is a personalized process of teaching and learning reading that allows individuals to seek and select a wide variety of interesting and challenging reading materials, which are then used to develop students' reading skills. It is not a single method of instruction but a *general approach* that allows for many variations in materials, presentation format, and skill instruction. At the heart of any individualized reading program is the concept of self-selection, which is the motivating force behind promoting students' interest in books and their desire to read. One must remember, however, that

> [the individualized program of reading instruction] ... can never be effective in improving children's abilities to read if it becomes a patent procedure, a senti-mental devotion, a rite or ceremony, an exclusive ideology, a vacuous symbol, a standardization, a slogan, a dogma.... It ceases the moment that procedures replace perceptiveness, routine supersedes reflection or the moment that things take over for thinking or custom begins to curb creativity (Jacobs, 1958, p. 5).

The purpose of this chapter, then, is *not* to offer a standardized, patent procedure but to provide a plan—a set of suggestions and ideas the beginning teacher can use to individualize a program of reading instruction.

## THE TEACHER

It is an accepted fact that the teacher is a significant—if not the primary—factor in the success of any program of instruction. Thus, teachers who design individualized programs of reading instruction must recognize in themselves those characteristics that can promote or impede the effectiveness of the program. Characteristics that are considered important in effective teachers, specifically those for teachers of reading, are listed in Figure 16.1. Honestly evaluate yourself by checking the yes, no, or sometimes column in response to the ten questions asked.

How did you rate yourself? The teacher who successfully uses an individualized program of reading instruction is likely to achieve high ratings on this assessment of personal characteristics. All are important in helping children become successful at independently seeking, selecting, and pacing themselves in the reading program. Although all of the characteristics listed are important, independence, intellectual security, and enthusiasm will be highlighted in this discussion. The independent teacher is secure and allows students to become independent. The independent teacher has no need to create environments in which children must adhere to the teacher's preconceived style of learning. Children can, and must, be self-directed and make choices for themselves.

The teacher who is intellectually secure is confident in her ability to teach. The secure teacher does not depend on manuals that dictate each day's lesson or specific skill-reinforcing activities for the class. Such a teacher knows the field of reading, and understands how children develop cognitively and learn to read. The intellectually secure teacher is able to detect deviations and gaps in children's reading development and can prescribe activities to fulfill children's needs as they are revealed in conferences, group activities, and informal interactions.

Show me a teacher who is enthusiastic about children and what children read, and I will show you children who enjoy reading. The teacher who knows books, shares them with children, and is personally enthusiastic about reading inspires a love and an appreciation for reading in students (Huck, 1971).

Some teachers find it difficult to feel enthusiasm for basal reading programs. The individualized program of reading instruction offers such teachers an alternative to prepackaged materials and basal reading programs. The materials used in an individualized program of reading instruction can range from comic books to informational publications.

| Characteristics | Rating | | |
|---|---|---|---|
| | Yes | No | Sometimes |
| 1. Are you alert and enthusiastic in your work? | | | |
| 2. Are you interested in children and their activities? | | | |
| 3. Are you self-controlled, not easily upset? | | | |
| 4. Are you flexible in the way you plan activities? | | | |
| 5. Are you independent and without the need to have complete control over other people and situations? | | | |
| 6. Are you intellectually curious and knowledgeable in your field? | | | |
| 7. Are you well organized in your planning for instruction? | | | |
| 8. Are you patient? | | | |
| 9. Are you cheerful and optimistic? | | | |
| 10. Are you accepting of individual differences? | | | |

Figure 16.1. The characteristics of a good teacher.

The methods used for developing skills can range from tutorials to learning centers to whole-class participation. The individualized program of reading instruction, though not appropriate for all teachers or students, offers a viable alternative to the use of commercial reading programs. By definition, an individualized reading program can be tailored to meet the needs of the teacher and individual students and to foster creativity, excitement, and enthusiasm.

## THE BACKGROUND

The first step for a teacher who wants to adopt an individualized program of reading instruction is to read numerous children's books. Thousands of children's books are published each year and added to the multitude of books for children already on library shelves. When a teacher decides to implement an individualized reading program, it becomes his responsibility to familiarize himself with children's literature. Sources that provide such information include review publications such as *The Horn Book, Booklist, School Library Journal,* and the *Children's Catalog.* Book reviews can also be found in journals such as *The Reading Teacher, Young Children,* and *Language Arts.* Some excellent guides to children's literature include *Children and Books* (Arbuthnot, 1964), *Starting Out Right* (Latimer, 1972), and *Multi-Ethnic Books for Young Children* (Griffin, 1970). (These materials are described in the Recommended Readings at the end of this chapter.)

The teacher who implements an individualized program of reading must not only know which books are appropriate for children but also be able to supply at least five books for each student. A classroom library of 100 to 200 books is needed. Since a beginning teacher does not possess a personal library this large, how can she gather the collection of books she will need? The following are several suggestions.

1. Purchase inexpensive paperback books from supermarkets, novelty shops, and small bookstores.
2. Check out library books for short periods of time.
3. Visit garage sales and auctions to look for old but functional books for children.
4. Involve your class in a children's book club; most clubs offer bonus (free) books for every five or six books purchased.
5. Check with libraries; they may give you old or duplicate books.
6. Ask parents to contribute books from their libraries, attics, and basements.

Besides being asked to contribute books from their attics and basements, parents should be encouraged to help in the overall collection and selection of books for the individualized program of reading instruction. Parents then can understand more clearly the purpose of the program and the process that is used in instruction. Also, parental involvement in the reading program fosters support for the program.

## THE PREPARATION

Let us suppose that you are a second-grade teacher. First, you must determine the range of reading ability in your class on the basis of information from sources such as informal reading inventories, standardized tests, and reading levels established by previous teachers. (Refer to Part II of this book for specifics in this area.) A typical second-grade class will probably include students with a range of reading abilities; some students will be nonreaders, some will be beginning readers, and some will read at the fourth-grade level or beyond. Considering all the books you have read and the varied reading levels in your second-grade class, what will your selection of books look like? You may choose picture books, informational books, participation books, easy-to-read books, Mother Goose and riddle books, and joke books. Also, your collection should include books that are multicultural.

The books you choose for your collection should be functional and of high quality. Be careful to avoid books that promote stereotypes with regard to race, ethnicity, or sex.

After collecting an adequate number of books, you must determine the reading levels of the books you selected. On recently copyrighted material, you may find the readability level imprinted on the back cover or in the front of the book, since many publishers of children's books now provide this information. Also, check with your school or district reading coordinator, who may have already determined the readability of many of the books you will use. As a last resort, you can estimate the readability of your materials by following a readability assessment procedure such as the Fry Readability Graph (Fry, 1977), which is reproduced in Figure 16.2. Keep in mind that the readability level you obtain is only an estimate and that the "true" readability of a book may vary within a grade level or two of the estimate.

In addition to establishing the reading level of each book, you need to identify vocabulary words within the book that may be especially difficult for your students. In any basal reader's directed reading lesson, the teacher has the responsibility to help children to learn unfamiliar vocabulary words before silent reading. The individualized reading approach requires the same teaching strategy. How can a teacher who uses an individualized program of reading instruction possibly help each student with new vocabulary when every student has a different book to read? An example that illustrates a procedure that can be used, follows.

In *The Big Snow,* by Berta and Elmer Hader, the following words have been identified as words that second-grade children may need to be taught before they silently read the book: *ebbed, nibbled, beneath, attention,* and *pheasants.* Put the words in sentences, and then type the sentences on an index card. Next, place the card inside the front cover of the book. The card for *The Big Snow* would look like this one.

---

### Do You Know These Words?

The river *ebbed* slowly to the ocean.

The littlest rabbit *nibbled* another carrot top.

Her home was *beneath* the rock pile.

They paid no *attention* to the geese.

The *pheasants* roamed through the woods.

---

To help monitor comprehension, you need to formulate comprehension questions. Factual, inferential, and critical questions designed by the teacher can be either answered independently by the students or used by the teacher in the conference that is held after

## GRAPH FOR ESTIMATING READABILITY —EXTENDED

by Edward Fry, Rutgers University Reading Center, New Brunswick, N.J. 08904

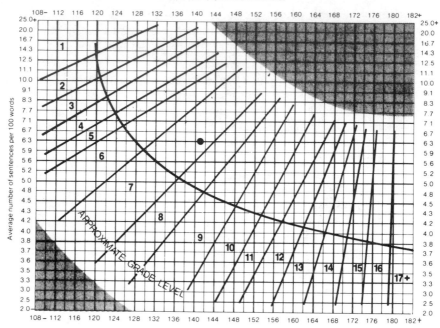

### Expanded Directions for Working Readability Graph

1. Randomly select three (3) sample passages and count out exactly 100 words each, beginning with the beginning of a sentence. Do count proper nouns, initializations, and numerals.
2. Count the number of sentences in the hundred words, estimating length of the fraction of the last sentence to the nearest one-tenth.
3. Count the total number of syllables in the 100-word passage. If you don't have a hand counter available, an easy way is to simply put a mark above every syllable over one in each word, then when you get to the end of the passage, count the number of marks and add 100. Small calculators can also be used as counters by pushing numeral 1, then push the + sign for each word or syllable when counting.
4. Enter graph with *average* sentence length and *average* number of syllables; plot dot where the two lines intersect. Area where dot is plotted will give you the approximate grade level.
5. If a great deal of variability is found in syllable count or sentence count, putting more samples into the average is desirable.
6. A word is defined as a group of symbols with a space on either side; thus, *Joe, IRA, 1945,* and & are each one word.
7. A syllable is defined as a phonetic syllable. Generally, there are as many syllables as vowel sounds. For example, *stopped* is one syllable and *wanted* is two syllables. When counting syllables for numerals and initializations, count one syllable for each symbol. For example, *1945* is four syllables, *IRA* is three syllables, and & is one syllable.

---

Note: This "extended graph" does not outmode or render the earlier (1968) version inoperative or inaccurate; it is an extension. (REPRODUCTION PERMITTED—NO COPYRIGHT)

Figure 16.2. The Fry Readability Graph.

the student has read the book. Like the vocabulary words, these questions should be typed on a card, but the comprehension card is placed at the end of the book. The following are examples of comprehension questions.

---

**I Can Answer These Questions.**

1. Why was the book called *The Big Snow*?
2. What were some of the signs that winter was on its way?
3. Which animals were able to survive outside during the winter months? Why?
4. What time of year was the happiest time for most of the animals? Why?

---

The comprehension questions that can be used for the books in an individualized program of reading instruction do not always have to be so specific as those used for *The Big Snow*. In addition to questions like those listed above, which are specifically tied to a particular book, general questions can be asked about any book. If the book is a narrative, for example, questions like the following would be appropriate.

1. What character did you like best? Why did you like him or her?
2. What part of the story was the hardest for you to understand?
3. Do you believe that everything in the story actually happened? Why or why not?
4. Can you make up a different ending for the story?

A good strategy for monitoring students' comprehension and helping them to prepare for the pupil-teacher conference involves having students talk with other students who have already read the same book. Children of all ages who have successfully read a book are excellent evaluators of those who finished reading the same book more recently. They are able to evaluate the correctness of responses to questions and generally to discuss the book. A form that shows the names of students who have read each book should be kept in a file that students can examine. A card from such a file for the book *The Big Snow* would look like Figure 16.3.

## THE SCHEDULE

After the books have been selected, readability determined, and vocabulary sentences and comprehension questions written, you must establish a schedule that provides students time for independent reading and for the other components of the individualized reading program, such as individual conferences and group skill instruction. For example, for a teacher who had established a 90-minute period for daily reading and language arts instruction, the weekly schedule displayed in Figure 16.4 would be appropriate. Although this is a generalized schedule, note that specific times are set aside for self-selection and reading, skill instruction, and pupil-teacher conferences. Also note that major activities are in capital letters and supplemental activities or explanations are in lowercase letters.

## THE PROCESS

It is critical that students be fully introduced to an individualized reading program before the program is initiated. You will need to work your students into the program

I HAVE READ _____ The Big Snow

Tommy Johson

Rita Martinez

Michael Jefferson

Miss Matthews (Teacher)

Rachel Stein

Figure 16.3. A sample file card.

|  |  | 8:30–9:00 | 9:00–9:30 | 9:30–10:00 |
|--|--|-----------|-----------|------------|
| Monday | | BOOK SELECTION Silent Reading | SKILL GROUPS Silent Reading | LANGUAGE ARTS Functional Grammar |
| Tuesday | | CONFERENCES | CONFERENCES Silent Reading | CONFERENCES Silent Reading |
| Wednesday | | LANGUAGE ARTS Individualized Spelling | SILENT READING Book Selection | SILENT READING Conferences |
| Thursday | | CONFERENCES Prepare for Sharing Time | SKILL GROUPS | LANGUAGE ARTS Creative Writing |
| Friday | | SKILL GROUPS | SHARING TIME | SKILL GROUPS |

Figure 16.4. A weekly schedule for an individualized reading program.

slowly and carefully. The following synopsis of the first five days in a typical individualized reading program should give you a sense of how, and at what pace, children should be introduced to an individualized reading program.

*First Day.* Meet with the children to explain the process. The teacher's introduction might take this form.

"Girls and boys, we are beginning a different reading program. I have many new and exciting books just for you. Today, you will choose one of the books you would like to read.

"To help you select a book that is not too hard for you, I have arranged the books in our classroom on three different shelves: a red shelf, a blue shelf, and a green shelf. In your folders you will find a card that is red, blue, or green. You may choose books from the shelf that are the same color as your card."

The teacher has arranged books according to readability level. If this were a third-grade class, for example, the readability levels of books on the red, blue, and green shelves would be of second-, third-, and fourth-grade difficulty, respectively. Also, the teacher would have estimated each student's instructional reading level so that each student would be assigned to one shelf. Keep in mind, however, that both readability and instructional reading level determinations are *estimates;* therefore, be flexible when assigning students to shelves.

"Also, to help you choose a book you are interested in and one that you can easily read, I have listed some words that might be difficult for you to read. The words are in sentences on a card inside the front cover of your book and are underlined in red. If you miss more than half of the words, the book may be too hard for you. There will be time to select another book, and I will help you.

"You may set your own pace when you read. Read the book you choose for as long as you need to today, tomorrow, and the following day. When you have completed your book, there are questions you need to answer about what you read. You can find these questions on another card at the back of your book.

"I will be available to have conferences with you on each of the days that we read independently. Tell me when you have finished your book, and we will schedule a time for a conference. At conference time, you can tell me about your book and read orally your favorite part of the book. This will help me to see how well you read and to find out about any problems you may be having understanding your book.

"Are there any questions? All right, go ahead and select your books now. Then, find a comfortable place to read and enjoy yourself."

*Second Day.* On the second day, some students begin to sign up for conferences with the teacher. The teacher should have a file card for each child that includes space for titles of the books read, the level of the books read, and word identification and comprehension skills that may need development. It is also helpful in your planning for skill development to have a checklist available for evaluating individual student's progress. A sample checklist can be found in Figure 16.5. Note that the checklist includes categories that allow the teacher to evaluate each students' sight vocabulary, word identification skills, and comprehension skills.

Three aspects of reading that Veatch (1959) has suggested a teacher should investigate thoroughly during the conference are (1) the pupil's understanding of and reaction to the chosen book, (2) the pupil's ability to deal with specific reading skills (vocabulary, word identification, comprehension), and (3) the pupil's ability to read orally. If the teacher has dealt with all three of these aspects, there should be a wealth of information collected. After you have begun to gather this information for all of your students, you will find that several children may need instruction in the same skills. Skill groups that address only the skills that are needed can then be formed. These groups are sometimes small and involve only a few students; other times, they are large. The skill groups, however, must be kept flexible and can exist only as long as two or more children need the same instruction. (Refer to the discussion of skill groups in Chapter 14 for additional information.)

*Third Day.* The third day is another for individual reading, self-selection, and conferences. By this time, some children have already read their books, conferred with you,

## INDIVIDUALIZED READING PROGRAM
## PUPIL-TEACHER CONFERENCE CHECKLIST

Student Name: _____   Date: _____

Book read from: _____   Readability level of book: _____

| SKILLS | COMMENTS |
|--------|----------|
| Basic Sight Vocabulary | |
| Phonic Analysis | |
|   consonants | |
|   vowels | |
|   generalizations | |
| Structural Analysis | |
|   base words | |
|   affixes | |
|   compound words | |
|   inflections | |
|   contractions | |
| Contextual Analysis | |
| Comprehension | |
|   literal | |
|   inferential | |
|   critical | |
| Oral Reading Fluency | |

Additional comments: _____

Figure 16.5. A sample checklist.

and selected second books, while others are still reading their first books. It is important, therefore, that you closely monitor each student's time and progress. To ensure that students are reading and conferring with you, it is wise to keep a record of conferences with students. A simple record sheet like Figure 16.6 would be sufficient.

*Fourth Day.* By the fourth day, you have formed reading skill groups. The groups are formed only on the basis of identified student needs and are maintained only as long as the members of the group need instruction. Teachers using the individualized reading approach must be knowledgeable about techniques for teaching phonics, sight words, structural analysis, context clues, and comprehension skills. They must know the scope and sequence of reading skills and use them as children acquire various reading skills.

*Fifth Day.* The fifth day is the day for sharing. Children are encouraged to share portions of their favorite books. Sharing can take many forms, and the more varied the ways that children learn to share their readings, the more interest children will develop about the books they are reading or have read. Some activities in which children can engage after completing their books and waiting for conferences include the following.

1. Dramatizing sections of the book they read. This can be done individually or in groups.
2. Constructing a book diorama from a box and placing scenes from the story inside.
3. Drawing a cartoon that tells an entire story or short parts of a book.
4. Preparing sequels to a favorite story.
5. Making mobiles that depict characters from a book.
6. Writing a letter to a friend describing and recommending a book without giving away the ending.
7. Using puppets or pencil people to dramatize the story.
8. Reviewing a book as a newspaper or television critic would.
9. Making an "I Liked This Book" bulletin board on which students write short reports on the books they enjoyed.

This list is not all inclusive, for there are many other ways of sharing books or parts of books with the class. Some students prefer more personal ways, such as keeping their own vocabulary word list of new words or making pictures to be shared with their families.

## SUMMARY

The individualized program of reading instruction, which is currently practiced in many elementary classrooms, is a personalized method of reading instruction that allows

### TEACHER'S RECORD OF CONFERENCES

| Student's Name: _____ | Week of: _____ | Week of: _____ | Week of: _____ |
|---|---|---|---|
| _____ | M  T  W  Th  F | M  T  W  Th  F | M  T  W  Th  F |
| _____ | M  T  W  Th  F | M  T  W  Th  F | M  T  W  Th  F |
| _____ | M  T  W  Th  F | M  T  W  Th  F | M  T  W  Th  F |

Figure 16.6. A sample record sheet.

individual students to choose from a variety of reading materials of interesting and challenging content. An appealing feature of this reading approach is that it permits students and teachers to personalize reading instruction much more than if a basal reader program were used.

A prerequisite for an effective individualized program of reading instruction is the availability of many varied reading materials at a range of difficulty levels. From these varied reading materials, students are able to *seek* and *select* books that they themselves find readable and interesting. The individualized program of reading instruction, which requires both teacher and student involvement, is successful only when all of those involved share their enthusiasm for the independence, the variety, and the flexible structure that takes into consideration the student's natural pace, interest level, and readiness.

## REFERENCES

Fry, E. Graph for estimating readability: Extended. *Journal of Reading,* 1977, **21**, 242-252.

Huck, C. S. Strategies for improving interest and appreciation in literature. In H. Painter (Ed.), *Reaching children and young people through literature.* Newark, Del.: International Reading Association, 1971.

Jacobs, L. Individualized reading is not a thing! In A. Miel (Ed.), *Individualized reading practices: Practical suggestions for teaching.* New York: Bureau of Publications, Teachers College, Columbia University, 1958.

Veatch, J. *Individualizing your reading program: Self-selection in action.* New York: G. P. Putnam's Sons, 1959.

## RECOMMENDED READINGS

Arbuthnot, M. H. *Children and books.* (3rd ed.) Chicago: Scott, Foresman and Company, 1964.
   Arbuthnot's anthology of children's literature covers all years.

Gerlach, G. How to direct directed reading. *Teacher,* 1981, **98**, 72–73.
   The direct directed lesson is another variation of the individualized reading approach that was used effectively in a university elementary school.

Griffin, L. *Multi-ethnic books for young children.* Washington, D.C.: National Association for the Education of Young Children, 1970.
   The annotated bibliography of books for young children emphasizes American Indian, Appalachian, Afro-American, Jewish, Asian, and Latin American populations.

Latimer, B. I. *Starting out right: Choosing books about black people for young children.* Madison, Wis.: Department of Public Instruction, 1972.
   This book contains reviews of books for preschool through third-grade children and criteria for judging books involving black people.

Spache, G. D., and Spache, E. B. *Reading in the elementary school.* (4th ed.) Boston: Allyn and Bacon, 1977.
   In this text, the authors devote two chapters to the individualized reading approach. One chapter is devoted to the assumptions and principles underlying the reading practice. The second chapter offers the reader practical steps toward individualizing reading.

Veatch, J. *Individualizing your reading program: Self-selection in action.* New York: G. P. Putnam's Sons, 1959.
   Veatch's book discusses the principle of self-selection of reading materials.

### Periodicals

*Children's Catalog:* The first part of this source arranges the books according to the Dewey decimal system, and the second gives an excerpt of a review from some source.

*Booklist:* Published by the American Library Association twice monthly, but once in August, this periodical's reviews give plots and criticisms. All books in this source are recommended.

*The Horn Book:* A periodical published bimonthly, it is an excellent source for articles about book-related topics as well as selected reviews of children's books.

*Language Arts:* Formerly called *Elementary English, Language Arts* is published eight times a year by the National Council of Teachers of English. It includes recent publications of books, with plot summaries.

*The Reading Teacher:* This journal publishes a limited number of reviews of children's books. It is published by the International Reading Association monthly.

*Young Children:* Published by the National Association for the Education of Young Children, this journal occasionally features books for preschool and primary-grade children.

*School Library Journal:* For a wide variety of books at different reading levels, this journal published by R. R. Bowker Company is an excellent source. The books are reviewed by diverse critics and summaries go beyond simple plot synopses.

# CHAPTER 17

# Managing a Classroom Reading Program

Joan P. Gipe
University of New Orleans

*The first three chapters in Part III have discussed several* methods *and* materials *used in reading instruction that are appropriate for beginning teachers. To end our discussion there, however, would be a disservice to beginning teachers, for a third and crucial component is missing—the* management *component. A reading program based on an elaborate set of basal readers or a sophisticated individualized reading plan does not succeed automatically. A teacher still must manage classroom reading instruction. In other words, a reading teacher must organize classroom reading time wisely and organize instruction so that children perform the tasks required in an orderly manner. Without adequate class management, no program can succeed. In this chapter, Joan Gipe discusses this critical component of reading instruction. She begins by offering the reader guidelines for effective classroom management, which describe how to design and allocate tasks, supervise students and maintain discipline, provide feedback, and inspire commitment and cooperation. After these preliminaries, Gipe suggests ways a beginning teacher can establish a management plan, and she concludes the chapter with a detailed discussion and concrete examples of three alternative management techniques: (1) units, (2) independent learning systems, and (3) special groupings.*

For a beginning teacher, the task of putting into practice the instructional strategies learned in teacher–education programs can be overwhelming. Add to that challenge the realities of dealing with 25 to 40 students, and you have a considerable management task. Classroom management problems, which include organizational as well as disciplinary concerns, are probably the beginning teacher's most formidable problem. Understanding the principles of reading instruction and implementing a reading program are two different things. One could go so far as to say that, if a classroom teacher is *not* competent in classroom management, achievement suffers. In fact, the more time a teacher spends on management chores, which include disciplining students, the less time there is available for instruction (Cooley and Leinhardt, 1980; Stallings and Kaskowitz, 1974).

The purpose of this chapter, then, is to provide guidelines and a number of alternative techniques for managing a classroom reading program so that the beginning teacher is aware of some potential solutions to some fundamental problems.

## DEFINING TERMS

Teachers who become effective classroom managers stimulate their students' achievement. As Guthrie (1980) has written:

> Classroom teachers contribute to reading achievement by optimizing the scheduled time for reading and related activities, selecting materials that insure learning, minimizing the interruption of student attention, and assessing the amount of learning as a guide to assigning new materials. When these conditions are met, time in school has a handsome payoff (p. 502).

"Classroom management," as the term is used in this chapter, refers specifically to what Guthrie has called "optimizing the scheduled time" and "minimizing the interruption of student attention." In other words, the effective management of a reading program allows all students to use a maximum amount of "time on task." Let us say that the time scheduled for reading instruction is 60 minutes each day. Ideally, during most of those 60 minutes, students would be involved in reading instruction, whether direct teacher instruction or self-directed instruction.

The remainder of this chapter deals with two topics: (1) general guidelines for effective classroom management and (2) special management techniques related specifically to reading instruction (although these techniques may be useful in other subject areas as well). The techniques to be discussed are appropriate for all grade levels and all types of classrooms (self-contained, open, team-taught, and departmentalized).

## GUIDELINES FOR EFFECTIVE CLASSROOM MANAGEMENT

### Can You Identify a Well-Managed Classroom?

Take a few minutes to think about the classrooms you have observed or those with which you have been involved. Try to list the characteristics of those classrooms that indicated to you whether each was well managed. If possible, you might try to complete a semantic feature analysis to identify the relationships among what you think are features (characteristics) of a well-managed classroom. (See Chapter 3 and Table 17.1 for the beginning of a semantic feature analysis.)

### Considerations for Effective Management

It may be apparent from examining your list or semantic feature analysis chart that the type of classroom organizational plan (i.e., achievement groups, skill groupings, individualized programs) did not determine whether a classroom was effectively managed.

**Table 17.1. Section of a Semantic Feature Analysis for the Well-Managed Classroom**

| Classroom Organizational Plans | Students Working With Others of Same Ability | Skill Needs Being Met | Much Independent Reading | Many Learning Centers | Groups Rotated Often | Student Input Into Assignments |
|---|---|---|---|---|---|---|
| Achievement groups | + | + | – | – | – | – |
| Skill groups | + | + | – | + | + | – |
| Interest groups | – | – | + | – | + | + |
| Friendship groups | – | – | + | – | – | + |
| Individualized | + | + | + | + | + | + |

Rather, effective management occurs when students are meaningfully engaged in learning activities. According to Intili and Conrad (1980, p. 62), there are four interrelated management concerns: (1) task design and allocation, (2) supervisory strategy, (3) feedback system, and (4) student cooperation and commitment.

### Task Design and Allocation

Task design and allocation involves the decisions a teacher makes regarding the tasks on which students are to work. The tasks should be analyzed so that the teacher can determine the best way in which the tasks should be performed and who will benefit most from the tasks. For example, learning how to use a glossary is a task important to every student, so large-group instruction might be most appropriate. On the other hand, a task dealing with auditory discrimination of initial and final sound *b* would call for small-group instruction including only specific individuals. In addition, the clarity of the task is crucial to how well it can keep students involved. Understanding the directions and understanding the teacher's expectations are parts of the clarity of the task. The problem of task clarity becomes more important as the classroom structure becomes more individualized. The appropriateness of a task for specific students assumes that the teacher has performed some type of diagnostic work to determine the needs of individual students. (See Chapter 9.)

Once a beginning teacher has become familiar with the rest of the teaching staff and the materials available, a system of classifying instructional materials, called the Annehurst Curriculum Classification System (ACCS), may be implemented. Briefly, this system enables the teacher to classify materials for any curriculum area according to a variety of identifying characteristics for ease in storage and retrieval. For example, using the ACCS thesaurus, a material that works on short vowel *a* can be classified 4551. The first digit (4) refers to the major discipline: language and literature. The second digit (5) refers to the subject area: phonics. The third digit (5) refers to a division within the subject area: short vowels. The last digit (1) refers to the topic within the division, in this case, the short vowel *a*. The system is flexible enough to be expanded and, in fact, was designed to be expanded. For example, materials could be coded for media format. If the phonics material were recorded on a cassette tape and tapes received a code of 2, the classification could be 45512. Materials could also be coded for the amount of space they require or the amount of noise they involve. Any piece of information that would help the teacher understand at a glance the task design could be coded. According to Frymier (1977), the ACCS "includes detailed descriptive information about curriculum materials that relates directly to those characteristics of individual learners that affect their learning: previous experiences, intellectual ability, motivation, and visual and auditory perceptual skills, among other things" (p. 121). In summary, the ACCS is a complete task-analysis system worth investigating, especially for use in an individualized reading program, which involves a wide variety of materials.

## Supervisory Strategy

The second management concern, the selection of a supervisory strategy, involves the degree to which the teacher can monitor how well tasks are being performed. Only during whole-group instruction can the teacher directly observe which students are working, which are not, and why they are not. In any other organizational plan, the teacher must delegate supervisory responsibility to others, usually to the students themselves. Making students, or groups of students, responsible for their own supervision requires the teacher to invest appreciable amounts of preparation time.

The supervisory aspect of classroom management is closely related to classroom discipline. Welch and Halfacre (1978) have discussed ten guidelines for helping students assume more responsibility for their own supervision in the classroom. These ten ideas constitute a synthesis of three classroom management systems: behavior modification, Glasser's reality therapy, and teacher effectiveness training (Glasser, 1965, 1969; Gordon, 1974; Skinner, 1968). Summarized, the guidelines are:

1. *Be involved.* Recognize and treat children as human beings by sharing relevant childhood experiences, mutual feelings, frustrations, and expectations and by listening.
2. *Establish rules.* Five or six clear, specific rules developed with the help of the students are sufficient. The consequences of breaking the rules should also be determined ahead of time. The rules can be posted or copied for everyone.
3. *Involve students in decision making.* Class meetings, rap sessions, class councils, and suggestion boxes provide excellent opportunities for obtaining students' reactions and recommendations.
4. *Use specific language.* Avoid using vague affective terms to describe students' behavior. Instead of saying that "Johnny is lazy," it would be better to say that "Johnny does not complete his assignments."
5. *Be consistent.* It is important that children know not only what they are expected to do but also what the consequences will be when they do not do what is expected of them.
6. *Emphasize acting instead of talking.* Developing a plan of action ahead of time is more efficient than talking about problems as they arise. One such plan is discussed by Glasser (1965, 1969) as part of his reality therapy approach. In essence, the plan involves (1) stopping the misbehavior, (2) getting the student to identify the misbehavior and to make a judgment about whether it was helpful to anyone, (3) requiring the student to come up with a plan to improve classroom behavior, and (4) reporting back to the teacher about how the plan is working.

7. *Develop contracts.* Formal, written agreements between teacher and students are valuable tools for handling disciplinary problems as well as academic behavior. In developing contracts, it is important to:
   a. Involve the students in the wording of the contract,
   b. Be specific about the responsibilities of the student, teacher, or parent, whoever is involved,
   c. Be specific about the consequences of not fulfilling the contract and about the procedures for changing the contract,
   d. Designate dates for reviewing the contract's results,
   e. Have all the parties involved sign the contract.

   Contracts can be used with a whole class, with individual students, or with groups. Learning contracts are discussed further, and examples are given, later in this chapter.

8. *Recognize appropriate behavior.* Instead of only recognizing the students' misbehavior and "wrong" responses, encourage positive behavior by recognizing acceptable responses and good performances on reading assignments.

9. *Ignore inappropriate behavior.* Many students misbehave, or make no attempt to do well, in order to get attention. When appropriate behaviors (see the preceding guideline) gain attention while inappropriate behaviors do not, inappropriate behaviors eventually cease. Potentially dangerous situations, however, cannot be handled in this way. Guideline six should be followed in such situations.

10. *Call a time-out.* Calling a time-out is similar to sending a student to a corner or to the principal's office. Additional suggestions for using time-outs effectively include:
    a. Be sure the student understands why she is being removed from the classroom.
    b. Establish a specific amount of time for the time-out. This time could vary depending on the misbehavior, but similar actions should result in equal time-out periods. Be consistent!
    c. Do not use time-outs as the only way of dealing with misbehavior. Emphasize positive, responsible behavior by employing guidelines eight and nine.

Many excellent resources are available to help the teacher handle classroom discipline. Some of them are listed in the Recommended Readings at the end of this chapter.

### Feedback System

The third management concern, the design of a feedback system, becomes more important as teachers move from whole-group instruction to individualized instruction. Record keeping is a major aspect of the feedback system, and since a discussion of record-keeping systems was included in Chapter 16, the topic will not be discussed here. Other approaches for providing feedback on the students' progress, however, include the following.

1. Individual conferences, lasting 20 minutes each, can be scheduled about once every two weeks.

2. Brief observations about individual students can be written down in a notebook every day. At the end of the day, the teacher goes over the comments in the notebook and uses them for future planning. For example, "John is not finishing his work—check to see whether it is appropriate for him." "I missed Susan today—be sure to see her tomorrow." "The whole group has trouble with the directions at the vowel digraph learning center—clarify these directions."

3. Students post weekly learning contracts or schedules so that they are visible to all. The teacher can more easily check each student's progress and work with individuals to make changes when necessary.

4. Students keep journals, or logs, that describe what they have done and how they feel about their work and why. Scheduling 20 minutes at some time during the day for journal writing is sufficient. The journals also can be used in individual conferences.

5. Class meetings (Glasser, 1969) can be held at least once a week to discuss specific problems or to clarify certain concepts.

6. Regular reviews of the management scheme are needed to check on interaction patterns, especially the teacher's ability to respond to students' requests and needs.

### Student Cooperation and Commitment

The fourth management concern involves the students' cooperation and commitment. This ongoing process centers instruction, as much as possible, on the students' interests and involves students in decisions about how they spend their time in the classroom. The number of decisions students are allowed to make about how they spend their time should be kept to a minimum until the students become skilled at making such decisions and until the teacher feels comfortable with managing such a system.

## HOW TO GET STARTED

How do you begin to establish a management plan for your classroom? A six-step procedure for implementing a well-managed reading program follows.

1. *Become familiar with your teaching environment.* This step is important, since some aspects of your teaching situation are unchangeable. For example, the philosophy of your school's reading program may be very different from your own. You may see reading as a language or communication skill, while the school may view reading as a set of discrete skills, each to be mastered before moving on to other skills. Other questions to answer include: How is the school day divided? Are classrooms self-contained? What are the physical aspects of the classroom? What funds are available? What textbooks are available? Who are your colleagues? Are parents involved in school activities? What are the backgrounds of the children? Do you harbor any prejudices or fears about the community in which you work? Your answers to these questions will reveal some of the factors that can affect how well the reading program you design will work.

2. *Establish general goals.* Once you recognize the physical realities of your teaching situation and have achieved some understanding of the people with whom you will be working (students, fellow teachers, principal, parents), you can develop some general goals for your reading program. Many school systems adopt curriculum guides, which can be helpful in developing these general goals. For example:

*Skills:* To improve students' language skills in reading, writing, and listening.

*Knowledge:* To help students to discriminate fact from opinion and acquire basic information about the various forms of propaganda.

*Interest:* To encourage students to read more for enjoyment.

Whether you achieve these general goals for every student will depend on your ability to meet the specific needs of the individual students in your classroom. Students in any one group will be at different places on the road to attaining your general goals. The next step, therefore, is a crucial one.

3. *Assess students' abilities and interests.* To meet the individual needs of students, you must know what those needs are. Diagnosing students' strengths and weaknesses can be done through both formal (standardized) and informal measures. Chapters 9, 10, 11, and 12 should be reviewed for more detail on how to administer tests and what to do with the results. Also, the reading interest inventory in Chapter 20 is an instrument that informally assesses students' reading interests.

4. *Assess materials.* Now that you have some information about the specific abilities of your students, you need to determine what materials you have available and which of those are suitable. Do not overlook classroom aids. A variety of aids can be used to provide direct instructional input. Generally, these fall into three categories: audio, visual, and multisensory aids. The more commonly used audio aids include record players, radios, language labs (such as for teaching a foreign language), and tape recorders. Visual aids include chalkboards, bulletin boards, overhead and opaque projectors, filmstrips, and textbooks. Multisensory aids include films, television, language masters, sandpaper cutouts, felt boards, and computers. The use of computers as aids to instruction is discussed at length in Chapter 19. The information you gather about students' interests (step three) should also be utilized in assessing instructional materials.

5. *Establish grouping patterns.* A wide variety of choices can be made at this point. Chapter 14 discusses several grouping plans, and Chapter 16 discusses individualized reading programs. Later in this chapter, some alternative groupings are discussed. After studying all of this information, you will have to choose a plan that works best for you. Regardless of which plan you choose, *move slowly!* Do not try to implement any plan fully during the first day or week or month of school. Become comfortable with a plan, using it first with only a few students before expanding it to include larger groups.

6. *Determine specific objectives.* Instructional objectives should be based directly on the results of your assessments of the students' needs and interests. For example, if the assessment showed that many students could not discriminate factual

statements from statements of opinion, a specific objective such as the following could be developed: "Following a lesson that introduces differences between statements of fact and opinion, each student will be able to identify at least three statements of fact and three statements of opinion from a set of taped television commercials."

Ideally, you would prescribe an instructional program appropriate for each student. Fortunately, you will probably have in your class several students who have similar needs or interests so that some form of grouping may be appropriate. It will be impossible for you to be directly involved with every student or group for the entire reading period. Thus, good management becomes essential, and it can pay off. The techniques that follow should help you to manage a reading program that involves some kind of grouping plan or individualized instruction; that is, a program that occasionally requires students to work independently without your direct instructional input.

## ALTERNATIVE MANAGEMENT TECHNIQUES

The classic classroom organization puts the teacher's desk at the front of the room, the students' desks in rows, and the students in their desks with basal readers and accompanying workbooks. The teacher directs all learning activities. Usually, the basal program suggests three reading groups. (See Chapters 14 and 15 for information on how to use basal readers effectively.) While the teacher reads with one group, the other two are either reading a basal story silently at their desks or working independently in their workbooks. Figure 17.1 depicts the organization of an hour-long reading period for a class organized into three basal reading groups. Within such a plan, students have little opportunity to read for fun or to contribute much to their own learning. Also, the teacher holds sole responsibility for supervision, which can, and often does, use up time needed for instruction. The alternatives discussed here, however, *are not* meant to replace basal reader programs. Rather, they *are* meant to provide more opportunity for student input, which includes assuming supervisory responsibilities and reading for enjoyment. These alternatives are similar to what O'Donnell and Moore (1980) have called the transitional classroom, which lies somewhere between the classic classroom and the individualized classroom.

### Units

The unit approach is not a new technique by any means, but it is one often overlooked as a means of managing a reading program. The unit approach permits the integration of reading instruction, related language skills, and subject area topics (e.g., the planets, famous explorers, the weather). This approach accommodates the individual needs of students in many ways. Perhaps the best technique for meeting individual needs is differentiating reading assignments, a topic discussed below. The unit approach also provides the teacher an opportunity to incorporate students' interests (e.g., units on horses, sports, computer games) into the reading and learning process. The units can be of short duration (one week) or can span a longer period of time (four to six weeks).

To implement a unit approach, you must know the independent and instructional reading levels of each student. (See Chapter 9.) The results of an interest inventory

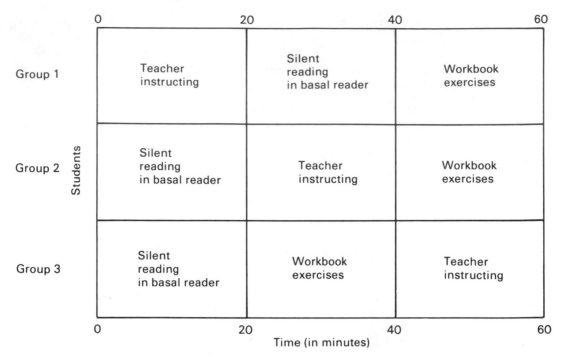

Figure 17.1. A classic management system for a traditional three-group reading program.

(Chapter 20) can be useful, since you will want to plan units around your students' specific interests as well as around subject areas.

In planning the unit, you develop objectives for the unit, questions to be answered, representative activities and projects, and perhaps a culminating activity. Finally, you gather a wide variety of materials that span several reading levels. Individual needs in a unit approach are met through the use of differentiated reading assignments. According to Mangrum and Forgan (1979), "The differentiated reading assignment allows the classroom teacher to use the unit approach with its common objectives but to vary (differentiate) the reading assignments according to individual children's reading levels" (p. 593).

Examine the sample differentiated reading assignment in Figure 17.2. By studying the resources and activities assigned to each of the children, you should be able to infer something about their reading abilities. See whether you can identify differences in reading achievement for this hypothetical fifth-grade class.

If you want to individualize instruction (but fear the challenge of preparing individual programs for each child), you may find the unit approach a helpful way to begin individualization, since there is a common theme in the instruction. The approach also allows for whole-class instruction, which helps reduce management problems. In addition, reading instruction is meaningful to the students, since they have definite purposes for reading: to answer specific questions or to complete a project. To understand how you can develop many types of reading skills through a unit approach, refer to Heilman, Blair, and Rupley (1981, pp. 406–407).

*Unit Title*: Oceans

*Unit Theme*: Oceans are a valuable resource.

*Directions*: For the next two weeks, you will be learning about oceans. Each of you will be trying to find answers to the questions below, but each of you will not be looking for the answers in the same material. After the questions listed below you will see a list of sources and activities. Find your name under the Reading Assignments to see which sources and activities you must complete. The schedule we will follow comes after the reading assignments.

*Reading Questions*
1. What kind of life is found in oceans?
2. How is this life helpful to people?
3. How do ocean products provide livelihoods for people?
4. How long have people explored and traveled the oceans?
5. Why have people explored and traveled the oceans?
6. What kind of recreational activities do oceans and their shorelines provide?
7. Are oceans a limited resource?
8. How might future uses of the ocean affect people's lives?

*Reading Sources and Activities*
1. *City Beneath the Sea*, fiction book
2. *Miss Pickerell Harvests the Sea*, fiction book
3. *Island of the Blue Dolphins*, fiction book
4. *The Garden Under the Sea*, fiction book
5. *Oceans*, nonfiction book
6. *The Sea Around Us*, nonfiction book (teacher's note: easy reading)
7. *Wonders of the Living Sea*, nonfiction book
8. *Man Explores the Sea*, nonfiction book
9. *Fresh Water From Salty Seas*, nonfiction book
10. *The Sea, Ships, and Sailors*, poem
11. *What Is Under the Ocean*? movie
12. *Gray Gull the Hunter*, movie
13. *Life on the Sea Floor and Shore*, filmstrip
14. *Oceanography*, filmstrip
15. "Water All Over the World," in science textbook
16. "Outgoing Tide," in science textbook
17. Word game—Alphabet Soup—in Learning Center #1
18. Word game—Double Trouble—in Learning Center #2
19. Crossword puzzle, in Learning Center #3
20. Vocabulary game—Sealab 2020—in Learning Center #3
21. Vocabulary activity—Fishing: Not Just for Fun
22. Activity—Make a mobile showing types of sea animals.
23. Activity—Make a globe. Show routes of some early explorers.
24. Activity—Make a display about beach or boating safety.
25. Activity—Make a display about foods from the ocean. Include some favorite recipes.
26. Activity—Look at a Coast Guard chart, and identify shallow and deep water, rocks, sunken obstructions, and current markers. Why are these important to sailors?

Figure 17.2. A sample differentiated reading assignment designed for a fifth-grade class studying oceans.

27. Activity—Prepare an oral reading of *one* of the following poems: "Where Go the Boats?" "Break, Break, Break," "After the Seaships," "Fog," and "The Whale."
28. Activity—Role-playing skit: Persuade boaters not to throw their junk into the water.
29. Activity—Gather newspaper or magazine articles about something that has affected ocean, lake, or river life in our town or state. Read the materials, and be prepared to share what you have learned.
30. Activity—Make a list of ways to save water.

*Reading Assignments*

| *Students* | *Sources and Activities* |
|---|---|
| Jan, Tom, Sue, Pete, Ed, Charles, Helen, Mary | Sources/Activities: 1, 5, 9, 11, 14, 16, 20, 21, 26, 29 |
| Jim, Fred, Barbara, Melissa, Beth, Jean, Kathy, John | Sources/Activities: 3, 4, 8, 11, 14, 15, 19, 21, 23, 28 |
| Ralph, Jerry, Paul, Betty, Jed | Sources/Activities: 2, 7, 10, 12, 13, 18, 21, 24, 25 |
| Dwayne, Joe | Sources/Activities: 6, 12, 13, 17, 21, 22, 27, 30 |

*Schedule*   (Each class period lasts 50 minutes.)

Week 1

| | |
|---|---|
| Monday | Whole class discusses unit plan; the class divides into two groups to see one of two movies. |
| Tuesday | Class divides into four groups, and rotates among sources/activities. |
| Wednesday | Class divides into two groups to view filmstrips, and then works according to interest. |
| Thursday | Same as Tuesday. |
| Friday | Whole class discusses questions 1, 2, 3, 4, 5; groups make presentations on activities 22, 23, 25, 26. |

Week 2

| | |
|---|---|
| Monday | Class divides into four groups, and rotates among sources/activities. |
| Tuesday | Same as Monday. |
| Wednesday | Class divides into groups according to interest, and examines unassigned sources and activities. |
| Thursday | Whole class discusses questions 6, 7, 8; groups make presentations on activities 24, 27. |
| Friday | Groups make presentations on activities 28, 29. |

**Figure 17.2** (*continued*)

## Independent Learning Systems

To maximize "time on task," teachers must help students to develop independent learning skills. More specifically, what this independence means is that the student can *find* necessary materials, can *read* the directions (or know what they are), can *perform* the task, and can *check* the results. Independent learners do not need constant supervision from the teacher. Materials should be made accessible, and a routine should be established for communicating to students how they are to manage their time (other than through the teacher's oral directions). In this way, the teacher is available to provide individual assistance or direct instruction when and where it is needed. The fact that a student is working independently does not necessarily imply that the student is receiving individualized instruction. Only when the student is working on activities specific to his distinct needs does truly individualized instruction occur.

Teaching children to become independent learners can be a slow process. Initially, the tasks should be easy enough and rewarding enough that the teacher's assistance is not necessary. Before students can participate in the kinds of alternative management approaches discussed here, they must first develop the ability to work independently. The appropriate use of learning centers, learning contracts, and incentive programs should help students to develop this independence.

### Learning or Reading Centers

From the preceding discussion of the unit approach and the following discussion, it should become apparent that management techniques can and do overlap. The organization of the unit was based on students' achievement levels, and the management of the unit was partially achieved though the use of learning centers.

Regardless, then, of what organizational structure is used, learning centers (learning stations, reading centers, all synonymous terms) can be used to help manage a variety of instructional activities. Centers are designed to provide interesting and appropriate activities that students can complete independently. The centers usually occupy designated areas of a classroom set off from other classroom areas by shelves, tables, groups of desks, or portable dividers. Each center provides the space, furniture, materials, or equipment necessary for the activity to be completed there. Most centers can accommodate only five or six children; therefore, it is desirable to have one more center than there are reading groups (i.e., with 30 children, you would need six or seven centers).

Centers can be set up for many different purposes. Some common examples include listening centers; library centers; centers for decoding skills, vocabulary, comprehension, study skills, and rate building; and book making centers. A wealth of information on the various types of centers and instructions for setting them up are available. (Refer to the Recommended Readings at the end of this chapter for specific sources of information.)

To achieve success using learning centers, the teacher must establish a routine for their use. The first step in this routine is assigning students to centers. Center assignments should take place at a designated time (e.g., every Monday and Wednesday morning, or every day at the beginning of the reading period). Second, students need to know exactly what they are to do at each center, and so the directions supplied at the centers must be clear. Whenever a new center is set up in the classroom, the teacher must explain its use to everyone. Third, some form of record-keeping system is needed. It may be an evaluation form to be completed after each use of the center or a student journal or a teacher-student conference. Fourth, every time a student uses a center, it must be restored to its original condition after the student has completed the activity. The students should be made responsible for this task, and directions for restoring order to the center should be fully explained when the center itself is initiated. Finally, a schedule should be established for using the centers. An example of a schedule is shown in Figure 17.3. On this schedule,

| Group | Monday | Tuesday | Wednesday | Thursday | Friday |
|-------|--------|---------|-----------|----------|--------|
| 1 | A | B | C | D | E |
| 2 | F | A | B | C | D |
| 3 | E | F | A | B | C |
| 4 | D | E | F | A | B |
| 5 | C | D | E | F | A |

NOTES: Each group has 15 minutes at the assigned center. Centers are labeled A through F. For each group one center is not assigned. The extra center is available as a free-time activity or when another center is too difficult or easy for a group.

Figure 17.3. A simple rotating assignment schedule for five groups and six centers.

five groups work in six centers. Each group is assigned to one center for a 15-minute period each day and uses at least five of the centers by the end of the week. Schedules for using the centers should be posted, since they provide information on how the students are to manage their time.

### Learning Contracts

Learning contracts are another way of helping students learn how to manage their time. The format of the learning contract varies according to the age, interests, reading ability, and needs of the student. A child of any age can follow the sequence of events in a contract when the design is appropriate. Instead of only written directions, shapes, drawings, and colors can be used to designate which centers or activities are to be completed. Farr and Roser (1979, pp. 390–395) have provided some excellent examples of formats for learning contracts. Two variations of contracts are illustrated in Figures 17.4 and 17.5.

### Incentive Programs

Sometimes, students need extra help becoming independent learners. Incentives can be used to motivate those students who need a little push toward working independently. Incentives are rewards, and they have been used in education for many years. The most common incentives are grades and teacher's approval, but for some students, these are not enough. A smiling face drawn on a paper well done can go a long way. Some teachers have had great success using tokens, such as gold stars or play money, that can be collected and then redeemed for prizes or privileges at the end of the week, or they could be saved for an auction at the end of the month. Many objects can be used as tokens, and the tokens can be used in a wide range of activities. Let your imagination, and your students, help you think of some.

Incentive programs are discussed last in this section, because they should be viewed as last resorts to getting students to work independently. Wallen (1981) has put it well.

In this early-primary example, Joey started at the "Triangle Center" designated by that shape in the room. (The center did not deal with triangles. It may contain any kind of activity. The triangle is just a way to designate the center.) When he finished there, he put a check in the box. He then went to his teacher. At that time, a story was dictated, which Ms. Jones wrote down for future lessons. She then wrote her comment and checked off that box. Joey then is to proceed to the "Circle Center" and then to the "Square Center." Note that each day (or perhaps each week) signatures from the student, teacher, and parent are needed.

Figure 17.4. An example of a learning contract for an early-primary-grade student.

Incentives should be viewed as crutches to be dropped as soon as students progress to the place where extrinsic motives are no longer necessary. If incentives are used routinely, students may never learn to feel rewarded for simply completing a task they set out to do, or mastering a new skill, or satisfying an interest. The routine use of incentives teaches students to do things only to satisfy the teacher. One does not read for personal enjoyment; one reads in order to please the teacher. Unfortunately, when the teacher is no longer around to provide incentives, the reason students have learned for reading is gone, and so they don't read if they can help it (p. 102).

### Special Groupings

Grouping according to achievement is probably the most common organizational technique used in classroom reading programs. Figure 17.1 illustrated the classic approach to managing such a reading program. As I pointed out earlier in this chapter, however, when the teacher wants to maximize the amount of time each student spends on relevant reading tasks, students must be taught to work independently and not to rely on the

Hi Betty! I hope you enjoy your work today.

Look at the filmstrip called *Life on the Sea Floor and Shore*. Then come tell me what you learned. *You learned the names of some unusual fish.* ✓

In your notebook write answers to question 1 on the assignment sheet.

Find the paper in your folder with the blanks on it. Fill in the blanks. Check your answers. Discuss some of your answers with a friend. See if any other words would make sense.

Now read "The Case of the Hair Dryers" in *Encyclopedia Brown Solves Them All*. Write down the solution here *before* you check your answer. *One of the women could read lips.*

*You are becoming a quite good detective. After some practice, you're now able to find the clues.* ✓

Some things to choose:
☐ go to the library
☑ put new words in word file
☐ play a reading game in game center
☐ do the puzzle in your folder

Name _____

Teacher _____

Parent _____

This intermediate-level contract demonstrates how you might incorporate the use of contracts into the unit approach. From the unit material on oceans, Betty is directed to view a filmstrip and to write down what she has learned. Note that as she progresses through the contract, her teacher monitors her progress and provides written comments in several instances. Betty knows she does not have to do every activity in order, and if she finishes before the scheduled reading period is over, she is free to select one of several activities. Again, parents are asked to sign every contract. This not only lets parents know what their children are doing in school, but it also allows them to see the teacher's comments to the child, which may provide them direct feedback on their child's learning.

Figure 17.5. An example of a learning contract for an intermediate-grade student.

teacher to find out what to do next. In addition, at least initially, students must be motivated to work independently. The traditional three-group approach does not always provide the necessary motivation. Several alternative strategies include a procedure called "groups of four" and peer tutoring.

### Groups of Four

Several alternatives to the classic high-, middle-, and low-achievement group plan were discussed in Chapter 14. The present chapter's description of the unit approach introduced another variation of achievement groupings. This section offers a promising alternative called "groups of four" (Burns, 1981), a grouping plan that is *not* based on achievement. The groups-of-four plan is a "system of cooperative learning that requires reorganizing the classroom physically, redefining the students' responsibilities, and carefully structuring" the teacher's role (Burns, 1981, p. 46). The physical reorganization involves *physically* placing students in groups of four, each group with a separate table or cluster of desks. (In classes that cannot be divided evenly into groups of four, one group may include three, five, or six students.) Students are assigned to groups randomly. Burns suggested using a deck of cards to assign students to groups. For example, each group of four is assigned the number of a playing card (ace, two, three, four, etc.), and the corresponding playing cards are then shuffled and distributed to students. The four students dealt aces go to the ace group, those receiving twos go to the two group, and so forth. The groups stay together one or two weeks after which time they are disbanded and new groups are formed. In this way, students work with everyone in the class over the course of the school year.

As with any new plan, the rules must be explained to the students carefully. Three rules apply to groups of four.

1.  Students are responsible for their own work and behavior. Other instructional strategies (e.g., learning centers or contracts) can be used in conjunction with groups of four, since all members of a group need not be working on the same assignments.

2.  Each student in the group must be willing to help any other group member who asks for help. This rule forces students to work cooperatively. Also, random assignment solves some of the problems encountered with peer tutoring, which is discussed in the next section.

3.  A student may ask for help from the teacher only when everyone in the group has the same question or when other group members have been unable to help. This rule helps the teacher provide more time to students in need of instruction. Instead of asking questions like "I don't understand the directions" or "How do I do this assignment?" the students first ask for help from other members of their group. Usually, someone in the group is able to help, since groups are not based on achievement. This rule is probably most valuable in helping students learn to rely on themselves and become confident, independent learners.

As in introducing any new management technique, start slowly. Groups of four can be used for only 60 minutes a day if you prefer. Keep in mind your own philosophies about learning, however. If you agree that interaction is an essential ingredient in learning, then groups of four is a management technique you may want to try, since it maximizes interaction among students. If you are not an advocate of interactive learning or if you are uncomfortable with such an arrangement, the groups-of-four plan is not for you.

### Peer Tutoring or Pair Learning

"Peer tutoring" is a one-to-one teaching and learning relationship between students, which is also called "pair learning" or the "buddy system." The range of uses for such systems varies widely. Sometimes, the tutor is a student the same age as the tutee, and sometimes the tutor is from a higher grade level and is actually the student in need of some help. Arranging pairs of peer tutors who are students in the same classroom requires a comfortable, risk-free, trusting classroom atmosphere. Providing a slow reader with an opportunity to practice reading skills by reading with a student in a lower grade is probably one of the better uses of peer tutoring.

## ORGANIZING TIME

Successfully managing a reading program according to one of the systems discussed in this chapter depends on the teacher's efficient organization of time. There is, however, no easy way to explain how you can efficiently organize your time. First of all, the way you schedule your reading period depends on your goals and priorities in reading instruction. If you place a high value on providing children time to read every day, then your schedule will certainly include time for independent reading. If you think skills instruction is very important, then that aspect of reading instruction will attain an important place on your schedule.

The more time you spend planning your program, the more time you save. That is, a reading program that is well organized and managed runs smoothly and provides more "time on task" for the students involved. This observation brings us back to where we started—increasing the time spent on task. That is what classroom management, regardless of the subject area, is all about. Two excellent and detailed examples of how two teachers scheduled (minute by minute) their first three weeks of reading instruction can be found in Chapters 16 and 17 of Smith and Johnson's (1980) *Teaching Children to Read*. (This source is listed in the Recommended Readings at the end of this chapter.)

## SUMMARY

A wide variety of techniques can be used to help teachers manage reading programs. Only a few of them were discussed in this chapter. The original sources listed in the References and Recommended Readings provide more information about management techniques. One last word of caution: Do not be impatient—effective management takes time.

## REFERENCES

Burns, M. Groups of four: Solving the management problem. *Learning*, 1981, **10**, 46–51.

Cooley, W. W., and Leinhardt, G. The instructional dimensions study. *Educational Evaluation and Policy Analysis*, 1980, **2**, 7–24.

Farr, R., and Roser, N. *Teaching a child to read.* New York: Harcourt Brace Jovanovich, 1979.

Frymier, J. *Annehurst curriculum classification system: A practical way to individualize instruction.* West Lafayette, Ind.: Kappa Delta Pi Press, 1977.

Glasser, W. *Reality therapy.* New York: Harper and Row, 1965.

Glasser, W. *Schools without failure.* New York: Harper and Row, 1969.

Gordon, T. *T.E.T.: Teacher effectiveness training.* New York: Peter H. Wyden, 1974.

Guthrie, J. T. Time in reading programs. *The Reading Teacher*, 1980, **33**, 500–502.

Heilman, A. W., Blair, T. R., and Rupley, W. H. *Principles and practices of teaching reading.* (5th ed.) Columbus, Ohio: Charles E. Merrill, 1981.

Intili, J. K., and Conrad, H. Planning the well managed classroom. In D. Lapp (Ed.), *Making reading possible through effective classroom management.* Newark, Del.: International Reading Association, 1980.

Lapp, D., and Flood, J. *Teaching reading to every child.* New York: Macmillan, 1978.

Mangrum, C.T., II, and Forgan, H. W. *Developing competencies in teaching reading.* Columbus, Ohio: Charles E. Merrill, 1979.

O'Donnell, M. P., and Moore, B. Eliminating common stumbling blocks to organizational change. In D. Lapp (Ed.), *Making reading possible through effective classroom management.* Newark, Del.: International Reading Association, 1980.

Skinner, B. F. *The technology of teaching.* New York: Appleton-Century-Crofts, 1968.

Smith, R. J., and Johnson, D. D. *Teaching children to read.* (2nd ed.) Reading, Mass.: Addison-Wesley, 1980.

Stallings, J. A., and Kaskowitz, D. H. *Follow-through classroom observation evaluation: 1972–73.* Menlo Park, Calif.: Stanford Research Institute, 1974.

Wallen, C. J. *Competency in teaching reading.* (2nd ed.) Chicago: Science Research Associates, 1981.

Welch, F. C., and Halfacre, J. D. Ten better ways to classroom management. *Teacher,* 1978, **96,** 86–87.

## RECOMMENDED READINGS

Bierly, K. Taking a new look at learning centers. *Instructor,* 1978, **87,** 80–84.
Bierly's article suggests 20 new and different ways to think about learning centers. Each one is discussed, and examples are given.

Chernow, F. B., and Chernow, C. *Classroom discipline and control: 101 practical techniques.* West Nyack, N.Y.: Parker, 1981.
In this collection of tips for maintaining discipline from the very first day of class, topics include maintaining group discipline, enlisting parents' help, overcoming vandalism and violence, and encouraging self-discipline.

Cunningham, P. M., Arthur, S. V., and Cunningham, J. W. *Classroom reading instruction K–5: Alternative approaches.* Lexington, Mass.: D. C. Heath, 1977.
This book presents six teachers' records, month by month, in journal fashion, showing their teaching strategies and classroom-organizing techniques. The same class of 24 children is followed throughout. Beginning teachers can see a variety of approaches as well as read about the first-year teaching experiences of Miss Nouveau. The same six chapters are also reproduced as Part II in P. M. Cunningham, S. A. Moore, J. W. Cunningham, and D. W. Moore's *Reading in elementary classrooms: Strategies and observations.* New York: Longman, 1983.

Forgan, H. W. *The reading corner.* Santa Monica, Calif.: Goodyear, 1977.
Many examples of activities for individualized instruction from this book can be used as learning center activities. The book also includes a section on how to set up learning centers.

Good, T. L., and Brophy, J. E. *Looking into classrooms.* New York: Harper and Row, 1973.
Concrete suggestions are provided through observational checklists for many classroom interactions, including management problems. Example management problems are presented, and possible solutions are discussed.

Indrisano, R. Managing the classroom reading program. *Instructor,* 1978, **87,** 117–120.
This article discusses three types of variables essential in managing a reading program: the pupil, the process, and the procedures. Guidelines for managing each of these variables are provided.

Joyce, B. R. Learning strategies for learning centers. *Educational Leadership,* 1975, **32,** 388–391.
The range of teaching strategies available is discussed: person centered, group centered, information centered, and others that focus on tasks and reinforcement schedules. The article implies that competent teachers utilize a range of teaching strategies.

Smith, R. J., and Johnson, D. D. *Teaching children to read.* (2nd ed.) Reading, Mass.: Addison-Wesley, 1980.
The two final chapters in this text, Chapters 16 and 17, are especially relevant to managing reading programs. Each of these chapters provides week-by-week, minute-by-minute accounts of reading instruction for the first three weeks of school in grades one and four, respectively. These accounts provide the beginning teacher with an idea of how to organize time and handle several groups of students in a self-contained classroom.

Wallen, C. J., and Wallen, L. L. *Effective classroom managment.* Boston: Allyn and Bacon, 1978.
This book discusses thoroughly eight management strategies that facilitate teaching. Examples of schedules, charts, and checklists useful in managing reading programs are presented.

# CHAPTER 18

# Teaching Poor Readers in the Regular Classroom

Deborah B. Cureton
University of South Carolina at Lancaster

Roger G. Eldridge, Jr.
East Carolina University
Greenville, North Carolina

*The subject of Part III is organizing and managing a reading program, and Chapters 14 through 17 have comprehensively discussed the methods, materials, and management options for a developmental reading program. A management concern that has not been discussed, however, is how a beginning teacher can work with poor readers in the regular classroom. Beginning teachers will probably have assistance in working with children who have severe reading disabilities, but regardless of the amount of help available, several poor readers who do not qualify for special remedial instruction usually must be taught in the regular classroom. In this chapter, Deborah Cureton and Roger Eldridge address the difficult problem of how a beginning teacher can organize and manage reading instruction for poor readers. They begin by presenting a rationale for why poor readers should stay in the regular classroom and outline three necessary conditions for working with poor readers: The teacher must teach them, individualized instruction must be administered, and poor readers need to be given time to read. The heart of the chapter is the presentation of specific strategies teachers can use to work with poor readers. An in-depth discussion of how basal readers can be adapted for use with poor readers is included, and a complete discussion of how teachers can help poor readers to cope with content area textbooks concludes the chapter.*

Students with poor reading skills are a continuing source of concern for educators. It seems that poor readers have always been with us, and nothing indicates they will disappear any time soon. You, the beginning teacher, should be prepared to meet the challenge of teaching students who read less well than others. Beginning teachers are sometimes at a loss for strategies to cope with poor readers in regular classroom instruction. Many feel that they should not be expected to teach such students, that all poor readers should be sent to a specialist. Certainly, some poor readers—those with severe reading disabilities—should receive remedial instruction from a special reading teacher. Students with less severe reading problems, whom we usually refer to as "corrective" readers, however, usually are not eligible for special remedial classes and remain in regular classrooms for reading instruction, as perhaps they should. Such students may actually benefit more from remaining within their own classrooms for reading instruction than they would from being sent to special reading teachers. Their reading skills are not at the "average" level of others in their grade placement, but they do exhibit the capacity for academic growth when given specialized, corrective help. The purpose of this chapter is to persuade you, a beginning teacher, that you *can* and *should* teach poor readers within your classroom. In addition, this chapter provides practical suggestions on *how* to teach reading to students who read poorly.

## WHY POOR READERS SHOULD STAY IN THE REGULAR CLASSROOM

There are several reasons why the regular classroom teacher should teach poor reading students. One reason is that he knows (or should know) the students' reading strengths and weaknesses. With this knowledge, the classroom teacher is in the best position to tailor instruction to the needs of individual students and thus to maximize reading growth. Also, because classroom teachers know their students well, they usually are the most qualified to select appropriate reading materials at a level poor readers can read and comprehend. Thus, when poor readers are taught in the regular classroom, the teacher can plan instruction based on the students' needs and can directly monitor the students' progress.

A second reason for classroom teachers to teach poor readers in the regular classroom is that then the poor reading students do not suffer the stigma associated with leaving the classroom for special instruction. The impact of reading achievement (or the lack of it) on individual students is formidable. The students' reading performance may determine their class placement, their success or failure in school, and even their status with teachers, peers, and sometimes even parents. Difficulty in learning to read may lead to serious emotional problems that can affect children throughout their lives. Reading is more directly related to the child's self-concept than any other area of schoolwork. Ask students in a class who the poor readers are, and they will be able to tell you. Poor readers may develop a negative self-image by being sent out of the room for special help. The classroom teacher can and must establish a learning environment that promotes a positive self-image. The learning environment must reflect an acceptance of the readers as potential learners and worthwhile individuals. Learning environments must be constructed so that students experience success.

Finally, classroom teachers should teach poor readers within the regular classroom, because they are ultimately responsible for the academic progress of their students. Taxpayers, administrators, parents, and students themselves turn to teachers for answers when children fail to meet educational objectives.

## WORKING WITH POOR READERS: THREE NECESSARY CONDITIONS

We make three other assertions with respect to beginning teachers and poor readers. The first is that the classroom teacher, and not the teacher's aide, should provide the instruction. Second, individualization of instruction is the most promising method for promoting reading progress. Third, poor readers should be given the opportunity to experience real reading.

## The Teacher Must Teach

Sometimes, teachers assign poor readers to the classroom aide so that the teacher can spend more time with the better readers. We contend that the poor reader needs, indeed deserves, the best instruction available. The teacher, not the paraprofessional, is the one who can provide this instruction. Teachers must realize that poor readers need more time, more intense instruction, and more focused instruction than better readers. This is not to say that the rest of the class should be neglected. Nevertheless, average and above-average readers are more capable of working independently than are poor readers. The teacher should take advantage of the independence of better readers and plan extended activities that the more capable students can accomplish alone or with the help of a teacher's aide. (See Chapters 14, 16, and 17.) That way, the classroom teacher can devote more time to teaching the slower readers.

## Instruction for Poor Readers Must Be Individualized

We believe that individualization of instruction is the most appropriate way to promote reading progress for poor, or corrective, readers. By "individualization," we mean that the teacher finds the most effective means of teaching each student, whether it be one-to-one, small-group, or whole-group instruction. Each strategy, however, has both advantages and disadvantages.

One-to-one instruction may seem to be the best method because the teacher can focus all attention on the learner to ensure that learning is taking place and skills are being mastered. This is an impractical method for most teachers, however, because it is time-consuming. In addition to the time factor involved for the teacher, the student may feel uncomfortable working alone with the teacher, since this situation is a further declaration that she has a reading problem. The alternative is small-group instruction, which allows the student to work with other students who are experiencing similar problems. The teacher can plan instruction for the entire group and solve several problems at the same time. If the members of the group are all at the same low reading level, however, they probably have little opportunity to learn from each other. Whole-, or large-, group instruction—another alternative—allows poor readers to learn from better readers. Large-group instruction gives poor readers the opportunity to see and hear good reading models. Nevertheless, during whole-group instruction, poor readers may be intimidated by those who read better than they do. As a result they may become withdrawn and reluctant to participate.

There is no one *best way* to teach problem readers. We recommend a flexible teaching strategy whereby the teacher determines the best method, or combination of methods, for each task to be taught, thus capitalizing on the strengths of each method.

## Poor Readers Must Read

Finally, we maintain that poor readers should be given the opportunity to experience *real reading*. Studies have shown that poor readers spend a great amount of time struggling through word pronunciation skill exercises (Allington, 1977, 1980). Most of their work is broken into tiny increments, and they rarely get a chance to put the pieces together and experience the whole of the reading process. Once they attain some degree of mastery at one level, they are ushered to the next level of skills, beginning the struggle again. *Poor readers need the chance to read!* After they finish work on a story, can pronounce all the words, and are familiar with all the words' meanings, let them read the story in its entirety. Let them feel like good readers—and experience the joy of fluency and the flow of thoughts instead of a series of words. As has always been the case, poor readers (as well as "good" readers) learn to read by reading.

Keeping these three conditions in mind, we will now present and discuss specific strategies for teaching poor readers in the regular classroom. Two sets of techniques and strategies are discussed: (1) how to teach poor readers through the use of basal readers and (2) how to help poor readers cope with content area reading materials.

## TEACHING READING THROUGH THE USE OF THE BASAL READER

The suggestions we offer here are not extraordinary and do not require any special training. They are of a common-sense nature and have been used by us in our own teaching. Student teachers we have worked with have also found them helpful when working with poor readers.

In all likelihood, as a first-year classroom teacher, you will be expected to use a basal reader program that has been adopted by your school or school system. Although most basal reader programs are designed for children of "average" ability at each grade level, we will explain how basal reader material can be used with poor readers as well.

### Establishing a Working Relationship

Before beginning in-depth work with poor readers in a basal reader text, you must first strive to establish an amicable working relationship with your students. As a teacher, you must realize that children who are designated as "poor readers" have been identified as such on the basis of many factors. Regardless of how your students have been labeled— good readers or poor—it is your responsibility to accept the poor readers for what they are—ordinary children who happen to read less well than others—and to refrain from blaming them, their parents, or their previous teachers for their lack of reading progress. We cannot emphasize enough the importance of a teacher accepting the poor readers as children who have feelings, needs, abilities, and aspirations just as their more skillful reading peers do. Do not isolate poor readers from the rest of the class; they have no contagious disease. Allow the poor readers the same opportunities you provide the best readers in your classroom, and expect them to achieve and make progress. The lower your expectations are, the lower their progress will be. Conversely, set "high" (but reasonable) expectations, and your poor readers will achieve at a higher level. Also, involve your poor readers in discussions and decision-making processes from the outset. Encourage poor readers to contribute to, and participate in, classroom and reading group discussions until the lines of communication between the poor readers, their classmates, and you become self-generating. The relationships and lines of communication you initiate and develop with poor readers will be positively related to the reading progress the poor readers make during the rest of the year in your classroom.

## Getting Started in a Basal Program With Poor Readers

In all likelihood, the poor readers who enter your classroom will have been identified by preceding teachers, special reading teachers, or a school psychologist or diagnostician. Your task is to provide instruction to these children at the level at which they are currently reading. One task is to group together the children who are reading at the same level and to assign them a reading text. Before you hand out the reading books, however, we suggest that you administer the placement or skills test that accompanies the basal reader series you will be using. This placement or skills test, which is usually a form of informal reading inventory (see Chapter 9), will provide you with information concerning the specific skill needs of the poor readers. That is, the tests will indicate which skills the poor readers need to be taught. You should work extensively on those skills. If there is no test accompanying your basal reader, construct and administer your own informal reading inventory, for the information you obtain will be invaluable in individualizing instruction for your poor readers.

Teaching poor readers can be slow and methodical. Do not be concerned with completing a set number of books or stories or skill exercises with these children; only be concerned with providing the *best* instruction you can at a pace the poor readers can handle. A general overall goal to keep in mind when working with poor readers is to add to their reading skill base so that eventually they will be able to read independently a variety of materials. We recommend that you work, either individually or in a group setting, with each of your poor readers at least once a day. If you decide to work with poor readers as a group, try to give individual attention to each group member. Also, encourage individual members to participate and contribute to the discussions of assigned stories.

We feel that poor readers should not be left on their own to work on their reading skills assignments. Just because a child is not as skilled at answering questions or reading orally as others does not mean that she should be ignored and not be expected to participate. The poor readers' lack of skill provides all the more justification for getting them to respond.

Teachers cannot assume that poor readers will learn and assimilate the information provided if the instruction the children receive amounts only to explanations of how to complete an assignment. What poor readers need most is direct instruction in specific reading skills. Poor readers should also be given step-by-step directions for completing reading skills assignments. Also, they need to have immediate feedback about the appropriateness of the answers they give. Only when the teacher provides direct instruction, guidance, and feedback to the children will reading skills take on importance and relevance for the children.

## Using the Basal Reader With Poor Readers

### Limit Skill Instruction

Once you have assigned the basal texts and begun to use them with the poor readers, you can follow these suggestions. First, familiarize yourself with the content and skills to be taught with each story. We suggest that for poor readers you select only *one* skill to be taught with each story. Decide which skill to teach on the basis of information obtained from the initial skills or placement test and your knowledge of the reading process. That is, for each lesson, select the skill that provides the reader with the greatest assistance in improving her reading ability. For example, if two comprehension skills are offered, such as finding story details and drawing conclusions, and the reader needs instruction in both, we suggest that the story details skill would have more relevance to the reader. This does not mean that we consider the skill of drawing conclusions unimportant. On the contrary, we would provide instruction in drawing conclusions *after* the reader becomes more secure and adept at reading and finding story details.

Selecting the appropriate skills to be taught is not an easy task, but it is important to limit the number of skills you teach to poor readers, since it is more desirable to have poor readers acquire a few skills than it is for them to have little or no proficiency in many different skills. Also, do not be concerned that the child will never be exposed to a skill you temporarily skip. Basal readers are designed to provide repeated exposure to many skills. That is, after a few stories, the drawing conclusions skill will be presented again, and then you can use both exercises (the exercise you skipped and the current exercise) to teach drawing conclusions.

### Prepare Poor Readers to Read in a Special Way

One of the first steps in introducing a story is presenting the children with the new words they will encounter in the story. The basal manual will recommend that certain words be pretaught before the children read the story. We maintain that *you* will have to read through the story and select additional words you know your poor readers will have difficulty decoding. When presenting the words to the children, select a sentence from the story that contains the word you want to introduce. In this way, the children can recognize and relate the meaning of the word *as it occurs in the story;* that is, you should present and teach new vocabulary in meaningful situations for poor readers.

Before asking poor readers to read a basal reader story, you need to set the stage for reading. Ask the children specific questions about what they think the story will be about. For example, ask your students to read the title of the story, look at the pictures accompanying the story, or skim the first paragraph of the story. Ask the children to make guesses (i.e., hypothesize) about what they will read. This process gets students thinking about the possible content of the story, which dramatically enhances their reading comprehension. Also, pose a few questions that require the children to search for answers as they read. These questions give your poor readers one or two specific purposes for reading. In sum, what you need to do is to expand and embellish the "prereading" activities that you find in the basal reader's teacher's manual.

### Guide Poor Readers Through the Story

We suggest that you have poor readers read only short portions of a story at a time and discuss each section before asking the children to continue reading. You should be careful not to assign the children too many pages to read at one time. The exact amount of reading you ask children to do, however, should depend on the story's content, the complexity of the ideas expressed, the vocabulary used in the story, and the experience and abilities of your students.

Once children have completed reading a section, ask them to talk about and share what they have read. A teacher can lead a discussion through the use of questions. Concerning questions, we strongly suggest that you do not limit yourself *only* to the questions provided in the teacher's manual, for they may not be appropriate in light of the goal you had for having children read the story. Use the teacher's manual questions as *guides* for developing your own questions.

Also, provide your poor readers with different types and "levels" of questions. (See Smith and Barrett, 1979, pp. 63–66.) Do not rely on the exclusive use of literal questions that ask children to repeat details and facts from the story's text. In addition to literal questions, ask inferential questions, which require children to relate information from the text to their own experience, intuition, and knowledge. Also, ask children to judge the validity and appropriateness of the author's ideas in relation to their own ideas. By all means, ask questions that require children to explore the author's purpose for writing the story, the author's use of words and ideas, and the children's feelings about what they have read. Poor readers do have difficulty *reading,* but that does not mean they have difficulty *thinking* and expressing their own feelings and opinions. Poor readers can think, make judgments, and express opinions and feelings just as well as their more competent peers. In fact, we have found that, in many instances, poor readers' interpretations of stories are more interesting, creative, and imaginative than those of more skilled readers.

### Provide Silent and Oral Reading Experiences

Having all children read both silently and orally is valuable. We recommend, however, that children be given the opportunity to become familiar with the story's vocabulary and content before they are expected to read aloud, which can be more difficult than silent reading.

Oral reading can be very helpful, especially for poor readers. Oral reading seems to be very reinforcing for poor readers, perhaps because they hear what the words say. Oral reading can also help students develop fluency if the teacher provides materials that are easy enough for the students to read themselves without hesitating at every word. The common practice of having students take turns reading a sentence or paragraph within a reading circle—a practice commonly referred to as "round-robin" reading—is to be avoided, however. Oral reading in the round-robin manner can intimidate and embarrass poor readers. Also, round-robin reading is terribly inefficient, because only *one* student is reading at a time. *Less*-intimidating strategies that allow for *more* oral reading include the following.

1.  Have students read in pairs, each alternately reading a page.
2.  Have students read to a peer tutor or parent volunteer.
3.  Have students practice reading a book that they later read to a first-grader or kindergarten student.

For additional alternatives to round-robin reading, refer to Chapter 23 of this text.

### Use Workbooks and Worksheets Judiciously With Poor Readers

Before ending our discussion of the use of basal readers with poor readers, a few comments about the workbook and skill-sheet activities that accompany basal reader texts should be added. We recommend that you ask children to complete only those activities that focus on the skill needs of the poor readers and the skills you have already taught. The students' skill needs can be identified through the use of basal text skills or placement tests previously mentioned. For example, when a poor reader is capable of identifying a main idea in a paragraph or story, you need not ask the child to complete skill sheet after skill sheet on main ideas. Rather, spend the time teaching other skills the student has not mastered. Also, do not use skill-activity sheets that have little relevance to the special needs of poor readers. For example, workbook pages containing accent exercises add little to the reading ability of the poor reader, and such exercises often confuse more than clarify the reading process for the poor reader.

We feel the use of workbook pages and skill sheets should be held to a minimum. Use only those exercises that follow up instruction you have previously administered, make sure the worksheets are relevant to skills that are necessary and realistic for your poor readers, and make sure that the activities actually do provide practice of the skills they claim to reinforce. Our experience has been that many teachers use workbooks and skill sheets as "controlling" devices. That is, they use the activities to keep children quiet and busy. We reject this use of workbooks and skill sheets, and we believe that reading skill activities should only be assigned to enhance children's abilities to read and understand.

### Establishing Independent Reading Time for Poor Readers

We also strongly recommend that teachers *provide time* and *encourage* poor readers to select and read trade or library books on their own as part of the daily classroom reading program. We believe that the overall objective of reading instruction should be to make children independent readers. By providing poor readers with an opportunity to read independently, teachers are reinforcing the skills they are teaching children, allowing children to develop their individual interests, and encouraging children to employ the skills they have learned.

Establishing independent reading time is an easy task that does not require the implementation of elaborate rules or extensive preparation. First, you select and set aside a time that the children can use every day for independent reading. Teachers we have worked with have put aside the time immediately after lunch and recess for children to read independently. These times were selected, because they gave children an opportunity to calm down after exciting activities. Children should learn that during the independent reading time they are to be reading books or other materials they have chosen. There is to be no talking, walking around, doing other classroom work, or exchanging books. Once the reading materials have been selected, the reader works with those materials until the silent reading period is over. You should also read during this period. Never underestimate the power of your modeling behavior.

We recommend that kindergarten and first-grade teachers allow at least 10 minutes of independent reading every day and that teachers in grades two through eight set aside at least 20 minutes every day. Please realize that time for independent reading periods beyond that regularly scheduled for classroom reading instruction should be set aside. The silent reading time provided should be free of pressure to write reports or to give oral presentations. The time should be devoted to allowing children to read and enjoy the books they have selected to read.

When initiating independent reading time, you will find that children have difficulty selecting a book and sticking with the books they choose. We suggest that teachers implement this activity in stages. That is, begin by allowing 10 minutes at first and gradually increase the time until the children are reading 20 to 30 minutes per day by themselves. We also suggest that young children and poor readers select two or three books to read during each independent reading time. Initially, children with reading problems find it difficult to concentrate on any one book for more than a few minutes. With two or three books, poor readers can switch from book to book without going to the bookshelf or library.

In conclusion, within this section, we have attempted to provide suggestions for teaching reading to poor readers within the regular classroom setting. Although the suggestions were made in connection with the implementation of the basal reader program, we feel the suggestions can be applied to any type of reading program a teacher chooses to implement. In the following section, we will discuss ways you can help your poor readers to cope with the content reading materials they encounter in subjects such as science and social studies.

## TEACHING POOR READERS IN CONTENT AREAS

The skills needed to perform reading tasks in the content areas include many of the same skills that a child acquires from a well-rounded basic reading program. Many of the suggestions in the previous section, therefore, can be adapted for use in the content area classroom. Nevertheless, we will present two specific techniques that we have found to be particularly helpful for content area teachers who must work with poor readers: group informal screening and diagnostic tests, and reading guides.

### Using Group Informal Screening Tests and Group Diagnostic Tests

Often, only one textbook is available for content teaching. When this is the case, you may decide to administer a cloze test to determine how well your students are able to comprehend the text. (See Chapter 9.) For those who would have significant difficulty with the regular textbook, you might need to provide alternative reading materials.

When more than one content textbook is available, and when the textbooks vary in difficulty, you need to know which readers will benefit from using each text. Two strategies you may find helpful are the group informal screening test (GIST) and the group informal diagnostic test (GIDT), procedures developed by Allington and Strange (1980). Advantages in using GISTs and GIDTs are: (1) they can be administered quickly to an entire class, (2) they assess students' specific strengths and weaknesses in skills that apply to particular content areas, and (3) the students are tested on materials that are to be used for instruction.

Three tests are included in a GIST series: the GIST, $GIST_2$, and GIDT. The GIST is administered to the entire class. From a chosen text passage, a set of questions is developed to assess the skills relevant to the content area. The questions could query areas such as (1) using parts of the book, (2) using resource materials, (3) noting main ideas, (4) following directions, (5) drawing conclusions, (6) recalling information directly stated in the text, (7) making inferences based on information contained in the text, (8) demonstrating a knowledge of the specialized vocabulary found in the text, and the like. An example of a GIST is reproduced in Figure 18.1. This particular GIST corresponds to a life science text designed for middle-school students (*Focus on Life Science*, Charles E. Merrill, 1977).

After you administer and score the GIST, you must determine which students will be able to handle the text and which will find it too difficult. We recommend that students who score 70 percent or above on the GIST be assigned the textbook used to construct the GIST. For those who score below 70 percent, the text probably will be too difficult. Administer to these students a second GIST (GIST$_2$), which is based on your alternative— and, it is hoped, easier—textbook. See Figure 18.2 for an example of a GIST$_2$ that corresponds to the text *Concepts and Challenges in Life Science* (Cebco Standard, 1979).

Assign students who score 90 percent or greater on the GIST$_2$ to the text that corresponds to that instrument. For students who score between 70 percent and 90 percent, administer the GIDT, an informal diagnostic test that provides you with specific

---

*Passage Readability:*
Fog Index = 9.2
Fry Graph = 8.3

*Text Reading Assignment:*
   A 581-word passage discussing the circulatory system of animals (pp. 102–105).

*Procedure for Administration:*
   Explain the purpose of the test to the students so that they will be relaxed and not nervous about making a bad grade. Give the following ten items face down on a single sheet of paper. Direct the students to read the passage in their book, close the book, turn the sheet over, and complete the items without referring to the material.

   I. Place the letter of the correct answer in the blank beside the question.

(recall of directly stated information)

_____   (1) Hemoglobin is a part of the blood which combines with _____.
         (A) oxygen   (B) nitrogen   (C) carbon dioxide.

_____   (2) Earthworms obtain oxygen through their _____.
         (A) spiracles   (B) urea   (C) skin

_____   (3) Kidneys remove _____ from the blood.
         (A) wastes   (B) oxygen   (C) food

_____   (4) _____ connect arteries and veins.
         (A) systems   (B) capillaries   (C) lungs

(vocabulary knowledge)

_____   (5) _____ are vessels which carry blood away from the heart.
         (A) arteries   (B) kidneys   (C) lungs

_____   (6) The atrium is a part of the _____.
         (A) stomach   (B) heart   (C) lungs

_____   (7) A system for carrying food, oxygen, and wastes is called the _____.
         (A) respiratory system   (B) nervous system   (C) circulatory system

Figure 18.1. A GIST for *Focus on Life Science* (Charles E. Merrill, 1977). (This material was developed by Judy Sanderson, a teacher in the Chesterfield County School District in South Carolina. It is reproduced here with her permission.)

(questions requiring an inference based on textual material)

_____ (8) A horse would probably have _____ chambers in its heart than a fish.
(A) more (B) less

_____ (9) In a starfish, ocean water moves through its body to bring food and oxygen to all parts and remove wastes. In a cow, what material does this job?
(A) milk (B) fat (C) blood

II. Write the following statements in the correct order:

(10) In a frog:
Urine is carried to a storage area.
The blood carries food through the body.
Urine leaves the body through the anus.
The kidneys filter the blood.

1.

2.

3.

4.

Figure 18.1 (*continued*)

*Passage Readability:*
Fog Index = 4.3
Fry Graph = 6.0

*Text Reading Assignment:*
A 553-word passage about the respiratory system (pp. 102-105).

*Procedure for Administration:*
Same as the first GIST.

I. Place the letter of the correct answer in the blank beside the question.

(recall of directly stated information)

_____ (1) The bronchi are small tubes which enter the _____.
(A) heart (B) lungs (C) alveoli

_____ (2) The lungs are made up of many _____.
(A) air sacs (B) bones (C) muscles

_____ (3) The _____ in the nose trap dirt in the air we breathe.
(A) cells (B) sacs (C) hairs

Figure 18.2. A GIST$_2$ for *Concepts and Challenges in Life Science* (Cebco Standard, 1979). (This material was developed by Judy Sanderson, a teacher in the Chesterfield County School District in South Carolina. It is reproduced here with her permission.)

_____ (4) The air that enters the lungs must be _____.
(A) moist    (B) dry    (C) cold

(vocabulary knowledge)

_____ (5) The sticky liquid found inside the nose and the windpipe is _____.
(A) cilia    (B) alveoli    (C) mucus

_____ (6) Tiny hairs found in the windpipe are called _____.
(A) alveoli    (B) cilia    (C) mucus

_____ (7) The windpipe is divided into two smaller tubes called _____.
(A) alveoli    (B) cilia    (C) bronchi

(questions requiring an inference based on textual material)

_____ (8) All of the organs that help us breathe belong to the _____.
(A) nervous system    (B) digestive system    (C) respiratory system

_____ (9) We sneeze when we are sick, because _____.
(A) our nerves in the nose are not working properly.
(B) there is extra mucus in the nose.
(C) we are not getting enough oxygen.

II. (10) Put the following words in order to show how air moves as it enters the body:

windpipe
nose
bronchi
lungs

1.

2.

3.

4.

---

**Figure 18.2** *(continued)*

information about skills your students need to develop to be able to read that text. Figure 18.3 shows an example of a GIDT that corresponds to the *Concepts and Challenges in Life Science* textbook. For students who score below 70 percent on the GIST$_2$, you may need to find even less difficult reading materials. Figure 18.4 summarizes the scoring criteria for using the GIST, GIST$_2$, and GIDT sequence.

Decisions about which book and method of instruction should be used for each student should be based on more than test results like those just described. Also included in the decision should be (1) observations of learners' reading behavior, (2) evaluations of learners' performance on other tests and papers, and (3) judgments about learners' background knowledge and interests. Making such evaluations should be a continuous

This test will help determine the kind of text learning assistance these students will need to be successful working with this book. Ask the students to read a much shorter segment of text (235 words; pp. 106–107). This section is titled "How do we breathe?" Before the students begin reading, go over the main ideas they should look for in this passage. Have them listed on the board to point to as they are read.

1. What is a diaphragm?

2. What are two things that help us use our lungs to breathe?

3. What happens when we inhale?

4. Explain why air leaves the lungs when the ribs move down and in.

Instruct the students to read the passage in their book, turn the question sheet over, and answer the questions, referring back to the book if necessary. This type of test, with a shorter selection and the important information identified, allows the teacher to determine whether providing this structure will help the students learn from this text.

I. Place the letter of the correct answer in the blank beside the question.

(vocabulary knowledge)

_____   (1) The diaphragm is a _____.
(A) sheet of muscle   (B) piece of bone   (C) large blood vessel

(recall of directly stated information)

_____   (2) What are two things that help us use our lungs to breathe?
(A) blood vessels and ribs  (B) diaphragm and stomach  (C) diaphragm and ribs

_____   (3) When we inhale, _____.
(A) air leaves the lungs  (B) air enters the lungs  (C) the space inside the chest becomes smaller

(question requiring an inference based on textual material)

II. (4) Explain why air leaves the lungs when the ribs move down and in.

Figure 18.3. A GIDT for *Concepts and Challenges in Life Science* (Cebco Standard, 1979). (This material was developed by Judy Sanderson, a teacher in the Chesterfield County School District in South Carolina. It is reproduced here with her permission.)

process. Students should not be put into a slot and left there. The students' progress should be carefully monitored throughout the school year.

## Using Reading Guides

Reading guides are written guides that help students to read, understand, and learn from content area textbooks. Constructing reading guides is a time-consuming process, but it is well worth the effort when you consider that, once they are made, only minor revisions will be needed during subsequent years. When constructing reading guides, you

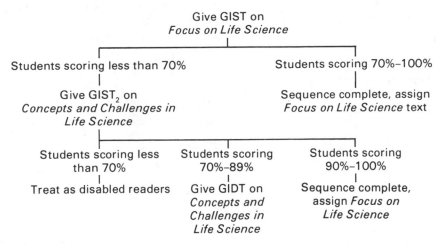

Give GIST on *Focus on Life Science*
- Students scoring less than 70%
  - Give GIST₂ on *Concepts and Challenges in Life Science*
    - Students scoring less than 70%
      - Treat as disabled readers
    - Students scoring 70%–89%
      - Give GIDT on *Concepts and Challenges in Life Science*
    - Students scoring 90%–100%
      - Sequence complete, assign *Focus on Life Science*
- Students scoring 70%–100%
  - Sequence complete, assign *Focus on Life Science* text

*Students scoring 70%–100% on the GIST*: These students should be able to work from the *Focus on Life Science* text.

*Students scoring 90%–100% on the GIST₂*: These students may be able to work from the *Focus on Life Science* text with teacher's attention and instructional assistance. The answers on the first GIST for these students will be evaluated. It is possible that they missed a particular type of question. Their scores on the GIST should fall in the 50%–60% range. If not, there may be factors other than reading ability affecting the scores.

Students scoring 70%–89% on the GIST₂: Recommendations for these students depend on the results of their GIDT. If they answered most questions from each category correctly, they can be placed in the *Concepts and Challenges in Life Science* text with a structured assignment that helps them find the important information. If they missed questions from one or two particular categories, their assignment can be adjusted to help them work in these areas, but the bulk of their work depends on answers in the areas in which they are successful. This gives them the best chance to gain the scientific knowledge required by this class, to feel successful, and to gain some experience with questions they have been unsuccessful with in the past. Students who have no success with the GIDT can be treated as disabled readers (discussed in the following paragraph). Since this GIDT is a very short test, recommendations based on the number of questions missed in each category may not be completely accurate. The students should be observed carefully and switched to another type of assignment if necessary.

Students scoring below 70% on the GIST₂: These students can be treated as disabled readers. Although they do not read well, they are not necessarily poor learners. They still need access to content area information. They can be expected to listen to lectures and participate in class discussions and projects. An effort should be made to locate and make available simpler materials that cover the topics under study. Assignments can be adjusted so that they are shorter and less complex. Whenever possible, audio and audiovisual materials should be provided to aid these and all students in the acquisition this course's content.

Figure 18.4. A GIST-GIDT testing procedure and instructional decisions. (This material was developed by Judy Sanderson, a teacher in the Chesterfield County School District in South Carolina. It is reproduced here with her permission.)

*Assignment*: Unit 7, "The Immigrant Experience," *The American Dream* (Lew Smith, Scott, Foresman and Company, 1980, pp. 293–331).

*Organizing Concept*: America has changed over time from a melting pot to a pluralistic society.

I. These are words you should know:

| | |
|---|---|
| immigrant | Americanization |
| emigrant | melting pot |
| ghetto | ethnic |
| machine government | pluralistic society |

1. From your readings, decide which word goes into each blank.
   Ify Fatuyi of South Carolina is an American _____.

   (A)  emigrant                          (B)  immigrant

   Mr. Fatuyi _____ from Nigeria in 1960.

   (A)  emigrated                          (B)  immigrated

2. Read the meaning of *ghetto* on p. 293.
   What does the word *ghetto* commonly refer to today?

   _____

   _____

3. Read p. 318, and then tell how immigration led to the development of machine governments.

   _____

   _____

   _____

   _____

4. On p. 326, you will read about ethnicity. What does the word ethnic mean? (You may need to use the dictionary.)

   _____

   _____

5. Read pp. 304 and 322–327. Which of the following terms best fits in each blank: *melting pot, pluralistic society, Americanization*?

   a.  A _____ is a society composed of many cultures and traditions that coexist despite their differences.

Figure 18.5. A reading guide (one to two weeks).

b. _____ refers to an idea that immigrants would undergo a process that would combine individuals of all nations and yield a new race. It suggests a society in which everyone has similar customs, beliefs, and life-styles.

c. _____ generally meant encouraging immigrants and their children to reject their native languages and traditions.

II. Let these questions guide your reading. Be prepared to discuss your answers in class.

Reading 1—"Why They Came," pp. 297–304.

Give four reasons why immigrants came to the United States.

1.

2.

3.

4.

Reading 2—"The Idea of the Melting Pot," pp. 304–305.

Why do you think it was difficult for non–English-speaking immigrants to "melt" into America?

_____

_____

_____

Reading 3—"Humanitarianism," pp. 306–309.

Did America act in a "humanitarian" manner toward immigrants? Explain. _____

_____

_____

_____

Reading 4—"Reactions to Immigrants," pp. 310–312.

Give two reasons for negative reactions to immigrants.

1.

2.

Give two reasons for positive reactions to immigrants.

1.

2.

**Figure 18.5** (*continued*)

Reading 5—"Problems in the New Land," pp. 314–318.
  Although most immigrants came to America for a better life, many encountered problems. Name three problems that the immigrants encountered.

  1.

  2.

  3.

Reading 6—"Political Machines and Immigrants," pp. 318–321.
  Compare the advantages and disadvantages of political machines for the immigrants.

Political machines

| Advantages to Immigrants | Disadvantages to Immigrants |
|---|---|
|  |  |

Reading 7—"Americanization," pp. 322–326; Reading 8—"The Idea of Ethnicity," pp. 326–329.
  Which concept, "melting pot" or "pluralistic society," is the better dream for the United States today? Why?

_____

_____

_____

_____

_____

_____

**Figure 18.5** (*continued*)

must carefully think through the behaviors and outcomes that you want your students to attain. The guides must be so constructed that they will lead the students to those goals. An example of a reading guide is shown in Figure 18.5. This guide was developed from a United States history text (Smith, *The American Dream*, Scott, Foresman and Company, 1980).

When using reading guides with poor readers, you need to model the behaviors that you are attempting to elicit. Initially, the guides should be worked through in group discussions. You should point out beforehand the kinds of information that you want the students to seek. You should then lead them through the steps needed to locate the information. Modeling helps the students know exactly what is expected of them. At first, you may supply almost all of the answers; however, you should gradually lessen your input until the students can complete the guides independently. During this weaning process, students should be asked to support and defend their answers, whether they come directly from the text or result from logical thinking processes. This helps students reinforce the appropriate skills and keeps you informed of the students' progress in developing those skills. Throughout this process, your readers learn independent strategies for processing textual information.

## SUMMARY

What we have done in this chapter is to present a few suggestions that may help beginning teachers cope with problem readers. In the Recommended Readings at the end of this chapter, you will find a list of additional sources that explain in greater detail some of the techniques that we have mentioned.

## REFERENCES

Allington, R. L. If they don't read much how they ever gonna get good? *Journal of Reading*, 1977, **21**, 57–61.

Allington, R. L. *Poor readers don't get to read much.* East Lansing, Mich.: Institute for Research on Teaching, Michigan State University, 1980.

Allington, R., and Strange, M. *Learning through reading in the content areas.* Lexington, Mass.: D. C. Heath, 1980.

*Concepts and challenges in life science.* Fairfield, N.J.: Cebco Standard, 1979.

*Focus on life science.* Columbus, Ohio: Charles E. Merrill, 1977.

Smith, L. *The American dream.* Glenview, Ill.: Scott, Foresman and Company, 1980.

Smith, R. J., and Barrett, T. C. *Teaching reading in the middle grades.* (2nd ed.) Reading, Mass.: Addison-Wesley, 1979.

## RECOMMENDED READINGS

Allington, R., and Strange, M. *Learning through reading in the content areas.* Lexington, Mass.: D. C. Heath, 1980.
Chapters 3, 5, 6, 7, 8, and 10 provide excellent background information and techniques for differentiating instruction based on textual material in the content areas.

Bond, G. L., and Tinker, M. A. *Reading difficulties: Their diagnosis and correction.* Englewood Cliffs, N.J.: Prentice-Hall, 1973.
A comprehensive discussion of diagnostic and remedial techniques for problem readers is presented.

Otto, W., and Smith, R. J. *Corrective and remedial teaching.* Boston: Houghton Mifflin, 1980.
This book should be required reading on the subject of children who have reading problems.

Smith, R. J., and Barrett, T. C. *Teaching reading in the middle grades.* (2nd ed.) Reading, Mass.: Addison-Wesley, 1979.
Middle-grade students (grades four through eight) are given little attention in the educational media. Smith and Barrett provide a detailed look at middle-grade readers and offer practical suggestions on how to improve reading in the middle grades.

# CHAPTER 19

# Computers, Literacy, and Teaching Reading

Michael L. Kamil
University of Illinois at Chicago

*The final chapter in Part III considers a different managerial-organizational problem facing beginning teachers: dealing intelligently with computers in the elementary reading program. Computers in education are here to stay, and it is imperative that beginning teachers become knowledgeable in basic computer concepts and potential uses of computers in reading instruction. In this chapter, Michael Kamil provides beginning teachers this needed information. He begins by defining computer literacy, the computer, and some basic computer terminology; then, he discusses the advantages and limitations of the use of computers in education. Guidelines for selecting and evaluating computer hardware and software are included (since teachers are often involved in selecting instructional materials), and some reading and language arts applications of computers are described. The last portion of the chapter consists of an annotated list of the computer software currently available.*

Perhaps the question most frequently asked by teachers about computers is: Will computers replace teachers? The answer to that question is simple. Within the limits of our current technology, only the poorest of teachers would be in danger of being even partially supplanted by a computer. Every teacher can be greatly assisted by computers, however, particularly since microcomputers are now relatively inexpensive and widely available.

The purpose of this chapter is to provide you with an introduction to basic concepts about computers, computer literacy, uses of computers, and evaluations of computers and the instructional materials used with computers. A sample of some available software for teaching reading and language arts is also included.

## WHAT IS LITERACY?

At one time the ability to make one's mark was a sufficient sign of literacy. Changes in technological, professional, educational, and military requirements have necessitated changes in the definition of literacy. It was once a requirement that one be able to sign one's name to be literate. More recently, literacy has been defined as being able to read and comprehend new material (Resnick and Resnick, 1977). Today, the definition of literacy must include the ability to use and interact with computers.

Even this definition undergoes frequent changes. When the first electronic computer was developed, it had to be rewired for each function it was to perform. Later, computers required that users be able to keypunch cards for the computer to use. Present-day microcomputers rarely have the option of using computer cards.

A thorough knowledge of what a computer is and what computers can be used for is part of what we mean by "computer literacy." Most students in elementary school today will need to be computer literate before they reach college; it is imperative that their teachers be familiar with computers so that they will be able to teach them. It is equally important that computers be used to help teach students when appropriate.

## WHAT IS A COMPUTER?

A computer is simply a machine that performs electronic manipulations of information. So long as the information can be reduced to appropriate codes, there is no restriction on the type of information that can be handled by a computer. Since a computer is a series of switches, all the information it uses must be reduced to a form that is like a switch. Since switches are either on or off, the codes used for information must use only two symbols, one for on, the other for off. Hence, computers operate on the "binary number system"—a system that uses zeros (off) and ones (on).

In dealing with computers, an important distinction must be made between their hardware and software. "Hardware" consists of all the physical components that you can feel, touch, and operate. The computer and its case are parts of the hardware. Similarly, the monitor, or display screen, is a piece of hardware, as are all the "attachments" to the computer. "Software," on the other hand, represents the programs that tell the computer what to do. A "program" is a sequence of instructions for the computer. It can be something you purchase or create. Most computers even have programs that are stored internally, so they begin operating when you turn on the power.

### Why Are Computers Useful?

Computers can perform several functions better than people can. Computers can do repetitive tasks that people do not do well. Computers can perform calculations at speeds that humans cannot approach. These abilities enable computers to make decisions faster than people can. In education, this translates into the ability to deliver instruction that is precisely based on the performance of the student. In short, each student could be given an individually tailored program of instruction that would be optimal in terms of rate of achievement, motivation, and the like. That is, the computer does not need to consider for a long time what to do for a particular student. Teachers often make inappropriate decisions, particularly when they have little or no time to reflect (as during a class).

Computers may be able to take over many functions of teachers at a much lower cost, with greater objectivity and flexibility. Finally, computers allow access to vast amounts of software. This means that a teacher does not have to be expert in all areas of instruction. (In fact, it might be possible to use computers for in-service work and the like.) In short, the use of computers would allow teachers to provide their students (and themselves) with a far wider range of materials or instruction than they could if they had to depend on their own expertise and knowledge. Certainly, computers do not perform these sorts of tasks today as well as teachers can, but as we learn more about teaching and the content of instruction, computers will play an increasingly important role in education.

## What Are the Drawbacks of Using Computers?

Mason (1980) has listed several problems associated with using computers for instruction in reading. First, computers must have displays, usually on a television screen or a cathode-ray tube (CRT), which create critical problems with legibility and eye fatigue. Many computer users complain that they can watch the screen displays for only short amounts of time. A second problem is that the computer cannot listen to students read and check for fluency. A related difficulty is that the voice quality of computers (speaking to users) is often poor. Third on the list of problems is the fact that the computer cannot respond to novel answers; it is restricted to responding to the answers that have been programmed. In short, the computer is flexible only up to the point that flexibility was built into the software. Finally, there is the cost of producing materials for use in instruction (software). One conservative estimate is that the cost for computerizing an entire school curriculum could be as high as $92 million (Isaacson, 1981).

One partial solution to these problems will be the development of effective, easy-to-use "authoring languages" with which teachers can create their own software. This is not the ideal solution, since a large investment of time, effort, and expertise is required. Such investments are rarely made for the development of conventional materials; it is unlikely that they will be more common for computer instruction, for which the investments and necessary skills are even greater.

## SELECTING HARDWARE AND SOFTWARE

Many decisions to buy computers are made relatively independently of decisions to purchase software. This is definitely a mistake. The capabilities of the hardware should be used as a criterion for software selections. The availability of software should also be a criterion for hardware selections. The exception, of course, is the case in which the computers are already in place.

In the following sections, two evaluation schemes will be presented: one for hardware and one for software. For clarity, they are discussed independently; they should, however, always be used together.

### Hardware Evaluation

If you have no computers and are planning on buying them, you should evaluate the available hardware in a systematic fashion. Not all computers have the same capabilities, and you should not pay for capabilities you will never use or need.

The first step in this process is to define carefully the purposes for which you will use the computer. Teaching beginning reading may require computer capabilities very different from those required in teaching study skills. If the computer is to be used for many different types of instruction, all of the goals and purposes should be considered. At the same time, the software to be used should be considered. Often, the computer's capabilities determine what type of software can be used. For example, a program that uses color or sound cannot run as effectively (if at all) on a computer with a black-and-white monitor and no sound output. Careful consideration must be given to the *availability* of software as well as to the capabilities of the computer required by the software. If little software were available for your computer, the hardware would be of little use to you.

In general, evaluation of hardware must take into account factors such as cost, memory capacity, display characteristics (e.g., upper and lower case, color, graphics, legibility, etc.), sound or speech, expandability (i.e., how easy it is to add to the computer), available accessories, and, of course, software availability. A fully developed method of performing such an evaluation is discussed in Billings and Gass (1982). In their scheme, each factor is weighted by the evaluator before the computers are rated on each factor. An overall evaluation is obtained by multiplying the rating by the weights and then summing. Suppose, for example, you decided that cost is the most important criterion. A very low cost computer might be your choice, even though it did not have a capability you rated low in priority, say, sound capability. Although this is a lengthy process, it is too important to neglect.

Any technique for evaluating hardware, however, must be used interactively with software evaluation schemes. That is, if you are contemplating the purchase of computers and other equipment, you should consider the software available at the same time. Remember, not all software will run on all computers, nor can it be converted to run on all machines.

## Software Evaluation

The overriding question in the evaluation of software is: Does the program do something better than what could be done without a computer? That is, the particular program or piece of software should accomplish some goal or objective in a way that conventional instruction cannot. For example, if the computer were simply used to present workbook-page exercises, there would be no value in using the computer. Conventional ditto sheets would be cheaper and have the advantage of being transportable; kids could take them home if they wanted. When the program does offer some unique capability, then it must meet ten criteria to be a "perfect" instructional tool.

### Availability

The first of these criteria is simply whether the program exists. Often, programs are described in brochures, magazines, and the like but are not yet commercially available. If you cannot see a running version of the program, do not buy it.

### Content

Does the program or software cover the material that you want or need covered? An important point here is that you, as a prospective user, need to know precisely what it is that you want to teach (or have the computer teach). Another concern is the issue of related courseware. While software is the program that runs on the computer, "courseware" is the material that allows you to integrate the software into your curriculum. Questions to be raised in this regard include: Are there appropriate manuals? Is the basic teaching approach compatible with your teaching? Are there supplementary materials for the students?

### Appropriateness

The software package must be appropriate for the students who will be using it. They must be able to deal with the material and the computer program themselves. That is, if a teacher is needed to monitor the student constantly, using the computer has no advantage.

Software must be "user-friendly." That is, it must not place demands on the user that require special knowledge or skills. Simple errors or mistakes must not destroy the sequence of instruction. Students should be able to get help at any point in the program and be returned to where they were when they requested help. In addition, it is desirable that a student can start or stop at any point in the program and return later to the same point.

Another important consideration involving the software's appropriateness is whether the concepts are at the proper level of cognitive difficulty. A program that contains highly abstract concepts or requires sophisticated thinking would not be useful for very young children. Similar questions have to be asked about the readability level of text in the program. Is it too difficult or too easy, or is the level of difficulty at or near the students' instructional reading level?

Finally, the software should have a diagnostic-managerial component. That is, it should determine whether it is appropriate for the student to work through the program. Students who already know the reading skills a program teaches should not have to work through the entire program; rather, they should be directed to more-advanced activities or to other programs.

### Feedback

All programs should provide students with feedback about their performance. Correct responses should be reinforced, and incorrect answers or responses should be explained. Mistakes should not cause difficulty in the program but should elicit a helpful explanation of what is required. In addition, students should have the option of requesting help or reviews at any point in the program. Another important concern is the variety and type of feedback. Programs often fail to provide a "very good" feedback message when the student finally succeeds after many attempts. More appropriate is to make the feedback fit the performance, with less enthusiastic feedback for less satisfactory work.

### Attention

One of the particular strengths of computers is their ability to attract and maintain the students' interest, even in repetitive tasks. Good software should take advantage of this asset. Graphics (e.g., pictures, animation, graphs, charts, etc.) should be used appropriately, as should sound, music, color, and other capabilities. Explanations, feedback, text formats (e.g., amount of text, size of type, etc.) and the like should be varied from time to time throughout the program to maintain the students' interest, motivation, and attention.

### Pacing

The speed of instruction should be sufficient to keep students moving ahead while learning. It should not be so quick as to impair achievement. When a student makes an incorrect response, the program must have appropriate "branches" to help the student correct the mistakes and learn the material. For example, when a student does not perform well, the program should automatically move to an explanatory segment, or branch.

### Record Keeping

Each piece of instructional software must monitor the students' progress. Records should be kept of the students' performance, and those records should be available to the instructor. The students also should be given evaluative information about their performance.

### Reliability

The program should run reliably. That is, it should perform as expected each time it is run. Students only experience frustration when the programs do not "work" the way they are supposed to. In addition, the program should consistently produce learning experiences for students. Using a program that does not promote learning is no better than not using a program at all.

### Cost Effectiveness

The question that most software purchasers ask is: How expensive is the program? Other equally important issues related to cost must also be considered. For example, will there be sufficient numbers of students who can use or benefit from the program? Are special pieces of hardware required to use the software? Often disk drives, color monitors, printers, speech synthesizers, and other special components are required before the full capability of a program can be realized. All these factors must be taken into account in considering the cost effectiveness of software.

Two related concerns are the program's memory requirements and whether a special language is required to use the program. Memory requirements are crucial, since a program will not run when there is insufficient memory space. "Computer memory" is defined in terms of the number of bytes. A "byte" is one "word" of computer memory. Usually, one character can be stored in one byte of computer memory. Most microcomputers have from 4K (4096 bytes) to 64K (65,536 bytes) of memory. (The abbreviation $K$ is used for the value $2^{10}$. Hence, 64K represents 65,536 instead of 64,000 bytes.) A few have more—up to 512K in some instances. Memory requirements are inflexible; when a program requires a certain amount of memory, it will not run in less space. This also applies to computer languages (e.g., Pascal, Fortran, Pilot, etc.). When the language is not available on the computer, the program will not run.

A final concern involves the types of machines available. If software is intended to be used on several different machine types (e.g., Apple, TRS-80, CBM, IBM, etc.), caution should be exercised. Few pieces of software are compatible with more than one or two types of computers. The programs you purchase, therefore, may run only on one brand of computer.

### Environments

The software should not interefere with other computer activities or other classroom activities while it is being used. Sound is the most obvious problem. A large number of computers in the same room could create an unbearable din if they all generated sounds at the same time. (Have you ever visited a crowded videogame arcade?) Color, animation, game paddles, and printers can also add environmental distractions in a classroom.

## After the Evaluation

If you find a piece of software that meets all of the preceding criteria, buy it! It may be the only one around. Remember, however, that this scheme is a guide to finding good software; perfect software does not exist, just as perfect conventional instructional materials do not exist. So, before you buy, make sure the software meets the most important (to you) or the largest number of the criteria discussed.

If the software that you evaluate does not meet these criteria (or most of them), there are three choices: First, simply refuse to purchase it and look for something else. Second, buy it and plan to work around the limitations that you have already discovered while doing the evaluation. Your last option is creating your own software.

This last alternative is not for every teacher. For those who are inclined, programs can be written in computer languages such as Basic, Pilot, or Pascal or with special authoring systems for particular computers. Be warned ahead of time: This is a difficult, often frustrating, task that is even more complex than producing conventional instructional materials. The final product, however, might turn out to be precisely what you need (and were unable to find available commercially).

## A Final Word About Evaluation

Remember, the two evaluation systems given here—for hardware and for software—should be used *together*. Unless you already have hardware available, the decision to buy one computer or another is most efficiently made when you simultaneously consider software options.

## SOME USES OF COMPUTERS

Without differentiating between large and small computers, the following applications represent a small sample of specific uses for computers in education, with the greatest emphasis on reading and language arts.

1.  Determining reading or readability levels.
2.  Producing cloze test materials.
3.  Teaching survival skills (e.g., balancing checkbooks).
4.  Teaching Latin and English vocabulary.

5. Providing record-keeping and grading facilities.
6. Teaching basic skills to adults and children.
7. Teaching phonics.
8. Teaching bilingual reading.
9. Teaching multiply handicapped children.
10. Teaching critical reading.
11. Generating stories and story structures.

This is not an exhaustive list. Moreover, there is no judgment implied that these are the best uses for computers. Space limitations prevent a complete description of these programs. Rather, the following sections describe materials that provide information about programs, techniques, hardware, and software.

## A SAMPLING OF READING AND LANGUAGE ARTS SOFTWARE

Reading software is being introduced at a rapidly accelerating rate. Applications are limited only by the incapacity of computers to accept voice input. That is, computers now cannot "listen" to students read. (There are a few voice-input devices on the market, but they have to be calibrated for each student and have capacities of only a few words—usually 32 or 64. Moreover, they do not approach 100 percent accuracy. The future holds promise for new developments in speech-recognition devices.)

There are two general categories of software for reading and language arts: instructional and managerial. In the following sections, a small sampling of these is presented. The list is, of necessity, only a sample, and approval is not implied.

### Instructional Software

The following is a partial list of some of the instructional programs currently available.

1. *Borg-Warner Educational Systems: MicroSystem 80:* Microsystem 80 is a collection of programs dealing with word structure and critical reading. A management system is included.
2. *BLS, Inc.:* BLS has programs available to teach word skills, reading comprehension, inferences, writing, and grammar skills.
3. *Milton-Bradley Educational Software:* Milton-Bradley programs teach vocabulary and punctuation skills. A management system is included.
4. *Milliken Publishing Company:* Milliken produces programs in language arts (grammar) and reading comprehension. A management system is included.
5. *Minnesota Educational Computer Consortium:* The MECC has programs available in language arts and spelling.
6. *Radio Shack Educational Software: High Motivation Reading; Reading Is Fun:* Radio Shack's programs teach main idea, sequence, details, and fact versus opinion. Other Radio Shack programs teach spelling and keyboard skills.
7. *Random House School Division:* Random House produces various programs in alphabet knowledge, phonics, spelling, grammar, and other language skills.
8. *Scott, Foresman and Company: Reading Skills Courseware Series:* The Scott-Foresman series is a complete reading series, grades one through six, that includes a management system.

9. *Scholastic, Inc.:* Scholastic publishes a catalog of computer software that has been screened by the company. The software comes from a variety of producers.

10. *Society for Visual Education:* The SVE produces a catalog-detailing program in reading, grammar, vocabulary, punctuation, and spelling.

## Management Systems

The following list contains a few management systems that are program independent. Also listed are those that are keyed to specific reading programs.

1. *Corporation for Public Information in Education:* A program called Curriculum Manager can be used in association with all computer-assisted-instructional materials (or conventional instruction).

2. *Educational Progress Corporation:* MMICRO is a custom-designed management system to be used with a set of objectives for any curriculum.

3. *Ginn and Company:* Ginn produces a management system keyed to the Ginn Reading Program.

4. *Holt, Rinehart and Winston, Inc.:* CLASS is designed for use with *Holt Basic Reading Series.*

## Authoring Systems

Many of the authoring systems available are versions of PILOT, which is available for most microcomputers. Bell and Howell Microcomputer Systems produces two systems, PASS and GENIS I, for use with Apple computers. Radio Shack also produces an authoring system for use with TRS-80 computers.

## A Final Word About Software

The amount of software available for reading instruction can only increase. Current instructional software is good but not great; it does not yet offer a substantial improvement over conventional materials, although there are some advantages to using computer assisted instruction. Management packages are more advanced, in general. They presently offer more advantages for the teacher than do many instructional packages. In both cases, the future holds much promise.

In the meantime, authoring programs offer an alternative to commercial software, although they require a substantial investment of time and effort. If educators produce a concerted demand for high quality, the result will be vast improvements in software.

## SUMMARY

When it comes to the use of computers in elementary schools, the results have been extremely favorable. Vinsonhaler and Bass (1972) and Edwards, Norton, Taylor, Weiss, and Dusseldorp (1975) have reported nearly unanimous agreement among studies of the effectiveness of computer-supplemented instruction at the elementary level. Kulik, Kulik, and Cohen (1980), however, have assessed the effects of computer-assisted instruction at the college level to be modest although positive. By extrapolation, the effects in middle and secondary schools should be somewhere between.

The rapidly increasing number of microcomputers in schools will provide a solid testing ground for computer instruction of all sorts. As teachers begin to accept and use microcomputers, the results of computer-assisted instruction should become even more striking.

## REFERENCES

Billings, K., and Gass, S. Adding a micro to your school picture. *Electronic Learning,* 1982, **1**, 35–40.

Edwards, J., Norton, S., Taylor, S., Weiss, M., and Dusseldorp, R. How effective is CAI? A review of the research. *Educational Leadership,* 1975, **33**, 147–153.

Isaacson, D. What's holding back computer use in education? *Classroom Computer News,* 1981, **1**, 1, 28–29.

Kulik, J., Kulik, C., and Cohen, P. Effectiveness of computer-based college teaching: A meta-analysis of findings. *Review of Educational Research,* 1980, **50**, 525–544.

Mason, G. Computerized reading instruction: A review. *Educational Technology,* 1980, **20**, 18–22.

Resnick, D., and Resnick, L. The nature of literacy: An historical exploration. *Harvard Educational Review,* 1977, **47**, 370–385.

Vinsonhaler, J., and Bass, R. A summary of ten major studies on CAI drill and practice. *Educational Technology,* 1972, **12**, 29–32.

## RECOMMENDED READINGS

### Books

Coburn, P., Kelman, P., Roberts, N., Snyder, T., Watt, D., and Weiner, C. *Practical guide to microcomputers in education.* Reading, Mass.: Addison-Wesley, 1982.
This volume covers almost all of the topics of interest to educators. It is one of the best general introductions to the use of microcomputers in education, although reading and language arts are not specifically considered.

Doerr, C. *Microcomputers and the 3 R's.* Rochelle Park, N.J.: Hayden, 1979.
Doerr presents a survey of applications and uses for microcomputers in schools that deals with all subjects and includes a number of program listings.

Frederick, F. *Guide to microcomputers.* Washington, D.C.: Association for Educational Communications and Technology, 1980.
This good general reference provides information on almost all aspects of microcomputers and their application.

Mason, G. E., Blanchard, J. S., and Daniel, D. B. *Computer applications in reading.* (2nd ed.) Newark, Del.: International Reading Association, 1983.
Mason and Blanchard's thorough book summarizes the uses of computers in teaching reading.

### Reviews in Professional Journals

Blanchard, J. Computer-assisted instruction in today's reading classroom. *Journal of Reading,* 1980, **20**, 430–434.

Gleason, G. Microcomputers in education: The state of the art. *Educational Technology,* 1981, **21**, 7–18.

Kamil, M. Technology and reading: A review of research and instruction. In J. Niles and L. Harris (Eds.), *New inquiries in reading research and instruction.* Thirty-first Yearbook of the National Reading Conference. Rochester, N.Y.: The National Reading Conference, 1982.

Mason, G. Computerized reading instruction: A review. *Educational Technology,* 1980, **20**, 18–22.

Thompson, B. Computers in reading: A review of applications and implications. *Educational Technology,* 1980, **20**, 38–41.

## Computer Education Journals and Magazines

*Classroom Computer News*
Intentional Educations, Inc.
341 Mount Auburn Street
Watertown, Mass. 02172

*The Computing Teacher*
University of Oregon
Eugene, Ore. 97403

*Creative Computing*
P.O. Box 789-M
Morristown, N.J. 07960

*Courseware Magazine*
4919 North Millbrook #222
Fresno, Calif. 93726

*Educational Computer*
P.O. Box 535
Cupertino, Calif. 95015

*Educational Technology*
140 Sylvan Avenue
Englewood Cliffs, N.J. 07632

*Electronic Learning*
Scholastic Corporation
902 Sylvan Avenue
Box 2001
Englewood Cliffs, N.J. 07632

*School Microware Reviews*
Dresden Associates
P.O. Box 264
Dresden, Maine 04342

## Other Sources of Information

CONDUIT
P.O. Box 338
Iowa City, Iowa 52240

MICRO-IDEAS
2941 Linneman Street
Glenview, Ill. 60025

MicroSIFT
Northwest Regional Educational Laboratory
710 Second Avenue Southwest
Portland, Ore. 97204

Minnesota Educational Computer Consortium
2520 Broadway Drive
St. Paul, Minn. 55113

Project LOCAL
500 Nahaton Street
Westwood, Mass. 02090

# PART IV

# Affect and Reading:
# Motivating Students to Read

Part IV examines the development of the student's motivation to read, interest in reading, and lifelong desire to read, that is, the affective dimension of reading instruction. Chapter 20 offers many ideas a beginning teacher can use to bring children and books together in the classroom. Chapter 21 presents strategies a beginning teacher can employ to guide children from the basal reader to the realm of children's literature. In Chapter 22, many ideas are offered concerning how teachers can "create" readers in the classroom and how teachers can actively involve parents in the development of their child's literacy. Chapter 23 presents suggestions teachers can use to help students to practice and enjoy oral reading, and Chapter 24 describes strategies for motivating children's critical reading and writing through sports-based activities.

# CHAPTER 20

# Bringing Books to Children and Children to Books

Olive S. Niles
University of Lowell
Lowell, Massachusetts

*Before children can develop a desire to read and so acquire the reading habit, they must become familiar with various reading materials. The teachers who introduce children to books must themselves be knowledgeable about children's literature and aware of strategies to promote children's interest in books. In this chapter, Olive Niles discusses bringing children and books together. She begins by describing the broad content of children's literature and then suggests ways teachers can evaluate students' interests so that this knowledge can be used when suggesting or providing books for children. Many suggestions are offered to help the beginning teacher to become acquainted with children's literature and create a classroom climate conducive to reading for pleasure. The remainder of the chapter describes specific activities a beginning teacher can initiate to motivate children's reading and so to bring children and books together in the classroom.*

Everyone agrees that teachers must know as much as possible about teaching children *how to read,* and this book has dealt with many techniques and procedures to help you effectively teach reading skills. Another important issue, however, has yet to be addressed: How do teachers help children to *acquire the habit of reading;* that is, how do we promote the desire to read among children?

Encouraging children's enjoyment of reading is not an easy topic to discuss, because so much depends on the personality of the individual teacher and the often unpredictable and idiosyncratic ways in which different teachers interact with children. No firm "rules of the game" exist. Teachers must discover what works for them. The purpose of this chapter is to discuss some general principles, and a few specific procedures, that have worked for *some teachers* with *some children* and may work for you.

On the whole, American schools do a good job of teaching children reading skills (Micklos, 1980). We cannot claim the same success, however, with our efforts to sell voluntary reading to our students. Studies of the reading habits of the American people are not encouraging; although more books are read today than ever before, only a small part of the population does most of this reading (Cole and Gold, 1979).

The two parts of a complete reading program (the cognitive and the affective) are closely related. If a child does not possess the requisite skills (i.e., the cognitive abilities), it is very hard to persuade her to read for pleasure (i.e., the affective component). Reading is just too hard, and the child always fears failure. On the other hand, if the child does not read voluntarily and extensively, she does not gain practice with the skills that promote increasingly efficient reading.

The habit of reading results from a long series of satisfying experiences; therefore, involvement with books should begin early in a child's life. Parents who do not (or are unable to) share reading experiences with their preschool children place their children at a disadvantage. Whether or not involvement with books has been started in the home, however, the school plays a major role, and you, the classroom teacher, are the central figure in helping children become enthusiastic readers. Two main factors are involved in bringing books to children and children to books: good books and wise teachers. Let us examine these two factors.

## WHAT BOOKS?

Critics of children's literature have set forth criteria for judging books that most of us accept. We adults acknowledge that books winning the Newbery Medal and the Caldecott Medal, for example, represent some of the finest children's books available. Interestingly, however, children do not always agree. From their perspective, a good book (as determined by adult standards) may be no good at all. The question should be: Good for whom? A book that seems good to one child may be of no interest to another. For this reason, it is important to make many books available to children and to allow the children to choose their own books as often as possible.

What kinds of books should be made available? Books of fantasy like C. S. Lewis's (1951) *The Lion, the Witch, and the Wardrobe,* which help children stretch their imaginations; books like Elizabeth Speare's (1958) *The Witch of Blackbird Pond,* which introduce children to people with other ways of living and different values; books like Neta Frazier's (1973) *Stout-Hearted Seven,* which tell children about their heritage in history, myth, and folklore; easy-to-read books like Arnold Lobel's (1972) *Mouse Tales,* which encourage literacy by helping beginners and newly literate children practice their developing reading skills; books like Robert McClung's (1979) *America's Endangered Birds,* which excite children's curiosity about the world in which they live; books like *Saturday's Child,* edited by Suzanne Seed (1973), which illustrate many different kinds of careers and help children to answer the universal question: what will I be when I grow up; books like Norma Mazer's (1973) *A Figure of Speech,* which deal with the problems of relating to families and peers, to the changes that come as children grow, to different beliefs about religions and ethics, and to the rewards and responsibilities of citizenship. Children need humorous books like Judith Viorst's (1972) *Alexander and the Terrible, Horrible, No Good, Very Bad Day*, for times when they want to laugh; beautiful picture books like Robert McCloskey's (1952) *One Morning in Maine*, which foster children's appreciation of art in many forms. They need books of poetry and plays like Nancy Larrick's (1968) *Piping Down the Valleys Wild*, which introduce them at an early age to the various forms of literature. Finally, children need books like Peggy Parish's (1963) *Amelia Bedelia*, which are just for fun, nothing more. Magazines such as *Highlights for Children, Ranger Rick, National Geographic World,* and *Cricket* should also be made readily available.

We also need to remember that everyone has three different reading levels. One is the frustration level, at which no child should ever be forced to read. This is the level at which reading is so hard that there can be little comprehension and certainly no enjoyment. The second level is the instructional level, which is the level of difficulty appropriate for teaching materials such as basal readers and social studies textbooks. Children can, and should, read these materials when we help them read; that is, when we *teach.* Then there is the independent level, at which reading is easy, fluent, natural, and unimpeded. Materials for promoting the reading habit should be concentrated at this level. The materials intended for voluntary reading should be at a readability level easier than that of materials designed for study reading, research projects, and the like. The teacher must be sensitive to differences in reading levels when helping children select books for independent reading.

Acquiring an appreciation of literature is a developmental process similar to the acquisition of reading skills. This fact must be considered both in helping children select books and in organizing activities to promote the use of these books. There are three main stages in this process. At first, when they are little, most children love books, but they generally do not know why. Even when they do have some idea about why a book appeals to them, very few can verbalize it. The teacher should not ask that they attempt to do so. If all they can say is that the book was "good" or "fun," that should be enough.

The second stage usually occurs during upper elementary school, middle school, or high school (probably in a literature class) when students learn why some literature is better than other literature and about such things as imagery and tone and irony and connotation. A few fortunate readers may attain the third and final stage (at which they not only love books but can explain why they do) before they leave elementary school, but most readers fully attain it only later, when they have become mature readers.

Before I turn to suggestions about how the beginning teacher can help children to move through these developing stages of appreciation, let us examine children's reading interests, for a knowledge of their interests is essential to bringing children to books.

## CHILDREN'S READING INTERESTS

A great deal is known about the reading interests of children of various ages. This information, which is probably more useful to authors and publishers than to teachers, is readily available in many professional books (e.g., Sutherland and Arbuthnot, 1977). What the teacher needs is not this general information but a knowledge of the interests of individual children in his class. Many times, these interests do not conform to the general pattern.

There are several ways to find out about individual interests. Here are a few.

1.  Listen and observe. When there is free time for reading, what materials do individual students choose? If you are using basal readers, to which selections do individual children respond most enthusiastically? During oral discussions, what do children reveal about themselves, their experiences, and their concerns?

2.  Use an interest inventory, a simple one that can be given orally with some modifications to small children or in written form to a whole class of older children. The success of such an inventory depends on whether you and your class have a relationship of trust. When trust is absent, children often tell teachers whatever they think the teachers want to know rather than the truth. For this reason, interest inventories should not be used until you have had time to build a trusting relationship. Figure 20.1 presents a sample inventory.

3.  Write the class a letter. Tell the children personal details: your out-of-school interests and activities, things you have done, trips you have taken, even problems you have had, all, of course, within the limitations of good taste and the children's ability to understand. Then, invite (not require) each child to respond in kind. In this way much valuable information is exchanged, and you will gain insight into your students' interests. This exchange works best with children who have developed some fluency in writing.

---

**Favorite Activities**

1.  What games or sports do you like best? _____

2.  What is your favorite television program? _____

3.  How would you like to spend next Saturday if you could do exactly as you wished? _____

4.  If you could have only one pet, what would you choose?

_____

**Experiences**

Circle places where you have been.

| | | |
|---|---|---|
| Farm | Picnics | Concert |
| Zoo | Circus | Seashore |
| Museum | Park | Big city |
| Library | Art gallery | Airplane ride |

**School**

1.  What school subject do you like best? _____

2.  What subject do you like least? _____

Figure 20.1. An interest inventory.

Reading

1.   About what subjects do you like to read? Circle the three you like best.

| | | |
|---|---|---|
| Animals | People of other lands | Nurses and doctors |
| War | Indians | Humorous stories |
| Knights | Machinery | Sea stories |
| Automobiles | Airplanes | Science |
| School | Home and family | Biography |
| Love | Travel | Adventure |
| Pioneers | Mystery | Sports |

2.   How much time do you spend each day reading at home? _____

3.   What part of a newspaper do you usually read first? _____

Second? _____

The Future

1.   What do you wish for most? _____

2.   What kind of work do you hope to do when you finish school? _____

_____

**Figure 20.1** (*continued*)

4.   If you are a little reluctant to approach the matter in so personal a way, ask your students to complete this sentence (orally, if they are not yet fluent writers): "If I could have an author write a book just for me, I would ask for a book that _____." To give you an idea of just how powerful this exercise can be, here are some actual responses made by students in grades four, five, and six.

*By a boy who may have seen too much television:* "I want a scary book, a book that will give me the chills to read each page. I want a book with scary monsters such as werewolves, vampires, ghouls, and behemoths. I want many people to get killed by the monsters."

*By a girl who is a dreamer:* "If I could have an author write a book just for me, I would ask him to write about a girl who wanted a horse. She saved her money to take riding lessons. When she could ride well enough and handle a horse, her parents fell in love with a ranchlike house in the country, so they moved to that house. When they finally settled in the house, her parents thought they would surprise her and fill up those empty stables in the barn. Then she could be in the 4-H club and enter some horse shows."

*By a girl who is a "romantic":* "If I could have an author write a book just for me, I would ask him to write it about a beautiful princess. The princess would have beautiful clothes and jewelry. She would run away with a handsome prince. They would both get married. When they got married, they would come back and tell the king. The king would get angry and throw them out. Then they would build a little cottage. And they would live happily ever after."

*By a no-nonsense kind of boy:* "If I could have an author write a book just for me, I would ask for a book about the Air Force. Some day I will join the Air Force and fly one of the big bombers."

*By a heartbroken boy:* "If I could have an author write a book just for me, I would ask him to write about my dog who got hit by a car on the day before my birthday. I miss him so much. When Whitey and I went fishing together and were together all the time, we could go places and see things. He loved children and kissed the little ones. And we could play in the grass. How I wish he was still alive. No other dog was as good as him. And I wish I could hear him bark again."

These examples were chosen because they are brief and could be included here. Sometimes, children write pages detailing the whole content of a book they would enjoy. This procedure provides more information about children than just what may be a current, perhaps a passing, reading interest.

5. Develop a simple cumulative record form on which children list the books they have read. Such a record reveals many things about individual children, their interests, and particularly changes in their preferences (often abrupt, as when a girl suddenly stops reading Nancy Drew). When kept in a folder and passed from teacher to teacher as children move from grade to grade, these records provide valuable insights into children's reading habits. Figure 20.2 shows a sample form. As children read, they should keep their own records, checking the spaces to indicate the types of books they have read. Other categories may be added. Children usually take pride in their lists as they grow. Since it is easy for the teacher to observe children's current and past interests, children who need to broaden their interests can be easily identified.

Teachers need to know about children's individual interests, because motivation must start with the interests they already possess. Teachers also have a responsibility to help children develop new interests. The easiest time to do this—in fact, the easiest time to influence children's attitudes about the value of reading in general—is at the ages of 9 or 10 (when most children have developed considerable fluency) to 13 or 14 (when the consuming interests of adolescence absorb so much time and energy).

## TEACHERS WHO KNOW BOOKS

Teachers can help children to develop their interests in printed materials best when they have read those materials themselves. Children can easily tell whether a teacher is or is not knowledgeable about children's literature. When children sense a lack of knowledge, they react much like the shopper in the midst of the Christmas rush who encounters a minimally trained clerk behind the counter. Shifting from one aching foot to the other, the shopper asks for some item, the clerk fumbles around and comes up with something that resembles what is wanted but misses the mark in some way, and (unless it is actually Christmas Eve) the prospective buyer walks off without making a purchase. Unfortunately, some teachers do not read the books written for the children with whom they

School System ——————

Name ——————

Grade ——————

**Reading Record**

| No. | Title | Author | Animals | Folklore | Fairy tales | Mystery | Adventure | Travel | Humor | Sports | Western | History | Biography | Home/school | Inventions | Machines | Science | Science fiction | Careers | Poetry | Arts | Plays | Religion | Personal problems | Public problems | Other | Read whole book | Liked very much | Liked fairly well | Did not like |
|---|---|---|---|---|---|---|---|---|---|---|---|---|---|---|---|---|---|---|---|---|---|---|---|---|---|---|---|---|---|---|
| 1 | | | | | | | | | | | | | | | | | | | | | | | | | | | | | | |
| 2 | | | | | | | | | | | | | | | | | | | | | | | | | | | | | | |
| 3 | | | | | | | | | | | | | | | | | | | | | | | | | | | | | | |
| 4 | | | | | | | | | | | | | | | | | | | | | | | | | | | | | | |
| 5 | | | | | | | | | | | | | | | | | | | | | | | | | | | | | | |
| 6 | | | | | | | | | | | | | | | | | | | | | | | | | | | | | | |
| 7 | | | | | | | | | | | | | | | | | | | | | | | | | | | | | | |
| 8 | | | | | | | | | | | | | | | | | | | | | | | | | | | | | | |
| 9 | | | | | | | | | | | | | | | | | | | | | | | | | | | | | | |
| Etc. | | | | | | | | | | | | | | | | | | | | | | | | | | | | | | |

Figure 20.2. An example of a cumulative reading interest record.

work. Like the clerk in the Christmas rush, they know very little about the books they are trying to sell, or they know only those books they met in a course in children's literature. Like the prospective customer with the aching feet, the children walk away from the books.

A very important part of every teacher's preparation for teaching reading is a knowledge of children's books (with continuous updating while teaching). How can this knowledge be acquired and kept up-to-date? Here are some suggestions.

1. If you have never taken a course in children's literature or if the one you took was given more than five years ago, take such a course as soon as you can. It will provide you with all sorts of shortcuts to the world of children's books that might take you years to discover for yourself. Since many books for children are published every year, you need these shortcuts.

2. Focus on *authors* rather than individual *titles.* Come to know what to expect from certain authors, not forgetting that the best writers are often the least likely to follow a pattern from book to book. Nevertheless, if you have read one or two books by a certain author, it is fairly safe to predict what other books by the author will be like. For example, if you have read Beverly Cleary's (1954) *Henry Huggins,* you should be able to predict fairly well the style and content of *Henry and the Paper Route* (Cleary, 1957).

3. Subscribe to *Horn Book, Language Arts, The Reading Teacher,* or all three. Read the articles about children's books and authors and especially the reviews of new books as they are published. The reviews reveal how "styles" in children's books are changing, what new books well-known authors have written, and what new authors are being recognized for their work.

4. Try to persuade your fellow teachers to form a children's book review club. Each member pledges to read at least two children's books each month. When you meet, perhaps once a month over coffee and cookies in the media center, you exchange information and views about the books you have read. When it comes time to suggest new books for your classroom library or media center, you will be more knowledgeable about what is available and so probably will be happier with the new acquisitions.

5. Haunt the children's room of your public library. Browse, talk to the librarian, ask questions about books that circulate rapidly (and those that sit on the shelves), borrow books, and *read.*

6. Perhaps most important, when you teach, *read books to your students and discuss them.* Be aware of the books your students are reading, and ask them to discuss their favorites. Some of your best sources for information about children's literature sit right in your classroom.

Does all this sound like a lot of work? Maybe it is, but you will rarely undertake a more pleasant job.

## THE SETTING FOR MOTIVATION

Now that we have looked at the books themselves and at your readiness as a teacher to sell them, the next question relates to the kinds of experiences children will have with the books.

You will need to give some thought to your classroom itself. Does it have a reading climate? Where are the props: bookshelves, reading table, bulletin boards, book nook, pillows and carpeting, maybe even a rocking chair or a divan? How do you obtain such things? You will find ways, as many teachers have, if you believe strongly enough that the climate makes a difference. Parents are often glad to build bookshelves; secondhand shops sell furniture at prices low enough to make even your bake-sale proceeds valuable. In short, use your imagination.

Perhaps more important than such physical accessories is the time factor. In your crowded day, when can you find the time to help children learn to love to read? If you do not make time, there will be no time. How can you set aside time to enjoy books? Here are a few ideas.

1. Consider how efficiently you may presently be using your time and the children's time. Are the materials in your room so well organized that children can move from one activity to another with a bare minimum of preparation time? In other words, reduce the amount of transitional time required.

2. Ask yourself how much attention you are paying to individual differences. Do all the children in each of your reading groups do all the practice exercises you plan? This is rarely necessary. Some children can put their time to much better use—by reading what they choose to read! Just to be excused from a "ditto" is motivating.

3. Have you thought about integrating some aspects of your program? For example, a handwriting lesson and a spelling lesson are natural partners. Why have two separate lessons? Why not teach children to read for main ideas and to write good paragraphs in the same series of lessons? Why not teach use of the card catalog when children have actual social studies or science topics to explore rather than having a separate "study skills" lesson? Teaching children to use context clues in a "real" lesson rather than an isolated one saves time and enhances the chances of transfer to other "real" lessons.

4. Use a dramatic way to enhance the reading climate of your classroom, or, better still, your whole school, by implementing the technique called uninterrupted sustained silent reading (USSR), or just sustained silent reading (SSR). Its effect is impressive, because it tells children that personal, independent reading is so important that a special time is set aside for it. During your SSR period, everyone reads: children, teacher, and, if the program is schoolwide, even the principal, secretary, custodian, and parents when they are in the building—everybody reads! And everybody reads whatever they want to read, no questions asked. Time is used to its fullest (McCracken, 1971).

## ACTIVITIES FOR CHILDREN

Children are often better motivators than their teachers. Peer influence, which reaches its climax in the secondary school, is not absent among elementary school children. It is important to set up situations in which children frequently share with each other their experiences with books. These may be either group or individual activities. Some of the following activities might work in your class.

1.  Children can be taught to play "That reminds me . . . ." On a preannounced date (so that children can prepare ahead of time), start things by talking for a minute or two about a children's book you have just read. This lets children know *you* are reading their books. Then wait until some child is ready to say "That reminds me . . . ." She builds a bridge from your book to hers. She may point out that her book had a similar character, the same author, or an event that had something in common with an event in your book. For example, after you have mentioned all the wondrous sweets described in Roald Dahl's (1976) *Charlie and the Chocolate Factory*, a child might respond, "That reminds me of the character named Fudge in Judy Blume's (1980) *Superfudge*." Some bridges are frail—never mind. They serve the purpose if they keep children listening to each other so that they can build the bridges and keep on talking about books they have read. After the bridge has been built, the child talks briefly about the book he has read. After a number of children have built bridges and talked about their books, set a time for the next session and stop. When you keep going more than 15 or 20 minutes, time begins to drag. Children should be allowed time to exchange books if their interest has been sparked.

2.  Another group experience that leads to sharing is a special kind of oral questioning. Again, set a date in advance and have children sign up if they wish to share. A child who has read a book goes to the chalkboard and writes the name of the book and its author. The teacher then asks one question about the book, to which the child responds. Then, two children are allowed one question each about the book. This procedure, as a bonus, encourages children to learn to ask good questions.

3.  A group of four or five children who have read books that have something in common (all animal stories, for example) may sit with a tape recorder and talk informally about their books. After the conversation has been recorded, they listen critically to the recording, and if they believe they could do better, they are given the privilege of rerecording until they feel their tape is good enough to share with others. Then, you might place the tape, the recorder, and the books the children discussed in a convenient place so that other children can listen to the tape, examine the books, and perhaps choose one of the books to read.

4.  A group or class can be encouraged to read for a period of time materials related to a common theme. For example, some fifth-graders might choose adventure as their theme and read anything related to this topic. The more obvious choices are books such as *My Side of the Mountain* by Jean George (1975) and articles about Neil Armstrong's famous first step on the moon. Better readers soon realize that there are other kinds of adventure, like that recorded in William Gibson's (1957) *The Miracle Worker*. After three weeks of reading, the teacher can ask the children to write personal definitions of "adventure" and to illustrate their definitions by recounting incidents from their reading. In such an activity, one child actually wrote, "Adventure is anything that makes you stronger and wiser."

5.  A whole class can use a shared event such as an assembly, a class visitor, a field trip, or a movie as the basis for reading experiences. For example, one sixth-grade

...ss learned that a visitor from India had been invited to speak to all the fifth- and sixth-graders at a school assembly. Their teacher asked how much the children knew about India. Not much, they had to admit. There was to be a chance at the assembly for the children to ask the visitor questions, but how could they ask questions? Good questions do not come from ignorance. They went to work reading about India, but they kept their activity a secret. The resulting question-and-answer period amazed the principal and all the other teachers and pupils. For a few days, the class was famous. Their reading had paid off.

Many of these activities are more appropriate for upper-elementary or middle-school children than for younger children, but young children, too, need opportunities to share. Here are some possibilities.

1. Children could be asked to select just one paragraph or page from a story or a book and read it orally to a group. They then state why this particular paragraph was chosen. This activity is a meaningful oral reading experience and may arouse the curiosity of other children.
2. Children could write brief notes to classmates recommending a particular book. These notes are then placed on a bulletin board to be picked up by the children to whom they are addressed. Second- through fourth-graders who love to get mail become excited about receiving the notes and may heed their peers' suggestions and read the recommended books.
3. Reading partners or threesomes could work together. Set aside a period of time, perhaps 30 minutes twice a week, when the partners or threesomes read orally to each other from books they are enjoying.
4. After you have shown your class an old-fashioned quilt or a picture of one, the students could make a "quilt" for the bulletin board out of drawings (on six-inch-square paper) of characters or scenes from a favorite book. The title and author of the book should be written on the square. Then, the class "sews" the quilt together by assembling the squares on the bulletin board.
5. Children could write one paragraph about "the character in [name of book] I would like to be" or "the character I would not like to be." The students should be prepared to read their paragraphs to the class and to answer questions about their characters.
6. Eight or ten books of appropriate difficulty could be chosen for a group of students. The group reads as many of the books as they can over a period of one or two weeks. The day when the books are to be discussed should be announced ahead of time. After the discussion, the children "elect" their favorite book from the preselected group of books. This activity is more fun if two or three groups are reading the same books at the same time and can compare their choices for "book of the month."

## SUMMARY

The key to sharing is enjoyment. The traditional written book report, venerated by generations of teachers, may not promote enjoyment at all and may, in fact, inhibit the development of interest in books. Recall the fact that most elementary school children are at the first stage in the evolution of appreciation: the stage of unconscious enjoyment. When young people have matured and have advanced into the second stage of literary appreciation, a book review has its place, but it has no place before that time.

Consider how a love of reading is like an infectious disease. You catch measles only from someone who already has measles. A love of reading is *caught* more often than it is *taught*. So these questions must be asked: To what extent do you value reading in your own life? To what extent do you use reading to extend your horizons, to have experiences you will never have in real life, to meet people you will never see, to find solace, to escape forever from boredom, to make meaningful decisions, to relax and enjoy your leisure time? Children have uncanny ways of knowing whether we practice what we preach.

Love of reading grows by what it feeds on—good books, more good books, and still more, in the hands of wise teachers and curious children.

## REFERENCES

Blume, J. *Superfudge.* New York: E. P. Dutton, 1980.

Cleary, B. *Henry and the paper route.* New York: Morrow, 1957.

Cleary, B. *Henry Huggins.* New York: Morrow, 1950.

Cole, J. Y., and Gold, C. S. (Eds.) *Reading in America.* Washington, D.C.: Library of Congress, 1979.

Dahl, R. *Charlie and the chocolate factory.* New York: Alfred A. Knopf, 1976.

Frazier, N. *Stout-hearted seven.* New York: Harcourt Brace, 1973.

George, J. C. *My side of the mountain.* New York: E. P. Dutton, 1975.

Gibson, W. *The miracle worker.* New York: Alfred A. Knopf, 1957.

Larrick, N. (Ed.) *Piping down the valleys wild.* New York: Delacorte, 1968.

Lewis, C. S. *The lion, the witch, and the wardrobe.* New York: Macmillan, 1951.

Lobel, A. *Mouse tales.* New York: Harper and Row, 1972.

Mazer, N. *A figure of speech.* New York: Delacorte, 1973.

McCloskey, R. *One morning in Maine.* New York: Viking Press, 1952.

McClung, R. *America's endangered birds.* New York: Morrow, 1979.

McCracken, R. A. Initiating sustained silent reading. *Journal of Reading,* 1971, **14**, 521–524.

Micklos, J. J. The facts, please, about reading achievement in American schools. *Journal of Reading,* 1980, **24**, 41–45.

Parish, P. *Amelia Bedelia.* New York: Harper and Row, 1963.

Seed, S. (Ed.) *Saturday's child.* New York: J. Philip O'Hara, 1973.

Speare, E. G. *The witch of Blackbird Pond.* Boston: Houghton Mifflin, 1958.

Sutherland, Z., and Arbuthnot, M. H. *Children and books.* Glenview, Ill.: Scott, Foresman and Company, 1977.

Viorst, J. *Alexander, and the terrible, horrible, no good, very bad day.* New York: Atheneum, 1972.

## PERIODICALS FOR CHILDREN

*Cricket,* Box 2670, Boulder, Colo. 80302.

*Highlights for Children,* 2300 West Fifth Avenue, P.O. Box 269, Columbus, Ohio 43216.

*National Geographic World,* Seventeenth and M Streets NW, Washington, D.C. 20036.

*Ranger Rick,* National Wildlife Federation, 1412 Sixteenth Street NW, Washington, D.C. 20036.

## PERIODICALS THAT CONTAIN REVIEWS OF CHILDREN'S BOOKS

*Horn Book,* 585 Boylston Street, Boston, Mass. 02116.

*Language Arts,* National Council of Teachers of English, 1111 Kenyon Road, Urbana, Ill. 61820.

*The Reading Teacher,* International Reading Association, 800 Barksdale Road, Newark, Del. 19711.

## RECOMMENDED READINGS

Coody, B., and Nelson, D. *Successful activities for enriching the language arts.* Belmont, Calif.: Wadsworth, 1982.

Coody and Nelson's "cookbook" volume is filled to the brim with ideas for things to do in the classroom to help children enjoy reading and other aspects of the language arts.

Coody, B., and Nelson, D. *Teaching elementary language arts: A literature approach.* Belmont, Calif.: Wadsworth, 1982.

This book describes in detail a practical language arts program that is full of ideas for making enjoyment of literature the heart of the program.

Cullinan, B. *Literature and the child.* New York: Harcourt Brace Jovanovich, 1981.

A comprehensive book about children's literature, *Literature and the child* is particularly valuable for its many suggested activities for children and for its criteria for the selection of books of various types.

# CHAPTER 21

# How to Use Good Books: With and Beyond the Basal

M. Jean Greenlaw
North Texas State University
Denton

*Many ideas beginning teachers can use to bring children and books together were presented in Chapter 20. This chapter also considers the problem of dealing with children who can but choose not to read, although the perspective is somewhat different. In this chapter, Jean Greenlaw suggests ways beginning teachers can use basal readers as springboards to developing students' interest in good children's literature. She suggests that a beginning teacher start by becoming comfortable with books—that is, by becoming knowledgeable about them—and then survey the basal reader being used in the classroom to determine what kinds of literature it contains. Given a knowledge of what narrative, informational, and poetic selections the basal reader contains, the teacher can develop activities that take children from the basal reader to the realm of children's literature. Some of the ideas she suggests include forming classroom reading clubs, corresponding with authors of children's books, inviting children's authors to speak or interviewing them, using literature to promote creative writing, and acquiring freebies from publishers to promote interest in specific titles.*

The purpose of teaching students *to* read is to attempt to make certain that they *can* and *will* read. A student who can read but does not is as much a problem reader as one who cannot read. Often the school curriculum has created this type of "nonreader." Our emphasis on skill instruction; sounding out words; and the inevitable use of worksheets, ditto sheets, and round-robin reading has convinced many students that reading is a bore and certainly not something they would do voluntarily.

This chapter provides specific suggestions for implementing the use of library books as supplements to basal reader instruction. Activities are presented as *examples* for you to apply to whatever basal reader you use to teach skills. Titles of specific children's and adolescents' books might be named, but it is the *idea* that is important. Each activity, therefore, can be adapted to many other books.

## WHERE TO BEGIN

### Become Comfortable With Books

The beginning teacher should develop and nourish her own love of books. Nothing is more motivating to a student than an excited teacher who wants to share a good book. Read many books and begin your program with those you particularly enjoy.

The following is a short quiz on books popular with students. See whether you can name the title of each book. (Answers can be found at the end of this chapter, on p. 297.)

---

### Name That Book

1. Wilbur is "Some Pig."
2. Jim Hawkins hid in an apple barrel.
3. A horse faces much cruelty.
4. He is a bear of very little brain.
5. There was a parade to Boston Commons.
6. The man in the marmalade hat arrived in the middle of March.
7. Jess and Leslie create a magical kingdom.
8. Ben wants to become a jazz musician.
9. Two animal friends share many adventures.
10. A caterpillar eventually becomes a butterfly.

---

Chances are you were able to name the first five titles easily. These are classics that have been read and shared for years. The second five are newer books, but they are all award-winning books and are very popular with students. It is important that you become familiar with old and new books that can be shared with your students.

How can you accomplish this? Get to know your school and public librarians. Teachers who show an active interest in books are rare, and librarians will love you. Take a *good* children's literature course, one that covers more than the history of children's books and Newbery and Caldecott winners. Use bibliographies like the one provided each year in the October issue of *The Reading Teacher,* which publishes an annotated list of "Children's Choices" for the preceding year. These are books selected as favorites *by children* as part of a project sponsored by the International Reading Association and the Children's Book Council. The project has been in existence since 1975. Then, *read!* You will be surprised at the pleasure you can derive from reading well-written children's books.

### Survey Your Basal Reader

Spend part of your preschool in-service time analyzing the basal reader you will be teaching. Decide on the stories and poems and informational pieces that you want to extend. Remember, you do not need to do a fancy project for each selection in your basal reader, and neither do you have to do everything the first year. You will probably use the same basal reader for five to ten years, so build your program to maintain your interest as well as to motivate your students.

Begin by surveying the table of contents. Are there any authors you recognize and enjoy? One second-grade teacher discovered there was a story by Beatrix Potter in her basal reader, and she was able to arrange for someone who had visited the Potter home in England to come and show slides to her class. The teacher provided a library of all the Potter books and shared a biography of Beatrix Potter with the students. The second-graders then read through the entire Potter library and wanted more. They created a mural showing the characters from the stories and selected their favorite characters to write about. *Authors* write books, and most authors have written more than one book. Students should learn that their basal stories are written by *people* and that these and other stories are available in the library.

The table of contents also tells you the types of selections in the basal reader. Perhaps you will want to put aside the basal reader for a bit and pursue a unit on mythology or folktales or historical fiction or whatever seems intriguing to you and the students. Tangents such as these can be fruitful and absorbing, and the school and public library can provide you the books you need to pursue these interests.

Check the acknowledgments page for the books from which the stories in the basal reader are excerpted. Try to obtain a copy of each book when students read the story in the basal reader. These can be shared with students, and many children will be interested in reading the original version. For at least one basal story, try to obtain multiple copies of the original book and conduct a lesson on critical reading stressing likenesses and differences. It is amazing how perceptive even young children can be when they are shown what an adaptation is.

Study the illustrations in your basal readers. Most basal readers incorporate a variety of artwork. How the artwork is produced may interest many students. The development of woodcuts is one form of artwork you could pursue. Try to get someone from the high school to come to your class and give a demonstration of how a woodcut is made. Have numerous books available that use this medium. Allow the children to make potato prints, which use a similar technique.

Look at the informational selections in the basal reader and see whether there are ones that can be correlated with science, social studies, or math projects. Reading is not an isolated subject, and planned activities that foster an integration of subjects enhance the transfer of learning. For example, if there is a selection in your basal reader about Louis Braille, you might wish to study a science unit on sound. An excerpt from *The Cloud Book* (de Paola, 1975) could lead to a study of weather.

Study your teacher's guide and see whether there is a list of suggested books to be used with each basal selection. This list could be a starting point for providing a reading table or corner of free-reading books to be made available to the students. Your librarian will be able to suggest others, and as you read more books, you will find ones you want to add.

## Organize

Good intentions have paved the way to the "hot place" for many a poor soul. Unless you organize and plan your specific program, you are going to find that you never have time or that the books you want are checked out or that the speaker you called today to come to your class tomorrow has other plans or.... In other words, do your homework and be prepared!

It would be advisable to plan your units several weeks in advance. This gives the librarian time to make sure books are available to you (popping in on Monday morning with a "By the way, could I have at least 20 Japanese folktales by ten o'clock" will not win you love and affection) or for you to locate the books yourself. Planning ahead allows you or the librarian enough time to order any media you want to use and to be *sure* the equipment is reserved. Also, it gives speakers, for whom you may have specific goals and objectives, time to collect materials and prepare their presentations.

So what happens if you are not quite ready for the story when the speaker is scheduled to appear or if the movie comes a week early and must be returned tomorrow? Be flexible. The basal reader is your *tool*. It is a *guide* for your reading program, but you control it, it does not control you. Skip a story when you need to. Take time to expand an idea. Do what is necessary to make it easy for your students to enjoy reading.

## ACTIVITIES FOR INVOLVEMENT

Many suggestions will be given here, but keep in mind that these are only suggestions. You will generate your own ideas as you become familiar with your basal reader and your library. Also, remember that you are not expected to do all of these things at once.

### Free Reading

The best way to become a good reader is to practice reading. The more the students read, the better readers they will become. This means reading all types of materials: books, magazines, newspapers, original stories written by class members, and so on. This also means giving students time for reading alone, with freedom to make mistakes.

Your classroom library, or reading center, should change constantly. New reading materials that complement current class activities should be added as they become appropriate. Have you ever gone to the doctor's or dentist's or hair stylist's and found the same old dreary magazines visit after visit? You listlessly poke at them, but you are not raring to read them. Your reading center should draw readers. Change the scenery at least once a week. Once your students realize that the reading center is going to change frequently, they become responsible for alerting the librarian to the next topic, exchanging the materials, and bringing contributions from home.

Be sure to include magazines in your reading center. There are excellent children's magazines that will add to your classroom reading. For example, *Cricket* is a superb magazine that includes stories, poems, and biographies by the finest children's authors writing today. Students will be able to go from a magazine story to a book by the same author or illustrator. *Ranger Rick* and *National Geographic World* are photo-essay magazines that concentrate on nature and the world around us. *Cobblestone* is a magazine about American history.

Choose your books to extend your basal selection in some way. You might want to have stories or poems by the same author. When a story about a possum appeared in the basal reader, one class read fiction and nonfiction about marsupials. A story set at the seashore might inspire reading of fiction, nonfiction, and poetry selections about the sea.

You might want to select books that are of the same genre or literary type: biographies, folktales, science fiction, and so on.

## Reading Clubs

Rather than traditional reading groups, you could allow students to form reading clubs occasionally. The basis for the groupings would be interest, rather than ability, which would probably be a welcome change for many students.

Suppose you wanted to extend a folktale that was adapted in the basal reader. After students explored the elements that define a folktale, they could break into small groups to read folktales from many countries. They could read African, Japanese, German, Irish, English, and Scandinavian folktales as well as tales from any other ethnic group for whom you could collect books. The students could share books within their group and discover common traits in a country's tales, and then all groups could collectively share information. A chart could be made as each group presented its information. The chart could show how the tales of the individual groups met the requirements for being folktales. Figure 21.1 lists the elements of traditional folktales, as determined by folklorists.

Several clubs could operate at the same time. Their interests could include mysteries, sports, fantasies, biographies, and science fiction. Each would have an appropriate name and a separate goal.

## Plays, Puppets, Skits

Basal readers often include selections from plays. Rather than having the students read the story around the table or up and down the rows, exhorting them to use expression, present the play as a *play*. Choose parts, using several people for each part and therefore having several casts. Have students practice their reading; many will surprise you and memorize all or most of their parts in a short time.

Decide whether you are going to use puppets. Keep scenery and props simple. Discuss the actions, movements, and emotions of the characters. Practice the play several times

### FOLKTALES

| Groups | Beginnings | Magic | Good Characters | Bad Characters | Endings |
|--------|-----------|-------|-----------------|----------------|---------|
| African | | | | | |
| English | | | | | |
| German | | | | | |
| Irish | | | | | |
| Japanese | | | | | |

Figure 21.1. A sample chart for a reading club interested in folktales.

with each cast. The students can perform for their own class, invite guests, or videotape and show the play at an open house.

Once the method has been learned, each play takes less time to prepare. It would probably be a good idea, however, only to do this as an occasional treat (two or three times a year). Otherwise, it becomes mechanical.

Students will be able to find additional plays in books and magazines. They can develop these as supplementary or independent activities.

### Reading and Writing

Reading books can stimulate writing in many ways. A second-grade class with whom I worked studied books by Tomie de Paola, because there was an excerpt from *The Cloud Book* (de Paola, 1975) in their basal reader and because he was going to be speaking at a nearby conference. Also, I promised to deliver letters the students wrote to Mr. de Paola. The class located and read dozens of books by de Paola, wrote to his publisher and received posters and a biography, and discovered stories by him in *Cricket* magazine. Their letters represent a diversity of interests and ability. Several letters are reproduced here.

Dear Mr. de Paola,

I like the cloud book. It has good illustrations. I think you are the best illustrator. At least I think you're the best one I have ever heard of.

Shane

Dear Mr. de Paola,

I like the book, *The Knight and the Dragon*. It is funny. The pictures are hilarious. It is my favorite.

Paul

Dear Mr. de Paola,

In class we are learning about clouds. I heard about the three main kinds of clouds. There are cirrus, cumulus, and stratus.

Jennifer

Dear Mr. de Paola,

I like your book especially the *Popcorn Book* because I like popcorn a lot.

David

Each letter is an individual effort, and each child was able to express personal reactions to books.

Another type of writing can be stimulated by responses to a story in the basal reader. For example, the story *The Dragon in the Clock Box* (Craig, 1962) was the basis for a discussion of critical reading. The basal adaptation of the story was compared with the original book. In addition, descriptive words were generated about three very different dragons that were brought to class. The students then wrote their own stories about dragons, which were collected in a class book. The book was placed on the reading table and was chosen often by individual readers. The following are stories from this book. The students' errors were not corrected, since the emphasis was on ideas and since the students were writing regularly; every story was not polished.

### Wonse There Was a Dragon

by William

Wonse there was a dragon you see—you see. he went to hevan he came back down. Where ever he gos he gos up or down !!!!! Yea!!

### My Best Friend

by Casey

My dragon has red eyes. And he is sparkling purple. He is smooth and he has sarp claws. He is pink. He is small. His wings are copper.

### The Big Green Dragon

by Julie

I have a big green dragon. He is gigantic. I love my dragon very much. He is hard and lumpy. My dragon sits on my bed.

A basal story by Byrd Baylor, author of *Guess Who My Favorite Person Is* (Baylor, 1977), prompted a fifth-grade teacher to read the original book to the class. In the book, an adult and a child share their favorite things. The fifth-graders also shared.

### Favorites

by Todd

My favorite food is Mexican food. Mainly tacos, but I like any Mexican food. You know how it makes you feel when you eat the meat, lettuce, etc. I don't know what I'd do without it.

### My Favorite Animal

by Tiffany

My favorite animal is a pretty paint horse that runs through the meadows and will be my friend for the rest of my life. I wish I could ride it all day long bareback; that's what I want.

### My Favorite Smell

by Brad

Is a cherry pie after it came out of the oven and you can smell the cherries and can't wait to sink your teeth into the cherry pie and a cold glass of milk.

A class studied pourquoi, or why, stories in the basal reader and then wrote their own. These were shared with the class and displayed on a bulletin board.

### Why the Moon Has Black Spots

by Michael

The reason the moon has black spots is that one day Germany sent a spaceship to the moon to take photographs. Then when the astronauts were leaving, their oil started to leak. Then the oil fell down to the moon, and that is why the moon has black spots.

### Why Do People Dance

by Jenny

Once, a long, long time ago there used to be a country of flies. The flies would bother the people who lived in this country. Flies would be in the food, in beds, and especially bothering to the people.

The flies would swarm around any person sitting, standing, or walking. The people thought of what to do to keep the flies away from them. So they thought and thought. Finally they decided that if they wiggled a lot, the flies wouldn't bother them.

So the people of this country wiggled and wiggled around to keep the flies off of them. Soon the flies disappeared. The people were so used to wiggling around, that that is what they did instead of walking. To this day people dance.

A haiku poem in a fourth-grade basal reader generated the reading and writing of haiku. Here is one such poem.

The thick, bubbling clouds,
Bursting with smoggy droplets,
Floated in the breeze.

by Luke

Writing can be motivated by creating class books, keeping individual journals, or displaying individual written pieces in various ways. Also, some magazines solicit children's writing, which provides a perfect way to teach editing and polishing skills. *Stone Soup* is a magazine composed solely of children's writing. The *Christian Science Monitor* occasionally runs a children's page on which they publish writing by children. *Cricket* holds seasonal contests for children's writing. Students should read these magazines and newspapers carefully to discover the style, length, and form of materials required.

### Scripts for Interviews

Guest speakers can be invited to work with a class. There are many possibilities for interesting guest speakers, so only a few will be described here.

Invite a local writer. An author who lives nearby is a prime prospect. Also, consider inviting writers for a local newspaper or magazine writers. Another option is to invite a speaker who has a special hobby that relates to a basal story. Someone who has traveled and brought home artifacts and slides of a locale of one of your stories or someone whose job relates to an informational selection in the basal would make a wonderful guest. How can you locate such people? Ask around. They will not come to you, you need to seek them out.

A second- and fifth-grade teacher were discussing the fact that they were unable to find much Native American poetry or information on Native American folktales to use with selections on Native Americans in the basal reader. Another person who overheard this conversation indicated that she had a friend, a Native American who collected artifacts from the Southwestern tribes. The woman was contacted and came to school to meet separately with the second and fifth grades. She brought many of her artifacts, wore the clothing of her tribe, and showed slides of a famous potter creating her work in the desert. The students and teachers were entranced; they had an opportunity to listen, touch, look, and discuss. A videotape was made of the demonstration so that other classes would be able to share the valuable experience.

Inviting speakers places a responsibility on the speaker, teacher, and students. The speaker should be told clearly what the purpose of the visit is, what the grade level of the students is, and how many students are to be involved. The teacher and speaker should discuss the time allotted, any equipment needed, and the best setting for the presentation.

Most important is the preparation of the students before the demonstration or talk. If an author is coming, the students should read the books written by the author. The teacher should prepare a loose script for questions to be asked. Far too often, the questions stay at the level of "Where do you get your ideas" and "How long did it take you to write _____?" Such questions are usually followed by a flood of questions asking how long it took to write each of the author's books. Before the speaker comes, it is useful to have students arrange their questions in categories, such as personal information, questions about specific books by the author, and questions about writing in general. The questions can be discussed, with some eventually discarded and others modified. Although the students should be somewhat spontaneous, the author will be pleased to know that the students have been prepared, and the students will benefit from a greater depth of knowledge because they were prepared.

The same general format works for any guest speaker. Since you have invited a guest, you should have a purpose in mind. Prepare the students and yourself to get the most from the experience.

## Art

Be alert for the possibility of including art in the curriculum. An excerpt or adaptation of a story by Ezra Jack Keats in a basal reader, for example, could lead to a study of collage (Keats is well known for his work in this art form) and extend to other illustrators such as Leo Leonni and Gerald McDermott who also use this technique. Studying such illustrators' books and informational books on creating art could lead students to making collages. A basal selection on giants, for another example, could inspire the students to create a giant for the classroom, and a story on signs could generate the building of useful signs for appropriate spots in the school and classroom.

## Media

Be open to the use of media as a means for expanding your basal reader and leading students to good books. Filmstrips and cassettes can be used to introduce students to authors and illustrators. Students get to see and sometimes hear the authors and illustrators and come to realize that they are real people. Be sure to make books by the author or illustrator discussed in a filmstrip available for *immediate* use in the classroom. Students (and most teachers) are not good at handling postponed gratification.

Other media include recordings of poetry and stories, filmstrips and films about books, and teaching films and filmstrips that discuss the production of a book or a film. Weston

Woods and Random House/Miller Brody are two companies that produce numerous media materials suitable for the elementary classroom.

Be sure to use media to record your ongoing project. A 35-millimeter camera is simple to use, and when you keep one in your classroom, you can catch on film those moments and activities too good to lose. Your slides could be used at an open house to show parents all the projects completed during the year. Videotaping can be saved for special projects and used in the same manner. Remember that good public relations are part of our business, and your interest, enthusiasm, and professionalism help the school system.

### Freebies

Some materials for use in your classroom are free for the asking, or at least very reasonably secured with a stamped, self-addressed envelope.

Publishers offer posters, book jackets, bookmarks, biographies, and bibliographies. You can learn about these giveaways by reading your professional magazines carefully. In one recent issue of *The Reading Teacher,* I saw an ad for a contest entitled Build Your Own Robot. The prize was a spinner rack filled with children's paperbacks and free robot T-shirts for the winning class. Whether my students won or not, the contest would be fun and would involve reading. In the same issue was an announcement offering a free illustrated pamphlet providing step-by-step instructions for setting up and running telephone interviews with authors; there was also information on a program called Dial-an-Author. At about the same time, *Early Years* and several other magazines carried an announcement on a contest to win Jean Fritz, a well-known author of children's books, for a week in a school. All this and more was available in one month's worth of professional reading.

Another source of information is the Children's Book Council, a nonprofit organization that promotes the use of children's literature. A one-time fee of $10 puts you on their mailing list. Several times a year, you then receive a wonderful publication called *Calendar,* with articles by authors, illustrators, editors, and book people of all kinds. It also presents bibliographies on various subjects (e.g., mysteries, sports stories, stories about handicapped people) and publishes pages of freebies available from publishers. The address is: The Children's Book Council, 67 Irving Place, New York, N.Y. 10003.

## SUMMARY (AND A WORD OF CAUTION)

Teachers who implement a plan such as the one outlined are likely to have students who *enjoy reading* and are excited about coming to class. Parents are likely to think you are a good teacher and ask to have their children placed in your class. Administrators and librarians will sing your praises. Still, to steal a line from Lewis Carroll, "Beware the Jabberwock, my son! The jaws that bite, the claws that catch!" There may be Jabberwocks in your school: those lounge lizards whose tongues flick out to sting any teacher who wants to be a creative professional. Do implement a sound developmental reading program; do use the basal reader; and, yes, do teach those skills; but do not stop there. Get your students involved with books. If you do these things, the Jabberwocks will be foiled.

## ANSWERS TO QUIZ

1. *Charlotte's Web*
2. *Treasure Island*
3. *Black Beauty*
4. *Winnie-the-Pooh*
5. *Make Way for Ducklings*
6. *A Visit to William Blake's Inn*
7. *Bridge to Terabithia*
8. *Ben's Trumpet*
9. *Frog and Toad Are Friends*
10. *The Very Hungry Caterpillar*

## REFERENCES

Baylor, B. *Guess who my favorite person is.* New York: Scribner's, 1977.

Carle, E. *The very hungry caterpillar.* New York: Philomel, 1971.

Carroll, L. *Jabberwocky.* New York: Warne, 1977.

Craig, J. *The dragon in the clock box.* New York: Grosset and Dunlap, 1962.

de Paola, T. *The cloud book.* New York: Holiday House, 1975.

Isadora, R. *Ben's trumpet.* New York: Greenwillow, 1979.

Lobel, A. *Frog and Toad are friends.* New York: Harper and Row, 1970.

McCloskey, R. *Make way for ducklings.* New York: Viking Press, 1941.

Milne, A. A. *Winnie-the-Pooh.* New York: E. P. Dutton, 1926.

Paterson, K. *Bridge to Terabithia.* New York: Thomas Y. Crowell, 1977.

Sewell, A. *Black Beauty.* New York: World, 1872 (1877).

Stevenson, R. L. *Treasure Island.* New York: Scribner's, 1982 (1883, 1911).

White, E. B. *Charlotte's web.* New York: Harper and Row, 1952.

Willard, N. *A visit to William Blake's inn.* New York: Harcourt Brace Jovanovich, 1981.

## RECOMMENDED READINGS

Greenlaw, M. J., and Wendelin, K. H. *Literature and learning centers: K–3.* Atlanta: Humanics, 1983.
Suggestions for numerous learning centers are based on children's books and include concepts, numbers, wordless books, fantasy, and other activities.

Hopkins, L. B. *More books by more people.* New York: Citation Press, 1974.
Authors and illustrators of children's books are interviewed.

McClure, A. A. Integrating children's fiction and informational literature in a primary reading curriculum. *Reading Teacher*, 1982, **35**, 784–789.
This practical guide to creating a reading program based on thematic units includes an excellent bibliography.

Mikkelsen, N. Celebrating children's books throughout the year. *Reading Teacher*, 1982, **35**, 790–795.
Numerous possibilities for using children's books in the classroom are suggested.

Reasoner, C. F. *Bringing children and books together.* New York: Dell, 1979.
One of four excellent teacher's guides available from Dell, this publication provides specific, practical, and creative suggestions for using children's books.

Somers, A. B., and Worthington, J. E. *Resource guides for teaching children's books.* Urbana, Ill.: National Council of Teachers of English, 1979.
Specific activities in lesson-plan form are provided for 27 children's books.

## PERIODICALS

*Cobblestone:* Cobblestone Publishing Company, 28 Main Street, Peterborough, N.H. 03458.

*Cricket:* Open Court Publishing Company, 1058 Eighth Street, La Salle, Ill. 61301.

*National Geographic World:* National Geographic World, Seventeeth and M Streets NW, Washington, D.C. 20036.

*Ranger Rick's Nature Magazine:* National Wildlife Federation, 1412 Sixteenth Street NW, Washington, D.C. 20036.

*Stone Soup:* Children's Art Foundation, P.O. Box 83, Santa Cruz, Calif. 95063.

## MEDIA REFERENCES

Random House/Miller Brody, 400 Hahn Road, Westminster, Md. 21157.

Weston Woods, Weston, Conn. 06883.

# CHAPTER 22

# Strategies for Creating Readers

Sandra S. Dahl
University of Wisconsin–Madison

*Chapters 20 and 21 have discussed how classroom teachers can bring children and books together. In this chapter, Sandra Dahl continues this theme by providing suggestions beginning teachers can use to create readers both in the classroom and in the home. The classroom strategies she suggests involve surrounding children with high-quality literature. Many anecdotal accounts of how teachers have successfully motivated children to read for pleasure are included in the first part of this chapter, and beginning teachers should find these first-hand accounts interesting and informative. In the second part of this chapter, Dahl discusses how teachers can involve parents in developing their children's love of books and desire to read. Some of the home-based strategies suggested include activities in which children's oral language development can be promoted, ways in which parents can read to and with their children and make it a pleasurable experience for all, and methods by which parents can reinforce reading skills the classroom teacher has identified as causing individual students difficulty. Of special interest are the section on management techniques teachers can share with parents to help them to schedule time for home reading and the section on ways beginning teachers can involve parents as support personnel in their classrooms during reading instruction.*

One of your goals as a teacher will be to help children to become skillful readers. An equally important goal, however, should be to instill in your students a lifelong desire to read; that is, it should be your goal to create readers. This chapter is designed to help you to meet the responsibilities entailed in reaching this second goal. Strategies you can use to promote reading for enjoyment in the classroom will be discussed first. Strategies you can implement to initiate or encourage good home-reading practices will be presented next.

# CREATING READERS IN THE CLASSROOM

A well-rounded school literature program is an essential ingredient in creating readers. Children's books are delightful, and ideas for incorporating books into daily lesson plans are limitless. The following sections discuss how you can familiarize yourself with children's literature and use children's books effectively in the classroom.

## Getting to Know Children's Books

In order to be effective in your quest to create readers, you must become familiar with large numbers of children's books. Knowing what books are available is essential in establishing credibility with your students and in developing effective lesson plans. How can you become familiar with children's books? One way is to enroll in a children's literature course as part of your professional training. Another way to learn about children's literature is to study one of the excellent textbooks on children's literature. Informative, outstanding textbooks by Huck (1979), Stewig (1980), and Sutherland, Monson, and Arbuthnot (1981) provide enjoyable reading for the elementary teacher.

Once you have developed a basic understanding of children's literature, you will want to update and broaden your knowledge continually. Here are some suggestions you may wish to consider.

1. Talk to children and find out what they are reading. Keep lists of books and authors mentioned frequently and try to become familiar with at least one book per author.
2. Seek advice from specialists in children's literature. Children's librarians, clerks in bookstores, and fellow teachers are certain to know what children are reading.
3. Read professional periodicals (e.g., *The Reading Teacher, Language Arts, Horn Book*); they often contain reviews of children's books. Good reviews include a book summary along with information on the appropriate age and interest level.
4. Keep abreast of award-winning books such as those earning the Caldecott or Newbery medals yearly. A list of the yearly winners from the inception of these awards to the present is given here. Also refer to the "Children's Choices" published annually in *The Reading Teacher* each fall (see Chapter 21 for specifics) for the best newly published books.

## Using Children's Books Effectively

Surrounding children with high-quality books is one of the surest methods for creating readers. The following are several first-hand accounts of techniques teachers have found to be effective in getting children involved with books.

Raymond, a fifth-grade teacher, follows a chapter-a-day plan for four days each week. (Fridays are devoted to an all-school literature-sharing program.) Raymond reports that he seldom has difficulty settling his class for the opening of school, since that is the time for reading aloud to his students. The children arrive on time, anxiously anticipating the high adventure, humor, suspense, or fantasy awaiting them as they explore good books together. This perceptive teacher seldom reads more than one book per author; rather, he stocks his classroom bookcart with multiple copies of other books written by the featured

## The Caldecott Award–Winning Books

1938 *Animals of the Bible.* Illustrated by Dorothy P. Lathrop. Text selected by Helen Dean Fish. J. B. Lippincott.

1939 *Mei Li.* Illustrated and written by Thomas Handforth. Doubleday.

1940 *Abraham Lincoln.* Illustrated and written by Ingri and Edgar d'Aulaire. Doubleday.

1941 *They Were Strong and Good.* Illustrated and written by Robert Lawson. Viking.

1942 *Make Way for Ducklings.* Illustrated and written by Robert McCloskey. Viking.

1943 *The Little House.* Illustrated and written by Virginia Lee Burton. Houghton Mifflin.

1944 *Many Moons.* Illustrated by Louis Slobodkin. Written by James Thurber. Harcourt Brace.

1945 *Prayer for a Child.* Illustrated by Elizabeth Orton Jones. Written by Rachel Field. Macmillan.

1946 *The Rooster Crows.* Illustrated by Maud and Miska Petersham. Macmillan.

1947 *The Little Island.* Illustrated by Leonard Weisgard. Written by Golden MacDonald (pseudonym of Margaret Wise Brown). Doubleday.

1948 *White Snow, Bright Snow.* Illustrated by Roger Duvoisin. Written by Alvin Tresselt. Lothrop, Lee and Shepard.

1949 *The Big Snow.* Illustrated and written by Berta and Elmer Hader. Macmillan.

1950 *Song of the Swallows.* Illustrated and written by Leo Politi. Scribner's.

1951 *The Egg Tree.* Illustrated and written by Katherine Milhous. Scribner's.

1952 *Finders Keepers.* Illustrated by Nicolas (pseudonym of Nicolas Mordvinoff). Written by Will (pseudonym of William Lipkind). Harcourt Brace.

1953 *The Biggest Bear.* Illustrated and written by Lynd Ward. Houghton Mifflin.

1954 *Madeleine's Rescue.* Illustrated and written by Ludwig Bemelmans. Viking.

1955 *Cinderella, or the Little Glass Slipper.* Illustrated and translated from Charles Perrault by Marcia Brown. Scribner's.

1956 *Frog Went A-Courtin'.* Illustrated by Feodor Rojankovsky. Text retold by John Langstaff. Harcourt Brace.

1957 *A Tree Is Nice.* Illustrated by Marc Simont. Written by Janice May Udry. Harper.

1958 *Time of Wonder.* Illustrated and written by Robert McCloskey. Viking.

1959 *Chanticleer and the Fox.* Illustrated by Barbara Cooney. Adapted from *The Canterbury Tales.* Crowell.

1960 *Nine Days to Christmas.* Illustrated by Marie Hall Ets. Written by Marie Hall Ets and Aurora Labastida. Viking.

1961 *Baboushka and the Three Kings.* Illustrated by Nicolas Sidjakov. Written by Ruth Robbins. Parnassus.

1962 *Once a Mouse.* Illustrated and retold by Marcia Brown. Scribner's.

1963 *The Snowy Day.* Illustrated and written by Ezra Jack Keats. Viking.

## The Caldecott Award–Winning Books (*continued*)

1964 *Where the Wild Things Are.* Illustrated and written by Maurice Sendak. Harper and Row.

1965 *May I Bring a Friend?* Illustrated by Beni Montresor. Written by Beatrice Schenk de Regniers. Atheneum.

1966 *Always Room for One More.* Illustrated by Nonny Hogrogian. Retold by Sorche Nic Leodhas. Holt, Rinehart and Winston.

1967 *Sam, Bangs & Moonshine.* Illustrated by Evaline Ness. Holt, Rinehart and Winston.

1968 *Drummer Hoff.* Illustrated by Ed Emberley. Adapted by Barbara Emberley. Prentice-Hall.

1969 *The Fool of the World and the Flying Ship.* Illustrated by Uri Shulevitz. Retold by Arthur Ransome. Farrar, Straus and Giroux.

1970 *Sylvester and the Magic Pebble.* Illustrated and written by William Steig. Windmill.

1971 *A Story, A Story.* Illustrated by Gail E. Haley. Retold by Gail E. Haley from an African folktale. Atheneum.

1972 *One Fine Day.* Illustrated by Nonny Hogrogian. Adapted by Nonny Hogrogian from an Armenian folktale. Macmillan.

1973 *The Funny Little Woman.* Illustrated by Blair Lent. Retold by Arlene Mosel. E. P. Dutton.

1974 *Duffy and the Devil.* Illustrated by Margot Zemach. Retold by Harve Zemach from a Cornish tale. Farrar, Straus and Giroux.

1975 *Arrow to the Sun.* Illustrated by Gerald McDermott. Adapted by Gerald McDermott from a Pueblo Indian tale. Viking.

1976 *Why Mosquitoes Buzz in People's Ears.* Illustrated by Leo and Diane Dillon. Retold by Vera Aardema. Dial.

1977 *Ashanti to Zulu: African Traditions.* Illustrated by Leo and Diane Dillon. Written by Margaret Musgrove. Dial.

1978 *Noah's Ark.* Illustrated and written by Peter Spier. Doubleday.

1979 *The Girl Who Loved Wild Horses.* Illustrated and written by Paul Goble. Bradbury.

1980 *Ox-Cart Man.* Illustrated by Barbara Cooney. Written by Donald Hall. Viking.

1981 *Fables.* Illustrated and written by Arnold Lobel. Harper.

1982 *Jumanji.* Illustrated and written by Chris Von Allsburg. Harcourt Brace Jovanovich.

1983 *Shadow.* Illustrated by Marcia Brown. Written by Blaise Cendrars. Scribner's.

## The Newbery Award–Winning Books

1922 *The Story of Mankind* by Hendrik Willem van Loon. Liveright.

1923 *The Voyages of Doctor Doolittle* by Hugh Lofting. J. B. Lippincott.

1924 *The Dark Frigate* by Charles Hawes. Little, Brown.

1925 *Tales From Silver Lands* by Charles Finger. Doubleday.

## The Newbery Award–Winning Books (continued)

1926 *Shen of the Sea* by Arthur Bowie Chrisman. E. P. Dutton.

1927 *Smoky, the Cowhorse* by Will James. Scribner's.

1928 *Gayneck, the Story of a Pigeon* by Dhan Gopal Mukerji. E. P. Dutton.

1929 *The Trumpeter of Krakow* by Eric P. Kelly. Macmillan.

1930 *Hitty, Her First Hundred Years* by Rachel Field. Macmillan.

1931 *The Cat Who Went to Heaven* by Elizabeth Coatsworth. Macmillan.

1932 *Waterless Mountain* by Laura Adams Armer. Longmans.

1933 *Young Fu of the Upper Yangtze* by Elizabeth Lewis. Winston.

1934 *Invincible Louisa* by Cornelia Meigs. Little, Brown.

1935 *Dobry* by Monica Shannon. Viking.

1936 *Caddie Woodlawn* by Carol Brink. Macmillan.

1937 *Roller Skates* by Ruth Sawyer. Viking.

1938 *The White Stag* by Kate Seredy. Viking.

1939 *Thimble Summer* by Elizabeth Enright. Rinehart.

1940 *Daniel Boone* by James Daugherty. Viking.

1941 *Call It Courage* by Armstrong Sperry. Macmillan.

1942 *The Matchlock Gun* by Walter D. Edmonds. Dodd, Mead.

1943 *Adam of the Road* by Elizabeth Janet Gray. Viking.

1944 *Johnny Tremain* by Esther Forbes. Houghton Mifflin.

1945 *Rabbit Hill* by Robert Lawson. Viking.

1946 *Strawberry Girl* by Lois Lenski. J. B. Lippincott.

1947 *Miss Hickory* by Carolyn Sherwin Bailey. Viking.

1948 *The Twenty-One Balloons* by William Pène du Bois. Viking.

1949 *King of the Wind* by Marguerite Henry. Rand McNally.

1950 *The Door in the Wall* by Marguerite de Angeli. Doubleday.

1951 *Amos Fortune, Free Man* by Elizabeth Yates. Aladdin.

1952 *Ginger Pye* by Eleanor Estes. Harcourt Brace.

1953 *Secret of the Andes* by Ann Nolan Clark. Viking.

1954 *. . . and now Miguel* by Joseph Krumgold. Crowell.

1955 *The Wheel on the School* by Meindert DeJong. Harper.

1956 *Carry On, Mr. Bowditch* by Jean Lee Latham. Houghton Mifflin.

1957 *Miracles on Maple Hill* by Virginia Sorensen. Harcourt Brace.

1958 *Rifles for Watie* by Harold Keith. Crowell.

1959 *The Witch of Blackbird Pond* by Elizabeth George Speare. Houghton Mifflin.

1960 *Onion John* By Joseph Krumgold. Crowell.

1961 *Island of the Blue Dolphins* by Scott O'Dell. Houghton Mifflin.

1962 *The Bronze Bow* by Elizabeth George Speare. Houghton Mifflin.

1963 *A Wrinkle in Time* by Madeleine L'Engle. Farrar, Straus.

1964 *It's Like This, Cat* by Emily Neville, Harper and Row.

1965 *Shadow of a Bull* by Maia Wojciechowska. Atheneum.

1966 *I, Juan de Pareja* by Elizabeth Borton de Trevino. Farrar, Straus and Giroux.

1967 *Up a Road Slowly* by Irene Hunt. Follett.

---

**The Newbery Award–Winning Books** (*continued*)

1968 *From the Mixed-Up Files of Mrs. Basil E. Frankweiler* by E. L. Konigsburg. Atheneum.

1969 *The High King* by Lloyd Alexander. Holt, Rinehart and Winston.

1970 *Sounder* by William Armstrong. Harper and Row.

1971 *The Summer of the Swans* by Betsy Byars. Viking.

1972 *Mrs. Frisby and the Rats of NIMH* by Robert C. O'Brien. Atheneum.

1973 *Julie of the Wolves* by Jeane Craighead George. Harper and Row.

1974 *The Slave Dancer* by Paula Fox. Bradbury.

1975 *M. C. Higgins, the Great* by Virginia Hamilton. Macmillan.

1976 *The Grey King* by Susan Cooper. Atheneum.

1977 *Roll of Thunder, Hear My Cry* by Mildred D. Taylor. Dial.

1978 *Bridge to Terabithia* by Katherine Paterson. Crowell.

1979 *The Westing Game* by Ellen Raskin. E. P. Dutton.

1980 *A Gathering of Days: A New England Girl's Journal, 1830–32* by Joan M. Blos. Scribner's.

1981 *Jacob Have I Loved* by Katherine Paterson. Crowell.

1982 *A Visit to William Blake's Inn: Poems for Innocent Travelers* by N. Willard. Harcourt Brace Jovanovich.

1983 *Dicey's Song* by Cynthia Voight. Atheneum.

---

author. Raymond notes that the bookcart usually contains a long waiting list of readers eager to get their hands on the alternative selections.

Sharing books can fulfill many instructional needs in the classroom. Susan's kindergarten plans frequently include beautiful picture books selected to help children with concept development. For instance, *Swimmy,* by Lio Lionni (1963), taught the concept "schools of fish," and Eric Carle's (1969) *The Very Hungry Caterpillar* vividly portrayed the life cycle of butterflies.

An exploration of different versions of the Cinderella story was carried out by Karen's third-graders. Lessons on setting and plot development were a natural outgrowth as the children witnessed the contrasting versions of Marcia Brown's (1947) Caldecott winner, *Cinderella,* and the expanded story in *The Glass Slipper* by Eleanor Farjeon (1956).

*Otherwise Known as Sheila the Great* by Judy Blume (1972) was Eric's fifth-graders' choice for a creative drama. Dividing into groups, the children designed scenery and costumes and wrote a script to portray a series of antics described in the book. The three preceding examples demonstrate the wide range of learning opportunities that can emerge out of the reading of children's books.

Whole-class book activities represent just one way to organize story reading at school. Classic selections drawn from folklore or fairy tales along with current literature such as *Charlotte's Web* (White, 1952), *M. C. Higgins, The Great* (Hamilton, 1974), and *A Wrinkle in Time* (L'Engle, 1962) appeal to most children and represent excellent choices for large-group reading sessions. There are times, however, when intimate book sharing pays high dividends.

For a two-week period, Tim's primary-age students were invited to participate in small-group reading activities. Along with aides who were senior citizen volunteers and select students from a high school service group, Tim planned unique experiences with literature. Such small-group activities are outlined below.

1.  Six children elected to meet daily to share *All-of-a-Kind Family* (Taylor, 1941), the story of a Jewish family living in New York during the 1930s. An elderly Jewish volunteer added insights into the lovely story and delighted the class with a special holiday treat that had been described in the book.

2.  Tim used this time to guide a group of readers as they read individual copies of *The Doll House Caper* (O'Connell, 1975), a delightful fantasy featuring a family of dolls that comes to life each night. A play script was written and presented by the children in the group.

3.  Several children, arranged in groups of three or four, joined high school volunteers in reading a series of books on the topics of magic, animals, and superheroes. Projects of a variety of types evolved from the readings (e.g., a magic show, an animal book using alliteration, and life-size figures of several superheroes).

4.  Several children read and discussed books dealing with difficult life situations. Benjamin, the only black child in class, was impressed with the lovely story *Two Is a Team* (Beim and Beim, 1945) along with the more recent book written in free verse by Arnold Adoff (1973), *Black Is Brown Is Tan*. The sensitive story about how a young blind child copes with life through the use of his remaining senses, *Sound of Sunshine, Sound of Rain* (Heide, 1970), was used to open discussions with Joey, who was having difficulties with mainstreamed schoolmates.

Creating readers involves putting children in touch with books that are personally meaningful. Providing intimate experiences requires careful planning on the part of the teacher. Volunteer groups can offer valuable assistance in individualizing instruction.

The age-old tradition of telling stories through pictures has become popular again. A wide variety of expertly created wordless picture books is now available for children of all ages. Few youngsters can resist the gentle humor of Mercer Mayer's (1967) *A Boy, a Dog, and a Frog* or fail to respond to the realistic fear and friendship portrayed in the soft-toned illustrations in Sonia Lisker's (1975) *Lost*. Older children enjoy more complex wordless books such as *The Silver Pony* by Lynn Ward (1973). Wordless picture books, often quite small in size, can be enjoyed by individuals or small groups. What are some ways teachers have used wordless books in the classroom?

Jennifer Erickson's sixth-grade class included a group of disabled readers who, among other problems, lacked basic sight vocabulary. A library display of newly acquired wordless books gave Ms. Erickson a novel idea for stimulating her students to practice needed sight words, expand writing skills, and gain a positive experience with books. Erickson carried a large supply of wordless books into her classroom, telling her poor readers that first- and second-grade children in the building, though delighted with the new stories, were disappointed because all of the words had been left out. In teams, the sixth-graders were asked to write stories for each wordless book drawing as many words as possible from a basic sight word list provided by their teacher. Edited story scripts were typed, bound, and attached to each wordless book. Sets of books and stories were placed in the library to be checked out by beginning readers. The disabled sixth-grade readers also rehearsed the new stories and read them to individual first- and second-grade children, which was a positive reading experience for these students.

Two gifted first-grade boys working with student teacher Joyce Kannenberg did a fantastic job of retelling *Who's Seen the Scissors,* a wordless book illustrated by Fernando Krahn (1975). After an oral storytelling session, the boys dictated and refined a script. Next, the entire script was illustrated on transparency sheets using colored magic markers. Once the script and illustrations had been completed, the boys moved from class to class telling their version of Krahn's delightful story. As a final project, the boys taped the story and filed the tape, book, and illustrations in the school library.

Designing follow-up creative responses to literature is a superb way to encourage the "hooked-on-books" syndrome. Think of the times you have read a book or magazine article and felt that you just had to do something suggested in the reading—take a walk in the woods, bake fresh cookies, or do a special favor for a friend. Children are no different and will respond enthusiastically to techniques you suggest. Some examples of book sharing include these.

1.  Turn out the lights, pull the shades, and gather around a classroom campfire (large electric skillet) and tell the story of *Stone Soup* (McGovern, 1968). As the story progresses, the children in the group carefully add spices, meat, and vegetables to the water and stone simmering in the skillet. Later in the day, serve the "stone soup" with crackers. Rest assured that children will fondly recall the day they made stone soup in school.

2.  Select and prepare a lengthy narrative poem such as *Casey at Bat* (Thayer, 1964). Choose children spontaneously to portray the poem's characters as you read. Be sure that your voice encourages the children's most dramatic responses.

3.  Choose some books that present ideas children must share with one another verbally. How could a group of third-graders do anything but discuss their feelings on sharing after hearing *The Giving Tree* by Shel Silverstein (1964)? I remember a group of sixth-graders so horrified by the opening pages of *Sounder* (Armstrong, 1969) that they chose to give up their recess period to share feelings of anger and disbelief with their teacher.

4.  Realize that children frequently enjoy using art projects to respond to children's books. A fifth-grade class spent hours of free time creating a papier-mâché replica of the beautiful Ozark Mountains where Billy adventured with his hounds, Dan and Little Anne, in Wilson Rawls's (1961) heartwarming story *Where the Red Fern Grows.*

You need not plan creative responses for every book your class reads. Not all books should have or need a planned follow-up activity. Some stories seem to evoke such deep personal emotions that children may just want to spend time alone reflecting on the author's ideas. For example, after reading *Molly's Moe* (Chorao, 1976), a child may prefer to spend time thinking about times when he has been scolded for misplacing mittens, toys, shoes, or other things. Creative responses, if planned too often, become dull, routine activities.

Creating readers can be incorporated into many areas of the curriculum. The more you learn about children's literature, the more possibilities you will recognize for working good books into your lesson plans. Nearly 2000 new titles flood the market every year; once you begin to explore children's books, the task that perhaps began as a quest for responsible teaching tools will become a task brimming with personal delight and fulfillment.

## CREATING READERS IN THE HOME

"Parents as partners" in education has become a familiar slogan. Parents have always been the child's most influential teacher, but until only recently, many schools discouraged parental involvement in children's education. At present, state and national educational organizations are promoting active parent committees and disseminate books, brochures, and videotapes designed to help parents to instruct children at home. From your perspective as a classroom teacher, parental cooperation can be an invaluable resource.

Most parents, though supportive and willing to promote their children's academic achievements, have not received training in educational techniques. Many feel insecure as they attempt to work with their children. This is where your assistance is necessary. What can you do to help parents develop positive reading-at-home activities?

First, you need to assure parents of the importance of their role in educating children. To secure home cooperation, bring parents together early in the school year. Perhaps a school open house could be scheduled at which a discussion is held that focuses on goals for the coming year. There, you need to explain the basic and supplementary materials that you will be using in school. Parents need to be reassured that (1) you are in control of the learning situation and (2) you have some definite plans for including the home as you work to meet the goals you have set. Carefully planned comments are crucial to the success of the meeting.

Parents, through their tax dollars, hire you to carry out the task of educating their children. You are expected to introduce new ideas, stimulate learning, reinforce needed skills, and manage a testing and record-keeping system. The parental role is one of support; that is, parents can very effectively help, assist, and aid you in teaching children both at home and in the classroom setting. The second thing you need to do, therefore, is to give parents some guidance and direction in providing educational support in the home and in school.

### Home-Based Reading Activities

Reading-related activities in the home setting should include (1) attention to language development, (2) reading to and with youngsters, and (3) reinforcement and review of specific reading skills as needed.

#### *Language Development*

Language development, a fascinating topic, has received much attention from educators. Language development begins at birth and is well established by the time a child reaches school age. Parents need to become aware of the importance of talking and singing to youngsters from birth on, referring to playthings with verbal labels, and encouraging children to use language to express themselves. When parents respond to baby talk with mature words and sentence patterns, youngsters are given models to follow as they grow in language ability. The child who enters school with a broad oral vocabulary, developing sentence patterns, and confidence in her ability to verbalize ideas has a good chance of becoming a successful reader.

As children progress through school, the language they acquire is drawn from a broader base. Adult models, peer interactions, media exposure, and reading all work together to increase language knowledge. Part of the work you do with parents through grade-level meetings, individual conferences, and newsletters should emphasize the continued need for verbal growth. Encourage parents to take time to talk to their children, listen to them, read together, and discuss programs they watch on television.

The richer a child's oral language (i.e., the greater the child's vocabulary and the more sophisticated the child's grammar), the more ammunition available as those same words and ideas are met on the printed page. Efforts must be made at home and in school to increase each child's ability to use language effectively. Several specific suggestions parents can use in the home include the following.

1. Encourage the infant to imitate movements and sounds (e.g., *wave* and say "bye bye," *clap* and say "pat-a-cake").
2. Make a practice of talking about common objects and encouraging the child to use correct verbal labels (e.g., at bath time use words such as *soap, washcloth, shampoo,* and *talcum powder* and praise any attempts baby makes to imitate the words).
3. Reinforce and praise all attempts a child makes to verbalize needs and wants. Accept immature efforts such as "wah-wah" (*water*) but warmly model mature language such as "Oh, do you want a drink of water?"
4. Give the child experiences that arouse sensory perceptions and help him to learn words to express ideas such as how bread dough *feels,* how chocolate *tastes,* or how a puppy *looks* after rolling in a mud puddle.
5. Use family outings to spur vocabulary development. A simple trip to the grocery store provides endless opportunities for word learning (e.g., *cauliflower, butcher, generic, aisle, counter*).
6. Take time to discuss new words that appear in children's storybooks, on television, or in newspaper articles the family shares.

### Reading To and With Children

Reading books to and with children should be the *number-one priority* for parents and teachers wishing to create readers. Lovely books are available for children of every age. Children fed a regular diet of literature at home bring a wealth of experience to the classroom. Part of that experience includes familiarity with the formal language used in books as opposed to that of informal conversation. Students who have been read to also tacitly learn how books are put together and that we read from left to right and from top to bottom. These children also learn about the "language of instruction"—what words such as *word, letter,* and *sentence* mean. Even more important, however, being read to helps children to expand their conceptual knowledge, encourages social and emotional development, and provides a stimulating, productive mode of recreation.

Throughout the school year, urge parents to read to their preschool and school-age children *daily.* Give the parents some helpful ideas on selecting books as well as some ideas on management or incentive programs they could try.

*Selecting Books*

Parents appreciate receiving guidance in selecting books with and for their children. Parents frequently ask questions about the types of literature available for children in specific age-groups. The information given below could be included in a handout that you

---

### Guidelines for Selecting Children's Books

Infants and Young Preschool Children (Ages Birth to Three Years)
* Bright, colorful picture books with simple designs and books with sturdy bindings are good choices.
* Counting books with simple objects are often favorites.
* Alphabet books with large, colorful illustrations encourage early recognition of letter shapes and names.
* Short stories about animals and people help children learn values, manners, and good behavior.
* Books with definite rhythm and repeated lines are excellent choices.

Older Preschool and Kindergarten Children (Ages Four and Five Years)
* Wordless picture books offer opportunities for creating stories.
* Fairy tales with excellent illustrations appeal to these children.
* Poetry, nursery rhymes, and Mother Goose should be used frequently.
* Pop-up and other toy books with corresponding puppets, dolls, or other items are favorite selections.
* Books with repeated lines encourage memorization helpful to the development of reading ability.

Primary-Age Children (Grades One, Two, and Three)
* Easy readers help the child to develop skills being learned at school.
* Riddles, jokes, and nonsense rhymes appeal to children at this age.
* Picture books must have solid story development and strong characters.
* Nonfiction titles are useful as children begin to develop reference and research abilities.
* Books on "things to do" gain popularity: magic, cooking, drawing, building.
* Books to be read to these children should be above the child's present reading ability level.

Intermediate Children (Grades Four, Five, and Six)
* Each child's individual tastes, hobbies, and interests dictate selections.
* Newspapers, magazines, and paperback books become popular.
* Titles under the heading modern contemporary realistic fiction appeal to older children.
* Books that go along with movies or television shows may appeal.

might wish to prepare and distribute to parents during a meeting. You would need to expand this list by including titles of appropriate books available in your classroom, school, or public libraries that fit the various categories listed. For example, *A Boy, A Dog, and a Frog* (Mayer, 1967) could be included in the older preschool and kindergarten wordless-picture-book category, *Go, Dog Go* (Eastman, 1961) would fit in the primary easy-reading category, and so on. Your school librarian could help you to identify good titles for each of the categories.

Bookstores, discount stores, and supermarkets have been known to cooperate with schools by offering discount coupons on books teachers feature at school. Perhaps a popular author or illustrator could be featured one month or books on specific topics of interest at another time. Cooperating stores might provide printed coupons ($1 off list price) that could be attached to the book list and sent home to parents monthly.

Some classroom teachers provide parents with lists of good books that supplement or enrich the basal reading program used in the district. Frequently, the manuals accompanying basal materials highlight specific books that go along with the instructional units. Featured books could be drawn out of libraries and placed on reserve for parents wishing to use them with their children.

Resources for use with parent groups are listed in the Recommended Readings at the end of this chapter. Many times, single copies of brochures are available free of charge or for a minimal fee. You would be wise to order these materials for your files.

### Management Techniques

Parents in today's busy households appreciate knowing about management techniques that encourage families to set aside time for reading. Home sustained silent reading (HSSR) is a plan whereby parents and children agree to read together silently for specified periods of time each week. Like uninterrupted sustained silent reading (USSR) time implemented in classrooms, during the HSSR time, each family member selects a piece of reading material to read silently. Modeling by parents is crucial to the success of this program. Children who see parents enthusiastically reading a magazine, newspaper, or book interpret the act to mean that reading is a valuable, worthwhile activity. Even young children can participate in HSSR. A book bag supplied with colorful picture books or the popular cloth-toy books can be made available. All members of the family benefit from the quiet reading time. Although the recreational aspect of family reading time is the main goal of HSSR, children gain valuable hours of reading practice certain to benefit their overall academic progress.

Alternatives to HSSR have been tried successfully. In McFarland, Wisconsin, the district reading coordinators (Ina Dick and Rose Mastricola) initiated a unique family reading program for grades kindergarten through twelve. Parents in the McFarland district were asked to turn off the television set(s) in their homes for 30 minutes each night for a week. Families who elected to participate in the program received the Family Reading Award certificate shown in Figure 22.1. The certificate, printed on a sturdy grade of parchment paper, was suitable for framing by the family. As you might expect, the program was highly successful, and many families continued the practice after the program was over.

# Family Reading Award

## Presented to the

_____

family

for turning off the TV and reading at least ½ hour each night for a week. We congratulate you! We hope you will continue!

Your McFarland Reading Coordinators,
Ina Dick and Rose Mastricola

Figure 22.1. The Family Reading Award certificate.

Hillcrest Elementary School in Ellsworth, Wisconsin, has followed a reading at home (RAH) program for the past five years. RAH is designed to increase students' recreational reading at home, thus supplementing reading programs at school. Michael J. Perkins, the school principal, supplied parents with a "Turn On Reading, Turn Off Television" contract. Families were asked to choose any half-hour time block between the hours of six and nine in the evening, Monday through Thursday, and use the time to read self-selected books. For each 15 books or 600 pages read by a child and certified by a parent's signature, the child earned the right to choose a free paperback book provided by Hillcrest's Parents Club. This program was also highly successful.

### Reinforcement of Reading Skills

Parents can offer assistance when a child is experiencing skill difficulties that usually respond to additional practice time. What are some reinforcement activities parents can implement?

Matthew, a first-grader, was experiencing difficulty with the basic vocabulary needed to read his primer. Mom and Dad worked daily with Matthew on words sent home by the teacher. Games the teacher had suggested and simple timed drills using flash cards were used daily. Following each brief drill session, Matthew selected words from the cards and used them in sentences he dictated to one of his parents. The sentences were printed on newsprint and kept in a folder for review. Word drills, plus the reading of words in context, transferred to the reading work required of Matthew in school, and his knowledge of sight words increased dramatically.

Third-grader Heather was an average reader in need of work on fluent oral reading. The teacher suggested that Heather and her parents use the following practice exercises to help Heather to develop greater fluency. (1) Using a rather easy book, one of Heather's parents would read with expression a few sentences into a tape recorder. Heather would listen and follow along in the book. Heather's task then was to reread the sentences in unison with the tape. (2) Selecting a fairy tale with a great deal of dialogue, Heather, her parents, and an older brother chose characters and, following a silent practice session, read the entire fairy tale into a tape recorder. The recording was replayed to family members' delight. As they read additional tales together, all the family members' oral character portrayals improved significantly.

In working at home on specific skills, parents need teacher-directed ideas and materials. A game-type atmosphere should prevail whenever possible. Also, be aware that not every skill deficiency is appropriate for home remediation. A child who requires intensive corrective or remedial work on vowel generalizations is best taught these skills in school by the teacher. Other, less academic activities (e.g., reading to or with the child), however, would be appropriate for home tutoring. Use common sense when involving parents in reinforcing reading skills at home. Records showing achievement and incentive charts work well with some children. Parents should be encouraged to work under quiet, *nonstressful* home conditions and *to terminate work when either the child or the parent becomes frustrated.* Under these conditions, parental assistance may help a child to overcome minor skill deficiencies that could combine eventually to cause major reading problems.

## Parents in the School

Parent volunteers can be used effectively and efficiently by classroom teachers at all levels. For plans for using parent volunteers to be successful, however, a clear organizational plan fully understood by volunteers and teacher is needed. How can parents best serve children in a classroom situation?

Parents can be trained to work with children on a number of different activities. Many of these activities require minimal planning on the part of the classroom teacher and supplement and reinforce the reading program's goals. With little advance preparation, a parent can perform the following activities.

1. Read books to individuals or small groups of children who have completed their daily work assignments. Suitable books can be placed on a parent's shelf along with a list of the children who would enjoy hearing the stories.
2. Play skill reinforcement games prepared by the teacher and left on a special shelf for tutors to use. Checklists can be used to identify children who would benefit from the activity.
3. Talk to individual children or small groups about any topic of current interest. Meaningful discussions with caring adults provide invaluable verbal and mental stimulation but also help the children to develop a positive self-image. All too often, entire days pass without any time spent in conversation between children and adults.
4. Offer assistance to children struggling with assignments. Helping children to discover answers by using problem-solving techniques is invaluable. The tutor can provide immediate feedback to the child and help with the correction of errors.

These represent just a few ways parents can be of assistance in the classroom. Note that, when the above strategies are used, classroom teachers are free to continue undisturbed with teaching tasks while the volunteer is present. The tutoring tasks do not require extensive extra planning sessions that rob teachers of valuable work time and often discourage volunteer help as well.

## SUMMARY

Creating readers is a monumental but valuable task requiring work in the school and the home. Teachers who encourage home reading activities while maintaining solid in-class literature activities are making strides toward reaching the goal of creating a reading population. Children who read are enriched throughout their lifetimes. The time teachers invest in that enrichment is well worth the effort.

## REFERENCES

Adoff, A. *Black is brown is tan.* New York: Harper and Row, 1973.

Armstrong, W. *Sounder.* New York: Harper and Row, 1969.

Beim, L., and Beim, J. *Two is a team.* New York: Harcourt Brace and Company, 1945.

Blume, J. *Otherwise known as Sheila the great.* New York: E. P. Dutton, 1972.

Brown, M. *Cinderella*. New York: Scribner's, 1947.

Carle, E. *The very hungry caterpillar*. New York: World, 1969.

Chorao, K. *Molly's Moe*. New York: Seabury Press, 1976.

Eastman, P. D. *Go, dog go!* New York: Random House, 1961.

Farjeon, E. *The glass slipper*. New York: Viking Press, 1956.

Hamilton, V. *M. C. Higgins, the great*. New York: Macmillan, 1974.

Heide, F. *Sound of sunshine, sound of rain*. New York: Parents Magazine Press, 1970.

Huck, C. *Children's literature in the elementary school*. (3rd ed.) New York: Holt, Rinehart and Winston, 1979.

Krahn, F. *Who's seen the scissors*. New York: E. P. Dutton, 1975.

L'Engle, M. *A wrinkle in time*. New York: Farrar, Straus and Giroux, 1962.

Lionni, L. *Swimmy*. New York: Pantheon, 1963.

Lisker, S. *Lost*. New York: Harcourt Brace Jovanovich, 1975.

Mayer, M. *A boy, a dog, and a frog*. New York: Dial Press, 1967.

McGovern, A. *Stone soup*. New York: Scholastic Book Services, 1968.

O'Connell, J. *The doll house caper*. New York: Thomas Y. Crowell, 1975.

Rawls, W. *Where the red fern grows*. New York: Doubleday, 1961.

Silverstein, S. *The giving tree*. New York: Harper and Row, 1964.

Stewig, J. *Children and literature*. Chicago: Rand McNally College Publishing Company, 1980.

Sutherland, Z., Monson, D., and Arbuthnot, M. H. *Children and books*. Glenview, Ill.: Scott, Foresman and Company, 1981.

Taylor, S. *All-of-a-kind family*. Chicago: Follett, 1941.

Thayer, E. *Casey at bat*. Englewood Cliffs, N.J.: Prentice-Hall, 1964.

Ward, L. *The silver pony*. Boston: Houghton Mifflin, 1973.

White, E. B. *Charlotte's web*. New York: Harper and Row, 1952.

## RECOMMENDED READINGS

Glazer, S. M. *Getting ready to read: Creating readers from birth through six*. Englewood Cliffs, N.J.: Prentice-Hall, 1980.

  Glazer's book contains excellent ideas for parents to use as they work with their children in the home setting. The ideas are practical and require little or no preparation and few materials.

Larrick, N. *Encourage your child to read: A parent's primer*. New York: Dell, 1980.

  This inexpensive pocket-size book outlines basic reading skills in easy-to-understand terms. Helpful hints for parents are offered.

Reasoner, C. F. *Bringing children and books together*. New York: Dell, 1976.

  Reasoner's paperback book offers graded titles of children's books along with ideas on motivating children to read.

Materials on parental involvement in the reading program are available free of charge or for a minimal fee from the International Reading Association. Ask for copies of brochures and micromonographs prepared for parents. Address: International Reading Association, 800 Barksdale Road, Newark, Del. 19711.

# CHAPTER 23

# Alternatives to Round-Robin Reading

Eugene H. Cramer
University of Illinois at Chicago

*The first three chapters of Part IV have presented suggestions that beginning teachers can use to promote children's interest in books and their desire to read in school and at home. This chapter, though also concerned with the affective dimension, discusses a different topic: how to promote reading skill and enjoyment through oral reading. Traditionally, oral reading in the school has been conducted in a reading circle, with each child in the circle reading a sentence or paragraph in turn, a practice commonly called "round-robin reading." In this chapter, Eugene Cramer argues that round-robin reading is an inefficient and potentially detrimental way for children to practice oral reading. As alternatives to round-robin reading, Cramer describes many ways teachers can provide children more opportunities to engage in oral reading and make oral reading a pleasurable experience. After discussing several principles of oral reading instruction, he presents three instructional techniques: the repeated reading procedure, the choral reading activity, and the neurological impress method. The remainder of the chapter suggests methods teachers can use to teach oral interpretation of literature and specific oral reading activities.*

Whenever the subject of oral reading comes up, I think of the old saying, "Don't throw the baby out with the bathwater." Before 1900, most reading instruction was done by having pupils take turns reading aloud, with the teacher correcting the pupils' reading when they made errors. This practice was known as "round-robin reading." Teachers emphasized proper pronunciation and articulation, often to the detriment of meaningful comprehension by their pupils.

Around the turn of this century, a number of educators became concerned about the overemphasis on oral reading and the absence of instruction in silent reading for comprehension. They argued that, since most adult reading is done silently, children should receive most of their reading instruction in the same mode. Accordingly, during the first few years of the twentieth century, oral reading was virtually eliminated from elementary school reading programs, and like the baby and the bathwater, much good was thrown out along with the bad.

Oral reading never completely died out as a classroom practice. Although there has been an upswing in the number of oral reading methods and practices reported in use during recent years, the controversy is far from settled. The purpose of this chapter, therefore, is to present reasons for including oral reading as an integral part of reading instruction and to give you some method, strategies, and sources of materials for doing it most effectively.

## WHY CHILDREN SHOULD READ ORALLY

There are several reasons why I believe that oral reading is an important part of the development of young readers. Reading aloud may help beginning readers better understand the relationship between oral and written language. Reading aloud may be used to increase pupils' sensitivity to language elements of voice, diction, pitch, stress, and juncture and thereby help them to become better communicators. As oral reading elements become internalized, I believe that pupils, in fact, become better silent readers. Goodman and Goodman (1980) agree: "In our view a single process underlies all reading. The cycles, phases, and strategies of oral and silent reading are essentially the same. The miscues we find in oral reading occur in silent reading as well" (p. 263).

Efficient silent reading is the ultimate goal of reading instruction, since it is the principal mode in which adults most commonly read. There are, however, at least three practical reasons for elementary teachers to include oral reading as a regular part of their reading instruction: (1) as a means of diagnosing pupils' reading abilities, (2) as a means of developing reading fluency and expressiveness, and (3) as a means of fostering positive attitudes toward, and appreciation of, the written word.

### Oral Reading for Diagnosing Reading Ability

Oral reading is commonly used by classroom teachers to gather information about their pupils' reading abilities. The informal reading inventory is basically an oral procedure for assessing pupils' reading strengths and weaknesses. Since this procedure is discussed in Chapter 9, it will not be discussed here.

Investigators have used oral reading miscues as a means of analyzing pupils' strengths and weaknesses in more formal procedures as well. The Reading Miscue Inventory (RMI) developed by Goodman and Burke (1972) and the Diagnostic Coding of Oral Reading Miscues (DCORM) developed by Pflaum (1979) are two such diagnostic methods that evaluate the quality and type of reading miscues made by pupils. The miscue-analysis procedures enable teachers to select appropriate teaching strategies and materials to match an individual pupil's needs.

## Oral Reading for Developing Fluency and Expression

When pupils are given many opportunities to read aloud meaningfully, I believe that improvement in their oral reading fluency and expression follows. Furthermore, such improvement in oral reading should result in improved silent reading. Much of this chapter is devoted to ideas for incorporating meaningful oral reading activities into your reading lessons in order to help your pupils grow into fluent, expressive oral readers. Consider these ideas as alternatives to round-robin reading that may help you to avoid the tedium of what Singer (1972, p. 23) has called "lock-eyed reading in groups," in which each pupil takes a turn reading aloud as the other pupils supposedly follow silently in their texts while awaiting their respective turns.

## Oral Reading for Fostering Positive Attitudes

To develop positive attitudes toward reading, pupils must be actively involved with what they are reading and aware of the purposes for which they are reading. The oral reading activities and strategies described in this chapter are intended to provide both involvement and purpose for the young readers in your classroom. Providing the opportunity for pupils to develop their oral reading skills in a variety of activities and in the relaxed atmosphere of their own classroom will result, I believe, in increased self-confidence in their abilities as readers and in better performance as readers in more formal situations.

## PRINCIPLES FOR GUIDING ORAL READING INSTRUCTION

Before presenting specific teaching activities and strategies for using oral reading in your classroom reading lessons, a number of guiding principles will be suggested to help you to obtain maximum benefit for your pupils from oral reading. When planning oral reading activities, always try to follow the six principles described in this section.

## Comprehension Before Oral Reading

Pupils must *understand* what they are to read aloud *before* they can do their best oral reading. Often, you can help pupils to improve their oral reading performance if you discuss the selection first and then let them read it silently. After this silent first reading, again discuss the selection and clear up any troublesome pronunciations. In your discussion of the selection, focus on pupils' comprehension of the author's ideas. When you are reasonably certain that they have grasped the author's intended meaning and sensed the mood and tone of the piece, pupils are probably ready to read aloud, conveying the meaning and tone to their listeners.

## Active Involvement

One of the best ways to eliminate the "lock-eyed" reader phenomenon is through the principle of active involvement. As one pupil reads aloud, have the others listen with one or more specific purposes in mind, such as listening (1) for specific ideas in the story, (2) for the main idea of the passage, (3) to generate questions, (4) to be able to retell, (5) to notice the sequence of ideas or events, (6) to draw a picture, map, or chart, or (7) to note a character's mood.

### "Real" Reading

Be constantly on the lookout for situations in which purposes for oral reading are real. Insofar as possible, try to eliminate oral reading practice as an end in itself. Children are more willing to rehearse their oral reading when they know that ultimately there will be an audience for their efforts. Many instances occur in which children can do oral reading for "real" purposes. The following are but a few examples: (1) to read aloud a part of the story that they especially liked, (2) to read aloud to settle disagreements or differences of opinion, (3) to read worksheet responses aloud, (4) to read directions aloud, (5) to read announcements sent from the office, (6) to read aloud letters from pen friends, (7) to read aloud the joke or riddle of the day, and (8) to read aloud original themes, stories, and poems written by the pupils.

### The Magic "If"

Opportunities for pupils to rehearse and present oral readings may not always be readily available. I have found that pupils are often motivated to improve their oral reading through imaginary situations. The great stage director Stanislavski noted the magic of the word *if* as a device for stimulating an actor's thoughts, imagination, and emotions. Similarly, pupils often can be motivated to improve oral reading while pretending to be radio or television news commentators, sports announcers, characters in a story, or radio disk jockeys. For example, you could furnish pupils with ready-made scripts adapted from articles in daily newspapers, or you could help them to prepare their own scripts with a language-experience type of activity after they have listened to a newscast. Many stories from basal readers or trade books can be easily adapted as scripts for dramatic oral reading. Information printed on record albums can be adapted to be read aloud as radio scripts. With a few props, your classroom can become an imaginary television studio, an enchanted forest, a recording studio, or Jack and Jill's hill. Simply say to your pupils, "What if this eraser were a microphone and this box a TV camera?" or "What if these desks and chairs were tall trees and undergrowth in a dense jungle?" or "What if...?" and their imaginations will begin to take over.

### Modeling

All teachers should read aloud to their students on a regular basis. In the lower grades, a period should be set aside every day for the teacher to read aloud. In the middle and upper grades, I believe the teacher should read aloud several times a week, if not every day.

By reading aloud to your class, you will provide a valuable model for pupils. Many children have not heard an adult of their personal acquaintance reading aloud. If you have a little bit of the "ham" in you (and who of us has not?), so much the better. Try to make the times you read aloud to your class warm, happy, and eagerly anticipated events. Occasionally, to help set the scene for your reading, you might wish to use background music or lower the lights or use a simple prop such as a cane or flower or wear a Sherlock Holmes–style cap while reading a mystery.

Be ever on the lookout for stories, essays, poems, articles, and plays that would be suitable for you to read aloud to your students. Most important, be sure that *you enjoy* the selections yourself, because your obvious enjoyment is itself a valuable model for your students.

### Practice

The goal in the preceding five principles is to provide opportunities through which your pupils can become fluent, expressive oral readers. None of the principles can have much effect unless the practice principle is applied. Practice that employs the first five principles can do much to increase the oral reading abilities of your pupils. They must comprehend the material, be actively involved with it, use it in real or imaginary situations, and have a good model to follow. In general, the more oral reading practice your pupils have, the better readers they will become. Keep in mind, however, that pupils should have an opportunity to read any selection silently before they read it orally. Try to help your pupils to develop a habit of rehearsing their oral reading several times before presenting it to any audience, whether it be their own classmates or some other group.

## BASIC INSTRUCTIONAL TECHNIQUES
## FOR DEVELOPING ORAL READING

The instructional techniques discussed in this section have a common purpose: to help young readers to develop fluency and expressiveness in their oral reading. These techniques have been tested by various researchers and found to be useful in a variety of situations. You may adapt any or all of them to suit your needs.

### Repeated Readings Technique (Individual Pupil)

The repeated readings technique is a method of instruction, described by Samuels (1979), in which a pupil first reads a short selection aloud and the teacher notes and enters on a chart the words read per minute and the number of miscues. (See Chapter 9.) The pupil rereads the selection silently a few times before again reading it aloud, at which time the words read per minute and the number of miscues are noted and charted again. The procedure is repeated until the pupil reaches a satisfactory words-per-minute rate (usually around 100) and reduces miscues to an acceptable minimum (usually no more than one or two per 100 words of text). After disabled readers had followed the repeated readings procedure over a number of passages, Samuels noted that, in most instances, they showed dramatic improvements in their oral reading fluency and a reduction of miscues even on unpracticed passages.

Figure 23.1 presents a sample chart, adapted from Samuels' repeated readings procedure, for recording an individual pupil's words per minute and word-recognition errors over six trials on the same passage. As a model of the repeated readings procedure, Figure 23.1 shows a record of the oral reading performance of a student named David as he progressed through the application of this procedure. Notice that on David's first trial he read at 30 words per minute with 16 word-recognition errors and that by the sixth trial, about a week later, he read at 90 words per minute with no word-recognition errors. Although David is a hypothetical student, the scores recorded on the repeated readings record chart in Figure 23.1 are typical of the performances noted for many individual students using this procedure.

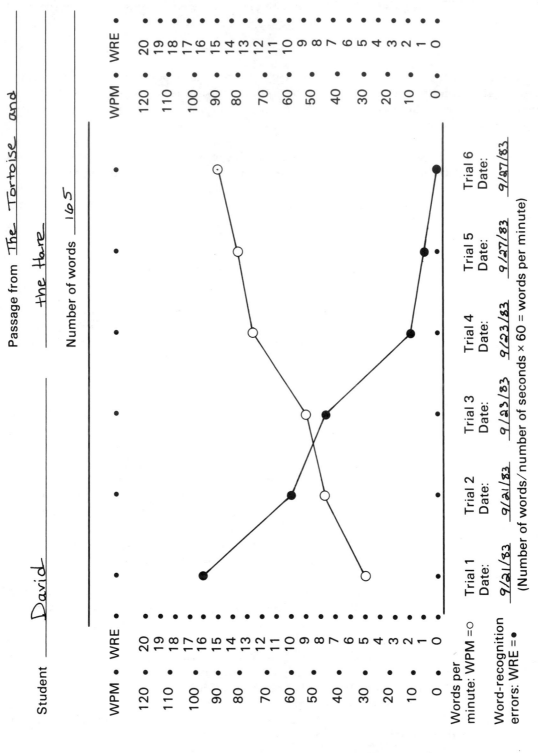

Figure 23.1. A sample repeated readings record chart.

### Repeated Readings Technique (Group)

Lauritzen (1982) modified the repeated readings technique to make it applicable to classroom groups of pupils rather than to individuals only. Several steps are followed in the procedure's application, all with the same general goal of having pupils repeat a selection until they reach a degree of fluency.

1. The teacher reads the entire selection aloud; the class reads the print silently.
2. The teacher reads a line, sentence, or paragraph; the class echoes it.
3. The teacher and the class read the entire passage in unison.
4. The pupils read aloud individually, in pairs, or in a small group, while the rest of the class listens.

The success of this technique depends to a large extent on choosing passages that the pupils will want to repeat a sufficient number of times for them to reach the desired level of fluency and expressiveness. Lauritzen (1982) reported that the best selections have a "sing-it-again" quality that children love, and she offered suggestions to guide your choices. Look for selections that have one or more of the following qualities.

1. A definite rhyme scheme, such as abab, aabb, or abcb
2. Strong rhythm
3. A compelling sequence
4. Patterns typical of oral literature, such as linking words, repeated words, or repeated syntactical patterns

A few examples follow.

> *Mix a pancake,*
> *  Stir a pancake,*
> *  Pop it in the pan;*
> *Fry the pancake,*
> *  Toss the pancake,—*
> *  Catch it if you can.*

> *Christina Rossetti*

### Advice from the Duchess

> *"Speak roughly to your little boy,*
> *  And beat him when he sneezes:*
> *He only does it to annoy,*
> *  Because he knows it teases."*

> *Lewis Carroll*

> *Captain: For I'm never, never sick at sea!*
> *Crew:    What, never?*
> *Captain: No, never.*
> *Crew:    What, never?*
> *Captain: Well,—hardly ever!*

> *from* H.M.S. Pinafore

## Choral Reading

Sometimes called unison reading, choral reading offers many opportunities for repeated readings of a particular piece and gives practice in oral reading to the entire class. Choral reading is particularly well suited to poetry. After an initial discussion of the selection, the teacher reads the entire selection aloud, with the class following along silently. Then, the class reads the piece together with the teacher. A few repetitions usually fix the piece in the children's minds, especially if it has the "sing-it-again" quality referred to in the preceding section.

Next comes the time for fun! An almost infinite number of possibilities exists for choral reading. Try to select the most appropriate vocal elements to reinforce the meaning of the selection. Here are just a few of the possible strategies.

1. Alternate slow and fast lines, stanzas, or paragraphs.
2. Alternate loud and soft lines.
3. Alternate low and high voices.
4. Emphasize key words and phrases by reading them louder or softer.
5. Pause for a specified number of silent "beats" before everyone again joins in.
6. Have various groups of readers read sections in loud or soft, high or low voices.
7. Have soloists read key parts of the section, with the class joining in as a chorus.

The following are a few examples of choral reading schemes to help you get started.

1. All (normal voices):      Simple Simon met a pieman,
   Half (light voices):      Going to the fair.
   All (normal voices):      Said Simple Simon to the pieman,
   Solo (high voice):      "Let me taste your ware."
   Half (heavy voices):      Said the pieman to Simple Simon,
   Solo (low voice):      "Show me first your penny."
   All (faster voices):      Said Simple Simon to the pieman,
   Solo (high voice):      "Indeed, I have not any."

2. All:      Solomon Grundy,
   Solo 1 (high and fast):      Born on Monday,
   Solo 2 (high and not so fast):      Christened on Tuesday,
   Solo 3 (normal):      Married on Wednesday,
   Solo 4 (normal and a bit slower): Took ill on Thursday,
   Solo 5 (groaning):      Worse on Friday,
   Solo 6 (low and slow):      Died on Saturday,
   Solo 7 (low and very slow):      Buried on Sunday,
   All (quickly):      This is the end of Solomon Grundy!

3. Half (high voices):      Jack Sprat could eat no fat.
   Half (low voices):      His wife could eat no lean,

| Duet: | And so between them both, you see, |
| All (loudly): | They licked the platter clean. |
| 4. All: | There once were two cats of Kilkenny, |
| | Each thought there was one cat too many. |
| Half (high voices): | So they fought and they fit, |
| Half (low voices): | And they scratched and they bit, |
| All: | Instead of two cats, there weren't any. |

When a selection has been well rehearsed, you may wish to tape-record it to play to another class or to a group of parents.

Choral readings can be kept simple or be made quite elaborate by adding background music, simple costumes, and a master of ceremonies for public appearances.

### Neurological Impress Method

The neurological impress method (NIM) was devised by Heckelman (1966) as a means for teaching beginning or very slow readers to read orally. The NIM is especially effective with small groups or in a one-to-one situation. The teacher reads a very short selection aloud and while reading moves a finger along the print to indicate exactly what is being read. The pupils are invited to join in with the reading and to imitate the teacher's voice pattern, rhythm, and inflection. After a few repetitions, the teacher gradually reduces the cues and lets the pupils take the lead. The teacher is ready, however, to join in whenever the young readers begin to falter. As the pupils become more competent, longer and more complex selections are used.

## ELEMENTS OF ORAL INTERPRETATION

For many of the activities suggested in this chapter, you need to make use of a few basic elements of oral interpretation. The elements described in this section do not comprise a complete list. The oral interpretation of literature is a complex art, which could be studied for a lifetime. What is presented here is an elementary-level list of certain basic elements commonly used in the oral interpretation of literature. Each of the elements is briefly defined, and an example given to show when and how the element could be used.

### Basic Vocal Elements

#### Volume

"Volume" refers to the loudness or softness of the voice. Loud voices suggest power and force or indicate great size. Soft voices show gentleness, small size, or cautiousness and reluctance.

#### Rate

"Rate" refers to the speed at which words are spoken. A fast rate suggests hurry, excitement, joy, or carelessness. A slow rate can mean calmness, deliberation, sadness, or caution.

### Pitch and Inflection

"Pitch" refers to how high or low a voice would sound on a musical scale. High pitch is usually used to indicate small size or youthfulness; low pitch indicates large size, maturity, or dominance. Changes in pitch, called "inflection," are used to show many different shades of meaning or emphasis in a piece. Pupils can experiment with inflection and pitch changes in their own voices to hear how many different shades of meaning they can convey in a single sentence, such as, "Can you tell me what time it is?"

### Stress

"Stress," or "emphasis," refers to the amount of force or energy given an individual syllable, word, or phrase. A stressed word is given additional importance over the words around it. The familiar children's game of emphasizing each word in turn in a short sentence, such as, "Where are you going?" can be used to demonstrate stress.

> WHERE are you going?
>
> Where ARE you going?
>
> Where are YOU going?
>
> Where are you GOING?

After each version is read, the pupils should be asked to explain how the meaning has been altered. Here are some other sentences for them to try.

> What did you say?
>
> I don't know who you are.
>
> Please watch where you are going.

### Pause

"Pause" refers to any silent spaces in oral reading. Pauses can be extremely effective devices if used carefully and sparingly. A short pause (silently counted as one or two) can indicate uncertainty or unwillingness. A longer pause (silently counted as five or more) can indicate deliberation, deep thought, extreme sadness, or great confusion. Teachers and students alike must consider the use of pauses carefully as they prepare selections for oral presentation. The effective use of pauses can enhance or support the meaning of a passage. Too many pauses, however, can interrupt the flow of the reading and may cause listeners to anticipate them and eventually become bored.

## Voice Types

Of all the elements of oral interpretation, perhaps the one that the teacher and pupils will find to be the most fun is using various types of voices to indicate different characters and moods. In the use of different types of voices, a little modeling by the teacher is very helpful. You should remember, however, that your main purpose is to increase your pupils' reading ability, not to prepare them to become actors and actresses. Usually, a brief suggestion of the appropriate voice type for pupils to use is enough encouragement to help them carry through the idea. Table 23.1 lists a few voice types to try with your students. I

**Table 23.1. Voice Types That Can Be Used in Oral Readings**

| Classroom Label | Speech Type | Uses | Teacher's Cue to Pupils |
|---|---|---|---|
| "Your own voice" | Normal | To express point of view of narrator, hero, heroine, or main character | "Just be yourself" |
| "Whispery voice" | Aspirate | To suggest hiding, fear, wonder, or awe | "Add more air as you speak to make your voice sound breathy; reduce normal voice" |
| "Whiny voice" | Nasal | To suggest a cranky, mean, or fretful person or animal | "Speak so voice comes through your nose" |
| "Squeaky voice" | Falsetto | To suggest a tiny person or animal or general silliness | "Push your voice up to the top of your head; try to sound like a mouse" |
| "Big voice" | Orotund | To suggest a very large person or animal or a politician, orator, or windbag | "Take a deep breath and push your voice from your stomach; pretend to be a big barrel and let your voice rumble" |
| "Growl voice" | Gutteral | To suggest a villain, a fierce animal, an old explorer, a pirate, a sea captain, etc. | "Tighten up your throat and push your voice hard; pretend to have a dry, sore throat, but be louder; use this voice sparingly" |
| "Ghost voice" | Pectoral | To suggest ghosts, evil creatures, moaning, voices from far away, etc. | "Let your voice moan and stretch out all long or open vowel sounds, especially *o*s and *u*s; your voice should be breathy, but it can be soft" |

suggest that you use the "classroom labels" rather than the speech types when teaching them to your pupils.

## PLANNING ORAL READING ACTIVITIES FOR YOUR CLASS

To help you to appreciate the wide range of possibilities for oral reading activities and to help you plan both real and "magic if" formats, here is a menu of ideas for oral reading activities. Shown in Table 23.2, the menu is based on the familiar model of the communication process:

Sender ⟶ Message ⟶ Receiver

Broken down to its most basic elements, all communication is included within this simple model. A fourth element, the medium, has been added to the model to show you the ways in which senders may encode their messages and to indicate some of the many opportunities available to you in planning oral reading activities:

Sender ⟶ Message ⟶ Medium ⟶ Receiver

## Table 23.2. Menu of Ideas for Oral Reading Activities

| Sender(s) | Message | Medium | Receiver |
|---|---|---|---|
| Teacher | Book | "Live" voice | Pupil |
| Pupil | Story | Tape recording | Teacher |
| Small group | Folktale | Audio cassette | Small group |
| Entire class | Fairy tale | Slides | Our class |
| (etc.) | Fable | Filmstrip | Another class |
| | Play | Radio | Our school |
| | Poem | Television | Another school |
| | Nursery rhyme | Video cassette | Parents at home |
| | Essay | Overhead projector | Parent group |
| | Commercial | Opaque projector | Community group |
| | News, weather, sports | Puppet theater | (etc.) |
| | Disk jockey show | Shadow screen | |
| | Announcement | (etc.) | |
| | Conversation | | |
| | Commentary | | |
| | (etc.) | | |

To use the menu, simply choose one or more items from each of the four columns in response to questions such as these.

1. Who is going to be reading aloud? (column one)
2. What is the material to be read? (column two)
3. Will the reading be done "live" or will it be recorded? (column three)
4. Will the reading be supplemented by background sounds or music? (column three)
5. Will the reading be supplemented by pictures or other graphic aids? (column three)
6. Who will be the audience for the oral reading? (column four)

As you use the menu, you should become aware of three advantages to having the list of ideas for oral reading activities displayed in this type of arrangement. (1) The menu can serve as a source of ideas for devising a wide variety of oral reading activities. (2) It can remind you of sources that you may not be using. (3) It may act as a stimulus to adding further items to any of the four columns. Note that each column ends with et cetera, which is intended to remind you that none of the columns is complete and that you are free to add new items as you think of them.

Literally hundreds of oral reading activities can be generated from the menu in Figure 23.2. These activities can range from simple to elaborate, depending on your time, energy, and resources. The following are just a few ideas to get you started. Certainly, you will be able to devise many, many more.

### Activity 1

Read a book to the entire class. *All classroom teachers,* I believe, should read to their pupils on a regular basis as a form of modeling. Formats you may wish to explore are (a) chapter a day (especially good for suspense stories), (b) seasonal or holiday poems and stories, (c) unfinished stories for creative writing activities, and (d) jokes and riddles following a theme (for example, elephant jokes).

### Activity 2

Tape-record a story for an individual or a small group. Although many excellent tapes and records with professional actors and actresses reading stories for children are available commercially, there is something special about a tape-recorded story prepared by teachers for their own pupils. Familiar and favorite stories and poems are best. You could record them during "live" reading sessions, as described in activity 1. Copies of the story or poem should be available for children to "read along with the teacher." This activity provides individual students with additional practice in oral reading, and it is a nice way to stock your listening center with books and tapes.

### Activity 3

Practice choral reading of parts of stories with groups of students. Tape-record the final product and share it with other classes or with parent groups.

### Activity 4

Read with sound effects in the background. Pupils choose a brief passage from a favorite story and select appropriate background sound effects that capture or enhance the mood of the oral presentation. Audio effects can be performed "live" or can be obtained from one of many sound-effect recordings available.

### Additional Activities

Many other ideas from the oral reading menu can be used to provide variety and fun, including the following.

1.  A slide and tape program could be based on a story or poem.
2.  A filmstrip or tape of a story or poem could be presented.
3.  A puppet show could be based on a story or novel.
4.  Opaque or overhead projector "movies" could be based on stories, poems, or novels.
5.  Oral reading practice could be provided through the use of audiotapes prepared by the teacher or older students.
6.  An old-time radio show could be taped.
7.  A disk jockey program could be recorded on audiotape, with students reading copy from record jackets.
8.  Slide and tape book ads could be created by students to "sell" other students on reading a favorite book.
9.  Students could tape-record their readings of famous speeches by present-day or historical figures.
10. Students could compose, read, and record narratives to accompany slides of family trips.
11. Students could compose and tape-record instructions for completing a simple task that others could follow.

12.  Students could tape-record discussions among famous historical figures or literary characters.
13.  Students could produce audio- or videotaped commercials they have prepared for real or imaginary products.
14.  Students could prepare and tape-record commercial announcements of real school events and play them over the public address system to the entire school.
15.  Teacher or students could record a riddle of the day or a joke of the day.
16.  Students could adapt, rehearse, and present short stories or sections of novels in a readers' theater format.

## SOURCES OF MATERIALS FOR ORAL READING

Materials for oral reading activities can come from many sources: basal readers, library and resource-room materials, daily newspapers, magazines, and students' writings, to mention only a few. You must always be alert to the world in which your students live. Try to develop a habit of noticing what sorts of materials seem most interesting to them. Remember that your goal is to find stories, essays, poems, folktales, fables, advertising copy, and books, both fiction and nonfiction, to which your pupils will respond positively.

One word of caution, however: *Not every piece of reading material is suitable for reading aloud.* Try reading potential selections aloud yourself to determine whether their content, vocabulary, and sentence patterns are appropriate to your pupils' reading level.

Many lists of materials that can be read aloud are available. Your school librarian or resource-room director should be able to help you locate such lists. One reading specialist I know assembled a graded list of read-aloud books by conducting a systematic survey of elementary school pupils by using the following six steps (Berg, 1981).

1.  Informal discussions about books were held with individuals or small groups of children of various ages. The most useful of these discussions, Berg reported, was held with six children in a car pool together. One of the children served as secretary, and the others told about their favorite books and indicated for which grade levels the books seemed best suited.
2.  Students filled out questionnaires in their classrooms. Twenty to 25 children participated at each grade level, in the fourth, fifth, and sixth grades. The questionnaires followed a simple format that asked pupils to name their favorite book titles and authors and to tell what kinds of stories they most liked to have their teachers read to them.
3.  Class discussions were held with pupils in the first, second, and third grades, with the reading specialist recording the children's suggestions about their favorite books and the kinds of stories they most liked to hear.
4.  Conversations about children's favorite books and authors were held with a kindergarten teacher, a librarian (to determine which books were checked out regularly), and teachers at all grade levels. Several of these conversations were held in the school lounge to preserve an air of informality.
5.  Discussions were held with remedial reading students at all grade levels, one through six.
6.  The classroom questionnaire was administered to pupils from another school.

Using these six steps, or any combination of them, you can quickly build a list of books, stories, and other reading materials for oral reading activities suitable for your own pupils. From time to time, update the list, keeping "old favorites" and discarding less popular items. Whatever method you use to select oral reading materials, keep in mind your main purpose: *to make reading materials available that are suitable for oral reading and that are of geniuine interest to your pupils.*

## SUMMARY

The ideas presented in this chapter should help you to increase the oral reading abilities of your pupils. Fluent, expressive oral reading appears to be a necessary step in the development of mature silent readers. Avoid using the round-robin reading approach. It is inefficient, tedious to pupils, and potentially detrimental to the development of their reading comprehension and positive reading attitudes. A number of alternatives to round-robin reading have been presented by which you may help pupils to increase their oral reading abilities while simultaneously growing in their appreciation of the written word. The key factor for success in oral reading development, however, is the *teacher*, who must provide inspiration, guidance, enthusiastic support, and the right idea at just the right moment.

## REFERENCES

Berg, M. Read aloud book lists for kindergarten through sixth grade based on children's recommendations. Unpublished paper, 1981.

Goodman, Y. M., and Burke, C. L. *Reading miscue inventory.* New York: Macmillan, 1972.

Goodman, K. S., and Goodman, Y. M. Learning about psycholinguistic processes by analyzing oral reading. In M. Wolf, M. K. McQuillan, and E. Radwin (Eds.), *Thought and language/language and reading.* Cambridge, Mass.: Harvard Educational Review Reprint Series number 14, 1980.

Heckelman, R. G. Using the neurological impress remedial reading technique. *Academic Therapy Quarterly,* 1966, **1**, 235–239.

Lauritzen, C. A. A modification of repeated readings for group instruction. *Reading Teacher,* 1982, **35**, 456–458.

Pflaum, S. W. Diagnosis of oral reading. *Reading Teacher,* 1979, **33**, 278–284.

Samuels, S. J. The method of repeated readings. *Reading Teacher,* 1979, **32**, 403–408.

Singer, H. Research that should have made a difference. In A. J. Harris and E. Sipay (Eds.), *Reading on reading instruction.* New York: David McKay, 1972.

## RECOMMENDED READINGS

Alexander, S. *Small plays for you and a friend.* New York: Scholastic Book Services, 1973.
    Five short plays, complete with directions for staging them with simple props and costumes, are included in this paperback. With help from the classroom teacher, pupils in grades three and above should enjoy producing them.

Hamilton, M. C. Read aloud to children. *Instructor,* 1974, **84**, 129–130.
    In addition to a well-written and well-reasoned rationale for reading aloud to children, this short article provides a graded book list of tried and tested titles from the author's own experience.

Janney, K. P. Introducing oral interpretation in elementary school. *Reading Teacher,* 1980, **33**, 544–547.
    With this article, Janney offers a nine-step guide for incorporating interpretative reading into an elementary school classroom. Also given are some suggestions for using the combined efforts of the classroom teacher, the media specialist, and the school administrator to enhance the project.

Jennings, M. *Tape recorder fun.* New York: David McKay, 1978.

Subtitled "Be Your Own Favorite Disk Jockey," the book presents many ideas that you can use to increase your students' involvement in oral reading activities, including programming ideas, recording sound effects, a history of radio broadcasting, and career pointers. It is suitable for students in the upper elementary grades.

Laffey, J. L. Oral reading: Beyond the bird in the round. *Reading Teacher*, 1981, **34**, 472–475.

This is a brief but excellent overview of current oral reading methods and purposes, including the neurological impress method, choral reading, creative drama, reader's theater, and listening while reading.

Manning, J. C. Reading echoic: An effective technique. *Instructor*, 1974, **84**, 65–68.

In addition to providing step-by-step instructions for using the echoic reading technique, the author lists many specific benefits children receive for being involved in oral reading activities: It assists in word recognition, reduces word-by-word reading, encourages context cue use, builds comprehension, and helps develop confidence.

Morrow, J., and Suid, M. How you can outclass TV with classroom radio. *Learning*, 1977, **6**, 87–91.

This article highlights the imagination-building power of radio and illustrates how to develop this power in students in a number of classroom activities, all of which require considerable amounts of oral reading: disk jockey shows, radio plays, newscasts, interviews, and sound essays. It also gives tips on how to improve performances of the pupils.

Widmann, V. F. Developing oral reading ability in teenagers through the presentation of children's stories. *Journal of Reading*, 1982, **22**, 329–334.

Although this article is presented as an idea for students in junior and senior high school, it could easily be applied to pupils in grades four through six. Overall, the article presents a sound approach for developing oral reading abilities of students, regardless of grade level.

# CHAPTER 24

# Using Sports to Motivate Critical Reading and Writing Skills

Lance M. Gentile
North Texas State University
Denton

*The final chapter in Part IV considers the motivational aspects of reading. In this chapter, Lance Gentile argues that, when a teacher is able to capitalize on the interest in sports so many youngsters have, reading for pleasure and reading skill development are enhanced. More specifically, Gentile suggests that, because developing skills in reading and writing and developing skills in sports are similar processes, teachers who can channel the students' interest and desire to excel in sports toward the development of literacy will find increased motivation and learning. After the relationships between reading and writing and sports and the role motivation plays in the development of literacy are discussed, numerous sports-based activities for reading and writing skill development in the content areas of English, mathematics, social studies, science, health, and study skill development are presented. Although many of the activities included in this chapter are adaptable to a wide range of grade and reading ability levels, upper-elementary and middle-school teachers may be especially interested in the suggestions, because they are organized along content subject lines.*

In a recent *Newsweek* article, George F. Will (1982) wrote:

In an age short on craftsmanship and long on shoddiness, anything done well—laying bricks, writing poems, playing games—deserves honor. Worked at intelligently, sport is not just compatible with academic purposes, it complements them because it involves striving for excellence but striving governed by standards of fairness and seemliness (p. 88).

The purpose of this chapter is to help beginning teachers understand and appreciate the role motivation plays in developing students' critical reading and writing skills.[1] The focus is on sports, because sports provide many young people a possible springboard for developing emotional, physical, and intellectual strength and joy. Because of the positive, enjoyable experiences so many students encounter in sports, capitalizing on them for developing reading and writing abilities is a sensible, effective strategy. Moreover, when students select or are introduced to reading materials or writing activities whose content and objectives reflect their athletic tastes and appetites, reading and writing cannot be inappropriate or distasteful.

## SIMILARITIES IN READING, WRITING, AND SPORTS

Reading, writing, and sports share many comparable elements. The prerequisites for success in both areas are listed below.

| **Success in Sports Requires:** | **Success in Reading and Writing Requires:** |
|---|---|
| 1. Good coaching (teaching) models | 1. Good coaching (teaching) models |
| 2. Enthusiastic, responsive players who pursue excellence | 2. Enthusiastic, responsive students who pursue excellence |
| 3. Sequential mastery of fundamental skills | 3. Sequential mastery of fundamental skills |
| 4. Continuous feedback and reinforcement to players from the coach | 4. Continuous feedback and reinforcement to students from the teacher |
| 5. Self-discipline, perseverance, motivation, and many hours spent in regular practice | 5. Self-discipline, perseverance, motivation, and many hours spent in regular practice |
| 6. A willingness among players to compete for recognition and higher levels of acheivement | 6. A willingness among students to compete for recognition and higher levels of achievement |
| 7. An ability on the part of a player to respond effectively to a wide variety of symbols and patterns | 7. An ability on the part of a student to respond effectively to a wide variety of symbols and patterns |

Although the list points out the likenesses between reading and writing and sports, there exists one noticeable difference between them. In sports, the majority of young people are drawn to performing, dedicated to practicing or competing, and strive for self-improvement and recognition. Many youths, however, never demonstrate equal fervor when it

[1]Some of the material included in this chapter appears in *Using Sports for Reading and Writing Activities: A Book for Parents and Teachers,* by L. M. Gentile. Phoenix, Ariz.: Oryx Press, 1982. This material is used by permission of the publisher.

comes to developing themselves as readers and writers. The most plausible and significant explanations for this situation include the following three.

1. Not uncommonly, reading and writing are taught as discrete, skills-oriented subjects throughout the elementary grades. Most youngsters who learn to read and write well do so despite years of repetitious drill and workbook "fill-in-the-blank" activities. After several years' exposure to this kind of instruction, many students view reading and writing as boring and turn to other more interesting, less academic areas of the curriculum such as sports, music, art, and shop for self-fulfillment. For many students, this attitude remains unchanged throughout their high school years and adult lives.

2. Unlike the Greeks and Romans and some present-day European and Asian societies, American society has tended to separate the development of the mind and the body in its educational approach. Consequently, a clear and detrimental distinction between intellectuals ("eggheads") and athletes ("jocks") is made very early in youngsters' lives.

3. In America, athletes are cherished and worshiped by many members of society. Reggie Jackson, the star baseball player, recently remarked, "Fifty years ago it was Bogart and Cagney; 25 years ago it was Elvis Presley and Chubby Checker. Now it's the age of the athlete." Many American sports figures are idolized and receive extensive recognition and rewards for their "work." By comparison, except for a few writers, no equivalent admiration or payment is accorded those Americans who distinguish themselves through their reading and writing achievements. In fact, the "bookworm" or "egghead" (two rather derogatory labels) is more likely to be judged by some to be insipid or immature and undeserving of approval.

It is argued, therefore, that the motivation toward achievement in athletics is far greater than the motivation toward achievement in literacy, because (1) instruction in literacy is too frequently fragmented and boring, (2) the development of the intellect is considered separate from sports and physical education, and (3) athletes are awarded status, prestige, and financial reward far greater than those afforded literary people.

## READING, WRITING, AND CRITICAL THINKING: MATTERS OF THE HEAD AND HEART

One of the most frustrating problems faced by teachers at all levels concerns not so much their students' inability to read or write but their inability (or resistance) to thinking deeply about what they have read or written. Teachers claim that most of their students can "bark" at print or write words and sentences, but they are not equipped or disposed to interpret or compose ideas critically. Frequently, they cannot grasp an author's meaning, or they struggle unsuccessfully to write logically, forcefully, creatively, and cohesively. The failure to generate this degree of "cognitive commerce" with the written page is perhaps the primary reason many students never acquire a sense of purposefulness for reading and writing.

Educators generally agree that *real* reading and writing involve a complex interactive thinking and questioning process. Furthermore, critical reading and writing are by-products of concentration, which is the outgrowth of an arousal of interest on the reader's or writer's part. This level of functioning can be expected to occur only when the material or activities suit (i.e., interest, motivate, inspire) an individual and when there is an accompanying positive emotional reaction to whatever is read or written. If what a person reads or writes is unsuitable (lacks meaning or is uninteresting), any measurable benefit related to the time spent in the process is short-lived or insignificant. In this respect, reading and writing are no different than sports. When a reader, a writer, or an athlete performs unemotionally or impassively, the results are feeble and uninspiring.

In addition, readers and writers must have had certain personal or vicarious experiences that provide the foundation for critical thinking. Students can and will think about something to the extent that their knowledge, experience, and interest warrants. Figure 24.1 illustrates the interrelated factors that lead to a reader or writer's critical thinking. The illustration indicates that critical thinking occurs when the reader reads or the writer writes something that has strong *personal meaning*.

## THE ROLE OF MOTIVATION IN THE DEVELOPMENT OF CRITICAL READING AND WRITING

Students develop critical thinking skills when they accept and resolve certain challenges posed by various reading material or writing assignments. Whenever what they read or write introduces new challenges that create the right amount of tension to encourage them to use what they already know, critical thinking takes place. Students who are unsuccessful readers or writers are those who cannot or do not make the appropriate intellectual and emotional adjustments during their literary activities and so fail to develop new thought patterns to meet ever-increasing needs and challenges in school. It is not surprising, therefore, to find that students who lack these essential skills resist or experience great difficulty thinking about, understanding, or valuing their reading and writing assigments. In short, the material or activity frequently makes no sense to them; in effect, it is "nonsense."

Unfortunately, it appears to me that the current thrust of research in reading and writing tends to dismiss the unquantifiable psychodynamic variables of "what is in the reader's or writer's head and heart" and by doing so dehumanizes the reading and writing process. This situation perpetuates the image of a reader or writer as a computer and encourages the use of instructional approaches and materials that become mechanical, predictable, and ritualistic.

The meaningless interaction between many students and books—and their failure to produce consummate ideas, opinions, or sentiments when they write—may account for why so many of them are quick to answer, "It's boring," when asked why they do not like this or that subject. Although other factors such as absence of teachers' enthusiasm, adversive peer influence, or negative attitudes of significant others (family members, etc.) may account for the apathy or disdain some students bear toward reading and writing, in essence, many of these young people are stung, bewildered, bored, and angered by the prospect of having to read and write about things that do not speak personally to them and that they perceive as providing little or no intrinsic or extrinsic reward. Recently, I asked one student why she had not read a 15-page homework assignment in history and written out the answers to several questions related to the reading. She responded matter-of-factly: "We ain't never gonna need this stuff!"

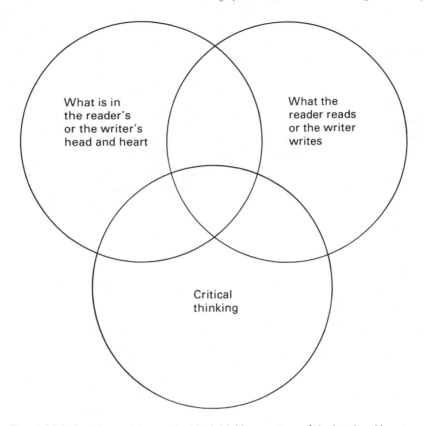

Figure 24.1. Reading, writing, and critical thinking: matters of the head and heart.

## READING, WRITING, AND SPORTS: CAPITALIZING ON STUDENTS' INTERESTS AND BACKGROUNDS

One reason for the "we ain't never gonna need this stuff" response is some students' failure to realize any *real* purpose or benefit from reading and writing in school. This probably occurs, because many students lack the language experiences to interact vigorously and knowledgeably with what they must read and write about in the various academic content areas. Often, teachers overlook or ignore these deficits and make no adjustments in their teaching to compensate for them. Their instruction lacks any use of concrete introductory examples of those facets of language (spelling or vocabulary) with which students may be unfamiliar. In addition, as was pointed out previously, many students lack the vicarious or personal experiences that allow them to read insightfully or to write critically. Many teachers also overlook or ignore these limitations and fail to adjust their teaching to compensate for them. Consequently, their instructional approach does not relate new terms, ideas, information, or learning experiences to students' lives by placing them in a context in which most youngsters can identify, value, and discover personal meanings.

For many young people reading, writing, and sports comprise one meaningful context. Although various topics can be motivating to students, in general, probably no single subject matter area other than sports has more potential to capture their full imagination and interest. At first this may seem to be an exaggerated statement, but upon closer consideration it becomes apparent that sports contain all the vital elements that make life interesting and exciting. Every day the features of human drama, tragedy, comedy, challenge, perseverance, romance, victory, and defeat are acted out in a myriad of sporting events around the world. These events are documented and chronicled in newspapers, magazines, and books and shown to millions of television viewers.

Teachers working to expand students' reading and writing skills will discover that, by involving them in instructional activities that make use of published sports materials, they can establish a provocative climate for learning. Many young people have developed an extensive store of language as well as personal and vicarious experiences in sports that teachers can use as a springboard to further learning. Such youngsters have not only actively participated in sports but have spent a considerable number of hours watching live and televised sports contests. They have listened to broadcasters, players, and performers describe the action or circumstances surrounding various games and events. In doing so, they have acquired a host of related vocabulary words and ideas.

Many students have also accumulated an abundance of knowledge and statistics concerning the history of sports, sports figures, rules, strategies, events, teams, and so forth. Thus, *they are motivated to apply or demonstrate what they know and want to learn more!* For this reason, teachers can employ sports-related materials and writing exercises as powerfully effective means of strengthening students' critical reading and writing abilities. Materials include sports magazines, sports sections of newspapers, biographies of sports heroes, publications containing sports quotes, trivia, superstitions, poetry, and humor. Such materials can be adapted to provide young people the following specific learning experiences that will contribute significantly to their critical reading and writing skills.

1. Opportunities to become active readers and writers instead of passive word callers or copiers.
2. Opportunities to gain vocabulary growth and language enrichment.
3. Opportunities to perform critical reading and writing skills, such as distinguishing between fact and opinion or cause and effect; locating likenesses and differences; identifying main ideas; sequencing events or character traits; critiquing authors' premises for strengths or weaknesses; and acting as authors to create clear, interesting pieces of writing for someone else to read.
4. Opportunities to collect and organize data, do inductive and deductive thinking, attempt interpretive and creative thinking, and experience a variety of situations that require problem-solving operations.
5. Opportunities to practice, apply, and develop general reading and writing skills in a sports context that transfer to school-based academic subjects.

As noted previously, reading, writing, and sports share many similar characteristics. Henry David Thoreau displayed support for this notion when he wrote:

> To read well, that is to read books in a true spirit, is a noble exercise which the customs of the day esteem. It requires a training such as the athletes underwent, the steady intention, almost of the whole life to this object (p. 180 of the 1962 paperback edition of *Walden and Other Writings*).

Many people, however, associate reading and writing with people who are only "academically" inclined. In effect, many see reading, writing, and sports as strange bedfellows and have difficulty understanding that people interested in sports or physical fitness can be good readers and writers, too. This perspective is injurious for several reasons.

1. It confines reading and writing to school-based curricula.
2. It disassociates reading and writing and the development of critical thinking skills from sports, sports figures, and sports fans.
3. It refutes the connections in learning between mind and body, thought and action.
4. It discounts reading and writing as favorable methods to bolster the acquisition of playing or performance skills; to make use of an individual's store of information, knowledge, and interest in sports as a basis for expanding learning and literacy; and to unfold innumerable mental and physical health concepts that students of all ages can develop and apply toward happy, wholesome living.

Teachers can make good use of supplemental reading and writing instructional activities that incorporate sports as an overall theme. These efforts should be made with the understanding that the listless connection that exists between many young people and reading or writing activities is not always the result of their inability to read, write, or complete assignments. More frequently, such students are not *motivated* to apply themselves, fail to evolve good study and work habits or skills, and consequently are not committed to becoming effective readers and writers.

## SPORTS-BASED ACTIVITIES THAT MOTIVATE STUDENTS TO READ AND WRITE

The following sports-related reading and writing activities have been developed to attract young people who are interested in, or identify with, athletes and athletics. The activities are not meant to be complete instructional packages; rather, they serve as *models* from which teachers can devise their own activities. The activities guide and suggest rather than dictate ways to enhance students' reading and writing skills. Thus, they should not be employed as paper-and-pencil drill work.

A more appropriate use for these ideas and materials would be as a differentiated means to stimulate group discussion or broader individual projects. At times, students may even be encouraged to develop alternative sports-based reading and writing activities that are more imaginative, comprehensive, or appealing to their personal interests. Teachers can also gain valuable assistance from older students, letting them act as tutors who use these activities with younger or less able youngsters. The activities also could be used as follow-up exercises and reinforcement for performance-based instruction or serve as a means of motivating many students who would not otherwise practice reading or writing.

### Sports in English

Using the following kinds of statements from newspapers and sports magazines, teachers can stimulate students' interest in vocabulary, language, math, and social studies while encouraging them to recognize simile and metaphor, perform deductive-inductive reasoning, and calculate solutions to arithmetic problems.

*Activity 1*

To stimulate youngsters to perform inductive or deductive reasoning and to introduce to them an abundance of figurative expressions, ask students to read statements such as the following and then respond to various questions or distinguish between true-false statements.

> "Last year, neither Baylor nor Singleton could throw a baseball through a spider's web. Baylor's arm has always been considered as useful as adenoids."

1. Why has the author used the image of a "spider's web" to describe Baylor's and Singleton's pitching? (Metaphor)
2. What does the statement "as useful as adenoids" mean? (Simile)
3. Baylor has the better throwing arm. (True or false? Defend your answer!)
4. Singleton's arm is much stronger than Baylor's. (True or false? Defend your answer!)
5. Baylor and Singleton both pitch. (True or false? Defend your answer!)
6. They both play baseball. (True or false? Defend your answer!)

> "The favorite sports of Bruce, Harvey, Ike, and Teresa are baseball, hiking, ice skating, and tennis."

1. Teresa and Harvey do not like team sports. (True or false? Explain!)
2. Harvey and Bruce do not like cold-weather sports. (True or false? Explain!)
3. What is each person's favorite sport?

> "More and more ball players, you may have noticed, are to be seen digging handfuls of small things from their pants pockets, popping them into their mouths, executing complex masticatory maneuvers, and spitting odd little flecks into the breeze."

1. Do you think the author is referring to football? (Defend your answer)
2. Do you think "masticatory maneuvers" refers to jumping up and down? (Explain!)
3. Does it appear that the ball players are popping raisins into their mouths?
4. Do you think the answer to number 3 is false? If so, what are the players doing?

*Activity 2*

To develop students' vocabulary and their ability to recognize various neologies or humorous, insightful remarks, have students read several quotations by various sports celebrities and write their interpretations of them.

> "Roger Staubach, ex-Dallas quarterback, at a roast for Kyle Rote, Jr.: 'He is a great competitor. He doesn't know the meaning of the word fear ... or cat ... or dog.'"

What is Roger trying to say? _____

_____

> "Vince Tralka, coach of a high school girls' basketball team: 'We play a man-to-man defense. Person-to-person sounds like a phone call.'"

What is Coach Tralka trying to say? _____

_____

"Mike Rice, Duquesne basketball coach, to a player who threatened to jump off a bridge into the Ohio River after hitting on just 2 of 14 shots: 'Wait until tomorrow morning. You might miss the river tonight.'"

What is Mr. Rice trying to say? _____

_____

## Activity 3

To teach sports poetry, have students read, for example, "To an Athlete Dying Young," by A. E. Housman (1968) and answer the following questions. This poem is a poignant description of the fleeting fame experienced by all athletes and the aftermath of their lives. It provides an excellent opportunity for teachers to develop some interesting insights among their students concerning the degree of importance that is typically assigned to various sports personalities and their sports achievements; finally, it points out how frequently the athletes and their notable feats are soon forgotten.

1. What is the tone of Housman's poem?
2. What sense do you get for an athlete's future?
3. Is there any value in having been a great athlete? Why or why not?
4. What is the author's advice to those who would so dedicate themselves?
5. Does the author leave you with a feeling that fame and glory are long lasting and highly prized?
6. Write a poem of your own expressing your feelings toward a sport or a great athlete.

## Activity 4

To get students interested in reading biography, introduce them to a brief episode taken from a book and use it as an interrupted story. For example, you might select a few pages from *Jesse,* by Jesse Owens and Paul Neimark (1978), and copy them for the class. Try to choose a portion of the story that relates a dramatic moment in the individual's life or a part that you think is sure to "hook" the group and stimulate real interest. After reading the selection and discussing it, make copies of the book available to the students. Ask them to report on other events in Jesse Owens's life.

## Sports in Math and Social Studies

### Activity 1

Have students read statements such as the following and perform the necessary computation to answer the questions.

"Last year Tony Dorsett ran for a total of 1680 yards. Ron Springs ran for 1120 yards. Robert Newhouse gained 890 yards rushing."

1. How many yards did Dorsett and Newhouse gain on the ground?
2. What is the total number of yards gained by all three runners?

What is the difference between the total yardages compiled by Springs and Newhouse? Between Dorsett and Springs? Between Newhouse and Dorsett?

"The same three running backs caught passes totaling 650 yards for Dorsett, 598 yards for Springs, and 425 yards for Newhouse."

1.  What is the total number of passing yards gained by the three players? Is it greater or less than the total rushing yardage?
2.  What is the difference between the number of yards Springs was able to gain on the ground and the number he gained through the air?
3.  Why do you suppose the totals are much less for passing than for rushing?

"Davis was paid $225,000 for his first fight—$185,000 by CBS and $40,000 by promoters in the 'Big Apple.' He has three more fights on the same contract with CBS, each calling for $185,000."

1.  What percentage of Davis's contract for the first fight was paid by CBS?
2.  What is the difference between the percentage paid by the promoters and that paid by CBS?
3.  How much will CBS pay Davis for all four fights?
4.  What are Davis's total earnings for this contract?
5.  In what city was the first fight held?

### Activity 2

Ask students to locate on a map (Figure 24.2) the cities in which the following famous yearly sporting events were played and then answer the questions. Many geographical concepts can be taught this way.

1.  Bing Crosby Pro/Am Golf Tournament (Monterey, Calif.).
2.  World Championship Tennis Finals (Dallas, Tex.).
3.  The 1982 World Series—both cities (St. Louis, Mo., and Milwaukee, Wis.).
4.  Superbowl XVII (Pasadena, Calif.).
5.  NBA All Star Game, 1982 (The Meadowlands, Newark, N.J.).
6.  Kentucky Derby (Louisville, Ky.).

Which event took place in the largest city?

Which event occurred farthest north? South? East? West?

Which event(s) could have been played in sunshine? Rain? Snow?

Which of these cities have Spanish names? Where are they located?

### Sports in Health and Science

The ability to keep records and read graphs, charts, and pictorial material is important in many content areas. Students must make assumptions, comparisons, inferences, and conclusions based on the diagrams. The following activity requires students to record, collect, organize, and interpret data.

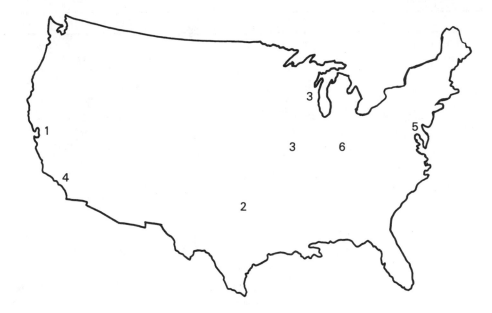

Figure 24.2. An exercise involving the locations of yearly sporting events in the United States.

## Activity 1

Provide students with stopwatches. First, pair students for recording each other's pulse rates at rest. Ask them to record the statistics on a chart. Discuss the differences among class members. Next, ask them to take turns running in place for two minutes and to record these figures as well. How do the rates differ? Why did they increase? Finally, ask them to measure the heartbeat after a two-minute recovery period. How many returned to their original rates? Why are some about the same as they were at rest, while others are still somewhat accelerated? (See Figure 24.3 for an example of the students' charts.)

As a follow-up activity, ask for volunteers to take part in a jogging program for two weeks. These students become the experimental group for purposes of this research project. The remainder of the class acts as the control group. At the end of the allotted time, have the whole class repeat the heart-rate experiment. Are there any differences between the volunteer joggers' rates and those of the rest of the students? Discuss reasons for these changes.

## Sports and Teaching Study Skills

### Activity 1

Identify an area of sports interest for student athletes. This may be a specific sport, coach, team, player, or general topic (e.g., the Olympics, the NCAA Playoffs, the Master's

| | Experimental Group | | Control Group |
|---|---|---|---|
| Pulse at rest | Richard Mafus | | Malcolm Crenshaw |
| | First trial | | First trial |
| | 94 | | 84 |
| | Second trial | | Second trial |
| | 86 | | 85 |
| Two minutes of running in place | First trial | | First trial |
| | 147 | | 142 |
| | Second trial | | Second trial |
| | 133 | | 144 |
| Two minutes for recovery | First trial | | First trial |
| | 117 | | 118 |
| | Second trial | | Second trial |
| | 105 | | 122 |

Figure 24.3. A data-recording chart for health or science (for one pair of students).

Tournament, the Belmont Stakes). Select materials or articles from newspapers and magazines that relate to these interests. Choose those that have accompanying pictures whenever possible. You should preread the material.

Present the material to students by using the following adaptation of Robinson's (1950) SQ3R technique.

### Survey

Create a background of experiences for reading and introduce unfamiliar vocabulary and concepts. Ask the students to judge the article's content by the illustrations accompanying it. After a brief discussion, tell them to scan the first part of the article (column or section) and underline or circle any word or phrase they do not understand. If a student fails to identify any words or phrases during the preview, you should ask for specific definitions and clarify meanings. Guide students over each succeeding column or section in the same way. The students should skim headlines and captions as well.

### Question

Set purposes for reading, and establish interest. After the students have looked over the article or material and you have discussed the illustrations and unfamiliar vocabulary and phrases, direct them to write down two questions they might ask about the content. Then, you write two questions resulting from the prereading activity. Typically, students' questions are literal, so teachers should try to ask questions at the interpretive or inferential level.

### Read

At this point, students are directed to read the article or material silently and to look for answers to their questions. They are also instructed to circle or underline any additional words and phrases that are unfamiliar. If students fail to do this, you should make a point of questioning them about those terms that may be misunderstood or unfamiliar and explain the importance of reading for meaning at all times.

*Recite*

Students are next asked to recite as much of the story or content as they can. After students have paraphrased the material, you should ask whether they can answer the two questions you had posed initially. Also ask students to answer the two questions they themselves have written.

*Review*

If students are unsuccessful in retelling the story and answering their own questions or if they cannot respond effectively to your questions, they should be referred back to portions of the text that reveal the required information. You should check for full understanding by watching for overlooked main ideas or details and helping students to uncover those as well.

## SUMMARY

For many students who have had personal and vicarious experiences in sports, reading activities involving sports-related materials make sense and seem to excite their interest immediately. Such activities provide teachers with an excellent instructional tool and a particularly good vehicle for stimulating those students who show disinterest in academic content and are reluctant to read from their textbooks or to write creatively.

## REFERENCES

Houseman, A. E. To an athlete dying young. In *A Treasury of the familiar.* New York: Macmillan, 1968, p. 361.

Owens, J., and Neimark, P. *A spiritual autobiography.* Plainfield, N.J.: Logos International, 1978.

Robinson, F. P. *Effective study.* New York: Harper and Brothers, 1950.

Thoreau, H. D. *Walden and other writings.* New York: Bantam, 1962, p. 180.

Will, G. F. Through hoops for a column. *Newsweek*, March 15, 1982, **99**, 88.

## RECOMMENDED READINGS

Gentile, L. M. *Using sports and physical education to strengthen reading skills.* Newark, Del.: Monograph number 225, Reading Aids Series, International Reading Association, 1980.
   The monograph contains a detailed discussion of the reading process and how it relates to the world of physical education and sports training. Although it is directed primarily toward coaches and physical educators, it can also be a useful tool for teachers. A wide variety of practical activities for improving players' performance-based skills and knowledge of games and events based on their ability to read and respond appropriately to various exercises is included.

Gentile, L. M. Using sports to strengthen content area reading skills. *Journal of Reading*, 1980, **24**, 245–248.
   Gentile's article contains examples of ways for teachers to supplement their content area reading assignments with related sports reading and writing activities. Examples include exercises for language, math, social studies, English, health, and science.

Gentile, L. M. Student athletes vs. literacy: One solution to the problem. *WCRA Fourteen*, Proceedings of the 14th Annual Conference, Western College Reading Association, 1981, pp. 96–103.
   The literacy problems existing among many college athletes are discussed, and some valuable insights for coping with these students' weaknesses are provided.

Gentile, L. M. Coaching student athletes to literacy. In R. Flippo (Ed.), *Innovative learning strategies.* Newark, Del.: International Reading Association, 1982.

A successful program for teaching college athletes to read and write effectively is described. The article introduces several cardinal principles for working with college athletes that should interest those involved in developmental literacy efforts at this level.

Gentile, L. M. *Using sports for reading and writing activities.* Phoenix, Ariz.: Oryx Press, 1983.

This book, designed for parents and teachers, contains an abundance of practical activities using the content of various sports to involve young people at elementary, middle, and secondary levels in reading and writing activities.

Maring, G. H., and Ritson, R. Reading improvement in the gymnasium. *Journal of Reading,* 1980, **24,** 27–31.

Maring and Ritson's article encourages physical education instructors to foster reading improvement in the gymnasium. It offers ten teaching strategies aimed at developing physical education content and gymnasium skills while at the same time enhancing students' reading.

Patlak, S. Physical education and reading: Questions and answers. In H. A. Robinson and E. L. Thomas (Eds.), *Fusing reading skills and content.* Newark, Del.: International Reading Association, 1969, pp. 81–88, 201–204.

Patlak's paper reports an interview between Sanford Patlak, a coach and physical educator at the University of Chicago Lab School, and Dr. H. Allan Robinson. Many interesting insights arise throughout the discussion between these two authorities on the role that physical education and sports can play in developing students' reading habits.

# Index

# Student Survey

## James F. Baumann & Dale D. Johnson
## READING INSTRUCTION AND THE BEGINNING TEACHER:
### A Practical Guide

**Students, send us your ideas!**

The authors and the publisher want to know how well this book served you and what can be done to improve it for those who will use it in the future. By completing and returning this questionnaire, you can help us develop better textbooks. We value your opinion and want to hear your comments. Thank you.

Your name (optional) _____ School _____
Your mailing address _____
City _____ State _____ ZIP _____
Instructor's name (optional) _____ Course title _____

1. How does this book compare with other texts you have used? (Check one)

   ☐ Superior    ☐ Better than most    ☐ Comparable    ☐ Not as good as most

2. Circle those chapters you especially liked:

   Chapters:  1  2  3  4  5  6  7  8  9  10  11  12  13  14  15  16  17  18
              19  20  21  22  23  24

   Comments:

3. Circle those chapters you think could be improved:

   Chapters:  1  2  3  4  5  6  7  8  9  10  11  12  13  14  15  16  17  18
              19  20  21  22  23  24

   Comments:

4. Please rate the following (check one for each):

| | Excellent | Good | Average | Poor |
|---|---|---|---|---|
| Logical organization | ( ) | ( ) | ( ) | ( ) |
| Readability of text material | ( ) | ( ) | ( ) | ( ) |
| General layout and design | ( ) | ( ) | ( ) | ( ) |
| Match with instructor's course organization | ( ) | ( ) | ( ) | ( ) |
| Illustrations that clarify the text | ( ) | ( ) | ( ) | ( ) |
| Up-to-date treatment of subject | ( ) | ( ) | ( ) | ( ) |
| Explanation of difficult concepts | ( ) | ( ) | ( ) | ( ) |
| Selection of topics in the textbook | ( ) | ( ) | ( ) | ( ) |

OVER PLEASE

5. List any chapters that your instructor did not assign. _____

_____

6. What additional topics did your instructor discuss that were not covered in the text?

_____

7. Did you buy this book new or used?            ☐ New       ☐ Used

   Do you plan to keep the book or sell it?       ☐ Keep it   ☐ Sell it

   Do you think your instructor should continue to assign this
   book?                                          ☐ Yes       ☐ No

8. After taking the course, are you interested in taking more

   courses in this field?                         ☐ Yes       ☐ No

   Are you a major in elementary education?        ☐ Yes       ☐ No

9. GENERAL COMMENTS:

May we quote you in our advertising?   ☐ Yes     ☐ No

Please remove this page and mail to:        Mary L. Paulson
                                            Burgess Publishing Company
                                            7108 Ohms Lane
                                            Minneapolis, MN 55435

THANK YOU!

## DATE DUE

| | | |
|---|---|---|
| DEC 9 1990 | | |
| OCT 1 1 1993 | | |
| NOV 2 1994 | | |
| DEC 1 8 1998 | | |
| 1-11-99 D.H. | | |
| MAR 2 9 1999 | | |
| | | |
| | | |
| | | |
| | | |
| | | |
| | | |
| | | |
| | | |

DEMCO 38-297